INFIDEL in
the TEMPLE

INFIDEL
IN THE
TEMPLE

A Memoir of the
Nineteen-Thirties

~

by Matthew Josephson

ALFRED · A · KNOPF: New York

1967

THIS IS A BORZOI BOOK
PUBLISHED BY ALFRED A. KNOPF, INC.

FIRST EDITION

Charles A. Beard: *Oh! those* respectable *ones—oh! their* temples *of respectability—how I detest them* . . .

The Author: *I have often found myself in the precincts of those temples and have always felt myself an infidel there.*

Foreword

AFTER MANY YEARS spent in writing biographies of famous men long dead the thought came to me that perhaps I might apply such historical-literary skills as I had acquired to the subject of myself, my friends, and our own times. My initial feelings of being daunted by such a project were dispelled by one of the most intelligent and forthright of my friends who exclaimed one day: "Enough of writing about how 'good' other men were; tell us about yourself and your own ideas."

I conceived of this book, nevertheless, as a memoir not only of my own experiences and thoughts, but of those of others who were my contemporaries. I would thus engage not only in the time-honored pursuit of self-knowledge, but also in recording some observations of history in the making during one of the most critical decades of this century, the thirties. In recent years writers of autobiographies have tended more and more to treat their lives as focal points of forces in history, with their own individual figures outlined against the historical horizon of their time. Such memoirs often reveal much about the interaction of individual experiences and world events. This history-minded method has long appealed to me. As Jean-Paul Sartre has said, the recapitulation, the reliving of one's ideas and experiences are of interest not merely because they are our own, but because they are similar to those of many others, and so help us to reconstruct the evolution of a larger group, a class, even a whole generation. Thus there may be value not only in the testimony of the leading actors in a given period, but also in that of decidedly lesser personages like myself—who at least tried to keep their eyes open to what was going on.

At the time of my conversation with my challenging friend we were in the early stages of World War II. The epoch of the thirties had really begun in late October 1929, with the crash of the stock market in Wall Street; it had ended with the sudden shower of Japanese bombs on Pearl Harbor in December 1941. The New Deal, with its social tensions, its sweeping reforms, and its vast welfare projects, was now well behind us. Our country, like nearly all the nations of Europe and Asia, had come under the arbitrament of war. We were to be in the hands of the specialists in violence thenceforth for some years to come. Everything around us was to change, even the very scale of human activities.

As the war got under way I felt that I must record, if only for myself, something of what I had seen in the time between the wars. Consulting my own notes and fragmentary journals of that period, I wrote a first draft of part of this book. But with the peace the Cold War soon blew in; and for several years after that the country was literally held *in terrorem* by Senator Joseph McCarthy. A book in which one tried to do justice to the men and ideas of the thirties, then in disrepute, would have been ill-timed, and so my project was put aside for a long while. When at length I returned to the old plan of a memoir, I began with an account of an earlier period of my life, during the twenties, when I was one of a group of young literary men living as so-called "expatriates" in New York as well as in Paris, and engaged mainly in the wars of art.[1] In the present volume of memoirs I continue with recollections of much the same group, save that it also embraced, during the thirties, a much wider circle, less exclusively literary and much more political in its interests. The reputedly carefree young men of the twenties were undergoing the trials of the long Depression; world history intruded into their private lives in the most immediate way.

If I were to try to epitomize the contrast between the twenties and the thirties I would say that before October 1929 Americans lived from day to day, without much thought of the future, believing themselves well favored by fortune. But after the Great Crash the American people really began to think. For years on end our capitalist economy was wholly out of balance, in a state of chronic cataclysm. At home there was much popular unrest, and revolutions and counterrevolutions in the world outside. The danger of general

[1] *Life Among the Surrealists: A Memoir* (New York: Holt, Rinehart; 1962).

war added to the anxieties of every day. Many who had never thought about the body politic, or the troubles of other people, felt themselves shaken out of their skins, yet also strongly challenged by the very dangers of the time.

In reality the Great Depression was not depressing. The lean years of the New Deal became a period of lively ferment. The old centers of power were being rudely knocked about; new opportunities opened for those able and ready to respond to them. Indeed, the thirties ushered in a revival of political education; whereas our national politics had formerly been perfunctory, an affair of Tweedledum and Tweedledee, now the very existence of millions of human beings depended upon national political action. Even those of literary and scholarly bent, who in the past were preoccupied with their special mental disciplines, forsook the study and engaged themselves in the struggles of common men. It was the heyday of the intellectuals and the experts in the professions, who were now courted by reformers and conservatives alike.

Because I had worked for several years in Wall Street—the real center of power in the old days—I felt equipped to measure the scope of the huge economic crisis. Moreover, as an active writer for the magazine press at the time I was able to rove freely "between the lines" from one camp to the other, which I always found diverting. I had close contacts not only with writers and painters, but also with politicians, social workers, economists, labor leaders, radical agitators, and conservative capitalists as well, and tried to write of what I learned objectively, or even blandly. But there were many things that were then considered not "fit to print," or that, on one ground or another, were censored out of my magazine articles. This material I preserved in what I called my "black notebooks"—and I determined to publish as much of it as might hold interest for the public of later times.

I had an abiding fear that with wartime prosperity and its attendant inflation of ideas as well as money men would tend to forget the lessons of the thirties and belittle their achievements. It has not been uncommon for the new breed to blame their elders of the preceding generation for present ills. In Restoration England public opinion denounced John Milton as well as Cromwell. In France after Waterloo the citizens welcoming back the Bourbons repudiated the prophets of the great French Revolution, as shown by their popular chant: *"C'est la faute à Voltaire. C'est la faute à Rousseau!"* In America we also had a Restoration of sorts after the war: the *Zeitgeist* of the typical intellectual spokesmen of the fifties was conservative. While busily propagating something known as the New Conservatism, they slated the liberals and radicals of the prewar era for their errors, follies, and even alleged "treasons." Many of the books and polemical tracts devoted to the intellectual movements of the thirties bore titles that were self-descriptive, such as: *A Generation on Trial, The End of Ideology, The Bitter Thirties, The God that Failed.* Even the usually judicious Dr. Reinhold Niebuhr declared that the men of the thirties must "stand trial" before posterity for their sin of pride, for having "vainly . . . attempted to manage human affairs . . . and control historic destiny" by seeking to improve man's material environment.

Worse still was said of the generation of the thirties by people who went about denouncing their former friends and confessing and recanting in public their "heresies" of the past. A Revisionist School of historians also appeared while the hunt for "un-American" persons and ideas was in full cry. Though the Revisionists were in no way associated with the McCarthian furor, they girded against the historical school of the thirties whose members had shown a strongly critical attitude toward the old establishment, with its "economic royalists" or "robber barons." Such works, it was urged, should be *rewritten* so that the old moneymen and industrial captains might be represented, not as men who had helped bring us to grief and depression, but as the true "saviors" of our country. The story of our business society, one of the Revisionists proclaimed, was to be given a new treatment, no longer in an apologetic tone, but one of "pride . . . in our dollars, our race to wealth, and our . . . materialism."

I felt, for many reasons, the strongest misgivings about the rewriters of history. The more they retouch and revise the story of the past, I reflected, the deeper will the truth be buried. It seemed to me urgent that I attempt another, different interpretation of the period I always thought of as the "brilliant thirties," while the memory of that time still remained vividly in mind.

§   §   §

I have not only consulted my own documents and those of others, but have also talked and corresponded with literally hundreds of persons who witnessed or figured in the events described here—they are too numerous to name and thank individually though some of them, at any rate, appear in the pages that follow. The Louis M. Rabinowitz Foundation provided me with a grant-in-aid given without restrictions of any kind, which helped me to complete this book; and I am under great obligations to them. I am also deeply grateful to Angus Cameron, of the editorial staff of Alfred Knopf, for his devoted readings of more than one version of this manuscript. As on many past occasions with my other books, I am heavily in debt to my wife Hannah Josephson for her very extensive assistance to me as a reader, critic, and copy editor.

Matthew Josephson

Rome, January 1966

Contents

INFIDEL in
the TEMPLE

Chapter One

∽

The Turn of the Tide

"AFTER US THE DELUGE"—thus men have sometimes cried out their defiance in the face of oncoming crisis. Yet when it comes they are utterly unprepared for anything of the sort. The French were caught by surprise when history presented them with 1789. So America, whose business society was the most prosperous in the world, found itself suddenly "overtaken by events" in the Crash of 1929. The Great Depression moved in upon us like a storm, and we were rudely buffeted during the evil seasons that followed. There was no revolution in the streets, but there was a fair amount of public disorder; many were in need, and even those who were not lived in fear. Later, when we had become accustomed to the somewhat different order of things, we marked the year 1929 as a great turning point in our history.

§ § §

In 1929 I had been back in New York about a year since my last long stay in France, and I found social life in the metropolis more stimulating and entertaining than ever before. Because of my two long absences abroad during the twenties I could more easily measure the gradual changes that had taken place. In the circles I frequented, mainly of literary and professional men, people seemed more knowledgeable, more alert to new ideas in books, art, and music. In New York, at any rate, the philistines whom H. L. Mencken assailed unweariedly were routed. Our old pleasure city had always provided a refuge from America's Main Streets, but now it was becoming "modern," a key word in the late twenties; you could feel this in the style of the new buildings which nowadays divested themselves of gingerbread façades and often, thanks to their set-back structure, assumed clean Cubist lines.

New York had long had its community of art lovers and culture-seekers, though they often seemed ill-nourished; as a music center, for example, it boasted two opera houses and a symphony orchestra. But the difference was that its public now had more chamber music than before. Contemporary American painters were being exhibited in galleries that had formerly sold only old European masters; some of them were also shown in the newly established Museum of Modern Art, then quartered in a small mansion at the site of its present elaborate structure. The little-theaters, helped by a growing public, invaded the midtown Broadway area; that is to say they moved uptown from Greenwich Village. Meanwhile publishers gave support to new authors through advances or commissions for literary work that was often "modern" or experimental in form. New cultural foundations such as Guggenheim's also awarded traveling fellowships to writers and artists. Thus a measure of security had come to the intelligentsia of the arts, as I could judge by the improvement in the condition of my formerly impecunious friends. Although few of them shared in the "golden boom" that Scott Fitzgerald enjoyed, they remained alive, and the terms of existence had become more agreeable. It was interesting that nowadays none of my friends thought of "escaping" to Paris or the Balearic Islands. On the other hand European visitors in New York were more numerous and freely expressed their enjoyment of our vertical city and its cheerful bedlam.

At the beginning of the twenties, however, the situation had been quite different: many intellectuals honestly believed American society to be undercivilized. In 1921 I had joined in the migration of American artists and writers to Europe, with which some of them had become acquainted during wartime service. If we were sometimes called "expatriates" the appellation had only a partial truth. We were really removing ourselves for a while from our business civilization, and from our middle-class families that counted fondly on our making our careers in an advertising office or a bank. It was our hope that we might "broaden" ourselves by foreign travel and by exposure to the great literary workshop that was Paris. We young Americans mostly lived in the frugal style of students; and it was no disgrace to be poor. Our ruling idea then was to approach the practice of our art from the point of view of serious craftsmen concerned, above all, with mastery of form and technique.

After our *Wanderjahre* we came home, some earlier, some later, with no little fear and trembling, to what we considered the non-culture of our native land. While abroad, we had thought a great deal about our own country and how its new arts might be developed. For a year or two we entertained hopes of creating an informed audience, such as we had seen in Europe, that would support experiment and the development of authentic American schools in the arts. Through our little magazines and our avant-garde movements and controversies we tried to expound a few ideas that were in advance of the time. At any rate it was our intention to stay here henceforth and fight for our ideas.

By 1924 two of the little reviews with which I was associated had suspended publication, and my particular group of friends broke up. Life scattered us, then at intervals brought us together in some common literary enterprise reflecting the old comradeship. In the early twenties it seemed hopeless to earn a living by writing that was not nakedly commercial; some of my friends who were poets worked in advertising offices; I was driven to take a job with a Stock Exchange firm.

Sometimes we thought we had wholly failed; and yet our voices, and others like ours, added something that kept echoing among successive coteries of the literary intelligentsia appearing at points in the country scattered between Boston and San Francisco. Other little magazines of the avant-garde replaced our own. By 1929 the arrival of a younger generation in American literature was generally accepted.

Several of my comrades of years ago in Paris, Malcolm Cowley, Slater Brown, and Robert M. Coates, were on hand in New York at that time and were regularly publishing their writings in established journals and literary reviews ranging from *The New Yorker* to *The Dial* or *The New Republic*. They were beneficiaries of the marked improvement that had taken place in the literary standards of the New York publishing center. The same was true of my other friends who had been associated with our little reviews. Kenneth Burke and Hart Crane were both winners of awards and grants from patrons of literature. Edmund Wilson, whom I had known since 1923, had lately become the literary editor of *The New Republic,* in which his critical interpretations of James Joyce and Marcel Proust were then appearing. E. E. Cummings came and went in his elusive way; the rebellious orthography of his poems no longer created shock, and he was now one of the most favored poets of the day. Periodically Dr. William Carlos Williams rode in from suburban New Jersey to join our evening parties; though he was a good ten years older than any of us, his were the most youthful spirits. A new member of our circle was Katherine Anne Porter, a native of Texas who had grown up in New Orleans. She too had undergone a period of "expatriation" in Mexico, during years of revolutionary conflict.

The personnel of one's circle of friends is constantly in flux in the course of a lifetime and especially in a distracting metropolis like New York. I have found it illuminating, nevertheless, to look back at my friends as a group, noting changes of direction and mood at different periods and using the record of their experience as a *point de repère,* a kind of guiding mark in the movement of time.

Seven or eight years earlier we had been virtually underground characters, whereas at the end of the twenties we were generally in flourishing condition and were establishing ourselves in the republic of letters. We were now, most of us, married; several were raising a child or two, and the papas among us owned little houses in the country outside of New York and were paying off mortgages. Going into our thirties, with the century, we were thicker of body and our hair was a bit thinner. In a word, we had become somewhat *embourgeoisés.*

The things we wrote were no longer the products of aesthetic rebels bent on shocking the respectable, but more often representative of earnest effort at communication with our audience. In my own case, after quitting my job in Wall Street and returning to writing, I had parted company with the literary avant-garde and the

Surrealists of Paris and by 1928 completed a biography, *Zola and His Time*, done in the leisurely manner of the English nineteenth-century studies of life and letters. The book had won a surprisingly large public for that period, which reflected the growing interest of Americans in history and biography.

Even the tempestuous Hart Crane had the support of a small loyal public for his reputedly obscure verses—despite the ridicule of conventional-minded reviewers. The publishing trade had prospered of late, and thus it was possible for one of the leading firms in New York to issue Katherine Anne Porter's first collection of short stories, *Flowering Judas*, in a limited edition. Several years earlier she had suffered from tuberculosis and undergone a lengthy cure somewhere in the Southwest. Living in New York, on bits of editorial work from publishers after 1928, had been a strain upon her health; her friends feared for her and bestirred themselves to find help. At last she was able to report that someone, "not Otto Kahn but like him," was endowing her with a small allowance for eighteen months. She was "saved from hunger," she declared, and would depart for Mexico, in whose dry air she would renew "the battle for my breath." The status and the economy of writers had measurably improved; but as a career, writing was still a quite marginal affair.

The subjects of our reading and our talk at that interval were determinedly unpolitical—it now seems amusing to relate. The concern of our coteries of intellectuals and literary men was mainly with the nature of the emergent American culture; we were constantly taking the pulse of our Leviathan-like society in order to note the qualitative changes taking place in it. That we were living in a Machine Age, among regimented mass-men, had become clear to us. Even before the days of the computing brain there was a growing measure of automatism in the rhythm of our existence. What, we asked ourselves, would be the future form of our civilization? What the role of the artist or scholar or the general scientist? How would they remain free minds in a world of giant factories, assembly lines, and cities of unending traffic jams?

A similar kind of inquiry, *Civilization in the United States*, edited by Harold Stearns in 1921 and written by thirty experts, had furnished evidence that there might be for us no civilization worth the name. (Henry Adams had felt the same terror when he inspected the new dynamos at the World's Columbian Exposition of 1893 and opted for the Virgin.) The recent publication of *Middletown* (by Robert and Helen Lynd) had exposed to our eyes an America that was a congeries of Main Streets—our industrial cities cursed with uniformity. "Can Artists and Writers Live in America?" was the subject of a symposium in *The Nation*. Still another, edited by Charles A. Beard, was characteristically entitled *Whither Mankind?* Its survey of our industrial society was, on the whole, optimistic; Beard, like John Dewey, was critical of our pecuniary culture, but he ventured the hope that the business-directed economy would undergo improvement through education and experiment. In the coming age of technology, which many now foresaw, reason and science, already applied by our engineers to industrial management, "would inevitably extend its area to the field of public policy," and Beard made the assumption that the principle of control would gradually be introduced into our unplanned economy; we would move from confusion to order.

In reviewing briefly some of the ideas we talked of at the turn of the decade, I find that they dealt principally with moral and aesthetic considerations. Here I am reminded of my utopian friend Lewis Mumford, with whom I became acquainted in 1928. Surely one of the most appealing of the young intellectuals of that era, he talked of men and machines in a way that reflected broader social interests than those of the literary fellows who were concerned mainly with form and technique in writing. While developing into an accomplished writer himself, this versatile young man, who was mainly self-taught (except for courses in night college), had pursued studies in the physical sciences as well as sociology and the liberal arts. His experience extended from operating one of the new-fangled radios on a naval vessel in wartime to investigating housing conditions in New York and serving as an adviser to its first City Planning Commission. A great inspiration had come to him from the "geo-technical" writings of Patrick Geddes, the Scottish scientist-architect-sociologist and city-planner in one, who labored to change England's industrial jungles into smiling garden communities. In Mumford's view, as in that of Geddes, the machine was the enemy and must be tamed in the interests of man, instead of letting man be turned into the machine's pawn or "robot" (a new term derived from Karel Capek's play *R.U.R.*). Artists and architects in particular were chosen to be the builders of the new society, in which men would be taken from their squalid quarters into the planned environment, rural or urban, in which, alone, the Good Life was possible.

The tall, handsome Mumford spoke of all this with a blazing conviction, with genuine eloquence, his dark eyes aglow with feeling. Even then he was as one *engagé*; he himself arranged to live according to his own austere scheme of the Good Life, going to reside with his charming wife Sophie and their infant son in the newly established cooperative community of Sunnyside in Queens. Here blocks of semi-detached houses were placed to enclose a common interior garden, from which vehicular traffic was excluded. The community of moderate-cost houses, moreover, enjoyed a measure of self-government operating through "town meetings" of the residents.

On visiting the Mumfords at Sunnyside, however, I found the place a rather homely imitation of a London suburb; its economy and sensible conveniences for families were evident, but in architectural form it was commonplace and in no way suited to inspire a renascence of art and civilization. To reach it one rode on the elevated railway over the squalid industrial suburb of Long Island City, which completely girt Sunnyside, a tiny island in an ocean of factories discharging grime and chemical waste on all sides.

Truly Mumford is one of our contemporaries who has served the Republic well: by his writings on our urban chaos he has provided us with a thoroughgoing critique of the naked commercialism that blights not only cities but millions of lives. Nevertheless, in my impatient mood of those times, I used to argue with him in friendly spirit that, by giving to city-planning priority over all things he was putting the cart before the horse. If important business interests drew revenue from cheap, depreciated slum properties, no sermons on ethical-aesthetic goals would ever bring them to change their ways. Only something equivalent to a social revolution, I remember saying, would ever release the death grip of banking and insurance corporations on their cherished slums.

Van Wyck Brooks, Mumford's older friend and confrere, also carried on his own sort of "war with the United States" for twenty years. In one book after another, following the *Wine of the Puritans* in 1912, he held that gifted writers, such as Melville and James, were alienated or ruined by our mercenary society, and he exhorted us to return to the Golden Age of New England, to the lights of Emerson and Thoreau. Brooks, too, wrote as a man with a social conscience, but his line of attack, like that of Mumford (whom he antedated), was also primarily ethical-aesthetic. More significant was Brook's continued effort to trace a "usable past," marking out with an intelligence superior to that of any American literary historian before him that which was notable and good in our earlier American civilization.

Concerned, like many others, with the dilemmas presented by the heedless industrialism of that postwar era and by the mass civilization it created, I too attempted in 1929 to study our present culture, such as it was, in the light of the past. The book I wrote that year was *Portrait of the Artist as American*, a group of nine essays in the literary history of the late nineteenth century, treating of those who came after the Golden Age of New England. These were principally Henry James, W. D. Howells, Mark Twain, Walt Whitman, Emily Dickinson, Henry Adams, and Stephen Crane. Inevitably my book became a chronicle of the process of alienation, in fact the near extinction of the literary species in the America of the post-Civil War era, the climactic years of the nineteenth-century industrial revolution. As Henry Adams wrote on returning from Europe after the war, it seemed that Americans had no thought except to develop their frontier lands and to build up the vast railway network and heavy-machine industries the country needed. Most of the writers and artists had no recourse but to remain here as "internal exiles," like the lonely poet Emily Dickinson, who sometimes asked herself: "How can people live without *thoughts?*" Others had gone away; Henry James in particular seemed to me to have made good his escape and to have achieved himself in the great novels and stories of his last phase—Van Wyck

Brooks notwithstanding. At the time I wrote, Henry James was considered disgraced by his expatriation, and very few Americans then read him.

Half a century after the Civil War, the tensions, the insecurity, the hazards of existence for the artist in this commercialized society seemed still unmitigated. Commenting on the scene of 1929, in a passage of *Portrait of the Artist as American* that now appears to be oddly prophetic, I permitted myself to protest the inhuman tempo of life in the United States:

> Our obsession . . . with speed, speed to be accelerated always is absurd and indecent, though it seem treason to say this. A period of reining-in must eventually come to retard the whole pace of life, if there is to be any breath left with which to live. We shall cease then to let machines appear to think for us . . . or determine what human needs shall be, whether populations shall thrive or famish.[1]

At the time my book appeared I was asked why, in view of my implied conviction that the United States was still essentially a nonculture, I ended by urging American writers living abroad to return home. I replied in an interview published in a newspaper literary supplement: "I too could go away to Europe and manage on a small income, but I want to live here and see the battle fought out, see the nature of the change that will take place . . . and find out whether the Machine will ultimately triumph over ideas."[2]

I knew that it was impossible henceforth for our people to exist without the assembly lines. There was no way for tens of millions of Americans to escape from the machines and go, like Henry David Thoreau, to subsist in a cabin by a lake and make their own lead pencils.

At the time, however, there was a group of writers calling themselves the "Southern Agrarians"—some of whom we knew and esteemed as poets—who now came out for a kind of Jeffersonian romantic revolt against the cities, urging return to the soil and, in their case, to the old Dixie way of life. Thus our friends Allen and Caroline Gordon Tate left New York toward 1929 and went back

---

[1] (New York: Harcourt, Brace; 1930), pp. 304–5. The manuscript was completed in August of 1929.
[2] Boston *Transcript*, January 23, 1930.

to live in rural Tennessee with a certain austerity and economy, but in the company of local literary friends such as Andrew Lytle, Robert Penn Warren, and John Crowe Ransom, the last a self-declared "unreconstructed Confederate." Insofar as they rendered in poetic form and with a fresh spirit the traditions of the old South and recaptured for us its dramatic past, their experiment seemed a valid one. Decidedly regionalism has its artistic attractions. But when the Southern Agrarians offered us the "ideals" of the old South as superior to those of the industrial North, some of them even defending the economy of slavery as if it possessed high spiritual values, then I found them intellectually absurd.

No, it was too late to turn back from the great cities, even from the evil gigantism of Chicago and Detroit, to Jefferson's rural utopia of forty acres and a mule per man. Even before 1929 the agrarian way of life was breaking down.

§   §   §

In the autumn of 1929 I made a little journey to Boston to do research at Harvard's Widener Library, staying for most of a week with my friend John Brooks Wheelwright and his mother at their home near Back Bay. Seven years earlier Jack Wheelwright, that rebellious dandy among poets, had been my collaborator in editing one of our little reviews from Europe, and I had seen him at regular intervals since then.

In Boston he introduced me to another literary group that seemed, like the Southern Agrarians, bent on escaping from the present and its discontents. They were the "Bards," as they called themselves; they even had their own little academy, the New England Poetry Society, of which for some reason they elected me an honorary member. (It was true that during the twenties I had written an experimental sort of poetry.) Like the Southern fugitives, the New Englanders had their own regional movement and a review, mainly antiquarian in interest, *The New England Quarterly*. They clung to Boston, pretending to love it, and they tormented and helped each other.

There was a core of solid character in the shabby old Boston of those days that made the city seem markedly different from New

York or Chicago. In her crooked old streets the tempo seemed slower and life more restful. The Wheelwright home on Massachusetts Avenue was high-ceilinged, spacious, and Victorian in style: Jack's long-departed father, a famous local architect, had decorated it with solid furniture and nineteenth-century paintings. Jack himself had finally taken up architecture, though there were few so reckless as to give him commissions. The friends who came to the house were all occupied with college teaching, book publishing, or editing, and a good many of them were related to the Cabots and the Lowells or married to one of their descendants.

In Boston the women of Yankee stock as a rule lived long and well-disciplined lives, hung on to their inherited wealth, and tended to dominate their menfolk. Jack's widowed mother, an imposing old lady and very opinionated, fitted the type, though there was warmth and sweetness in her.

The Harvard Bards (also called the "Aesthetes") had formed their group at the time of World War I, and they were the original contributors to the anthology *Eight Harvard Poets* (1917). Of its original members, Cummings and Dos Passos had been lost to New York; however Robert Hillyer, Stewart Mitchell, and Foster Damon were still on hand, as were the younger men Theodore Spencer and Winfield Scott and a few graduate students.

How they survived and continued to work at poetry was a mystery to me. Jack Wheelwright managed to live on his small income by balancing his extravagance in clothes, numerous pairs of shoes, opera subscriptions, and whisky, with humiliating economies in other items of consumption. One or two of the others enjoyed small annuities or, like Stewart Mitchell, a former editor of *The Dial*, lived off the bounty of an aged female relative. Hillyer, then an associate professor at Harvard, was already a bright star of its English faculty, while others had only minor posts as instructors or tutors. For the Boston intelligentsia, life seemed to revolve around the Harvard University cultural center; a similar situation was not to be found in other large American cities.

It amused me to attend one of the monthly reunions of the Bards, an exclusively male gathering. My diary notes of January 14, 1930, describe it:

Convening of the circle of older poets (thirtyish) plus very young poets. . . . The different readings are long. . . . Robert Hillyer, an old hand at versifying, and his young imitators too, all use well-worn poetic themes and rhymes: "Flesh—dust—flowers—lust." In their way they make a religion of literature. . . . It all has the air of a university class in polite letters. . . .

There is the economic motif always (as undertone): these attractive, well-spoken young men have a stake in the old regime. By behaving well, waiting patiently, they can inherit some position, some income, a little power of a sort. They talk of money respectfully as is never done in my own harum-scarum New York circle. When we were young we never dreamed of such an end as they come to in Boston. We had wicked or extravagant ideas of raising the dust in some way, living our free life. . . .

After the readings there was a good flow of bootleg Scotch lasting to 3 a.m.

Something of nineteenth-century Boston still lingered on, as I wrote in a letter of January 12, 1930, with the young people here "compressed in a mold of traditions which have somehow finally lost all significance or power to offer the novel and the unexpected." A case in point was that of the talented poet Theodore Spencer, who worked doggedly at teaching freshman English at Harvard for long years, living so frugally that he could hardly afford to be married. At last in middle age, in recognition of excellent work published, he reached the high honor and emoluments of the Charles Eliot Norton chair in literature. He could now have leisure to write as his heart desired. But almost immediately thereafter, at forty-five, a heart attack carried him off. His friends said: "Poor Ted Spencer—he waited too long."

For my part, I had resolved several years before to give up what we used to call pure literature. Instead of writing poems for a select circle of connoisseurs, or snobs, I intended to communicate with a large public. Working in the field of history and biography, choosing as my subjects men whose words assumed at some time the quality of heroic public actions, seemed rewarding in itself. Such a man had been the Émile Zola of the Dreyfus Case, who became "for a moment the conscience of all mankind," as Anatole France said; now in 1930 I was drawn to the study of Jean-Jacques Rousseau, the eighteenth century's "friend of man" and "father of revolutions."

In these days I lived really in the epoch of the eighteenth-century Enlightenment. The practice of biography also afforded me, through lengthy study of the private correspondence of the notable men of such a period, some fascinating glimpses of the behind-scenes movements of history.

Not long after Rousseau had passed on, a whole era had come to a sudden end in 1789. This could happen again, I reflected, as I considered the disorders threatening in various parts of the world. The author of *Émile* at one time was employed as tutor to the heir of the duke of Luxembourg, and it was observed that he taught the boy carpentry. "Why carpentry, for a duke's son?" he was asked. "Ah, he may need such knowledge some day," Rousseau replied.

In reviewing the various cults I encountered in the twenties, it comes back to me that during my visit to Boston I heard about the Neo-Humanist movement, then headed by Professor Irving Babbitt of Harvard, which that season provoked a spirited though short-lived controversy. To me the ideas of this group appeared neither novel nor humanistic, at least in the sense the Renaissance men understood that term. The Neo-Humanists had a strongly puritanical ethic and a pessimistic temper. Their precepts, they claimed, were derived from the Greek philosophers and poets, Aristotle and Plato, and from the neo-Aristotelian Christians. For them the modern world was all ugliness and vulgarity; assailing its new freedoms and its "anarchic" literature and art, they called for a reversion to an ethic of social balance and self-restraint under the discipline of something they called the "inner check."

Irving Babbitt, author of *Rousseau and Romanticism*, attributed all the alleged evil tendencies of contemporary mankind—democracy, naturalism, empirical science, and psychoanalysis—to Rousseau and his disciples. As a latter-day champion of Rousseau, I tried in my biography to restore him to his true stature as one of the world's seminal thinkers, thereby bringing down upon my own head the severe censure of the Neo-Humanists. In my view, the ruling idea in Rousseau's writings was that a culture that separated itself from awareness of the need for human welfare was spurious and decadent; and this stricture applied very well to our own society. As for the Neo-Humanists, when it came to curing our social and political ills, they offered only some vague proposals for setting up an aristocratic regime based on wealth, education, and decorous manners. Babbitt himself, in a lecture given in New York in 1930, actually sponsored a genteel form of fascism, though he had but a small bored audience.

The retrograde spirit of the Neo-Humanists seemed to infuriate our forward-looking intellectuals, such as Edmund Wilson, Hartley Grattan, and several others, who chastised the followers of Babbitt in the liberal press. For a while, nevertheless, the Neo-Humanists held appeal for a few wealthy patrons. In New York, a young man named Seward Collins turned the old literary monthly called *The Bookman* into an organ supporting their cause, and indulged himself in tirades against the "immoral" postwar breed as typified by Dos Passos and Hemingway. The son of a big stock market manipulator, Collins considered himself doubtless a member of the elite of wealth, education, and decorum Babbitt favored.

One day around this time, in 1931, I attended a cocktail party at the office of Harcourt, Brace in honor of the publication of my biography *Rousseau*. There to my surprise I encountered that rather pallid young Seward Collins with whom I had held argument on an earlier occasion.

"See you on the barricades, Mr. Collins!" I sang out cheerily.

Collins was taken aback, gave a feeble smile, then mumbled something about our certainly being "in opposite camps." A year or two later he moved on to active support of fascism.

The funny thing about the Neo-Humanists and their solicitation of the wealthy class, with whose aid they intended to elevate American society to the standards of ancient Greece (!), was that their prospective patrons all vanished instantaneously almost at the start of their campaign. In the autumn of 1929, suddenly, there was no money for such cults; we had more serious things to worry about.

II.

For years on end, during the twenties, the prolonged bull market in Wall Street provided the country with a cheery background music suggesting the clinking of many pieces-of-eight. The booming securities market accompanied and gave support to the postwar movement of industrial expansion. By their heavy and continued buying of common stocks at mounting prices, the investing and speculative public displayed the most unguarded optimism about the future. In later years, J. K. Galbraith, in his book *The Great Crash*, would describe the period as one of "mob lunacy" recalling the Tulip Craze in the Netherlands and the South Sea Bubble in Europe more than two centuries ago. Moreover the lunacy of the 1920's in America was systematically cultivated by armies of stock salesmen who were directed by men in positions of public trust. The typical moneylords of the twenties differed from the industrial barons of the late nineteenth century in that they were predominantly finance capitalists. Charles E. Mitchell, of the National City Bank, Samuel Insull, the Midwest's utilities magnate, and A. P. Giannini, the chain banker of California, were successful primarily in distributing to the middle-class public huge amounts of risk shares in their corporations, or in their pyramidal holding companies, while they themselves retained working control of those concerns through corporate legerdemain.

The great boom in Wall Street meant little to the writers and intellectuals, most of whom could never have understood the indenture on a debenture, nor find the money to buy any stocks or bonds. My own case was rather special: I had been exposed to the Wall Street power center when young and thus I had some first-hand knowledge of financial operations. My father, who had come to America as a young immigrant in the late 1870's, had risen in the business world of Brooklyn, ending up as a respected bank executive. It was his earnest wish that I, as the eldest of his three sons, should be trained in banking so that I might enter his business.

Being "addicted," however, to writing since high school days, I did little more than serve as a teller during summer vacations. After the years at Columbia College—where I figured, of course, as a fledgling writer—and a year of newspaper work and freelancing after the war, I was off to Paris with my young wife. When I returned home after two years' stay abroad, and tried to carry on here with experimental literature and with our avant-garde review *The Broom*, it became plain that we could not possibly survive. Even the United States Post Office fell upon us in January 1924 and suppressed the last issue of *The Broom* we managed to print, on charges of "obscene matter" that were laughable to readers even in those days.

Thereupon I executed an about-face and, with my father's approval, went to work with a Stock Exchange firm. For two years I directed the trading of a clientele of speculators and investors, and bore up under bear markets as well as bull markets. Had I continued as I had begun, I would have been advanced to the status of partner in the concern and held a seat on the Exchange.

Nights I went on writing, though in a desultory way, and regularly met with my literary friends—whose Bohemian milieu in Greenwich Village seemed thousands of miles removed from the great gambling casino of downtown Manhattan.

Malcolm Cowley, visiting me at my place of business one day, found me no longer threadbare, but dressed in conservative style and established in a luxurious private office beside my telephones and stock ticker. During the market session I seemed to him tenser than in former days, and had all the air of a young man of twenty-five who was highly resolved to win his fortune.

Wall Street, with its elaborations of financial techniques, possessed a certain glamour in those days. To be sure I was stationed in a lowly part of the corporate boiler room. Others, at the higher levels, in the old investment banks and in certain renowned law offices, carried on in elegant style with the flotation of new securities or with the mergers of small companies into big ones. My duties were but to help distribute the stocks manipulated by the Big Fish to a public of small fry, and to keep them trading. The people with whom I worked were much like any other Americans who were after the fast buck. But some of the old hands were originals; they had usually the impassive expression and beady eyes of inveterate gamblers—yet at intervals of exciting action in the market the passion for the game would break down all restraint, and our boardroom would resound with the cries of winners and losers.

At such times the place seemed like a jungle where each man's hand was turned against the other's. The Street, in fact, was full of its own varieties of snares and pitfalls. Almost every day a few touts bearing false rumors drifted through our boardroom, where, as in similar establishments all across the country, from fifty to a hundred persons gathered to watch the market quotations being posted from moment to moment. Those racing telegraph instruments brought not only intelligence but false intelligence. I had to learn to walk warily here, for even the managing partner of my firm sometimes communicated to me "inside tips" that brought my customers to grief. It was after one such episode—which had caused me to give vent to my sorrow over a schoolteacher who had lost all his savings—that the broker who had misled us came and admonished me to be without pity and put out of mind whatever happened to unlucky customers. "They all come here to get something for nothing," he said.

I remember the reports of a great strike of coal miners in the South in 1925 causing a temporary decline in the market. One day the Dow-Jones telegraph brought news that the union had suddenly given up the fight, acknowledging full defeat. It was a bad day for the miners, but a most happy occasion for the mine owners, who were actually great steel companies controlling those low-cost, "captive" mines. In our boardroom the crowd of speculators set up a great shout of joy as the market boomed. I felt profoundly disconcerted, recalling that I had always considered myself hitherto a liberal, and (in my student days) something of a socialist. What was I doing here, I wondered, among these people with whom I felt alone and bored. I had come to dislike my employers, those Babbitt-like commission brokers who wanted to turn me into a high-pressure operator. I had forebodings that life here would completely alter my character. "I will never be the same again," I used to say to myself.

In the evenings at home I continued to live a secret life, working happily over poems in an elliptical style that were published

(19)

in magazines like *The Little Review*; or over reviews of authors like D. H. Lawrence and Virginia Woolf. I dared not speak of such writings to the people I worked with in the Street. One of my clients by chance came upon one of my published pieces in the *Saturday Review* and declared with amazement that he could make nothing of what I wrote. He looked as if he wondered if he could trust my judgment in things financial.

In truth I enjoyed success of a sort, and even a rapidly increasing salary. But after two years of this I felt myself not only alienated and intensely unhappy in the Street, but also physically sick. One side of my head throbbed continually, and I was losing my hearing in one ear. I resigned and went to the hospital to undergo surgery; after I recovered I turned to writing again as a free lance.

In the year that followed it happened that both my parents died while only in middle age, leaving their children each an inheritance. My father, while believing me unwise or deluded, had nevertheless been uncommonly patient and generous in helping me from time to time. Now by the sad accident of his death I was bequeathed half a "living," for I had a young wife and child; at any rate, I was granted time, so terribly needed by young writers, to practice my métier. Within the year I was publishing magazine articles and literary pieces actively and had received a commission to write a book.

Occasionally thereafter I revisited Wall Street, but now in the role of a prudent investor selecting gilt-edged securities for long-term holding and income. I had also the responsibility of acting as an executor for my parents' estate in behalf of my younger brothers and a sister.

I had promised myself that someday I would write what I had learned about the real Wall Street. I was also curious about the history of the place and its legendary heroes. In the twenties one could still encounter some of the aged money kings, wearing sideburns and dressed in morning coat, who had come to fame in the preceding century.

In the autumn of 1928 I wrote a series of articles for *The Outlook*, a national weekly now defunct, traveling about the Midwestern industrial cities and interviewing some of the modern breed of financiers, such as Louis Swift of meat-packing fame, Julius Rosenwald, head of Sears, Roebuck, and the Van Sweringens of Cleveland. Later *The New Republic* asked me to write articles on the stock market boom and its aftermath, and *The New Yorker* also gave me the assignment of a series of "profiles" of Wall Street's leaders (whom I was to select). Thus at various times I renewed my contact with the financial community; in the later years I came as a detached observer, scanning the records of key men, weighing their characters and forming my own judgments of how they managed things. Some of the information I accumulated came to me in off-the-record talks with high officials of the New York Stock Exchange and the Federal Reserve System.[3]

Much has been written of how the contagious fever for easy money to be picked up in the market spread all about the country, even to the lesser orders of waiters and bootblacks who exerted themselves to overhear and act upon insiders' tips. The boom-and-bust cycle had long been America's history, but never had there been a bull market that had run up so long and seemed so "easy." By 1929 the get-rich-quick passion touched even our literary circles.

Burton Rascoe, the well-known literary columnist of the New York *Herald Tribune*, also told me of how—with the counsel of a big Wall Street insider—he was able to parlay $2,000 into $40,000 within the short period of about eighteen months. Thereafter, in 1929, he was emboldened to manage things for himself and increased his pile to about $200,000. Under the smile of fortune his way of life and his character itself changed; he acquired a big house, a mink coat for his wife, and an arrogantly big car. But what happened soon afterward to all that easy money is not difficult to imagine.

Like many others, I too was tempted to try to increase my portion; however, I used a prudence instilled in me by experience in the Street and avoided "pyramiding" on borrowed money. My gains were therefore more limited than those of the more speculative

[3] One of these, George L. Harrison, governor of the Federal Reserve Bank of New York, in later years permitted me access to his journal of daily conferences and business transactions during the years of crisis.

fellows. Yet I too was participating in the great barbecue provided by the bull market of the late twenties.

§ § §

The mounting inflation of credit for stock market gambling created severe strain on the nation's economy and on that of Europe as well. Early in 1929 the money managers in our central banking system, the Federal Reserve, shifted from the easy money policy they had formerly pursued and raised the rediscount rate to 5 per cent.

Later I heard there was loud wrangling among the big bankers before even this mild corrective measure was authorized. "I thought it would have been better to have the stock market fall out of the tenth story, instead of the twentieth later on," Governor George L. Harrison of the New York Reserve Bank said to me in reviewing these events years later. One of the leading commercial bankers—who was also one of the directors of the New York Reserve Bank—Charles E. Mitchell of the National City Bank, helped thwart this restrictive action by flinging many millions of his bank's funds into the tight call loan market. Many corporations having surplus cash eagerly placed it in call loans at the current high rates, 12 to 20 per cent.

In August the Federal Reserve moved again to halt the runaway boom, advancing the rediscount rate to 6 per cent. Traditionally, a sharp rise in money rates was followed by a decline in stocks. The bull market careened higher still, then retreated in September; a few weeks later the retreat turned into a rout, as margin calling and forced selling became widespread.

October 24, 1929, was to be known in our history as "Black Thursday." On that day full-scale panic raged throughout the country as a result of the tremendous decline of the New York stock market. As in other panics, selling came in floods and there were almost no buyers. The high-priced "blue chip" stocks had been very high indeed, and some of them, like General Electric and General Motors, now fell about $50 a share in a single market session.

I myself was no passive onlooker, for I had my own small stake in that demented market. Within the past year my portfolio of stocks had doubled in value; the competence, the independent income that would permit me to write as I pleased, had been all but won, and now it was "gone where the woodbine twineth," as the old Wall Street traders used to say. I had shared for a while the hopes and illusions of the American middle class, and now I suffered their common fate.

I remember taking the subway downtown on one of those days of terror to visit my broker's boardroom. It was nearly 10 a.m. as I reached the Wall Street exit of the subway; I can still hear the sound of hundreds of running feet, the sound of fear, as people hurried to reach their posts of observation before the gong rang for the opening of business. Hypnotized by panic, the crowds of customers in the boardrooms of the financial district stared in amazement at the stockboards or ticker tape recording their progressive ruin. Brokers and their clerks were haggard and red-eyed for want of sleep. Owing to the record-breaking volume of trading (more than twelve million shares), the telegraphic reporting service fell two hours behind operations on the Exchange floor, and no one knew what the going values were. The customers all reacted in different ways; some looked on in stony silence; others made exclamations of surprise, or nervously tried to jest, as news came of unheard-of losses.

Actually, panics were endemic under our system; in the three decades since 1900 there had been five good ones, but everything was growing bigger. The Crash of 1929 made a grand economic spectacle, but for a small investor like myself it was much too stunning. When the bulls and the bears were done for the session of October 28 that I attended, I reckoned that in a few short days I had lost more than fifty thousand dollars.

"Easy come, easy go," I heard one of the customers say wryly. "It will all come back; they always do," a broker put in reassuringly. I wanted to believe him, but terrible doubts assailed me. Things had gone wildly wrong in a way few living men had ever seen before.

As always, the bell rang at 3 p.m. for the close of the market, but everyone sat or stood there for two hours longer watching the retarded tape spell out the unthinkable losses of that day. The whole Wall Street citadel of wealth and power and all its paper symbols—"the Bastille of American capitalism"—seemed to have collapsed, leaving us the vista of a landscape of ruins.

III.

A decisive change of direction in the stock market is generally supposed to forecast barometrically the future trend of the nation's business. Such a *grande chute* as that of October 1929 also exercises an immediate psychological effect on businessmen, making capital "timid," slowing down expenditures for new plant and payroll expansion. How our leaders in industry and finance behaved at the time of the smash-up in the securities market, and how they dealt with the various stages of economic recession that soon developed, became for me the subject of close study.

At noon on Black Thursday, October 24, a meeting of the so-called Morgan consortium of bankers at 23 Wall Street took place; this was widely reported at the time, and was said to have "saved" the stock market. Charles E. Mitchell of the National City Bank was there; Albert C. Wiggins, the veteran president of the Rockefeller-controlled Chase Bank also turned up, as did George F. Baker, Jr., of the First National Bank, and the heads of Guaranty Trust and Bankers' Trust. Thomas W. Lamont, chairman of Morgan and Company, presided. The acting head of the New York Stock Exchange, Vice-President Richard Whitney, also came to the meeting (the president was abroad), together with George L. Harrison, governor of New York's Reserve Bank; both men afterward gave me their account of the proceedings.

At this moment the whole world waited to see what would be done by the giant banks to end the market panic. The prestige of those men of the countinghouses was then at its zenith. Soon watching eyes at the corner of Wall and Broad Streets saw "Dick" Whitney emerge—he was known as "Morgan's floor broker"—cross the street, and enter the Exchange floor, where he elbowed his way through the milling crowd of brokers. Advancing upon Post 2, the station of specialists in United States Steel shares, he called out in a loud voice: "I bid 205 for twenty-five thousand Steel." Then he passed on to other trading posts for leading industrial stocks and left similar bids at current quotations. Prices recovered strongly that afternoon. The newspapers reported: RICHARD WHITNEY HALTS STOCK PANIC—HEROIC ACTION RALLIES MARKET.

The bankers' conference had hurriedly raised a temporary credit of $240 million for a syndicate that would buy leading stocks in an effort to stabilize the market. Whitney had been given those buying orders for the bankers' pool. It was the old system, used by the Morgans and Rockefellers in the panics of the past; but this time it did not work as well as before.

The newspapers exaggerated not only Whitney's role and the effect of his grandstand play on the floor of the Exchange but also the martial courage of the bankers' syndicate for whom he acted. Much graver problems than those of calming the frightened sheep faced the bankers. After their lunch-hour meeting downtown they met again, as a much larger group, that same evening after dinner in the library of J. P. Morgan's house at Madison Avenue and Thirty-fifth Street. This conference, which dragged on until 2 a.m., was not reported in the press, nor was it mentioned afterward by financial historians; but it was described in George L. Harrison's diary.

The bankers knew that the whole world was selling the stock market, and that the force of liquidation was only momentarily stemmed. As loans were called, more weak positions would be uncovered. Harrison's account shows that the banking leaders anticipated a general collapse of the entire financial structure with all its brokerage firms and banks, and they proposed to close down the Stock Exchange, as in the wartime panic of 1914.

Some of America's oldest and largest Stock Exchange firms, and some of the big fish these brokers served, were known to be in serious trouble; the Van Sweringens, publicly sponsored by Morgan's, owed their broker almost $50 million against collateral that had become terribly insufficient, and the broker owed the Morgan banks. The bankers always know who is in trouble, and they were aware that the mighty Samuel Insull and even Mitchell of the National City Bank were unable to meet their obligations. The banks were overloaded with insolvent clients who were so "important" that they had to be "carried" until they could extricate themselves from their plight.

The gravest danger rose from the fact that many private or non-bank lenders who had recently gone into the call money market would be taking all their money out in a sort of mass exodus. Out of nine billions in call money, more than a third was owing to these private lenders. The old-line New York banks had to take over those loans; but vast as their resources were, it was impossible to do so unless large additional reserves of credit were created for them.

Harrison relates that he was among those who counseled against closing the New York Stock Exchange, saying: "That is just what we should *not* do." But in order to support the New York banks, the central banking system would now reverse its tight money policy and begin large "open market operations" designed to create an expanded volume of money. Harrison added: "As our part of the bargain, I undertook to purchase a hundred million dollars in Government bonds each day in the week that followed." Thus the semi-governmental institution would help the commercial banks tide over a desperate situation.

Governor Harrison's diary of activities at the Federal Reserve Bank of New York for October 28–30, 1929, reads:

> On the Monday, Tuesday and Wednesday following [Black Thursday] we purchased Governments in great blocks. Enormous shifts in Loans for Others [than banks] were being made. In two days a billion in loans had to be taken over by the New York member banks. . . . The reserves were provided by the Federal Reserve buying their Government securities and establishing reserves for them on its books.

Despite these heroic measures, the general carnage continued for three more weeks, until mid-November, and encompassed what the New York Stock Exchange Report for 1930 called "the greatest stock market catastrophe of the ages." On the culminating day of the panic, November 13, trading attained such a phenomenal volume that communications facilities broke down completely.

Whitney told me afterward that they just stopped counting, but expert guesses put the volume of sales at 23 million shares. The loss in values was about equal to the World War I debt of the United States.

During those parlous times the Board of Governors of the Exchange, with Whitney presiding, used to come together every day in a basement room directly under the trading floor. Those "cellar meetings," Whitney said, were drenched in gloom: "the people present kept nervously lighting and extinguishing cigarettes until the room was blue with smoke." Out of rumors about these underground meetings grew up the legend that Thomas W. Lamont and "Dick" Whitney sat near a hole under the trading floor watching the movement of "the Morgan stocks" through a periscope. They had no periscope, not even a compass. As they left the basement room at the end of their conference and, in a group, neared the door leading to the street—where thousands of eyes would be watching them—Whitney would be at their head, and on several occasions he reminded the others: "Now get your smiles on, boys." With their hearts dead within them and simpers frozen on their faces, the governors of the Exchange marched out into Broad Street, before the cameramen, financial reporters, and all the host of hangers-on, and so back to their own offices.

Here were some of the managers of the New Era in American capitalism, and it would seem to have been one of the great ironies of history that a Richard Whitney should appear at their head. The weakness that led him, of all people, to fraud and embezzlement was not to be exposed until several years later. Outwardly he was a tall and imposing figure of a man, grown somewhat paunchy at forty, though handsome in a heavy-featured way, and always impeccably dressed in striped trousers and frock coat, as befitted the acting head of the old Exchange. Wall Street claimed much credit for staying open in the face of world-wide panic, and Dick Whitney somehow acquired laurels in the process, as The Man Who Saved the Stock Market. Early in the next year he was elected president of the Exchange and was sent to Washington as the official spokesman for the *ancien régime* to lobby before Congress

(27)

against proposed measures for regulating the securities markets—which was why I happened to interview and write about him two years later for *The New Yorker.*

He was quite the type of white Anglo-Saxon Protestant who would in those days have been chosen for the role he played. Born in Boston, the son of a bank officer (though not of the rich Whitneys), he was educated at Groton School and Harvard, trained for a while at the old investment firm of Kidder, Peabody and Company, and so, after marriage to an heiress who was related to the Vanderbilts, established himself as a broker on his own in Wall Street in 1914. Thanks to the help of an uncle and his elder brother George, both then executives at Morgan's, the market orders of that house were regularly allotted to him. In those days many posts in the financial hierarchy were filled by the claims of nepotism. Thus Richard Whitney, who had distinguished himself at school and college principally as a regular fellow, an athlete, and a joiner of exclusive clubs, moved up to become a member of what would later be called the Power Elite, representing the Morgan influence in the Stock Exchange directorate and being chosen to make that grandstand play on the afternoon of Black Thursday.

In getting up the materials for his "profile" I searched through all the newspaper morgues and society columns and rounded up former Groton and Harvard classmates in the Street in 1931 who knew Dick Whitney and often didn't like what they knew about him. Those who were of an independent cast of mind criticized the business favoritism shown by Morgan's to friends of the firm's members who were "in society," like young Whitney, whose acquaintances sometimes described him as a wary climber. To them he enjoyed prestige as one of "Morgan's floor brokers" but seemed to carry himself with an air of self-importance and vanity that had no other justification.

Facing this reputed generalissimo of finance, I made earnest efforts to get through to the real person and cut the clichés he was handing out—"we must, above all, restore the public's confidence" and "the market always comes back"—but found it no easy task. I had always heard that people who worked for Morgan in the old days were brainy and energetic, but Whitney seemed only of average mentality, and this raised the suspicion in my mind that he was really an "empty valise." (Another high official of the Exchange said that he expected I might make fun of Whitney, but he begged me to "please spare the New York Stock Exchange.")

Assuming an air of polite interest, I listened to Whitney's cant about the unimpeachable probity of the Stock Exchange under his supervision and the vital need to preserve its "free and open market" from all regulation save that of the members of the club itself. I depended, however, upon my own interpretation of the dossier on Whitney that I had in my pocket. In short, I put him down as a proper stuffed shirt. He had exhibited, I wrote, the qualities of a typical American financial leader of our time: "coolness in action, the ability to talk freely without saying anything, and to manage big deals with a poker face, save when the situation was so bad that it called for a broad smile."

The president of the Exchange had the important duty of investigating member brokers charged with unethical procedures in trading or in dealing with clients. If any were found guilty by the committee on business conduct, Whitney was authorized to punish such members by expulsion from the Exchange. On such occasions he would mount the rostrum at one side of the trading floor, ring a little bell (such as they used in London's ancient Stock Exchange), halt all business activity, and announce the punishment of an errant broker.

One day, seven years later, that little bell would toll for Richard Whitney himself. Ever since, he has been associated in the public mind with the famous scandal of his embezzlements from clients' accounts and from trust funds in his charge, which, in 1938, resulted in his trial and sentence to a long term in prison. After 1929, when he made that brave charge on the United States Steel post, his own business difficulties were chronic, and while preserving a bold front to the world, he formed the habit of falsifying his accounts. Finally his condition could no longer be concealed. That "Morgan's broker" and the president of the Exchange should swindle his clients out of more than five million dollars was something unforeseen, and it came as a tremendous shock to the entire financial world. The prestige of the so-called Morgan dynasty in

Wall Street was never the same after that, though Whitney's elder brother George repaid all the money stolen.

A good many of the amateur plungers who found the sudden change from riches to rags intolerable jumped out of the windows of high buildings or dived off the yachts they had forfeited. During the year that followed the Crash, the newspapers were full of brief reports of suicides, whose total in 1930 rose by 22 per cent above the previous year's record.

§   §   §

In the winter of 1930 I heard from one of my "contacts" in Wall Street an account of a remarkable social gathering of the moneyed set in New York that called to mind one of the fictions of Scott Fitzgerald about the "golden twenties," except that it was stranger. Harrison Williams, a well-known magnate of public utilities, was then one of the richest of the new rich. Coming to New York from a small town in Ohio, where he used to manufacture bicycles, he had at first the air of a rustic, but he quickly carved out a sizable fortune in the stock market during World War I. By the mid-twenties he commanded an enormous combination of public utilities in the North American Company, a typical "pyramided" holding company by which Williams held the voting-control stock in his hands, while the public invested vast sums of money in classes of stock without control.

Just before the Crash of 1929 Harrison Williams had unloaded a mass of new investment trust securities upon the public through the old banking firm of Goldman, Sachs and Company, netting something approaching a hundred million dollars in cash. Moreover, there were rumors in Wall Street during the panic of October–November that Williams had also sold short the securities of his own companies. (These rumors were in later years borne out in investigations by the Senate.) Thus, the more prices fell, the more profit he garnered; the more the lambs wept, the more he rejoiced.

A widower approaching sixty, he had recently married the beautiful Mona S. Bush, who was about half his age and known in those days as "America's best-dressed woman." With his new wife by his side this *nouveau riche* pushed his way into New York society. Toward 1929 he had acquired a sumptuous mansion on Fifth Avenue, and on the very day in mid-November when the panic was at its worst and prices had fallen to their lowest depths, he had arranged a house-warming party and grand ball for several hundred guests. Those invited were mostly of the bankers' and brokers' fraternity. Though they had no reason to make merry, though their hearts were dead within them, they and their wives pulled themselves together and came to the Williamses to inspect the great new mansion and the new wife.

My informant, a bank officer who happened to be listed in New York's social register, described the display of lights, rare carpets, old masters' paintings, and rivers of champagne as producing an effect unequaled even in those days of conspicuous waste. Estimates placed the cost of the party for that one night at "two or three hundred thousand dollars"; and Mrs. Williams's gown and jewels were also not to be disregarded. Now all the guests were very blue over the losses they had suffered and the danger of ruin that faced many of them. Yet, though broken-hearted, they dared not give words to their anxieties, but stared in amazement at the extravagant display Harrison Williams was able to afford at such a time. In their state of gloom and doom their response to the entertainment was at best subdued and constrained. But the canny old Williams—who, all suspected, had gotten out completely from under—greeted everyone with an air of the greatest self-contentment, as genial as old Satan himself.

"That was a real hangman's ball," my friend remarked.

§   §   §

President Hoover, then well regarded by the public, did not stand idly by during the stock market panic, but acted as if he realized that it could excite forces making for a serious decline in business activity. As soon as things became stabilized, after mid-November, he began to issue a series of statements calculated to reassure the public that fundamental conditions were "sound." Other authoritative voices also added assurances that "prosperity may continue indefinitely."

Showing an initiative greater than that of other Presidents,

Hoover also called a large group of the country's business leaders to a conference in Washington at which plans for stimulating a forward movement in business were to be agreed upon. About fifty captains and kings of industry gathered at the White House and cheerfully promised the President their cooperation in maintaining employment and preserving the nation's purchasing power. Some of the big employers present—like Walter Gifford, head of the Bell Telephone System—added that they planned to spend even larger sums than in the past on plant and machinery. The President observed that the industrialists were under no compulsions of any kind, but they had undertaken to cooperate in an entirely voluntary way.

A while later I happened to check up on how those captains of industry actually carried out their promises. As soon as they got back to their desks, they began discharging employees by the hundreds or thousands. President Lovett of the Sante Fe Railroad was among those at President Hoover's conference who had promised to maintain employment. But in the early spring of 1930 I found a little news item in the back pages of my newspaper showing that the Sante Fe had discharged five hundred machine shop workers. Similar reports came from all the heavy industries.

Hoover's ruling idea had been to bolster business confidence and head off a possible retreat of capital. He must have been aware that the economic index figures compiled by the Commerce Department had already turned sharply downward. Nevertheless he made cheerful predictions that "the present level of prosperity is to continue."

By April 1930 the securities markets had gradually recovered about half the ground lost in the previous autumn, but reports of a rapid increase in unemployment were being received in Washington. Official government estimates of unemployment (2.4 million) were sharply challenged on the score of accuracy by statisticians outside the government service, and in May they reckoned the number of jobless at five million. One of the government's own experts in vital statistics resigned at the time, apparently in the course of an angry dispute over the issuance of misleading statistical reports of employment. The disturbing idea spread about that

President Hoover and some of his aides tended to minimize or even suppress unpleasant facts. Meanwhile the stock market resumed its declining habit. We were beginning to feel that we could believe no one who was in a position of authority.

Chapter Two

~⚬~

Our Refuge

in the Country

IN THE EARLY SPRING of 1930 I moved from New York, with my wife and two small sons, to the farm in northern Connecticut which I had purchased the year before. While business conditions grew steadily worse that season and the prospect became ever darker, ever more "bearish," in the world beyond our rural horizon, here in our valley the annual "bull market" of spring that had never let us down in millions of years was in full progress. First the willow branches turned yellowish along the streams; the pale shad-blow then appeared in the wood-lots surrounding our meadows; the first leaves opened, and big clumps of dogwood on the hill facing our house to the west put forth a mass of formal white flowers.

The time of the Great Depression was actually a season of euphoria for me. I had recently recovered from injuries sustained in a fearful accident, a fire at our apartment house in New York. My family escaped, but I, with distracted mind, returned, apparently thinking of saving manuscripts or a precious painting, was trapped in the flames and rescued at the last moment by firemen taking me down a ladder. My burns proved so severe that during several weeks of fever I was near death.

I had lost half of the money I had inherited, and after that, in the conflagration of February 1, 1930, all my worldly goods in the form of books, pictures, furniture, clothes. Surprisingly, these successive disasters did not seem to cast down my spirits, nor those of my wife—at such times a wonderfully sanguine person. She recalls that after my recovery I seemed filled with simple joy at finding myself alive, at watching the procession of spring in the country, and, after long delay, resuming my work at a typewriter, though with hands still scarred and painful.

Years ago I had formed the habit of going to the country outside New York and staying there until the blaze of autumn color died down. I liked as much as anyone the cultural facilities of big city life, but it was in no way needful for my kind of work that my study should be perched beside a roaring subway excavation, or that I breathe only soot and grime all the year long.

The ritual of escape from our urban Hades each year had begun in my youth, though I was city born. While we were at college together my friend Kenneth Burke and I had got the idea from some artists who made it their practice to go each spring to an abandoned cottage in upstate New York or Maine and, while painting, live off the country—it might be on plain fare from the A & P store, or rabbit or trout. The scheme was no doubt a residue of Thoreauvian and Tolstoyan thinking; but it worked. After being a shut-in literary animal most of the day, an hour or two of exercise in the sun, gardening or clearing ground, was a perfect restorative, renewing my strength, clearing my head for the sedentary labor of the next day.

In time, with increasing prosperity, most of us departed from our original idea of living the Spartan life in the country. Kenneth Burke rejected electricity and modern plumbing, but built a tennis court and a small artificial pond at his New Jersey farm. In August 1929, I had luckily disposed of some shares of stock, which were fated to become worthless soon afterward, and made a down payment on a farm in the foothills of the Berkshire Mountains. It was a larger place than we needed for a summer dwelling and with far too much land, the owner having refused to divide it. In fact it embraced a whole valley enclosed by steep hills through which ran a brook that often behaved like a river in flood.

Once the site of a thriving tobacco culture, Twin Willows Farm, as it was then called, had been used by its recent owners to keep summer boarders; its grounds and barns had been neglected, but the old farmhouse was sturdy. After we cleared away the rubbish, cut the surrounding brush, and touched the place up with paint, we had an old-fashioned dwelling that had been renovated in 1848 by the addition of two wings and colonnaded porches, in the clean, symmetrical style of the Greek Revival. The house was well situated in a wide lawn under century-old maples and elms, and upon a knoll that overlooked a rugged valley and its stream. Though we were only sixty miles north of the New York city line our valley offered an extraordinary variety of landscape, and one felt as "protected" as if one were in the big woods of Maine.

The magic of the place was in its lively trout brook that tumbled among large boulders, at one spot splashing over a miniature waterfall into a rock cistern about twenty feet square to form a natural pool, or swimming hole. The pool was placed beside a grove of low ironwood trees, about five minutes' walk down the hill from our house. As its bed was of fine gravel and smooth rock its water was utterly clear and cold. Here my children swam and splashed about all summer long, and friends gathered to rest and sun themselves. On days of great heat, after long morning sessions at my desk, I would come to bathe at noon and return to my work refreshed. When I had to go to the city for a day or two of business calls or interviews, I would think with longing of our "sacred grove" and the pool; returning to the farm and its valley would restore a sense of repose I no longer felt in the town. I found myself in full accord with Thoreau, who said that if he had not gone to the woods he might have died with the feeling that he had never really lived.

My wife worked swiftly about the house and gardens assisted by a gigantic young Finnish girl who loved the country and our children. Our boys, then eight and four, grew up permissively enough, but they were taught to help at weeding and the mowing of lawns. When our charming niece of five came to live with us and filled the place of a daughter—and we also accumulated a cat, a dog, a brood of hens, and even a handsome saddle horse quartered with us for his feed—then our life was complete. The volume of sound generated by children and animals around the house and yard soon became something to reckon with. I had been working in one of the rooms of our rambling old house.

"Either the children must go, or I go," I declared sententiously; and so I went, out of the house to one of the smaller barns located two hundred feet down the road in a clump of locust trees at the edge of a meadow. It was actually a corn crib I had chosen, with two of its walls slanting inward as in an ark and making a high-ceilinged room of odd form. I improved the place by cutting many windows in the walls and setting up bookshelves all around. Because of its twelve windows and its open views in all directions, I felt as if I were out of doors all day long.

I was then engaged, under a long-term contract with my publishers, upon a whole series of books of biography and history. For my preparatory research I would drive regularly to the Yale Library at New Haven, an hour's journey, or sometimes to New York or Washington, D.C., returning with copious notes and books which I deposited in my ark-shaped barn. The habit of concentration associated with the barn library became autohypnotic; it would begin to work on me the moment I entered the place. I must have written the greater part of twenty volumes there in the three decades that followed.

In choosing to live in this rural community well beyond the commuting zone I did so with the knowledge that we had some friends of our own sort nearby. On Quaker Ridge, in Patterson, New York, were Slater and Sue Brown. "Bill" Brown, my classmate at college, had been a member of our literary avant-garde in Paris in the early twenties. Friendship with his wife Sue, the schoolmate of Kenneth Burke and Malcolm Cowley in Pittsburgh, also dated back to my college years. Another of my companions of Paris days was large, red-haired Robert M. Coates, who established himself with his wife Elsa on a few acres I sold him at the edge of my property, a quarter of a mile down our road. The dedicated young artist Peter Blume, a youth of twenty-three whom we called even then "the old master," also turned up in a small summer cottage in our village. He too needed the peace of the countryside and space in which to compose his monumental canvases. Malcolm Cowley, who had visited Sherman for years for its trout fishing, often arrived at weekends; Hart Crane, when staying at Quaker Hill, sometimes drove over with the Browns or the Cowleys; and once each summer Kenneth Burke and his wife journeyed over from New Jersey. Thus, on occasion, our old literary clan of the early twenties, "the antilogrollers" as we called ourselves, was fully reunited and resumed with undiminished zest its habitual form of conversation, a mixture of bantering and baiting.

It seemed there were fine talkers in abundance in those days; within a radius of twenty to thirty miles of our house, in Connecticut or rural New York, practically everybody we might enjoy was available. At Amenia, New York, Lewis Mumford resided, and at regular intervals we exchanged visits. He was then at work on his *Technics and Civilization*. Beyond Mumford's, at Rhinebeck, lived the artist Henry Billings, who was highly articulate, and his tall, beautiful wife, Gladys, whose tastes were musical and literary. In the village neighboring ours were Katharine Anthony, author of many excellent scholarly biographies, and her lifelong friend Elizabeth Irwin, the educator. They were by then middle-aged heroines of the wars of the feminists in America; but, kindling to their vivacity and wit, we named them "the gay ladies of Gaylordsville."

It was at their house that we first met Charles and Mary Beard, who had long lived in the nearby village of New Milford. My first sight of the historian was in a square dance at the Irwin-Anthony place, his very tall, lean figure vigorously bobbing up and down to the tune of "Turkey in the Straw." The Beards extended their hospitality to us; we became fast friends from the start, and my wife and I came to their Sunday luncheon gatherings on many occasions during the next two decades.

Charles Beard, who was then in his middle fifties, his red hair just turning gray, was beyond a doubt one of the great talkers of his day, very alert mentally, his speech often marked by an old-fashioned eloquence and fire. A native of Indiana, he had studied at Oxford University, where he and his wife had established the first Labour college and named it Ruskin College in honor of the man whose prose he admired most. Later he became a much idolized professor at Columbia, while also working in the field of

municipal research and serving as an adviser on governmental reforms in such diverse regions as Japan and eastern Europe. For
many years Beard had produced widely read works of history and
text books while living in the country. But now the scholar liked
to play the Hoosier country boy, and in his spare time he enjoyed
managing two dairy farms he owned in the neighborhood of New
Milford.

The Beards lived in a large house (formerly a girls' school) at
the crest of a hill overlooking the Housatonic River. On Sundays
visitors arriving from points as far removed as San Francisco,
Tokyo, or Berlin would appear there, and with them some of the
Connecticut illuminati. After a hearty meal Mary Beard (always
called Jane by her husband) would lead the way to the living room
and, before anyone could resume the light chatter of the luncheon
table, she would announce firmly: "Dr. M——, former cabinet
minister, who has just arrived from Europe, will now tell us about
the crisis in his country." Everyone would fall silent and assume an
air both solemn and attentive. Charles Beard, noticing the serious
mien we put on, exclaimed on one such occasion, with a twinkle in
his sharp blue eyes: "I see that Jane means to *improve* us."

II.

Sherman was a hill village, formerly a center for
cattle drovers, named after a local hero who had signed the Declaration of Independence. Situated several hundred feet high in the
hills above the Housatonic Valley, it seemed to have been overlooked by history. In 1930 there were still dairy farms, which was
why our winding brook valleys still had an open and smiling appearance; the farms were owned by Swedes, Irishmen, Poles, and a few
old-native Yankees. There were only two or three estate owners
reputed to be passing rich. In essence the citizens were tolerably
democratic and strong on community spirit. Many persons drove
through the main street without noticing they were in a village
with a homely little town hall dated 1886 and a single general store
at the main corner.

(39)

In the early spring of 1932 we determined to become all-year residents, though our house was lighted then by kerosene lamps and we had only a primitive heating system. Thereafter we were accepted by the Sherman people as permanent settlers, and we registered to vote there. We attended community suppers and church socials as well as town meetings, and my wife was elected to the village school board. Thus we came to know our Connecticut Yankees well and learned all about their old village feuds.

Our sparsely settled township (population 400), spreading over a large and beautiful rural area unspoiled by billboards or roadside stands, was and still is a rock-ribbed Protestant Republican stronghold, forming a sort of electoral rotten borough for the state legislature. Though the local people were at first wary of artists in their midst and called our group the "Left Bank of Sherman," they thawed out after a while and proved neighborly enough. I came to esteem some of the good and skillful farmers among them. We hardly ever went to the local Congregationalist church, but its attractive young minister became our good friend. After we had lived there several years I fell seriously ill during a midwinter blizzard when the roads were blocked by high snow drifts. I remember with gratitude how some of our farmer neighbors brought the doctor in a horse-drawn sledge, while the postman came to deliver medicine on skis. After a few days the neighbors, headed by the minister, cleared our road by hand.

It should be remarked that our several families did not constitute a Bohemian colony. Save for Saturday nights or weekends ours were disciplined working habits; we were, in most cases, raising children and animal pets and cultivating gardens, and some of us were given to hunting and fishing, much like our rural neighbors.

The New England town meeting appealed to me at first as the pure and hallowed institution of local democracy in which all citizens were free to participate directly. I soon saw it for what it was: a businesslike steam roller run by the inner circle of Republicans. In such a small community partisan politics were in fact meaningless; our village business and treasury were of such small scale that things were managed in tolerably honest fashion.

The economy of writers and artists, unlike that of farmers or mechanics, depended wholly on the publishing enterprises and galleries of the towered Babylon sixty miles south of us. Now past the age of thirty, my literary friends (and I too) turned out work with a resolution and regularity not shown in earlier years, and in most cases we were resourceful in obtaining writing commissions or magazine jobs that carried us through the worst of the Great Depression. But it meant keeping in touch with New York week by week.

Country life, even at low cost, offered no security in itself. For example, one impoverished young writer, Edward McSorley, came with his wife to live near Sherman in a house that a friend had lent him for the winter. He was said to be doing a novel in the manner of James Joyce. But like many others he had to face the struggle with self: when spring came, he had nothing done; the McSorleys were not only hungry, they were about to have twins! After that they fled to the city with their babies. Big-hearted Malcolm Cowley and I—at his insistence, for I scarcely knew McSorley—had shared the cost of the accouchement. I used to remind Malcolm about our each holding a "mortgage" on one of those twins.

Slater Brown, in his fine novel *The Burning Wheel*, described the countryside of Quaker Ridge and Sherman much as it was then; his book also focused upon the drama of the lonely writer, weltering in melancholia and alcohol, coming to the dead end of his unfinished work.

I went forward however with my own work during two long sessions each day, and sometimes a third at night, until my doggedness became proverbial in the neighborhood. Malcolm Cowley wrote of me later that I was "like an addict going back to his drink again and again." Every year or second year a book was completed.

My publisher, Alfred Harcourt, came to fish our brook and mapped out my life for me for years ahead. He was a sharp-faced, astute Yankee from upstate New York who had made an extraordinary success of publishing, and during many years he commanded what was then considered America's most distinguished list of authors. He had taken over my contract from a smaller house after the publication of *Zola*, my first success at the bookstalls, and found that I continued to reach a serious reading public with my next two books. Despite the hard times he undertook to back me with small monthly advances against future royalties, so that I could live in the country.

On a warm night in June 1931 I drove back to the farm from the city with new friends, the young West Coast novelist Robert Cantwell and his wife. We had our dinner in the long, low living room around which our house was centered and which had a very wide fireplace. In our cellar there was always a little keg of bootleg applejack, all of six months old and drawn from local orchards, that we served our friends. After dinner Cantwell and I sat outside on the lawn under the great shade trees in full moonlight, the air heavily scented with mock orange in blossom. Cantwell looked about him in amazement. Finally he exclaimed: "My God, this place seems to me like the reward for a long and fruitful life!"

His words struck me as both odd and touching. At a little more than thirty, I had not really lived very long; my life had not yet borne much fruit, though I had certainly become more productive than before. Cantwell, seven or eight years younger than I, was at twenty-three the author of a novel of extraordinary power and poignancy, *Laugh and Lie Down*, a document of runaway youth in the Pacific Coast region. In his condition of poverty and insecurity, he may have seen me as already a venerable figure of a man living a serenely patriarchal life in a beautiful countryside.

Everything did seem to have been well calculated to ensure our independence, my continued functioning, and the pursuit of happiness in this fortunate place that appeared well defended against the evil and ugliness outside and the sight of masses of human beings agonizing in the large cities. Everything seemed perfectly arranged—until the heavy repercussions of the Depression reached us. The great slump threw a pall over our cheerful acres. My nearest neighbor, a tall young man of Irish descent with a wife and three small sons, remarked to me: "Here, in the country, at least a man doesn't have to go to the soup line; he can always manage to get something to eat." Bill was a fine dairy farmer too, but the price of wholesale milk sank to two cents a pound, and potatoes at retail went for fifty cents a bushel.

One day Bill came to me and said he had no cash whatsoever

left after paying the costs of feed and material. He asked me to give him repair jobs to do in his spare time around my old buildings. As long as I could afford to, I had Bill and a young friend of his shingling the roofs of my barns and sheds during the summer of 1931.

One of my French friends, Philippe Soupault, arriving in the United States on a summer lecture job in 1931, described an incident he had witnessed in the main square of State College, Pennsylvania. A farmer drove up in a big truck loaded with potatoes, climbed up on top of his van and—as if he had gone berserk—began hurling potatoes all about him in the street while passers-by ducked or ran for cover. "I'll throw them all away rather than sell them!" he kept yelling.

In the spring of the next year Montgomery Schuyler, a rolling stone of an engineer whom I had met a few times at parties in Greenwich Village, turned up at my farm and asked if he could exchange his part-time labor for food and shelter. Of middle age, well spoken, and somewhat distinguished in appearance though he wore a sad smile habitually, Montie was the son of the Episcopal bishop of St. Louis and had received an excellent education. He spoke of having known and admired Thorstein Veblen; long ago he had worked in Soviet Russia for a while as an engineer. That was in 1919, during civil war and famine. Lately there had been no jobs; his most recent wife, who had a job, had left him. We took him in; he chose to quarter himself in the old corn crib down the road which I later renovated as my study.

§   §   §

At the end of 1930 Malcolm Cowley, who had joined the staff of *The New Republic*, told me that well-informed economists were predicting a long cycle of depression. "They say that 1931, like last year, will show a drop of 20 per cent in business activity and employment; but 1932 will make us look back to 1931 as a year of splendid prosperity."

I had thought of my farm in northwestern Connecticut as a safe harbor in which to ride out the Depression. But no plans of providence seemed to work in those days. The declining business cycle assumed a catastrophic force whose repercussions reached us even in our neck of the woods.

In December 1930 the Bank of United States (so-called), one of New York's largest commercial banks, closed its doors. The failure of this branch bank, which had $200 million in assets and 400,000 depositors, locked up the savings of many people who were in straits and spread a pall of gloom over the city. It happened that this chain bank, in its expansion by mergers, had bought my father's Brooklyn bank two or three years after his death. Some of its shares were left in our estate and became worthless, bringing ruin to members of my family who had held onto them. I had disposed of nearly all my own shares after the Crash of 1929, though at poor prices. A first wave of bank runs spread about the country that winter and recurred periodically.

After the hope of keeping an independent income of any sort was gone, I sought at least to hold some reserve capital against emergency needs, but that too dwindled rapidly. The constant fall of market values became a torment to one in such a position as my own. Each morning one awoke to find himself poorer than the day before, yet helpless to resolve the dilemma. How many other members of the formerly comfortable classes must have been in the same straits? The most frustrating thing was to be deluded by hope.

One day in the summer of 1931, when even the British pound sterling had been devalued, I sold out all the securities I owned for what cash they could bring. The loss from 1929 values was astonishing—about 80 per cent of a small fortune. There were also some bad notes in my family's estate. And yet I felt a deep sense of relief at having cast off an intolerable burden of doubt and fear.

Earlier that same year I was in New York for several days to correct the manuscript of *Rousseau* (then going to press), when I heard a good deal of noise outside the apartment I was using temporarily; there were snatches of martial airs, loud voices, the tramp of many feet. My window gave on Sixth Avenue, a very broad thoroughfare. I got up to look out and saw a little procession of about two hundred men and women, carrying banners and placards, marching down the avenue followed by two or three police cars. These people seemed by no means ragged or ill-favored, but decent average Americans; some of them looked like clerks or white-collar workers. They were smiling and shouting "We want jobs!" as they strode along in the bright sunlight of that mild spring day, while a few brass instruments and a drum played some marching tune. The placards they carried read: WORK OR WAGES — NO EVICTIONS — WE WANT JOBS NOT CHARITY — WE WANT BREAD — ARMORIES AND PUBLIC BUILDINGS FOR THE UNEMPLOYED.

Here was only a small peaceful demonstration of persons marching toward the City Hall downtown, as they often did in those days; yet it gave me a shock that I have never forgotten. I was seeing with my own eyes one of the hunger marches of the early phase of the Depression. Up to now we had merely read about such things in the newspapers as happening somewhere else, in some distant city. Now we could see the hunger marchers in the flesh anywhere in our own neighborhoods. They were people just like ourselves, and they were beginning to band together and stage demonstrations in the street.

Only a year or two before the managers of the world's richest nation had been talking all too much, as it seemed, of our "road to plenty" and our universal "prosperity." Of late they had been pretending that our economic troubles would soon be overcome; the recession was only a temporary inconvenience. But now I began to entertain the darkest fears about the country's whole future; our difficulties would not just pass off. Actual conditions, I suspected, were far worse than anyone dared admit; and I resolved that I would find out about all that in some way. Anger rose within me— the people of the thirties were often filled with the *saeva indig-natio*—because good, able-bodied American citizens were forced to walk the street and cry out for food and shelter. These people still seemed good-humored and orderly; but how long would this be?

My first sight of hunger marchers gave me quite a turn. I asked myself were such affairs only a passing phenomenon, or were they the symptoms of larger disorders to come, of popular convulsions such as had in former times brought down long-established regimes in other lands? Those historic eruptions also had begun with jovial crowds of men and women joining each other in the streets.

In those days many of the well-to-do began to suffer from an abiding sense of guilt as they sat down to a breakfast of bacon and eggs and opened their morning newspapers. I had thought my own necessities were becoming rather oppressive, though we had enough to eat well and even to keep a maid as cook and nanny for our children. But I wondered how long I would keep the peace if my wife and children were without food or a roof over their heads. What made everything seem all the more insane was that our mindless society, under free enterprise, now suffered from a glut of every sort of food and material.

Many of the unemployed, who were forming themselves into Unemployed Councils from 1930 on, were now said in current newspaper articles to have communist agitators working among them. These were helping to organize a National Hunger March on Washington, much like Coxey's Army of 1894. "The communists have the right to speak for the unemployed," said *The New Republic* editorially in December 1931, "as long as nobody else does so."

I had premonitions that worse troubles than any we had yet seen were in store for all of us. In my small patriarchy of Twin Willows Farm we were now seven. How long could we hold out here, even living as modestly as we did? It was imperative that I increase my small current earnings based on book royalties. Therefore I halted work on a new book I had tentatively planned, and went to New York to look for magazine assignments that would bring in some cash promptly. During the summer of 1931 my free lancing kept me in the city for two or three days of the week, but in that time of anxiety it relieved my mind to be in New York and in close touch with the swiftly changing situation there.

Chapter Three

❧

At The New Republic

WHEN HENRY ADAMS returned to the United States with his father after their years in England during the Civil War, he recorded their amazement at the great social transformation that had taken place in their homeland: "Had they been Tyrean traders of the year 1000 B.C. landing from a galley fresh from Gibraltar they could hardly have been stranger on the shore of a world so changed."

Adams had come back at one of the turning points in the nation's history: our rural society had become a land of iron mills, steam-driven trains, and metropolitan cities; the Industrial Revolution was moving into high gear.

We too at the beginning of the thirties noticed marked changes in the condition of our country for which nothing had prepared our minds, but they were not of happy augury. I had lately been away from New York for about six months, but I could see signs of deterioration in the appearance of the city. A good many buildings along the main shopping streets looked as if they needed paint. In the region of Times Square many stores were vacant; some carried signs announcing bargain sales, signs that were sometimes featured by expressions of forced humor such as "Retiring from Business Unexpectedly" or "Closed for the Duration."

In my youth Times Square had been a center of elegant night life catering to the carriage trade; it now looked merely flashy with its cheap cinemas and entertainment centers of the flea-circus type. There were many beggars abroad. For the first time in years I was openly accosted by prostitutes who haunted the recessed entrance ways of shops along Broadway. The public squares and park areas were filled with crowds of threadbare men carrying their belongings in paper bags; these people sat on park benches, as if they were waiting for nothing, or stood about in little knots listening to soap-box orators.

Along some blocks in the central quarter of Manhattan, on Fifth Avenue itself, there were pushcarts of apple vendors, some of whom wore ragged old khaki uniforms and fatigue caps. The whole-sale shippers of apples had had the idea of allotting quantities of surplus apples on credit to unemployed persons. Thus during those hard days everybody went about munching apples until they grew tired of them.

In my rambles around town in 1931 I came upon scenes of a tenant being evicted from his home; there would be a heap of battered furniture set out along the curb, toys, old chests, kitchen utensils, iron beds, and people standing about looking on im-passively.

All about the city were big posters, sometimes banners hung above the street between buildings, announcing charity drives of the Red Cross, the Salvation Army, and the Catholic and Jewish wel-fare agencies. Organized charity was now one of the most active enterprises on foot.

§   §   §

It was an unquiet time to be living in seclusion and writing volumes of belles lettres; I was keen to move into the middle of everything and speak out as a journalist on the condition of our public affairs. Therefore I was delighted when Malcolm Cowley, with the approval of *The New Republic*'s editors, invited me to take a temporary post as an assistant on their staff and contributor of editorial and general articles. That summer of 1931 two of the editors were to be away on journeys to Europe and Asia. Beside Malcolm, my old and congenial friend Slater Brown was also on hand as an assistant editor. After living in the country, mainly on his own canned vegetables, while trying to write fiction, Brown had run out of capital. Edmund Wilson, the year before, had begun to tour the country and write on the Depression scene, bringing Cowley in to replace him as book review editor. For several months we younger men, with the help of the proofreader Elizabeth Huling, brought out *The New Republic* in our own whimsical way without much interference from the senior editors Bruce Bliven and George Soule, who were then absent.

The New Republic's headquarters were then at the far west end of Twenty-first Street in the residential district of Chelsea, an area featured by old brownstone fronts like that which housed the magazine. Across the street were the ivy-covered buildings of the Episcopal Church's Seminary whose gardens we overlooked. The place was a quiet backwater of Manhattan and had almost a monastic atmosphere well suited to leisurely rumination over the problems of the world by persons of light and learning. Moreover the magazine itself was immune to all commercial pressures or the bribes of advertisers, having been richly endowed long ago by Willard Straight and his wife, the former Dorothy Whitney. Hence H. L. Mencken's reference to *The New Republic's* writers as a gang of "kept idealists."

For nigh on twenty years *The New Republic* had maintained itself as the organ of progressive social ideas and critical thinking about America's body politic. It was the magazine of America's intellectuals, rivaled only by *The Nation* for editorial independence. In past times it had published the world's most famous authors and scholars, including Britain's H. G. Wells, Bernard Shaw, John Maynard Keynes, and Harold J. Laski, and John Dewey and Thorstein Veblen among Americans. Perhaps its prestige had been at its zenith in earlier days when the founder Herbert Croly was in his prime and Walter Lippmann in his liberal youth wrote many of its leaders. Theodore Roosevelt had taken his inspiration from Croly's early writings; Woodrow Wilson had borrowed ideas from *The New Republic's* articles, even a few phrases such as "Peace without victory." But after the war that ended in victory without peace *The New Republic* had its fallow seasons.

In the twenties its political articles were for the most part improving pieces on municipal reform, labor unionism, or episodes of political corruption. Toward 1928 the literary section developed greater interest, thanks to the literary editor Edmund Wilson. I came to lunch with him at that time and met Herbert Croly, who seemed both reserved and subdued; at sixty he suffered from ill health and was in the last year of his life. Neither he nor his magazine espoused any longer the plans for the "social engineering" through state control that he had urged in earlier days in his book *The Promise of American Life*. Wilson spoke of him with high regard as a political philosopher who had profound insights into social problems but was now relatively forgotten.

After Croly's death in 1930 no editor in chief had been appointed, but Bruce Bliven, a native of Iowa educated in California and a former editor of liberal newspapers in San Francisco and New York, was managing editor in association with a directing group that included George Soule, the economist, Robert Morss Lovett, professor of English literature at the University of Chicago, and Stark Young, the drama critic. Wilson and Cowley were newer arrivals on the editorial board, with interests primarily literary.

The staff met for lunch in a comfortable dining room on a lower floor. Often one or more guests were present, usually experts in their special fields who were visiting New York from the Middle West, California, or from Europe or even China. Occasionally there were also *New Republic* dinners held in honor of some distinguished guest. Herbert Croly had established the custom years ago with the idea of making these meetings the occasion for stimulating talk on public questions. Ideas came to us from everywhere; news reached us from many publications and from press services, and sometimes we received through private channels intelligence that the newspapers did not print. In short *The New Republic* was an excellent vantage point from which to look out at a world in crisis.

In our table talk (almost always bearing on the crisis) President Hoover and his "big business administration" often came under critical examination. Some of the older men had known him a little during World War I as a successful engineer and promoter who had managed war relief and later the Food Administration with good effect. The federal government had kept hands off in earlier depressions. Now the liberal view was that it should "do something." Had not the Republicans claimed credit for the postwar boom? But Mr. Hoover seemed to have become the very image of an economic conservative stuffed with early nineteenth-century ideas of *laissez-faire*. His public statements reflected the characteristic prejudices of men who had accumulated wealth: fear of Treasury deficits and of currency inflation as tending to diminish savings and fixed incomes. Though we now heard estimates of ten million unemployed for the coming winter, the President had opposed all but the most modest federal contributions for unemployment relief. Some small public works amounting to about $400 million had been initiated at a time when the national income was falling at the rate of twenty billions a year!

A writer on one of the newspaper financial bureaus came to lunch one day and reported that at the recent U. S. Chamber of Commerce convention at Atlantic City most of the business leaders present commented on the extreme severity of the Depression but admitted they could find no explanation for it. Hoover's Secretary of Commerce frankly confessed on this occasion that the administration had no plan of action and knew of none that might work.

My assignments were to write editorials and articles on unemployment relief, on the handling of the 1929 financial crisis, and similar subjects, so that I was following Mr. Hoover's record closely.

A specimen of Hoover's thinking on policy was his treatment of relief funds of $45 million that Congress had provided in 1930, with his approval, for aiding drought-stricken farmers. He had ruled that they could use seed for replanting and fodder for livestock, but could not use such funds for feeding human beings made destitute by the drought. The next year the farmers were on the warpath. On July 19, 1931, in an Oklahoma town a mob of two hundred, including children and led by a minister, staged a food riot and looted stores. In August farmers "on strike" blocked highways on the Pacific Coast and overturned trucks delivering milk to the cities.

That summer I could have set up a map of the United States with little colored flags to pinpoint the many places where public disorder, attributed to hunger and unemployment, showed itself. It was the first stage of popular unrest taking the form of hunger marches and strikes of desperation. The points extended from the

East Coast industrial cities and the coal fields of West Virginia, Kentucky, and the Pittsburgh district, to Detroit and Chicago, the rural Southwest, and finally Seattle and San Francisco.

I gathered up my out-of-town newspaper clippings and wrote of these incidents week by week. One press service, for example, reported from Detroit that the giant motor plants were nearly all shut down, and the city's treasury was exhausted by attempts to distribute food to the jobless. In Grand Circus Park, the dispatch ran, "a man falls dead from starvation every twenty-four hours."

In most civilized countries the government paid doles of some sort to those who could find no work. But here when Congress passed bills donating money for welfare bureaus in the cities, counties, or states President Hoover vetoed such measures, usually accompanying his actions with homilies such as "We cannot squander ourselves into prosperity."

In August 1931, from my office at *The New Republic,* I wrote in a letter to a friend: "I have heard and read so many evil things that my head throbs and I can no longer 'indignate' over massacred hunger marchers."

II.

If Mr. Hoover had no ideas about what should be done, the company at *The New Republic*'s lunch table had a great many and aired them freely, though discussion was conducted with a courtesy and tolerance of opposing opinion that was somewhat unusual in those trying days. Mainly the editors divided into a moderate group, over forty in age, and a left group, thirtyish or younger.

Felix Frankfurter, then a small, vivacious man of forty-eight teaching at Harvard Law School, liked to visit *The New Republic,* of which he was a contributing editor, at intervals of several months whenever he passed through New York. For liberals the fame of a "people's lawyer" had been attached to Frankfurter ever since his fight to save Sacco and Vanzetti in 1927. He had been unjustly assailed in the press at that period as a kind of extremist, but in truth he was a moderate and very pragmatic spirit, zealous for civil liberty but more concerned with the evolution of courts and constitutional law. Moreover, before going to Harvard to teach, he had had a rich experience as a young government lawyer prosecuting trusts in the time of Theodore Roosevelt and Taft and also as an aide to President Wilson in the mediation of wartime labor conflicts. Thereafter, while at Harvard during many years, his extra-curricular contacts had been mainly with eminent members of the bar in Wall Street and in Washington circles, to whom he recommended his law school graduates for employment. He could be a friend of capitalists, corporation lawyers, and jurists, and also of Sidney Hillman the labor leader. A prolific correspondent ("he wrote more letters than Voltaire"), he regularly communicated with many of these influential persons who often sought his advice. Indeed the warm, good-humored, gregarious Felix liked to serve as a sort of catalyzer of men and movements, a one-man ginger group in himself. Evidently he found it amusing to play the intrigant in a way that harmed no one, ignored personal gain, and often served the public welfare. At *The New Republic* when I needed to reach some public personage for information Bruce Bliven, the managing editor, would say: "Ask Felix about seeing them—Felix knows everybody."

It was significant that Felix, who had participated actively in the Square Deal and the New Freedom, now confidently anticipated a new reform wave with the foreseen victory of the Democrats in 1932. Nor did he see any legal barriers to a large expansion of federal relief activity and emergency action for the general welfare. "The federal government," he said, "can and must take bold action to start reemployment." His attitude was: "We can't go on like this—let's do something."

§   §   §

It must have been Felix Frankfurter who originally brought Harold Laski to *The New Republic*. The young prodigy among political scientists was a visiting instructor at Harvard in 1919 when the Boston policemen's strike occurred; he had dared to speak for them in a letter to the newspapers, creating some controversy and earning the censure of Harvard's President Lowell. Governor Calvin Coolidge of Massachusetts meanwhile won national fame by calling out the militia to break that strike. Coolidge wound up in Washington as Vice-President and soon succeeded Harding, while Laski moved on to the New School in New York and back to England where he too flourished in his fashion.

On a summer evening in 1931 Laski appeared as guest of honor at a *New Republic* dinner. He had not only risen high in the Labor Party of England, but also during its recent tenure in office served as secretary to two Royal Commissions while acting as an adviser to cabinet ministers such as Arthur Henderson, Lord Chancellor Sankey, and Ramsay MacDonald himself. This small, thin, pale, owlish-looking young professor of thirty-five appeared fabulous to us. When he held forth there was a fine glow about him; he had the spiritual fire of his ancestors who were rabbis, but he was invariably quick of thought and close gripping in argument. When on the platform faced with opposition he would rise to great eloquence, yet in the very heat of debate remained fair, even kindly.

Laski brought the world of power politics and in fact the whole international crisis to our dining table. That night, after we had eaten, he spoke at length of the accomplishments of the British Laborites and defended their ministry with ardor. Through the dole they extended security to the unemployed; inheritance and income taxes were being drastically raised. It was a "peaceful revolution" he described, one that promised to advance step by step until, one day, we would see England wholly transformed. Laski was quite carried away with his vision. Meanwhile some of the audience of a dozen persons tried to raise objections. Once or twice Edmund Wilson, with his nervous stutter, interposed skeptical queries: Could England with her dwindling resources actually manage to revive employment; was she in earnest about self-government for India? But to the doubting Thomases Laski answered that the revolution was steadily going forward without the cruel measures of the Bolshevists, and England's high traditions of legality and democratic process were being preserved. He wound up exclaiming in exalted tones: "Gentlemen, it is not easy to distinguish great historic changes going on right before our eyes, but I say to you we are now witnessing in England the bloodless social revolution we have long hoped for."

Next morning Laski embarked for England. Within a matter of days events proved him a very poor prophet. In August the troubles of the German Reichsbank, which was unable to meet large debts to the Bank of England, caused financial crisis in London and soon led to devaluation of the pound sterling. The Labor ministry fell. MacDonald, breaking away from the Labor Party, entered the National Coalition with Stanley Baldwin's Tories. Abandoned was the Socialist program, while the most ruthless economies were now imposed by the Conservatives even in the meager dole payments. All this came about within a few weeks after Harold Laski in New York had predicted so confidently, so fatuously, the "coming transition to socialism" in Britain.

Laski himself was greatly affected by these events. Whereas formerly he had been an exponent of British (non-Marxian) socialism, he became afterward much more the Marxian and moved over to the left-wing minority group of the Labor Party. During the Popular Front campaigns after 1936 he grew a great deal in stature; and afterward, during World War II, by his powerful stump speaking at soldier's camps—his rousing calls for "building a new England after the war"—he played a leading part in Labor's electoral victory of 1945.

§   §   §

One who enjoyed high esteem among the editors of *The New Republic* was Sidney Hillman, an *émigré* from Czarist Russia in 1907, and since long years president of the Amalgamated Clothing Workers Union. Other leading figures in America's trade union establishment seemed to us then mere "labor skates," but Sidney Hillman was something different. As George Soule assured me, he and his organization constituted "about all the progressive labor movement there was in the country." It was moreover based on the industrial union idea, taking in unskilled as well as skilled workers, and had long been independent of the AFL.

We were then publishing a series of articles by the well-informed labor journalist J. B. S. Hardman on Hillman and the Amalgamated Union; I was editing these articles and felt eager to learn about the subject. Leo Wolman, a contributing editor who was a professor of labor economics at Columbia and also research director for Hillman's union, took me to lunch with the union leader.

In his early forties already, Hillman was slight of figure and youngish looking, with a good square forehead and dark eyes with spectacles. He still had the reputation of a sort of boy wonder among labor leaders but, surprisingly, resembled at first glance the average American Jewish professional or business man and spoke the plain language of workers and management. All the care of managing one of the nation's largest trade unions, now hard hit by Depression, was upon him; he talked with us as if under tension and rode up and down in his chair.

As he warmed to his subject, speaking impetuously and rapidly, he recalled that the Amalgamated had advanced through a series of fierce industrial struggles toward unionizing 80 per cent of America's clothing factories. Then, having gained a dominant position, the union had fostered industrial peace by introducing its "impartial chairman" plan for adjusting the workers' grievances. In the early twenties it had virtually set up a miniature welfare state in its industry, forming a union-owned bank, financing cooperative housing for its members, and—first among American unions—establishing unemployment insurance funds.

At this point Wolman remarked: "By 1929 the Amalgamated dominated its industry to such an extent that it could have taken over the whole men's clothing manufacture, but one union alone can't establish socialism while the rest of the country is still capitalist."

But now, Hillman went on, in this unprecedented crisis everything was changed; even the strongest labor organization could not stand up with more than half of its members jobless. Their limited unemployment insurance was gone; sweatshops were making their appearance again, and gangs of racketeers protected them against the union men.

Hillman, riding up and down in his chair, exclaimed: "Think

of it—all the social gains of twenty years swept away in this national calamity!"

The newspapers lately had been reporting something new in the way of strike action by his union. Hillman explained that non-union shops were trying to ship cut cloth by truck to out-of-town sweatshops, where they were to be sewn up by cheap labor for as little as $4 or $5 a week. The Amalgamated Union had therefore organized a spectacular demonstration in the garment district of lower Manhattan, during which thirty thousand members gathered in the streets formed a living wall to block the "scab" trucks. The union men, imitating the ways of Gandhi's followers, flung themselves on the ground in the path of the trucks.

"We have to admire these men," Hillman exclaimed with emotion. "They are willing to lie down and be run over by those gangster trucks rather than let the scab cloth go to the out-of-town sweatshops." Meanwhile Hillman and his lieutenants had been repeatedly threatened with sudden death, and during that season's campaigns they were protected night and day by private guards.

That was why, on arriving for dinner at Professor Wolman's apartment on lower Fifth Avenue a few days later (while Hillman was there), I found myself being frisked by two tough-looking armed guards when I rang his bell. Wolman's wife came to identify me. A beautiful young woman (the child of Pennsylvania coal mine owners), she gave some signs of distress at the constant presence of guards who looked like hoodlums. Wolman said philosophically: "Oh well, Hillman has to fight fire with fire."

The union leader was an old hand at getting up public movements or demonstrations and winning publicity for them in the newspapers as a way of arousing public opinion. George Soule, discussing with him the extreme severity of the Depression, urged the need for central economic planning for recovery at the level of the federal government. The issue, Soule said, ought to be brought to the attention of Congress and the public. Hillman kindled to the idea and went to work on it.

Through his union's Washington representative, Charles W. Ervin, the suggestion was laid before Senator Robert M. La Follette, Jr., of Wisconsin, that a Senate Committee investigate the present stage of the business Depression and hold hearings on proposed remedies, including the idea of a government-sponsored national economic council. La Follette was in full accord, and soon had a subcommittee (of the Senate's Committee on Manufactures) under his chairmanship authorized to hold hearings on measures that might lead to recovery.

Some of the nation's leading employers of labor, including James H. Farrell of U. S. Steel and Alfred P. Sloan of General Motors, were called to the stand in Washington by La Follette to give their expert testimony on the nature and cure of the Depression. Two of the fading stars of the banking world, Charles E. Mitchell of the National City Bank and Albert H. Wiggin of the Chase Bank, also appeared as witnesses. George Soule, who attended the hearings and also testified as an economist, told us at *The New Republic* how Senator La Follette, by well-aimed questions, drew from these eminent financiers the admission that they really did not know what had happened or what should be done about it. Wiggin blamed the public for "the wild, speculative craze" of recent years. Whereupon the Senator quickly asked him whether it was not true that the great commercial banks such as the one Mr. Wiggin headed had encouraged such excesses. This charge was not denied by the witness. Was it not possible somehow to stabilize our economy by planning, he was asked. "I do not think so," was the reply. But how long could the people endure such conditions? Wiggin thought the human capacity to take punishment seemed unlimited. The only remedy was "nature's cure," the automatic working of the market.

The La Follette committee hearings constituted a first public forum before which, as Soule related to us, "the mismanagers of the nation's economy were exposed as having really nothing to offer us." Then, in accordance with the plan of La Follette and his advisers, a very different group of progressive economists and statistical experts was called to the stand. Among these witnesses were Miss Frances Perkins, then New York State's Industrial Commissioner, Isador Lubin, statistician of the Brookings Institution, and George Soule. Their combined testimony, illustrated by charts, revealed the great sweep of unemployment and the fall of buying power. Finally Sidney Hillman contended that the nation's sufferings were *not necessary*. He added: "I do not share the belief that we must stand by helplessly until good luck, or the operation of mysterious forces . . . bring us back to a state of prosperity." Hillman said at the time that the inept statements of the financial leaders inspired him with feelings of contempt. The press had been playing down the true facts of the Great Depression; the progressive witnesses, from their rostrum in Washington, were able to put those facts on the front page of the newspapers.

Neither La Follette nor Hillman had expected that a bill providing for a national economic council could be passed at that time, but at least the subcommittee started the procession of fallen moneylords to the public pillory in Washington where they endured, during years on end, critical investigation by other committees of Congress.

III.

The ruling idea of *The New Republic* group was formulated mainly by George Soule, writer on economics and labor questions: he advocated national planning of America's industrial activity by an economic council, to be established by Congress, in which capital, labor, and the consuming public were to be represented. Associated with Soule and the planning idea were Stuart Chase, a former accountant who was a popular writer on public affairs, and Professor Rexford Tugwell of Columbia's Economics Department. These men, then in their forties, had been partisans of the prewar reform movements headed by the elder La Follette and Woodrow Wilson. In World War I the industrial planning carried on under the War Industries Board particularly appealed to their imagination. It amounted to a sort of "wartime socialism," with its priorities control and the takeover of the railroads by government.

In 1927, when Soviet Russia announced its first Five Year Plan for industrial expansion, Chase and Tugwell had visited Russia to learn what they could of this momentous program. On returning

Tugwell had edited *Russia in the Second Decade* (1928), a survey of the central planning for new industries and for the construction of new cities. At heart Soule, Tugwell, and Chase were Fabians: they hoped that America might gradually adopt central economic planning without the evils of the Soviet dictatorship.

While we Americans sabotaged our productive system, Russia expanded hers. George Soule journeyed to Moscow in 1932 and interviewed the new breed of economic commissars, whom he found running their factories and collective farms much like our own big business administrators.

Wryly Soule admitted: "It was simple to start planning in Russia; no one ever dared oppose the all-powerful commissars. They began with a clean slate, building new factory towns in the Urals or Siberia."

In Britain some four million workers, and in Germany six million, subsisted on the dole, which meant "bread without circuses." And America now faced her third winter of massive unemployment.

"But in America every special interest will fight to the death against any planning done at their expense," I interposed. "Who will plan for whom?" The only planning our businessmen liked was for their future profits; anything else they would block in the courts and in Congress. "To put over your collective planning," I wound up, "you will need either a socialist dictatorship or a fascist regime."

George Soule, our balding, bespectacled Connecticut Yankee, low voiced and drily humorous, was nothing like a political firebrand. He was, however, staunch in his belief that rational planning could be managed here in democratic fashion and would eventually be adopted. Today we have central planning under capitalism in western Europe, and partial economic planning by our own federal government and reserve bank system through monetary and fiscal controls. But in 1931 not even John Maynard Keynes, one of the progenitors of such schemes, knew well the techniques for controlling nationwide industries and managing supplies, prices, wages, and employment.

At the core of the planners' thinking was the persistent conviction that *experts* in engineering and economics should run the system of production, instead of leaving its direction to the blind hand of the market. The idea derived in a way from Veblen in *The Engineers and the Price System,* and from others such as H. L. Gantt, who had similar visions of our society reaching toward a scientific productive efficiency under the command of experts, i.e. engineers, instead of mere businessmen.

Schemes for rescuing the economic system were now in spate. George Soule said he could have spent the whole year just examining the letters that came to *The New Republic* outlining different plans. Most of them were offered by people who only pretended to be experts or were simply cranks, and they usually ran to monetary devices such as Free Silver, or dated scrip, or issuing unlimited greenbacks. Still other schemes called for establishing self-sufficient communities living by the barter of goods and services. Such cooperatives of the unemployed were running in Minneapolis, Seattle, and other cities.

The heads of young men formerly addicted to belles lettres now buzzed with schemes for changing or saving our society. I too scribbled little plans of my own, one of which I laughingly presented at *The New Republic*'s lunch table as my "Twenty-four Hour Program." Five year plans took too long, I explained; my scheme was simplicity itself and aimed at starting up reemployment instantaneously. Wherever a factory or shop closed down the government, through some agency like the Reconstruction Finance Corporation (launched in December 1931), would take over the next morning, arranging to compensate the owners and rehiring the personnel dismissed. These would man the idle machines and produce food and merchandise. There were obvious objections to a scheme under which socialized concerns would be competing with privately owned industries, but there were objections to be raised to other plans and, most of all, to doing nothing. I did not know that around the same time, or earlier, the veteran novelist and pamphleteer for socialism Upton Sinclair had proposed an almost identical scheme of production-for-use: "End Poverty in California," which two years later acquired an amazing vogue on the West Coast.

§ § §

It was rather late in the depression cycle when a public furor suddenly arose over technocracy and its prophet Howard Scott, a tall, middle-aged gentleman of serious mien, given to wearing wide-brimmed hats, and formerly an engineer by profession. Scott and a few of his apostles had been quietly engaged for some time in drawing up a quantity of charts surveying the "techno-social" resources of North America; they also had ready their own diagnosis of our recent disasters.

The people of the United States, in the technocrats' view, had accomplished a wonderful advance in the technology of industry and agriculture during the last fifty years; labor's productivity had increased many times over, while our political economy still used the methods and concepts of the oxcart era. By 1930 a man could make 4,000 bricks a day compared with 400 in 1914; automobile workers on the assembly line could turn out a superior motorcar in 92 hours instead of the 1,300 hours needed before the war; and so with most other large-scale industries where—thanks to the engineering of labor-saving machinery—man had vastly increased his energy capacity and therefore his potential wealth. America then was, technologically speaking, a land of milk and honey; yet everywhere men were overburdened with debt, they were poor and hungry and destined to become more so. But were our social system to be soundly engineered like our machines and its money or price system eliminated, each head of a family would need work only four days a week for half time and yet would earn "$20,000 a year." Let us then abolish markets and price system, set up a commonwealth run by a council of engineers, start up full production, do away with money, and pay people in terms of the energy they rate (*ergs*, as Scott named it).

Howard Scott had been developing his survey of energy capacity and resources with several helpers in a room of the Engineering Department at Columbia University. Professor Walter Rautenstrauch sponsored his work; Leon Henderson, then a young economist of the Russell Sage Foundation, collaborated with him; and the eminent engineer Bassett Jones, retired banker Frank A. Vanderlip, and President Nicholas Murray Butler of Columbia helped him with grants. Another enthusiast for the new school of technocrats was Stuart Chase, who brought Howard Scott to lunch at *The New Republic*.

"Soon there will be *twenty million* unemployed," Scott predicted, "and the next depression will be much worse than this!" He delivered this terrifying statement with an air that would allow of neither argument nor criticism. On the other hand his promise of "$20,000 a year" income for workers under technocracy glittered as a lovely mirage during those dark days when most citizens would have settled for a tenth of that sum.

It was to Howard Scott's glory that he had provided a dramatic illustration of the paradox of want in the midst of plenty. He was a longwinded talker who used a pseudoscientific jargon (ergs, technosocial) that impressed some but disconcerted others of his hearers. The magazines, newspapers, and wire services soon began to publish numerous articles on his movement. A popular following was attracted to technocracy and later formed a society, one branch of which was able to hold a convention in Chicago with about 350 persons attending. But despite his confident air and his oracular style of expression Scott, as serious inquirers soon discovered, really had nothing new to offer. He seemed to have only the vaguest ideas of any modus operandi for his "engineers' society." One day, he used to prophesy, the capitalist order would break down completely; guns and bombs would go off, and the engineers would have to take over.

George Soule recalled having seen Scott just after the war, toward 1920, in a group that called itself the Technical Alliance. Sometimes they would meet with Thorstein Veblen and talk of the "planned mismanagement" wrought by mere businessmen and financiers for the sake of profit. The scientist Charles P. Steinmetz, head of the General Electric Company's research laboratory, also turned up at these gatherings and used to predict that the increasing mechanization of industry (now called automation) would steadily reduce masses of people to penury. Perhaps in jest Veblen once playfully suggested that some day the citizens might decide to throw out their blundering men of business and set up a "Soviet of engineers" backed by the "one big union" of the I.W.W. But before his death in 1929 Veblen had lost faith in engineers and American labor unions alike.

Marx had set forth much earlier his conclusion that the advance of large-scale industry and adoption of labor-saving machines would displace men absolutely. He had also pointed to the extremely fluctuating relationship of money and debt as measuring units of value and weighed their often drastic effects on wages and commodity prices. The non-Marxian economists after him, such as Irving Fisher and Maynard Keynes, had presented much the same views on money and the debt burden in modern terms.

When Scott was asked how the technocrats proposed to eliminate the "price system" (Veblen's euphemism for capitalism) he disdained to answer, remarking only that he was indifferent to political action. George Soule's assumption was that only a state dictatorship of the fascist or communist type could introduce the necessary controls of investment, production, and distribution. Else who would give political authority to the engineers? How could the technocrats reach for power if they began by "throwing out politics," as they claimed they would. Scott and his apostles had no answer. But some capitalists were interested in adapting some of the technocrats' ideas.

At that time one of my friends who was very much in the conservative camp—and I always found it amusing to rove between the different camps—was Forrest Davis, known as one of the star reporters for the New York *World-Telegram*. Though Davis came from Indiana he dressed like a continental dandy, wore spats, carried a cane, and sprouted a goatee, looking much like one of our oldtime journalistic celebrities. He would go buzzing about gathering up ideas and personalities that would make news. At his spacious apartment on Washington Square he regularly entertained a mixed crowd of New York financiers, stage people, and journalists, serving them an excellent bootleg whisky but also conducting debates on burning issues in fairly formal style. A liberal would speak against a conservative on one occasion, or a socialist against an advocate of fascism. On one evening Davis invited Howard Scott to talk on technocracy and arranged to have in his audience

Bernard M. Baruch, Frank A. Vanderlip, Orlando Weber (head of the Allied Chemical Corporation), and Eugene P. Garvan, director of the Chemical Foundation. Roy Howard and Henry Luce were also on hand to address some questions to Scott.

"Nobody could really make anything out of technocracy and Howard Scott," Davis remarked after that meeting, "but they find it's a great thing to think about."

At that gathering the men with capital pricked up their ears at the talk of the wonders of industrial technology that were to come. They dreamed of fabulous labor-saving machines; and the suggestions of a corporative state implicit in Scott's vision also held appeal for some of them. The sophisticated money men whispered about the idea of a Grand Council of corporation executives, headed by an American Mussolini. But, please, no "Soviet of engineers"—they were the sort of people you *hired*, as Henry Ford used to say. Moreover, we had even then our "great engineer" in the White House.

The Howard Scott legend became the great sensation of a season, the autumn of 1932. But in January 1933 Scott's address at a banquet of leading businessmen—broadcast by radio all across the country—was a complete and terrible fiasco. His replies to all queries were considered by the press, and by his backers also, as generally confused and also evasive. Unfriendly gossip about his earlier career (Bohemian-radical) and his association with the I.W.W. began circulating. His conservative patrons, suspicious of Scott's doubtful political character, soon disavowed him. The group of technicians working on the energy survey quarrelled and split up while Scott himself was ousted from the Columbia University premises. In the gray gloom of the Depression he had permitted us radiant glimpses of the heavenly cities technology might build, and he had been hailed for a brief period as a man of the ages. Now he disappeared completely from the public view.

IV.

When the moderate reformers Soule or Tugwell spoke up for economic planning, then John Dos Passos, who appeared at intervals at our luncheons, would begin in his high thin voice a stammering protest: "But—but—but—Marx—"

Among *The New Republic*'s literary contributors during the twenties Dos Passos was one of the few who wrote as a convinced Marxist, speaking for the oppressed against the oppressors and prophesying that our surging economy was destined to have a great fall. Before the Crash in 1929 Edmund Wilson had judged him overgloomy in representing our middle-class republic "as a place where no birds sing," and he deprecated his "infatuation . . . with the myth of the proletariat . . . and the social revolution."

The next year was different; Wilson's strictures gave way to encomiums for *The 42nd Parallel* when this first volume of Dos Passos's trilogy of novels, *U.S.A.*, appeared. Responding to Dos Passos's call, many of us now returned to reading *Das Kapital* and the brilliant historical analysis of *The Eighteenth Brumaire of Louis Napoleon*.

There was Karl Marx, that prophet of the early Victorian era with his old-fashioned, full-blown whiskers, who had faced society with the most searching questions about its system of production and exploitation and stigmatized the whole business of capitalist accumulation as an affair of pursuers and possessors. And his ideas were highly contemporary. Had he not foretold almost a century earlier that the capitalist system would suffer periodic crises of overproduction and veritable "orgies of destruction of wealth?" I had not read him since college days, thinking him outdated because of his Hegelian metaphysics of determinism and his quite formal theories of surplus labor value (which most modern authorities rejected). Yet long before others he had profoundly analyzed the business cycle and the ways of the market place, representing the recurrent depressions as endemic to the system and tending to become ever more massive and widespread. Like a good worker in the sciences, he had been able to *predict* the very social debacle we were now witnessing in our rich land.

It was significant to us that Dos Passos's novels in his mature phase of 1928–38 were deeply infused with the Marxist view of class conflict and history and evidently benefited from it. The three novels of *U.S.A.* were in no sense written as social tracts, but they made up large panoramas of our society filled with figures that were drawn with a compassionate irony. At worst his characters were types and only two-dimensional, but there was humane passion, the bite of anger, in short, "meat and potatoes," in the works of his Marxist period. All of these qualities have been terribly lacking in the thin books of his later years as a repentant conservative.

I used to meet Dos Passos occasionally during the twenties in Paris and New York, and I remember him as a tall young man with a round, thinly covered head and nearsighted gaze. In manner he was uncommonly gracious, with an air both shy and eager to please; but one soon perceived in him one of the most intelligent and knowledgeable of our young novelists. The son of a wealthy corporation lawyer who was of Portuguese descent (while his mother was of English stock), Dos had been educated at Choate School and Harvard. In his earlier years he wrote poetry in the manner of the Harvard Aesthetes and also painted watercolors passably. His service with the Norton-Harjes ambulance unit during World War I in France, in the vicinity of Verdun, produced a crisis in his life. Letters written from the front crying outrage at so much human sacrifice got him into trouble with the French authorities, and though he was not arrested, as was his friend E. E. Cummings, he found it advisable to move on to Italy.

His early novel *Three Soldiers* (1921) was the expression of an ardent pacifist and social rebel. Several years later, after his *Manhattan Transfer*, an experiment with the *roman fleuve* influenced by James Joyce, we find him returning to write plays and novels of social protest. Toward 1929 I sometimes encountered him among the left-wing group around the New Playwright's Theatre, with Michael Gold and John Howard Lawson. His own version of a Marxist play, *Airways*, consisted of caricatures of capitalists and

their servitors, all made very gross indeed, and policemen represented as unspeakable brutes, while the proletarian wage slaves were
idealized. Of Dos Passos at this stage it was remarked that he
sounded like the naive hero of Flaubert's *L'Education sentimentale*
who, on being asked if he were not appalled by the sight of the
Paris mob of 1848 sacking the royal palaces, replied: "I don't care;
I think the lower classes are sublime."

His close friend Edmund Wilson perceived in Dos Passos's early
work certain "adolescent grievances" and "some deeply buried
streak of hysteria" that inspired him to aggression against his class
and his family. Apparently Dos, during most of his life, was
separated from his father—corporation counsel to some of the most
ruthless industrial trusts ever prosecuted by the Department of
Justice—but received from his parent an income that gave him
independence. Thus he was able to travel widely in Spain, France,
and Soviet Russia, and usually, as his friends noticed, in good style.

In his youthful letters (as from France in wartime) Dos Passos
sometimes sounded like an anarchist who would gladly apply a
bomb to our "rotten bourgeois" society. By 1930 he was saying that
what America needed was "an Ivy Lee to sell Soviet communism"
to our benighted people. Not long after that he went off at his own
risk with a writers' delegation, headed by Theodore Dreiser, that
undertook to investigate conditions of violent labor conflict in the
coal fields of Kentucky. By his courageous example and his eloquent
reports from the field, Dos Passos pointed to the mission of leadership in the social struggle to which writers in the thirties might be
called.

A spirited controversy was stirred up in the literary world at
the same period by Michael Gold, the columnist of the *Daily
Worker* who in his trenchant polemical style attacked Thornton
Wilder as a mere hack producing light romances or fairy tales for
the diversion of the leisure classes. The article appeared not in some
communist organ but, by invitation, in *The New Republic* for
October 22, 1930. The engaging and philosophical author of *The
Bridge of San Luis Rey* seemed to me in no way guilty of the vulgar
purposes imputed to him—prostitution of his talents—and something of an innocent bystander in the wordy brawl that followed.

But the gravamen of Gold's indictment was that it was high time for writers like Wilder to raise their sights and address themselves to the social issues of the day.

Mike Gold was a very lively product of the old East Side ghetto in New York, who at age twelve had to quit school to help provide for his family as a manual worker. In 1914 he had taken part in the riots of the unemployed led by the I.W.W., and I always thought he remained an American syndicalist at heart. A self-educated journalist, he wrote articles and sketches for the communist press in a consciously tough-guy style, but sometimes with native verve and wit. With his mop of black hair and his expressive though irregular features, Mike could easily simulate the angry Bolshevik. But those who came to know him perceived under the surface the imaginative power and warmth of heart that emerge in his autobiographical novel *Jews Without Money*.

An even bigger bombshell was exploded by Edmund Wilson's "An Appeal to Progressives," a tract for the times that appeared in *The New Republic* for January 14, 1931. Here Wilson demolished the myth of a prosperous American society and the hopes of liberals that it might be gradually reformed. After one catastrophic year of Depression the world seemed to be plunging downward into an abyss, and there were no footholds of security anywhere. Those American optimists who had known only about "mere money making" had taken quite a beating: "The energy and the faith for a fresh start seem now not to be forthcoming; a dreadful apathy, unsureness and discouragement is felt to have fallen upon us. . . . The present depression may be one of the turning-points in our history, our first real crisis since the Civil War."

Wilson had tried to find meaning in his life by different paths: he had once thought to live for the arts, or to laugh with H. L. Mencken at the American Scene, "with our bad gin, our advertising jingles, our mass-produced gadgets, our moronic salesmen." He had also tried to function as a liberal in politics. Liberals and progressives, however, were really betting on capitalism. Now it was clear that not only democratic government but the whole economic system had broken down. Thus, as Marx had long ago foretold, the destructive forces within the capitalist system worked to prepare its final collapse. In contrast we had the Soviet Russians carrying on their constructive program whose great scale itself should attract the American temperament.

In conclusion Wilson announced that it was high time to give serious attention to the plans of Marx's revolutionary followers in this country, the American Communist Party. It still appeared "absurd" and confined to narrow Marxian dogmas. Nevertheless American radicals "must take communism away from the communists, and take it without ambiguities, asserting that their ultimate goal is the ownership by the Government of the means of production."

Wilson's article was distinguished primarily for its moral fervor; it was a cry of protest at our defeatism, at our helpless drifting. It offered no analysis of the dynamics of political action, nor did it give any hint of how a social revolution like that carried through in war-torn Russia might be managed in the very different environment of the United States. One felt that Wilson's statements, like those of Dos Passos, reflected mainly the antibourgeois tradition of earlier American men of letters, and of the classic nineteenth-century French authors Balzac, Flaubert, Stendhal, and Zola. Balzac's *Comédie humaine* pictured the social jungle; in Flaubert's novels civilization under the regime of the bourgeoisie appears utterly vulgarized, and even the power to love is corrupted.

America's twentieth-century writers similarly had tried to satirize our middle-class republic with its wealth-getting, its Main Streets, its Babbitts. But now in this historic crisis, as Wilson held, it was time to stop interpreting our "meaningless society" and, as Marx urged, "to change it."

"An Appeal to Progressives" was actually the first of a series of articles for *The New Republic* in which numerous writers were to carry on a debate over the crisis. George Soule, for example, remarked that the very proposal to take over communism was a symptom of the defection of the intelligentsia from the old order such as often preceded historic movements toward social change. For my part I wrote that writers, like other members of the "white-collar class" had become increasingly aware that they were being regimented and standardized under the regime of the American trusts. Not only were the men of letters and the professions limited to the most meager stakes under the capitalist arrangement, but they were also reduced to living in a "moral nightmare," for "the moment you are disinterested as scientist, artist, or teacher, you are hemmed in . . . harassed on every side by the stupefying principle that determines the whole environment: buy cheap and sell dear." Frustrated by the spurious values of our commercial society, our writers and artists should be particularly well disposed toward a socialist program. Yet I expressed some reservations about the American Communist Party as constituting "a strange and feeble group," whose doctrines would certainly require "translation into terms of the native American situation." [1]

Other contributors to this symposium, especially Charles A. Beard, firmly opposed the idea of cooperating with the American followers of the Soviets, whose regime Beard stigmatized as a tyrannical police state. Edmund Wilson was as jealous of his freedom as any man could be, but for the time being he seemed indifferent to reports of arbitrary rule coming from the Soviets. He argued that our own personal liberties were in great measure forfeit during the present crisis. If we needed socialism, he concluded, then we should not temporize but should go for it in the quickest and shortest way.[2]

In truth no one, least of all Wilson, knew what was meant by "taking communism away from the communists." The leaders of that small party now anticipated a veritable boom for their organization, for in those dark days the sun shone for them. I was told by several communists that they considered Wilson's proposal well intentioned but ill advised. Traditionally working-class groups regarded the intelligentsia, whom Wilson typified, with mistrust. After all it was they the workers who had borne the heat and dust of the struggle. Though they welcomed bourgeois recruits, they had no intention of being taken over by them.

[1] "The Road of Indignation," *The New Republic* (February 18, 1931).
[2] Edmund Wilson: "What Do the Liberals Hope For?" *The New Republic* (February 10, 1932).

Chapter Four

❦

"The Two Nations"

A BROAD GAP seemed to open up at this interval between the minority of intellectuals and the men of affairs who ran the establishment. During the postwar years the intelligentsia were generally indifferent, not hostile, to the Men Who Ruled America. But now in the midst of crisis they urged the businessmen's government to do something. Many persons seriously anticipated from one day to another a mass uprising of the unemployed. Surely provisions should be made to feed the hungry; but what was being done in the form of private charity was simply abject.

In my diary notes of August 1932, under the heading *The Valley of Depression,* I remarked: "The very idea of a regular dole is rejected with horror by our conservative leaders, who claim that good Americans abhor charity and desire only wages, and that help should be provided for the indigent through private initiative alone."

The reader of today must bear in mind that Hoover and Mellon had the mentality of parsimonious rentiers and therefore strove as long as possible to prevent drafts on the Treasury for public relief. They were for letting the economy find its own equilibrium, even if it brought us to a social abyss of almost universal unemployment. The federal budget could have supported public works and unemployment compensation such as the weakest European nations then provided. But the President vetoed a bill distributing a cash bonus for war veterans that might have helped things. For this action the former Republican Vice-President Charles G. Dawes, then head of a leading Chicago bank, eulogized Mr. Hoover as a "political hero" who defended the "American way of life" against the "dole principle."

Several months later, in June 1932, Dawes accepted direct relief from the U. S. Treasury in the form of an RFC loan of $90 million to his bank, which helped it to weather a depositors' run. Such it seemed was the "American way": to administer government funds to big banks or railways that were in trouble, but not to the little man. Hoover stoutly defended his course, declaring that hundreds of thousands of Midwest depositors had been helped. At *The New Republic* we called such rescue operations Hoover's "percolator system"; that is to say, the money distributed to large private corporations was expected to dribble down to the masses of people. But owing to the widespread hoarding of cash, and for other reasons as well, the system did not work.

As for the unemployed, the President did exert himself to help organize privately financed charitable activities on an expanding scale, as in the days of the San Francisco earthquake and the Mississippi flood. The President's Emergency Committee on Unemployment was set up as a coordinating body to maintain contact with and guide the nation's principal philanthropic agencies; it was headed at first by Colonel Woods of the Rockefeller Foundation and later by Walter S. Gifford, president of the American Telephone and Telegraph Company. The Rockefellers and Morgans generously dispensed millions through such agencies as the Red Cross. But I was assigned to cover the relief front for *The New Republic*, and on visiting the Emergency Committee headquarters in New York I discovered that the big philanthropists were not bearing their burdens unassisted. Persons who still held jobs in solvent banks or public utility corporations were virtually taxed by their employers for regular weekly contributions to charity. Thus the surviving middle class and the rich quickly raised $11 million in Chicago to feed the poor in the winter of 1932; in New York twice as much was gathered for the Red Cross, the Salvation Army, and the Catholic and Jewish welfare agencies. Yet all of it was not a tenth of what was actually needed.

Trade was then stagnant; I remember the department stores

were so quiet that their salespeople looked lonely. But relief operations were booming. At the Emergency Committee, which worked
with seventy-five different charity organizations, all the personnel
were hustling about or shouting nervously into telephones. It was
as busy as Wall Street in the old days.

In a large hall of the City Welfare Bureau I found two hundred
clerks and social workers engaged in running through lists and card
indexes for reliefers. A great many more agents were out in the
field as inspectors. At the head of this army was a veteran official
of charity organizations who said to me of the work going on there:
"We regard this as *preventive* work. If not for all this"—pointing to
his assistants and the long lines of applicants they were interviewing—"there would be riots and bloodshed all over this town."

Examination of the relief picture showed that the jobless were
not troubled by feelings of "shame" at receiving small relief payments, food packages, and free meals, but by the fact that they
were not getting *enough.* Further, by 1932 private charity was being
administered to less than a quarter of the jobless while the City
Welfare Bureau, out of municipal funds, provided the rest as
weekly doles for home relief: $2.39 per couple and $6.60 for
families with children. Some additional payments that were limited
to $25 were made in alternate months for rent. A second category
of the unemployed were benefited by job relief or "made work" in
parks or on public buildings. Funds for this purpose were supplied
by a businessmen's committee, headed by the banker Harvey D.
Gibson, that employed 12,000 persons half time at $54 a month.
Altogether the combined charity agencies and City Welfare Bureau
looked after about 90,000 families, while three fourths of the estimated 391,000 jobless heads of families in New York, as of the
summer of 1932, received nothing.

"New York is Hunger Town," a welfare agency official said to me,
"yet it's not the worst place in which to starve." In the heavy industry
centers community chests were empty; some of the big cities were
admittedly insolvent. Chicago, with 40 per cent of its workers idle,
was unable to borrow money to pay arrears in salaries to school-
teachers and even policemen. According to a dispatch from the
Federated Press, in the suburb of Cicero "hundreds of people

formed in long lines before garbage dumps" for masses of edible waste left by Chicago's food processing industry.

Mr. Hoover's notion that unemployment relief was a local question was mistaken; it was decidedly a matter of interstate commerce. As the Depression's radius broadened about two million persons, many of them minors, took to the roads and drifted into centers like New York or Chicago.

"This is the last gasp of private charity," the head of one agency said to me. Organizations such as the Salvation Army had been equipped to deal with a few bums or drifters, not with mass starvation, so that the private and city bureaus turned away at least three out of five desperate people, especially single men, with an effect that was demoralizing even for the welfare personnel.

I was not disposed to a sentimental humanitarianism, but the bald newspaper story of John Zobranskie, an unemployed miner in Pennsylvania who had shot and killed his wife and six children and then hanged himself, haunted me. "Nobody is starving," Republican Senator Simeon Fess of Ohio declared. "We are not going to lend money to people who will never pay it back!" But there were great numbers of hospital cases of malnutrition reported, of babies dying, of men falling dead in parks, and frozen unemployed found in abandoned warehouses during the winter.

II.

After pondering the grim reports of welfare bureaus I decided to go out to the various shelters and lodging houses and see them for myself. I rambled about the city visiting new and old municipal shelters and abandoned factories taken over by the Salvation Army. Formerly the regular clients at the city shelters had been drifters and seasonal laborers. "Nowadays, we're getting a very good class of people," one of the guards remarked to me. "Half of them aren't bums at all."

It was no easy matter to achieve a relationship of mutual trust—such as would invite their confidence—with those shelter clients, most of whom had been down and out for two years. They had

(75)

become "adjusted" to their special anxieties and their fallen state; and like neurotics they were alienated and manifested instinctive suspicion of those who appeared before them well clad and well fed. The established down-and-outer came to feel that his relatives and friends who were luckier than he, having jobs and a home, could no longer understand him, and instinctively he assumed a defensive attitude toward those belonging to a world from which he had been cut off. How would the others know how he and his fellows had adapted themselves to the plodding routine of their lives, so entirely unnatural it seemed to me with its leisure that mocked them, its emptiness, fatigues, temptations, disappointments, indignities? Yesterday a busy and optimistic citizen, today part of the gray army of the unemployed—better to drop out of sight and not to write home.

At length I singled out one man who responded amiably to my approach; I talked with him, accompanied him on part of his daily itinerary, and also met two of his buddies. "I'd rather talk with you outside, down the street," he whispered when I first addressed him. "Police watching us here."

The story of the man whom I shall call George Smith was a typical case history of the period. A large man, bald, with a pleasant and open expression and well-spoken, he was evidently in his late forties. After having worked for many years as a first-class machinist in an upstate factory, he had lost his job in the autumn of 1929, found not even odd jobs in the year that followed, and drifted away. His wife had left him to stay with their grown children, and he never wrote them for help while they forgot his existence during the years in which he lived in the "jungle" or on relief. He sounded as if he had scraped the bottom of Skid Row during spells of drinking, then had been rehabilitated at some hospital, so that now he appeared sobersided indeed and thin, his ragged, ill-fitting clothes hanging loosely about his big frame.

Smith's case recalls that an untold number of families were broken up during those years. The wife might take refuge with parents or other relatives, while the long unemployed and humiliated husband might wander off to fend for himself. Boys would run away from their unhappy families and ride the rails or hitchhike about the country.

For me Smith became the image of the unemployed American, and I found him a very decent, well-mannered person. He obliged by giving me a detailed account of conditions in his field, explaining how you applied for relief, where you got the most for your non-existent money, where to stay, and how to prolong your stay. I wrote this down ostensibly for the benefit of my readers (the educated middle-class subscribers to The New Republic) as a little manual of Helpful Hints for the Unemployed or those who were soon going to be in that situation.

§   §   §

Facilities for handling the jobless had improved, I was able to report in the autumn of 1932, owing to advances of federal funds reaching the city authorities. Chances of finding a peaceful retreat in New York with free board were now said by the grapevine to be excellent if you were not fussy about the accommodations or the cuisine. A man needed only to give up the business of hunting illusory jobs, swallow his pride, and go down to South Ferry where the Central Registration Bureau for the homeless was located in an abandoned ferry terminal. After waiting in a long line with other threadbare chaps, usually carrying all their belongings under their arms in paper parcels wrapped with string, he had to answer a welfare officer's cursory questions, fill out an identification card giving name, age, and other details such as "Where slept last night?"

He might apply for meals only, if he had a floor to sleep on somewhere or a nook in the subway, and receive a ticket good for two meals a day at a Salvation Army canteen. Or, upon request, he might have both bed and board in the city's lodginghouse system, the invitation being good for two weeks and renewable in both cases. These arrangements were granted only if a man claimed to be a New Yorker of two years' residence in the state and one year's in the city. Strangers, if they so declared themselves, were given only one night's refuge and then ordered to move on. What became of them no one knew.

This life had its special slow-beat tempo. There were always lines to be waiting in. At the entrance gates of the South Ferry terminal whose former waiting halls were used as dormitories for fifteen hundred persons, the crowds of workless men queued up in the street during the afternoon hours ahead of time, the line extending for several blocks and moving up the great staircase to the windswept gallery fronting South Street. For hours on end they waited for the supper that was to be served at five o'clock. Police drove this gray throng along the gallery much in the way cattle are driven into a barn. A guard stationed at the farther end would shout the signal: "All right!" and relays of men hurried across the gallery. They ran with the queer, shambling gait of men with broken shoes and flat feet. The harshness, the rude discipline attending the daily race for the bowl of stew were impersonal, bureaucratic.

The guests received a tin bowl of coarse brown vegetable stew which on one or two days a week might have a little meat of some kind in it, also three slices of stale bread and a tin cup of weak coffee. Suppertime was hurried; there was little conversation at those long pine tables, for other crowds of gloomy-looking men stood by with folded arms, awaiting their turn. As I described the scene in my notes of 1932:

> Now everybody makes ready to go to bed, though it may be only six o'clock, for there is literally nothing else to do. One may not smoke or read during the evening; all clothing, all belongings are handed to a checker in the huge dressing room adjoining the cafeteria. Our new man, along with scores of others, disrobes completely, puts on a string with a brass check, the receipt for his clothing which is rolled off on a conveyor-line to the fumigating chamber and baked at 220° F. Then he is given a swift medical examination, sent in a long line through a shower room, and, having been furnished with a rough nightshirt, joins a long shuffling nightshirt parade to bed.

It was like being in a combination prison and poorhouse of immense size. At the East Twenty-fifth Street main lodginghouse, which was well appointed, you felt you were in a hospital. But the South Ferry shelter looked something like the steerage quarters of an old ocean liner. At the East River dock annex there was a dormitory called "the world's biggest bedroom," made up of a pier-shed extending 700 feet into the river and housing 1,724 idle citizens. It suggested to me a well-organized, latter-day version of Hell.

Here a Forgotten Man was no longer left to his own devices but thrown together with an immense family of his fellows, who would be snoring and coughing all night. The two-story army cots stood in endless rows, and their occupants might be seen from a gallery in every kind of posture: asleep, sitting up, climbing out of bed or into bed, or just staring. There were whites and Negroes, Jews and Gentiles, with hair tousled and faces haggard and unnaturally pale in the hard light of the huge arc lamps overhead.

Most of those faces were old or middle aged. Yet I noticed quite a number of youths in their teens. An officer gave me an estimate that one out of six were minors of high school age but now forced to complete their education in the prisonlike barracks of the unemployed. Forbidding though the place might seem, many more applicants appeared than could be received. On one wintry December night of 1932, three hundred surplus men were driven off by the police because there were not enough beds; they gave feeble shouts of protest, but there was no fight in these people.

The place was warm enough, but filled with a mighty human stench. That would become the most familiar thing in the world to the guests of the city's hospitality: it was compounded of the odor of heavy disinfectants and that of the human body, less sweet than cows, less fragrant than horses. It would impregnate the guest's clothes when they were given back to him at 6 a.m., the hour of his only other meal of the day: porridge and black coffee. Then he would be marched out into a street still cold and dark at seven o'clock of the late autumn morning; he would go out with the army of men in baggy trousers, ragged coats, and worn shoes, the new men of leisure, without duties and the whole day before them.

How should a man pass his day pleasantly? My large, barrel-chested friend Smith told me he always felt weak and a bit sleepy for lack of sufficient food, though the fare he got was "good enough for what you pay for it." Where to go? He and the others liked to promenade about the city and its squares or parks. "The public libraries are a Godsend!" he remarked with feeling. But sometimes, out of fatigue, one fell asleep over a book or magazine and was ejected. Slowly wandering the streets, the unemployed might enjoy all the unreeling film of the city's movement. Lacking small necessaries, especially tobacco, they learned to seek these out; they gathered up cigarette ends or cigar butts from the pavement, as well as discarded newspapers and other rubbish from refuse cans. Finally about half their number, no matter how respectable, eventually began to "ask," that meant to beg, Smith explained. The number of mendicants in the central quarters of the city was now estimated at about six thousand. In the early afternoon the thousands of wandering drones would come creeping back to their soup lines.

At a subsequent meeting with George Smith he had his two friends with him, and I asked them to take coffee and sandwiches with me in a beanery where we could talk privately about conditions in the "munies" (municipal shelters). The other two were, like Smith, decent, well-spoken workingmen. I managed to win their confidence, and I remember that these men, who tended to be guarded in speech, sometimes gave me a glance expressing appreciation or gratitude. I felt greatly moved at this and also had the thought that though they seemed good and useful men, quiet and shy in manner, they were doomed. In their fifties, they were gray-haired and their faces were lined. I tried to cheer them by expressing the conviction that more help would be coming to them from the federal government in the form of relief and jobs at public construction—after the election. "Things just can't go on like this," I exclaimed. They gave me their faint smile and said nothing.

Why, I asked, did the people not protest, or band themselves together to petition the authorities for improvements; this Depression, as it looked to me, was going to last for a long time. These men who had been taken into the city's "lodges" answered in a manner that was wholly resigned: "We don't dare complain about anything. We're afraid of being kicked out." The police and public flophouse guards kept an eye out for troublemakers.

I cautiously mentioned some of the demonstrations in behalf

of the unemployed being made by radical groups in the city and asked what they thought of them. My guests replied that they were "good Americans" and didn't go for the "communist stuff." None of them would join in the organized rallies or hunger marches of the Reds, and thought very few of their fellows in the city shelters did so, out of fear of being singled out for punishment—no food or bed. Smith, however, spoke up, the others nodding assent to his words: "A blast from the communists in Union Square and somehow, the next day, things improve a bit at the munies." The coffee was stronger and a little beef would be introduced into their bean stews.

Among New York's shelters there was one that rated as the finest rest home for the unemployed then available, and much credit was owing to the Salvation Army for having established it. It was a big white-painted factory formerly the site of the Gold Dust Corporation, producers of household cleansers, located at Corlears Slip with splendid views of the East River. The Gold Dust Lodge, as its guests called it, was reserved for the Better Element, some two hundred white-skinned, English-speaking men without work: ruined lawyers, engineers, bookkeepers, bank clerks, and a few skilled mechanics. "All of these people come from good homes," a Salvation Army chaplain said proudly. (It was there I had met George Smith.)

Here the residents themselves, working in rotation, performed all the housekeeping services needed for this huge hostel. They made beds, cooked, cleaned up, laundered, and saw to all repairs and painting. The food was good, because meat or fish was served twice weekly; and the men on service got a third square meal in addition to breakfast and supper. Finally the men enjoyed more personal freedom than elsewhere, being allowed to rest and read and smoke during the day in the big living rooms downstairs or go out as they chose. Some were permitted to stay on for as long as six months, so that the place seemed like a good home, a resort for retired people—except that religion, though not forced on the guests, was "pushed" by the evangelistic directors. Here too the people moved in long lines to bed or lavatories. For the select class of men at Gold Dust Lodge this life in a crowd, as Smith perceptively remarked, "made the first two or three days the hardest."

Smith told me he had been walking all about the city looking for a machinist's job, but in vain. "It's these clothes," he said sadly, pointing to his broken shoes and ragged outer garments. "I feel ashamed when people look at me as a deadbeat."

He accepted a little money from me with a diffidence that seemed unfeigned. I also got some clothes for him from Henry Billings, that knowledgeable young artist who then enjoyed an independent income, and Smith soon wrote to me that owing to his improved appearance he was "in line for a job."

The hardier spirits among the unemployed shunned the public asylums and subsisted in unused cellars or abandoned lofts or slept in hallways or subway stations. After my articles had appeared, one of these men wrote me a penny postcard from "under a staircase in a hallway in Brooklyn," where he had been domiciled for several weeks. In his view I had not told half of the truth about present conditions, though I had tried.

Still other idle workers congregated in numbers that ran into the thousands in those shantytowns made of tin cans and packing boxes that had sprung up in vacant lots near the river's edge, in the swamps on the New Jersey side of the Hudson, and finally in the "jungle" at the north end of Central Park. These communities were named, in honor of our thrifty President, Hooverville.

In the autumn of 1932 I used to visit one of these Hoovervilles at the foot of East Tenth Street on the East River. It was a fairly popular "development" made up of a hundred or so dwellings, each the size of a doghouse or chickencoop, often constructed with much ingenuity out of wooden boxes, metal cans, strips of cardboard or old tar paper. Here human beings lived on the margin of civilization by foraging for garbage, junk, and waste lumber. I found some splitting or sawing wood with dull tools to make fires; others were picking through heaps of rubbish they had gathered before their doorways or cooking over open fires or battered oilstoves. Still others spent their days improving their rent-free homes, making them sometimes fairly solid and weatherproof. As they went about their business they paid no attention to curious visitors or the slum children playing under foot. Most of them, according to the police, lived by begging or trading in junk; when all else failed they ate at the soup kitchens or public canteens. They were of all sorts, young and old, some of them rough-looking and suspicious of strangers. They lived in fear of being forcibly removed by the authorities, though the neighborhood people in many cases helped them and the police tolerated them for the time being.[1]

I had not the stomach to stay long at the Hoovervilles I came upon here and there; they were sores on the body politic, and they stank. Here was the unsanitary by-product of our freewheeling economy, with its haphazard institutions of private charity and its limited local relief. I wrote at the time:

> There is being created in our midst *another nation,* in the sense that Lord Macaulay meant when he wrote long ago of the dark industrial cities of England, that the poor and the rich are really "two nations" living side by side. The morals of even those fortunate family men who benefit by "work relief" is not much better than their meager purchasing power. They, as well as the group enjoying "home relief" at a pittance, seem as yet only bewildered or stupefied at being thrust back to an abysmally low standard of living—Is it to be the *new* American standard? The very mentality, the reflexes of the people of "the other nation" are deeply altered. They strike me as weak, disheartened, apathetic; there is no fight in them, no revolt. Theirs is a sickness that is spreading.

[1] About a year after I made my rounds Edward Newhouse, a young writer with strong bowels, changed into old rags and went to live for weeks on end in the munies and in Hooverville, where he was able to document his story of the homeless unemployed in his excellent topical novel *You Can't Sleep Here,* published in 1934.

Chapter Five

∾

A *"Bear Hunt"*
and Other Disorders

IN THE SPRING of 1932 I moved my post of observation from Hooverville to Wall Street. I was then undertaking some new assignments: one was for articles for *The New Republic* reviewing the Great Crash of 1929; the other involved writing profiles for *The New Yorker* of Wall Street types, with some account of how they survived during the Depression.

It seems to have been my destiny in those days to rove back and forth between the different camps. Meeting some of the Forgotten Men of the flophouses and a few earnest communists who were trying to organize them for hunger marches had shaken me emotionally and left me with feelings of apprehension about the future. Now I tried to compose myself, and assuming an air of cool detachment I went to meet the sleek, well-heeled bankers, brokers, and monetary experts I was to interview.

The sudden devaluation of the British pound in September 1931 had produced a new crisis in international currency exchanges. That autumn the Hoover administration, as if realizing at last that this Depression would not cure itself, tried to initiate some measures to stem the continuing financial deflation. At first President Hoover tried to work through private business channels on a plan for a national credit pool financed by the large commercial banks, which were to begin expanding loans to business borrowers. To this end he called twenty-five of the country's leading bankers to a private conference in the White House in October and read them a "long and dull" memorandum proposing that they each put about $25 million into the combined operation (which was to be managed by Federal Reserve officials). Afterward I came upon a most curious report of that conference of which only vague rumors reached the press. Most of the bankers present were absolutely cold to the whole proposition, arguing that there were "no good business risks" worth lending money for. One of them said: "It's a fine afternoon and we would do better to go off and play golf." In a word most of these men of capital would not risk part of their banking assets on the chance of helping the country and thus helping themselves. President Hoover, at the time, expressed keen disappointment at their lack of "enlightened self-interest." [1]

The President was then compelled, as a last resort, to use the federal government's borrowing power in order to launch such a credit pool and expand loans. Thus was born the Reconstruction Finance Corporation, a huge government-owned discount bank, established by Congress in December 1931 with an initial capital of $500 million. (Several billions more were soon raised by issuing bonds.) In the spring of 1932 the RFC began making loans against the collateral of banks, insurance companies, and railroads that were in distress. In a more limited way it also financed farm credit agencies and self-liquidating public works such as toll bridges and roads.

The RFC worked for money and credit inflation, but it was a timid sort of inflation. Some of its loans that were then bruited about, such as $23 million to the Van Sweringen-controlled Missouri–Pacific Railroad and $90 million to the Central Republic Bank of Chicago headed by Dawes, led to charges in Congress of financial favoritism. Congress, now hostile to the President, passed a bill (over his angry protests) requiring public disclosure of all RFC loans. That in turn made for financial scandal and contributed to the panic moods of 1932. Though it was claimed by the President that the RFC helped small businessmen and farmers, there was no "percolating" of money perceptible during the early stages of the government bank activities (that is, before Roosevelt). The

[1] George L. Harrison, Diary (unpublished); also interview with author.

weak banks, faced with runs, turned over their best collateral to the RFC and so were left without capital to start new business lending.

Another massive monetary operation aimed at stimulating recovery was also timed for the spring of 1932 by the Federal Reserve banks acting with the approval of President Hoover. Employing the method known as "open market operations," the Reserve banks attempted to expand the supply of money and credit by buying each day masses of U. S. Government bonds mainly held by the commercial banks, until by May 1932 more than $1 billion worth had been purchased. This made for large additions of cash in the hands of Reserve member banks, permitting them to expand loans and investments in the ratio of 10 to 1. As Governor Harrison declared afterward, it was "the greatest central banking experiment up to that date."

Judging that the combined operations of the RFC and the Federal Reserve would generate powerful expansive forces, President Hoover again, in June 1932, ventured predictions to the effect that we would "have the Depression beaten that summer."

Nothing happened. The effort to halt deflation by pumping money into the market utterly failed of its purpose. The money managers were greatly disconcerted, as Harrison admitted; he attributed the failure of the open market operations to the heavy drain of gold from the United States at the time, with France alone taking half a billion dollars' worth. The loss of gold reserves caused a great fall in bank deposits; bank runs and hoarding continued throughout the United States.

Immediately after the President's latest message of hope the stock market plunged to new low levels such as had not been seen in the memory of most living men. Now I heard persistent rumors that each time President Hoover issued one of his cheery predictions a group of powerful bear speculators in Wall Street used this as the signal for staging a raid of short selling, spreading panic in the market and gathering large profits from the abrupt fall in prices. The dismal picture of leading securities ever falling, with General Motors and General Electric offered at $5 or $10 a share, certainly did nothing to revive confidence. It was a strange paradox of the free enterprise system that a band of hard-nosed speculators could make capital out of the nation's economic misfortunes; indeed they were taking in barrels of money while the rest of the country went to rack and ruin.

Through a broker I had long known I was informed of the exploits of a powerful ring of bear operators. Some of its members were oldtime market plungers such as Percy Rockefeller; others were little known to the public previously, and of these the name of one Bernard E. Smith was given to me as a leading figure. He was described as a roughhewn sort, who had knocked about the world and been knocked about himself; in fact he had lost one eye. That should make him fit very well the popular image of a Wall Street pirate, I reflected. I broached the idea of a profile of this financial corsair to Harold Ross, editor of *The New Yorker*. The gangling self-styled "country boy" from Denver (who had made himself very much at home in New York and in Broadway theater circles) admitted to a vast ignorance of stocks and bonds, but gave his approval. It seemed to him madness that such people were permitted to rig the market and trick the public—"It's worse than the horse races," he said. He wanted me, however, to give the lowdown on the present Wall Street situation. Since he regarded me with some suspicion as an "intellectual," he advised that I purvey the facts objectively and clearly while avoiding moral judgments— a method of approach that had its value.

President Hoover had heard of the same ring of bear raiders I was looking into and he saw them with a jaundiced eye, for he believed they worked to undermine public confidence. In March 1932 the Senate Banking Committee, at the instance of one of its members, Senator Wolcott of Connecticut—a friend of President Hoover—opened an inquiry into manipulative practices in the stock market and called several of the bear operators to testify about their business. One of the most forthright among these witnesses had been the same Mr. Smith about whom I was so curious. Was it possible, I wondered, that these Wall Street bears were working, knowingly or not, to overthrow the whole wretched system we lived by? Were they moneyed anarchists who were trying to clear the slate?

Bernard E. Smith was an elusive fellow, not even listed in the directory. A week or so after I had addressed several letters and left telephone messages for him at a certain brokerage office he used, a man named Emil Hurja finally called me to say he had been asked by Mr. Smith, whom he sometimes assisted in press relations, to see me; and so we met the next afternoon at a speak-easy in the financial district.

Hurja was a large, stout man with a moon face, who talked with a Western drawl; he had been a reporter and newspaper editor but now served as a contact man. (Later he became almost too well known as a lobbyist in Washington.) His purpose was to look me over. His employer, he explained, shunned publicity and ignored all gossip published about him in the financial pages. Like other important operators in the Street, "Sell 'Em Ben," as he was known locally, was a profoundly suspicious man. What, they wondered, was my angle? I declared that what I had already learned about Mr. Smith had filled me with admiration for his clearheaded views of our economic position. Here at least was a man who sized up things for himself and took no handouts from anybody, least of all from the Great Engineer in Washington. We drank our drinks. The upshot was that the contact man promised to arrange an early appointment for me with his client.

Two days later I went downtown to the main office of W. E. Hutton and Company, one of the wire houses on the Exchange with many branches all around the country. By working in anonymous fashion with such a large-volume concern Smith evidently concealed his pool operations. In one of Hutton's private offices, with a desk, two telephones, and a stock ticker, I found Ben Smith. He was then in his early forties, a stocky, thick-necked man with a plain workaday face, a square jaw, and one blue eye (the other covered with a black patch). In manner he was brusque, posing as a tough guy and much given to bantering. In a challenging way he said he was born in the west side district of Manhattan known as Hell's Kitchen, had left school and gone to work as a newsboy at twelve, then as a clerk in a broker's office. As he had been adept at rolling dice, he developed an appetite for gambling in stocks when he was a youth. When he lost money he shipped out as a sailor and became quite a rolling stone, sometimes working as a common laborer or a miner. Around the time of World War I he had prospered as an automobile salesman. After the war he had married a young woman of education and breeding, and then gone back to Wall Street in a serious way as office manager of a Stock Exchange firm.

For all his gruff, kidding tone in talking of himself, the former newsboy and roustabout was a sharp-witted and energetic operator who might have fared well in some more constructive work than the stock gambling he so evidently loved. Although he was an Irish Catholic and therefore an outsider to the select circles of the Street, some of the upper crust financiers such as James Stillman and Stuyvesant Fish had liked and befriended him. In time he had become one of the twenty to thirty men in America who were past masters at "making markets," that is manipulating the prices of stocks—buying with one hand and selling with the other—and doing it with so much skill that no one could say how it was done. He had wealthy associates who subscribed to partners' shares in the stock syndicates or pools he directed. Among them, I gathered, were the General Motors executives John J. Raskob and Fred Fisher, and also Bernard M. Baruch and Lord Rothermere. Other associates were such nouveaux riches as Michael J. Meehan, the spectacular floor trader in the stock of Radio Corporation, and Joseph P. Kennedy of Boston, who had become a large-scale stock speculator during the twenties.

A pool usually began with a group of capitalists contributing some millions of dollars, more or less, and an agreement to operate in a chosen stock. Its manager and his aides would begin to trade in a certain stock, matching orders to buy and sell at the same price or employing "wash sales" through hired agents to create an appearance of growing activity. Also, by spreading financial gossip and tips, they excited the speculative public to buy. Then the price would be bid up swiftly and the pool would unload, at a profit, in the rising market that had been created. A bear syndicate organized for short selling worked in the same way, but in reverse; it sold a chosen stock to begin with and bought it back at a profit at some later date (much as future delivery options in grains are traded in the commodity exchanges).[2]

In the unregulated condition of the securities markets of those days the false rumor or false tip was widely used, often through payment of outright bribes to financial journalists. (In 1933 Representative La Guardia of New York brought impressive evidence of such corrupt practices before Congress.) I was reminded of these methods, and received the impression that Ben Smith knew all about such things and had a low opinion of the men of the fourth estate, as the following incident suggests.

The first thing he said, in his blunt style, was that he did not want me to write anything about him under any circumstances.

"How much do you get for writing an article for *The New Yorker*? Five hundred dollars? Only five hundred dollars?" He gave me a broad grin and said: "Hell, I'll give you five hundred dollars and you won't even have to bother writing anything. No, I'll give you a thousand." There were two other persons present: Hurja, the contact man, and Smith's syndicate partner Thomas E. Bragg.

I rose from my chair and reached for my hat, inwardly unsurprised but resolved to make a fuss over this proposition. I remember saying in angry tones: "Mr. Smith, you don't know me, you are talking to the wrong kind of writer—maybe you are not aware of that. I consider this insulting."

Smith laughed, and the other men also laughed though uneasily. He said: "Now don't get mad; I was only kidding you. Sit down and we'll see if we can play ball."

It was the first time in my life anyone had offered me a bribe. Later when I wrote about tycoons so-called for the mass circulation magazines, bribes were tendered me indirectly or covertly, either by the subjects of my articles or their contact men, but never as bluntly as by Smith. I would be offered future jobs that sounded like sinecures or commissions for writing for the corporation itself.

I went on to say that if Mr. Smith chose not to talk to me he

[2] Under the elaborate technology of the modern stock exchange a system had been devised for borrowing from other brokers the actual certificates of stock sold short but not owned then by the seller, the certificates being returned when the stock was bought in.

was entirely within his rights; I would just gather my material from the outside, without interviewing him, as I had done in the past. But I pointed out that what I wrote might be more accurate and in the end less vexatious for both of us if he gave me the facts himself. I won the good will of this hardboiled operator in a quite legitimate way. It was the time of the horrible kidnapping in March 1932 of Charles Lindbergh's son, and terror possessed all the rich who had children. Ben Smith had two young daughters kept under guard then at his estate in Westchester County. I promised that I would omit mention of his children; his face brightened and he opened up.

Just at that time Smith was being denounced in the press as one of the irresponsible speculators who were selling America short and coining money out of human misery. After having been subpoenaed by the Senate, he had promised to "give them an earful" when he appeared before their Banking Committee, and he did so.

Was it true, a senator asked him, that he was "one of the biggest short operators"? Smith manifested pride because he did things in a big way, but protested vehemently: "We just try to make our living like anybody else." A speculator, bull or bear, merely tried to make a profit by buying cheap and selling dear, and that was lawful and honorable. "A bull buys something he hopes he can sell later at a higher price; a bear does the same thing, only he sells his stock first and buys it in for delivery later."

The Senate Committee showed great curiosity about the role of the specialists on the Stock Exchange floor and their possibly intimate relations with big pool managers like Ben Smith. The specialist is the floor broker who stands at a designated post and is charged with keeping book on buying and selling orders as they come in (above or below the current market) for his special stock, such as Steel or Radio Corporation. When the orders to buy and sell are identical in price the specialist executes the sale; he often makes the market himself by buying or selling on his own account. But in any case he has inside information at all times of the volume of orders to buy or sell coming to the floor of the Exchange.

Smith was asked: Was not such a specialist as M. J. Meehan, while in charge of all trading in Radio, also at the same time a member of the pool which had operated in that stock? Ben Smith replied solemnly, "I do not think Mr. Meehan has ever been a member of any pool. It is in his wife's name." There was prolonged laughter.

In his off-the-record talks with me he admitted that the passing of inside information from specialists to traders was a common practice. The Stock Exchange's rules forbade this, but it was a club whose members passed on their own business conduct through their own Governors' Committee.

The beauty of Smith's testimony was that it clearly illustrated the contradictions of our uncontrolled financial system. When he maintained that speculation was sacred and his own operations irreproachable, the senators, who devoutly shared his principles, had no reply.

Firmly denying that he was an irresponsible "bear raider" Smith wound up his testimony in challenging fashion, declaring that the cycle of depression was caused "by the kind of government we have been having for nearly four years."

Privately Smith told me that he had been on the bull side throughout the twenties and was badly hurt by the October slump in 1929. Then he decided to sell everything he owned for what it could bring. He had put a million dollars into the great pool operating in Anaconda Copper, in which men high in the financial world were participants. These shares were originally floated on the market by the National City Bank's securities affiliate, the National City Company, for distribution mainly among small investors at $125. During the 1929 crash, when Anaconda sank to approximately $50 per share, favored insiders were able to unload their shares with little or no loss at the expense of small investors. Other participants in the pool, including Ben Smith, who were not then on the "preferred list" of National City, were "knifed in the back," as he termed it, and suffered severe losses before they could extricate themselves. Smith at the time turned vengefully to active short selling of Anaconda in particular. He declared to his friends, "You'll see that lousy stock go begging at five dollars a share"— which it eventually did in 1932.

By now professionals like Smith knew that there were many

skeleton closets in Wall Street: important banks were carrying large accounts of old favorites like the Van Sweringens and C. E. Mitchell who were secretly insolvent, and they would have to let them go down some day. In the spring of 1930 when President Hoover made his optimistic speeches about an early recovery and issued reports that employment was *rising*, Smith, by his own means of intelligence, learned that such reports were fallacious. His own agents judged that the bad times would be long drawn-out. He, therefore, turned to the short selling side in an ever bolder way. As a member of the Exchange he often went out on the floor and negotiated sales in the crowd of brokers himself; his stentorian war cry: "Sell 'em—they aren't worth anything," became famous and made his *nom de guerre*. In the autumn of 1930 the financial pages of the newspapers carried gossip about him under headlines such as the following from the New York *World*: SELL 'EM BEN MADE TEN MILLIONS IN LAST MONTH WALL STREET HEARS.

Certainly Ben Smith and his fellow corsairs spread terror when they hit the market at moments of weakness with masses of stock offered for sale at ever descending prices. Thus he and his kind left their offices at the end of each day humming a merry tune.

Were not the bears generating panic, like persons who cried "Fire!" in a crowded theater? Was it not time to restrict such methods of trading for the decline, as had been done in European security exchanges and as some members of Congress urged should be done in the United States? The old guard in the New York Stock Exchange answered that all government regulation was wrong and curbs on any transactions would make the securities markets less liquid and free. But the genial pirate Smith talked of such matters without cant, which was what made his charm for me.

On the question of having a government agency regulate and police the securities exchanges "Sell 'Em Ben" exclaimed: "Hell, they've been gettin' away with murder down here. It's about time they were regulated—that's long overdue." He also expressed a fine contempt for the old establishment in Wall Street. The men with new money, like Smith and "Joe" Kennedy the young movie tycoon, who were not generally the favorites of the old financial hierarchs, desired a change of command in the Street. Smith told me he had donated $10,000 to the Democratic Party's presidential campaign fund for 1932 while "Joe" Kennedy, self-made millionaire son of a Democratic ward boss of Boston, gave far more than that.

I pointed out to Smith that if the Democrats came into power there might be a good deal of reforming and taxing that would bear hard on men like him. He replied good-humoredly: "I never worry about government commissions or tax collectors. I have personal trusts scattered around the world, in Canada, the Bahamas, Switzerland, and even in the East Indies. That keeps me flying around in airplanes occasionally. I tell you that anything the Treasury Department gets out of me in the way of taxes they are entitled to!"

How long, I asked Smith, could he continue to play for the downward trend? He replied: "Well, I am a bull on *gold!*" Hence he had recently bought control of a small gold mining company in Alaska; when the dollar fell, his gold mine shares would rise proportionately.

My portrait of Ben Smith became an ironical eulogy of an admirable sort of anarchist operating in the heart of the old-fashioned financial system and performing what I considered to be a salutary work of destruction. "Sell 'Em Ben" was represented as a perfect modern model of such nineteenth-century "robber barons" as Jim Fisk and Jay Gould. It could be said that I praised him for the wrong reasons. He had the virtues of animals of superior cunning who knew how to survive in the jungles, and seemed "alert and youthful, like the artist, the hunter, the gambler, the lover." Moreover he worked to destroy the myths men believed about the financial system. I concluded that while such a man might be denounced from rostrum and pulpit,

He lives in a world of sharper realities than most of us ever know. . . . The world we little people live in, the very scenery we look at is largely made of American buncombe. It is a papier-mâché world that may fall apart suddenly, as it did in 1929. We get our misinformation from the morning papers, from the White House and the Capitol, from the mouthpieces and flunkies of the supposedly great, the legislators, the financiers. We buy what we are told to buy; believe what we are told to believe; starve when we have to, docilely, unromantically. Now Ben Smith feels himself under no compulsion whatever to consume the thing called Hooey. He is a free soul, having his own mediums of information, indifferent to what Herbert Hoover or Bishop Cannon may say, he makes his own judgments, he takes his own line.

II.

The winter and spring of 1932 were memorable for waves of panic sweeping across the country. In that year more than three thousand small-town banks closed their doors, adding to the distress of farmers who were being ruined by low crop prices.

We had before us a panorama of unrest featured by isolated movements of violence erupting here and there around the huge country, then dying down. The metropolitan newspapers as a rule played down the sporadic riots that took place, treating them in brief stories from out of town and often dismissing them lightly as if it were all a poor joke. From my old newspaper clippings and notes I reconstruct in my mind the scene of 1932 as one of apparently minor disorders occurring always at some distance removed.

The scattered reports we had from the rural areas showed that the farmers were far more militant than any other group affected by the Depression. Most of the men who joined in the Farm Holiday movement in the Pacific Northwest and in the upper Mississippi Valley had been Republican voters in the past; they now thought nothing of breaking the law. Taking their shotguns they barricaded roads, overturned trucks delivering milk and other produce, and mobbed officers of the law carrying out mortgage foreclosures for banks, insurance companies, and tax collectors. The farmers in short were riotous in their agitation for a debt moratorium and higher prices. In several Midwestern states the governors called out the militia to keep order but also made efforts to stay mortgage foreclosures.

The farmers sometimes talked of "revolution," according to some newspaper correspondents touring the farm belt. They would drive into town on Saturday nights and congregate in the square before the shops from which they could no longer buy goods and say: "If things go on like this—" But it was not a socialist revolution they had in mind, rather an action in defense of their land, their homes, and against debt, against the "money power" of the eastern bankers.[3] Ideas of money inflation by way of greenbacks or free silver spread among the propertied farmers especially, as in the days of the Populists under "Coin" Harvey and William J. Bryan. Well-to-do farm owners as well as tenants took part in the Farm Holiday movement, led by Milo Reno.

A rank-and-file movement grew up even among the farmers of rich Iowa. A communist who went out to Iowa in 1932 to organize the farmer strikers for his party told me about his encounters with this militant group. To one of their leaders he remarked that he thought the man was ready to work with the communists for a true social revolution and collective farming. The man said: "When I talk about revolution I mean only *that*"—and he pointed to his shotgun hanging on the wall. "But I don't know about communism."

In the industrial cities such as Chicago and Detroit the unemployed held parades and demonstrations periodically. In one of his excellent pieces of reportage of that time John Dos Passos described how their occasional looting forays were carried out: "Forty or fifty men . . . would enter one of the big chain grocery stores and ask for credit. On being told that goods were sold only for cash, the men would ask the clerks to stand back, because they didn't want to hurt anyone, but they meant to take some groceries with them. . . . They take what they need and go off quietly. The manager avoids calling the police or reporting the incident, saying that if more people heard about affairs like this, there would be more trouble." [4]

Robert Morss Lovett, who traveled at regular intervals from the University of Chicago's campus to New York to work at *The New Republic*, told us in his dry, unemphatic way that conditions in his

[3] Mauritz Hallgren: *Seeds of Revolt* (New York: Alfred A. Knopf; 1933), p. 137.
[4] John Dos Passos: "Detroit: City of Leisure," *The New Republic* (July 27, 1932).

city were getting a bit out of hand. "The big Chicago financiers such as Dawes and Insull," Lovett said, "come downtown to their offices under guard of their hired gunmen, since the police whose pay has been in arrears can no longer be relied on to keep order. It is all like a scene out of the days of the Italian city-states in feudal times, when everyone who could afford to do so hired his own private guards to defend him. When public order breaks down in the cities then it may be said we are in a state of undeclared revolution!"

The schoolteachers and other municipal workers of Chicago went unpaid for long periods. On one occasion—it was by then April 1933—an excited crowd of five thousand city employees marched about the Loop district and a number of them suddenly invaded the bank operated by Dawes, where one of them cried: "There's the man who borrowed ninety million dollars of the government but won't lend any to the city to help the school-teachers."

"To hell with troublemakers!" the irascible General Dawes shouted back at the crowd. He stood his ground, swearing at the invaders, until they were driven out by his guards.

I do not remember that the slumbers of America's comfortable classes were seriously disturbed by these sporadic outbursts of mob violence, because the city police were numerous, well armed, and usually equal to their duties. Crowds numbering anywhere from two or three hundred to a few thousand marched peaceably to their city halls to present petitions for aid. Sometimes, as when five thousand Negroes gathered and paraded down Dearborn Street in Chicago, the police lost their heads and fired pointblank into the unarmed crowd, killing three, wounding dozens more, turning the peaceful demonstration into a bloody shambles. The condition of the unemployed Negroes in the black ghettos was at least twice as bad as that of the whites; in Harlem more than half the workers were unemployed in 1932.

The experienced reporter Mauritz A. Hallgren of the Baltimore *Sun*, who covered many of the demonstrations of the unemployed, concluded that they were for the most part spontaneous and ill organized. A small nucleus of communists worked here and there in the big towns to win control of these restive crowds and lead them in disciplined action. One of Hallgren's dispatches reads: "Chicago April 1, 1932: Five hundred school children in tattered clothes paraded through Chicago's downtown district to the Board of Education offices to demand that the school system provide them with food." This was one of the eye-catching affairs that reflected the planning of the local Unemployed Council.

Another that occurred in New York was described for me by an eyewitness who was an AFL union official. One of the periodic mass demonstrations of the unemployed was to be staged in Cooper Square; it had been announced in advance only by word of mouth. But quite evidently the police knew all about it, thanks to having spies for their Radical Squad working among the Unemployed Councils. A day ahead of time newspaper reporters and photographers had been tipped off to be on hand the next morning to "see the fun"; thus everything from cameras to ambulances was in readiness for the crowd that gathered at the time appointed. As the demonstration began the uniformed officers waded into the crowd, laying about them lustily and singling out leaders of the unemployed for especially brutal treatment. The affair soon became quite bloody.

A Red scare spread throughout the country, though the militant communists were very few. Bodies of state militia were given special training for handling crowds in the large cities. Nevertheless there were no armed insurrections by the workers in the cities such as had been seen during strikes in the 1880's and 1890's, though the police were aggressive and shot to kill, so that during the worst years of the Depression, from 1931 to 1933, scores died in riots, hundreds were wounded, and thousands were arrested.

The Ford Massacre at Dearborn, Michigan, in March 1932 was one of the more famous of such episodes. There a crowd of four thousand unemployed gathered at the gates of the River Rouge plant to petition for work were received by the Ford Motor Company guards with a murderous machine-gun fire, killing four and wounding more than fifty.

The incident that was most widely reported and aroused the greatest popular resentment was the violent expulsion of the Bonus

Expeditionary Force from Washington, D.C. For more than a year the several veterans' organizations had been petitioning the government for payment of the balance of their promised bonus, half of which had already been paid them. In the spring of 1932 the unemployed veterans began to march or ride to Washington from all parts of the country, finally congregating in the capital as an army of about eighteen thousand ragged lobbyists. Most of them camped in a great shantytown or Hooverville they had built up in empty lots and among some abandoned government buildings at Anacostia Flats. By all accounts the veterans maintained themselves in very good order, displaying American flags and affirming their patriotism.

In mid-June the Senate rejected a bonus bill that would have appropriated $2.4 billion for the veterans. About ten thousand of the BEF elected, however, to remain in Washington. On July 28, 1932, President Hoover gave the order for the military to drive the veterans from their encampment. Not only was he angered by their petition, but he considered them a potential threat to the public safety and charged that "communists and persons with known criminal records" abounded among them. Well-informed reports held that the self-declared communist group in the BEF camp of eighteen thousand numbered not more than a hundred persons.[5]

At the command of General Douglas MacArthur, Colonel George S. Patton with eight companies of cavalry and infantry went into action against the unarmed veterans. According to the newspapers the veterans offered slight resistance, throwing a few stones and taking to their heels as the soldiers moved in with fixed bayonets. Patton, however, in an interview I had with him in 1934, remembered the affray as more strenuous than reported; his recollection is borne out by the movie newsreels showing great clouds of tear gas being discharged at groups of the veterans, some of whom fought back with great zeal.

"After all, those veterans were only four blocks from the Capitol," Patton recalled. "It might have been a bad thing if they had got in there. I myself was hit on the head and had to be taken

[5] Hallgren: *Seeds of Revolt*, pp. 187–9.

to the rear." A heavy, well-aimed brickbat dropped Patton from his horse, rendering him unconscious. The veterans were put to rout without bloodshed, and the soldiers set fire to their city of shanties.

§ § §

Gaily the bears might frolic in the desolate market place, but for the little people who had invested their savings in the corporate securities promoted by the great American bulls of the 1920's, C. E. Mitchell, Samuel Insull, A. P. Giannini, M. J. and O. P. Van Sweringen, and by Sweden's "Match King" Ivar Kreuger, there was little to cheer about. Armies of salesmen had peddled the stocks and bonds of Insull's utility holding companies until more than a billion in such securities were held mainly by savers in the Middle West. By 1932 whole areas of Chicago's residential quarters were stricken by the default of the Insull companies bonds and preferred stocks that had been purchased for "sure" income. The same blight afflicted the rentier sections of Boston where Kreuger had raised much of the capital for his monopoly of the world's matches, with the help of eminent investment bankers. Aware of the ill feeling of the local population toward himself, Insull kept thirty-six body-guards for his protection at his headquarters in Chicago night and day.

The American banking syndicate that backed Kreuger refused to believe that this Machiavellian swindler could do any wrong, and up to the last hour they continued to extend him credits—as was done also by the Morgan banks for the Van Sweringens. But in the case of Insull the Morgan banking consortium finally decided to cut him off. At the moment Insull was also aware that the Illinois authorities were preparing suits against him on charges of embezzlement. "I have done nothing," he protested, "that every banker and business magnate has not done in the course of business." (He was later acquitted of the charges against him.)

On March 12, 1932, monopolist Ivan Kreuger, facing bank-ruptcy and the exposure of his colossal forgeries, committed suicide in his Paris apartment. A few weeks later Insull, whose billion dollar holding company had also collapsed, took flight from Chicago—

before being indicted—reached Europe, and journeyed from one country to another in search of asylum until he halted in Athens. Fantastic tales of his flight filled the world's press: while U.S. agents pursued him slowly Insull, according to current reports that were probably exaggerated, offered the heads of the Greek and Turkish governments in turn a million dollars for immunity from extradition. Eventually the old gentleman was arrested in Turkey and, early in 1934, brought back to face trial.

Two days after Kreuger's suicide George Eastman, founder and head of the Eastman Kodak Company, took his own life, though the man and the company were financially speaking *sans pareil.* Eastman was a melancholy billionaire who, according to his suicide note, found himself in old age without friends he could trust.

Truly the American capitalist system had never sunk so low since 1869, the year of Jay Gould's gold conspiracy and the exposure of the Union Pacific's bribes of Congressmen. And now the captains and the kings seemed to be departing.

I had the whim to attempt a sort of parting salute to those vanishing kings of industry and finance, in the form of an open letter. It was also my intention to exhort the surviving moneymen to "stay away from deadly weapons" and keep up their courage, as we little fellows were doing. But when I broached the idea of my little satire to an editor I would have thought friendly to such a scheme he shrank from it as something "gruesome."

The next day I happened to encounter Edmund Wilson and mentioned my vexations with that editor.

"Oh," exclaimed Wilson, "Men like * * * will all be *done away with* pretty soon." Their time was about up, he went on to prophesy darkly. "History will liquidate them." I remember feeling a pleasurable emotion at Edmund Wilson's assurance that history was on our side and against persons we disliked. For Wilson, then, was wholly obsessed with the notion that a great revolution impended in the most immediate sense, and sometimes he sounded like Marat.

He was then in the early stages of writing his book *To the Finland Station,* a study of the science of revolution after Marx and Lenin. How greatly Wilson had changed! I remembered his yellow neckties of the early twenties, his air of a minister's son enjoying New York and Broadway, and especially the "nuthouse" humor of our popular theater. In those days he used to carry his friends off in a party after dinner to vaudeville shows where we might enjoy "pure American Dadaism," in the shape of the comedian Joe Cook. But from his interest in the popular arts he turned to the study of Joyce, Proust, the French Symbolists—only to bid them farewell in his book *Axel's Castle*, published the year before. And now he was immersed in the state papers of Lenin as well as in Marx's theoretics on the predictability of history. Inasmuch as the economic cycle we were witnessing must follow the "laws of motion" of the class conflict, the successful insurrection of the oppressed must inevitably follow, and that would be the finish of that bourgeois-liberal editor, Q.E.D. It was a prediction that I found most comforting at the moment and believed almost as fondly as Wilson.

Chapter Six

∽

Turning Left

WE WERE AT the nadir of the Depression in 1932; some current estimates held that one out of three American families were in distress. A high official of the AFL had recently testified before Congress that moderate union leaders could no longer count on their members' continued patience. "The doors of revolt," he warned, were about to be thrown open.

I remember discussing the situation of organized labor with Professor Leo Wolman, after a gathering at *The New Republic*. "Whenever will the workers rise?" I asked him. "I find the endurance of our people, their submissiveness, the most surprising thing of all."

Wolman, then well regarded as an expert in labor economics, said: "The workers here will not rise. They do not care about socialist doctrine as the Europeans do. But the American workers can be the bravest fighters in the world when they see something tangible that they can win by fighting for it."

His views were borne out later by the forceful action of labor in the years 1933 to 1937, years of recovery, in contrast with their apathetic condition in 1932. At that time there were strikes of desperation against wage cuts, but these were nearly always lost since the employers in such hard times welcomed stoppage. George Soule also pointed out that men are more inclined to revolution in prosperous times than in periods of hunger. The years preceding the French Revolution of 1789 followed recovery from famine conditions.

The young men in the circle of *The New Republic*, unlike the older, cool-headed fellows such as Wolman and Soule, were impatient for the coming of the Revolution; they talked of it, dreamed of it. In those days when the decline in the nation's affairs continued inexorably—as it did also in all the advanced nations of Europe—we who watched the catastrophic process, feeling powerless to act, became all the more aware of the frightening gulf that was opening up between the will of multitudes to "do something" and the inertia of the body politic, the paralysis of its accredited leaders. Beginning in 1931, Congress, now with a Democratic majority, and the President had been deadlocked; the parliamentarians of both parties quibbled over absurd questions: Should the government lend money for relief or give it away?

At such intervals in history it is as if power has been left "lying in the streets" to be taken by anyone who cares to use it, as Leon Trotsky said of conditions in Russia in 1917. In America we were not left prostrate by the disasters of war, but the people were plunged into a state of extreme frustration and some voices cried out that we take courage and, like Brutus, "speak, act, redress."

One of the angriest of our young men wrote: "The lives of millions of useful people were being slowly but surely destroyed. A dreadful economic waste of our industry and agriculture was being perpetrated. But the waste of human resources was even more criminal . . . as the producing masses were reduced to a state of stupefaction and despair."

The words were those of Sidney Hook, a slender and vivacious person then in his twenties and an assistant professor of philosophy at New York University, but nevertheless a dedicated revolutionary. Born in Brooklyn, educated in the city's public schools and colleges, Sidney had been a member of the Young Socialist League in his teens, then had studied Marx and Hegel at the University of Berlin and also for a short period at the Marx-Lenin Institute in Moscow.

No one in those days expounded Marxian doctrine with greater force and authority than young Sidney Hook. Moreover he brought to our discussion of human affairs a cold logic that was remarkable in one so young. He was too logical, I often felt; and he was so quick in argument that he answered opponents without waiting to hear them out.

The essential thing about Marx, as Hook urged, was that although he was dead and gone nearly fifty years he actually exercised a stronger influence upon the present age than any contemporary social thinkers. No one before or since him had so completely examined and described the *homo economicus* of factories, railroads, and world-wide commercial exchanges. There were to be sure eminent modern economists of the classical or liberal school who dismissed Marx as obsolete. Yet the other writers in his field studied only parts of the economic structure: interest rates, money, or market competition. Only Marx, we discovered, had tried to explain the economic order as a whole. He had asked the key questions, those that concerned the movement of classes and the transfer of power, the recurrent crises of booms and depressions. He had also analyzed the technical progress in manufactures that moved from one stage of industrial efficiency to a higher one, combining small commercial units into giant monopolies until the whole system, as in nineteenth-century England, acquired the essential character of collective enterprise, yet, owing to the contradictions within the capitalist system, tended always to create deep crises within society. He predicted finally that when the concentration of production and regimenting of labor reached a point where it became incompatible with its "outer integument" of private capital, it tended to burst asunder. Marx also held that a condition of "overproduction" was regularly brought about by the operation of capitalists expanding (capital) savings without control, while the sale of the commodities they produced was limited by the demand of a society in which the majority were left poor and must always remain poor. Here he approached closely the widely shared view of modern commentators that maldistribution of consuming power was at the root of our depression troubles.

Marx doubled his role of sociologist with that of the social prophet; not only did he interpret the real world to men, but he boldly called on them to *change* it. Sidney Hook, who was one of John Dewey's favorite pupils, reinterpreted Marx's method as "the method of social behaviorism, and opposed to the idea of social process as automatic or passive. Man is not a machine, [but] men make history, acting through classes and institutions. . . . By acting on the external world and changing it, man changes his own nature."

As to the question of establishing a dictatorship of the proletariat by force, both Sidney Hook and Edmund Wilson then made light of the moral scruples many thoughtful people felt. Wilson argued that personal liberty in the United States was "not worth a cent . . . the moment you step out of your owning-class orbit—you are lucky if you do not land in jail or get shot at in Harlan or Lawrence." In a published debate with John Dewey, Bertrand Russell, and Morris R. Cohen, all of whom opposed communism in its authoritarian or Soviet form as a new tyranny, Hook replied: "Communism, despite the false emphasis of some of its adherents, is not the negation of democracy, but its fulfillment. The right to determine our own destiny . . . is an intrinsic good. . . . The way to get genuine democracy—social democracy—is to take power and overthrow the economic system which makes the ruling class within it dictators of the national economy." The oligarchy of capitalists must be replaced by a dictatorship that for Hook equated "workers' democracy." Nor would he temporize in any way with such spurious parliamentary democracies as England's or Germany's, which had failed us. Democratic forms to be sure were to be used for "agitational purposes." Though he did not explicitly counsel violent action, Hook held that since the capitalists themselves were creating chaos and despair it would be "nothing short of calamitous to make a fetish of legality." In the spirit of Lenin, Hook urged that "Power is bestowed neither by God nor the economic process. It must be taken." [1]

The idea of revolutionary action in the Marxian sense, and of engagement in the expected mass struggles of the workers such as Sidney Hook then advocated, was embraced by great numbers of young literary men and intellectuals of the thirties. They, like Thomas Mann, had been mainly concerned in former years with the private war of the individual artist against the society of philistines. Now they came to Marxism by diverse routes, though seldom through actual study of economics, with which many of them were quite unfamiliar.

[1] Sidney Hook: "Why I am a Communist," *Modern Monthly* (April 1934).

Among the group of literary men I used to meet with in 1932 there were a number who had come to Marxism after undergoing a sort of moral crisis or religious experience. There was the messianic Waldo Frank, fortyish, author of novels of ideas and studies in our civilization such as *Our America,* who had formerly urged that the diffusion of culture and the arts alone would be the salvation of this country. Recently, as he had declared, he had lost all faith in our money-seeking society and pinned his hopes upon artists "fighting . . . by the side of proletarians and farmers."

Granville Hicks, the literary critic, had lately begun to contribute to *The New Republic* and *The Nation.* He had formerly studied to enter the Methodist ministry, but had wound up as an instructor of English at a small college upstate. As a liberal Christian he had hoped, as he confessed, that our capitalist society would look to human needs with benevolence; but nowadays he felt himself overcome by feelings of moral revulsion every time he encountered one of the unemployed in the street. By a sort of Augustinian revelation he saw at last that there was "but one way out": he and all who felt as he did must join the mass movement of the expropriated.

In the early thirties I used to run into Hicks with his old friend Newton Arvin, professor of American literature at Smith College, a small, quiet-mannered but tense young man with delicate features suggestive of much finesse. Underneath the skin Arvin was evidently an emotional or psychological rebel (as shown by his letters). His highly original critical studies of Hawthorne, Thoreau, and Whitman seemed to me brilliant, and they preceded and influenced the work of his younger friend Hicks, whose "Marxian" book on American literature, *The Great Tradition,* attempted much like Arvin's writing to correlate the political radicalism of the "classic" American authors with twentieth-century communism.

Even more curious was the case of James Burnham, another of the bourgeois converts to Marxism whom I met in 1932. The son of a Chicago railroad executive, educated at Princeton and Oxford University, he was a lapsed Catholic now possessed by his apocalyptic visions of the salutary revolution that impended. Like Hook he taught philosophy at New York University but had also private means which enabled him to live in one of the charming federal mansions on Washington Square, where I came with a mutual friend to meet him. He had been publishing at his own cost an excellent review of literary criticism and aesthetics, *The Symposium*, which in 1931 he converted into an organ of Marxian sociology. I found Burnham a shy young mental prodigy of the type we tend to label "frosty intellectual." But in expounding the doctrines of Marx, Lenin, and Trotsky he sounded implacable; he became the true fanatic carried away by dreams of vast blood baths that would attend the overthrow of our society. I felt the cold flame behind the tortoise-shell glasses of that composed and well-mannered young man of twenty-six.

In his later "Machiavellian" phase, at the time of World War II, when Burnham would have completely changed his ideas and emerged as an extremist of the right, his rather violent intellect seemed again possessed, this time by dreams of the atomic massacre of hundreds of millions of Russians and Chinese in a "preventive war." (Later I shall have something to say about the reconversions and recantations of some who, like Hook and Burnham during the thirties, embraced the communist faith in its most dogmatic form.)

I was not one who experienced a religious conversion to Marxism and read *Das Kapital* as a breviary, but I found Marx wonderfully timely and apposite in those days. In my student years I had a taste for metaphysics but never for Hegel's dialectical system. While I felt skeptical of the neo-Hegelian dialectic in Marx, I found his perceptions of social movements and his historical and economic insights brilliantly reasoned and compelling. Marx's effort to project from capitalist chaos to socialist order has always appealed to men of a rational and scientific turn of mind. I remember that old Professor Franz Boas once told me in 1918 he had become a Marxist through long study and comparison of cultures, those of the American Indians and Eskimos and of the Europeans.

Marx, in short, was a true heir of Humanism and the eighteenth-century Enlightenment as well as an intellectual son of the great French Revolution. All his life, as he wrote to Engels, he had labored in the hope that men might be led to "walk erect" again instead of "crawling on all fours." He saw a continuous pattern in history which promised that the triumphant movement of liberation of the bourgeoisie of 1789 was to be repeated, indeed duplicated, in the social revolt of the proletarians whom the bourgeoisie in turn oppressed. That vision of the continuity of man's revolutions was a most appealing hypothesis in the 1930's.

To be sure, Marx had not left us any blueprints for a utopia. Socialism would have to be enacted by human beings—and bureaucrats too—a sobering thought that came up repeatedly in my conversations with Kenneth Burke.

Edmund Wilson, it might be said, surpassed all the rest in his enthusiasm for the rediscovered science of history, which he called "the only really vital intellectual movement in the Western world." The latter-day Marxists, Lenin and his fellow Bolshevists, Wilson maintained, had contrived "a veritable engineer's technique" for analyzing society and manipulating its forces.

In an article entitled "What Do the Liberals Hope For?" he again made one of his calls to arms: "So, American intelligentsia—scientists, philosophers, artists, engineers—who have been weltering for so long in . . . prostitutions and frustrations, that phase of human life is done. Stagger out of the big office, the big mill—look up and look through those barren walls—look beyond your useless bankrupt fields and pastures! Remember that discovery and freedom which you enjoyed for a little while—the discovery of humanity and the earth has only been begun! What we need now are *engineers of ideas*. . . ." [2] The closing phrase echoes the words of Stalin to the effect that writers are to be the "engineers of the human soul."

To read, to seek new illumination, even to try to educate others was not enough in these days. We must all work to "set the world aright."

[2] *The New Republic* (March 23, 1932).

II.

In the summer of 1931 we began to receive reports at *The New Republic* of widespread strikes of coal miners in Pennsylvania, Indiana, West Virginia, and Kentucky. These seemed to be strikes of desperation against wage cuts, unemployment, and hunger. The United Mine Workers Union, which had organized the workers in this industry on a nationwide scale (except for the South), had lately been losing ground in its Midwestern districts. Worst of all was the case of eastern Kentucky's Harlan County, where mine guards and sheriffs' deputies shot it out in pitched battles with the miners, leaving numerous dead and wounded on both sides. After one of these affrays, in May of 1931, a band of deputies raided Evarts, one of the miners' villages, arresting seventy workers, a couple of the town officials, and two clergymen. Thus a good part of the local working population was locked up in the county jail to await a mass trial for criminal syndicalism.

The United Mine Workers, led by John L. Lewis, simply abandoned the field. The communists promptly appeared with their independent or dual organization, the National Miners' Union, enlisted the local people, and continued the fight. The IWW also moved in to set up some miners' locals affiliated with its own federation. In their mountain villages the Kentuckians received the communist organizers with open arms. The important mining companies in the region then imported "scabs" from Detroit and Chicago and with the help of sheriffs' deputies fought to keep the district free of unions, especially Red unions.

"You'd be a Bolshevist too, if you didn't have enough to eat," was a phrase often heard at the gatherings of the miners, who were nearly all of old native stock. Guerrilla war in Kentucky-mountaineer style raged here: a soup kitchen for the strikers was attacked at night by sheriffs' deputies with submachine guns, and two miners were killed; another soup kitchen was dynamited. The striking miners replied with deadly fire from ambuscades, killing and wounding several of the deputies.

Although no news of the struggle appeared in the metropolitan press at the time (except for *The Daily Worker*), literary circles in

New York buzzed with talk of the "class war" that had begun in Harlan County. *The New Republic* was following the affair and I was writing editorial paragraphs on it then.

A young reporter named Boris Israels (formerly one of the literary expatriates in Paris) went out to Harlan for the Federated Press, a small wire service for socialist papers and a few labor unions. Israels was taken for a ride by local deputies and shot in the leg. He came to *The New Republic* to see me, looking pretty cheerful under the circumstances, and told me that one of the miners' hamlets had elected a complete Communist Party slate to run their local government. Then he took off to cover the Negro sharecroppers' movement in Alabama, hardly a peaceful assignment. Another young journalist, Bruce Crawford, visiting Harlan for his own local newspaper in Virginia, was also shot and wounded and issued appeals to the nation's press to send in brave men to the scene in Kentucky.

In New York the writers young and old took up the cause of the Kentucky miners with an ardor such as they had shown several years before in the defense of Sacco and Vanzetti. The International Labor Defense, an auxiliary of the Communist Party, held meetings to raise money and food for the strikers; special appeals were made to liberal writers to help call the attention of the public and the great press to the miners' plight. It was in this way that dour old Theodore Dreiser, a lifelong nonconformist, and John Dos Passos were persuaded to form a special Writers' Committee to visit the Kentucky mine fields and report on conditions there.

On arriving in Harlan County, Dreiser's committee made efforts to hear both sides. But the local authorities were hostile, insisting that no real strike was going on. There were only malcontents and "foreign communists," they claimed. Objections were made to the writers meeting with delegations of the miners, and tough-looking young men with guns kept at their heels as Dos Passos related. Yet they managed to visit some of the small hamlets where the miners and their families lived, half starved in squalid shanties. These people literally had hung out a red banner to welcome the Writers' Committee and the ILD agents. One of their leaders explained that the year before armed deputies had broken up their processions as members of the old AFL union, and he added: "By God, if they won't let us march under the American flag, we'll march under the red flag."

In his vivid yet objective account of the writers' journey to Kentucky in the autumn of 1931 (*Harlan Miners Speak*), Dos Passos described the miners of Appalachia as talking much like oldtime Masonic Lodge speakers, though they sometimes also used expressions taken directly from *Daily Worker* editorials. Dreiser, who carried on like a brave old warrior, speaking up for "equity" for the workers, suffered an amusing *contretemps* on the second day of his stay at the county center of Pineville, when he was served with a summons to appear in court on a morals charge. The attractive young woman he had brought along with him as his secretary had been seen entering his hotel room at night it was alleged. Unruffled, the old novelist put in a brief appearance in court, made his deposition of innocence, and went on his way.

After the whole group left Kentucky they learned that, in their absence, all of them had been indicted on charges of criminal syndicalism. Sherwood Anderson, on hearing of this indictment (never seriously prosecuted), declared: "What we need is more criminal syndicalism!"

Undaunted, the writers in New York held more indignation meetings and soon organized a second writers' committee, headed by Waldo Frank and including among others Malcolm Cowley, Quincy Howe, and Mary Heaton Vorse (an old hand at reporting industrial battles). In February 1932 they set off for Kentucky by car, accompanied by a truck carrying $3,000 worth of food. When they tried to distribute the food to the miners, however, local officers prevented them from doing so; two members of the committee were arrested while addressing groups of the union men. After only one day the visitors were forcibly escorted by sheriffs' deputies to the Virginia border, where Waldo Frank and Allen Taub, lawyer for the ILD, were severely beaten about the head with revolver butts.

It was thanks to the communist-sponsored Writers' Committee that *The New York Times* finally sent its veteran labor reporter Louis Stark to the embattled mine fields of Kentucky. Stark returned with an able, very factual account that fully corroborated the writers' reports. The lockout continued, but now the whole country knew about the affair.

More than twenty years later John Dos Passos, retouching his original account of the first writers' expedition to Harlan, treated the whole affair as a comedy and represented Dreiser as a clumsy old "pachyderm." Edmund Wilson, who had accompanied the second committee as a reporter for *The New Republic*, also reviewed the episode as if it were but a piece of folly; and both he and Dos Passos in afterthought aired their suspicions that the communists were trying to "use" them as "pawns." There is no doubt that the communists tried to use everyone who might help arouse public opinion or give money for the insurgent miners. Even in 1956, in his later guise as an ultraconservative repenting his former beliefs, Dos Passos testified: "I still felt that the communists . . . by their tireless dedication were filling a useful function."

We heard of their organizers—courageous, but inexperienced in trade union work as one correspondent described them—being arrested, beaten, and sometimes killed. Their dual union was reduced to a skeleton. Yet there is the old saying in the labor movement that "no hard-fought strike is ever really lost." The spirit of resistance would rise again under the local leaders in New Deal days and carry virtually all the Kentucky miners into the revived industrial union movement.

§   §   §

I remember one lively meeting held at the apartment of Theodore Dreiser on West Fifty-seventh Street in New York for the purpose of bringing help to the Kentucky miners. There were numerous writers present; also teachers, theological students, and a couple of representatives of the ILD.

Dreiser was then in the ripeness of age, a heavy man with a big head, underslung jaw, thick lipped, now shy and halting in speech, now truculent. There was a stubborn strength in the man that had carried him through the long, unrequited labors of his earlier Zolaesque novels of social protest. Success in terms of sales and a large public had come to him late in life with the recent publication of *An American Tragedy*. The lonely years as an out-sider, subjected to censorship, forced to do hackwork to live, had left their mark on him. Now he had admirers all about him. On this occasion he became almost inarticulate as he set out to describe the lawlessness of the mine operators and local authorities in east-ern Kentucky. When his talk tended to wander the ILD personnel spoke up briskly to call the meeting back to the order of the day: raising funds, gathering food supplies.

Another speaker, Benjamin Stollberg, a small, red-haired man with a sardonic turn of humor, then spoke up in sharp opposition to the proposals put forth by the communists for helping an in-surgent coal miners' union. They were wrong, he argued, to introduce dual unions in mining, just as they had been proven wrong by the crushing defeat they had suffered recently in efforts to form a breakaway union of the AFL garment workers in New York and Chicago. (Stollberg, it should be remarked, was said to have been formerly a communist who had been expelled from the Party after disputes with the leadership.)

Some of the company roared in anger at the pessimistic Mr. Stollberg, who smiled with delight at the effect of his words. There was danger that the meeting would break up in a violent quarrel. Lincoln Steffens was present and calmed the agitated little crowd, speaking in his characteristically winning and urbane manner. He was a small grayhead nearing seventy, wearing a neat little goatee, with his hair combed in bangs, and he dressed with an Edwardian elegance. This venerable man, who carried himself with an air of youth, had been one of America's most famous journalists and editors; he seemed like an apparition out of the days of William J. Bryan and John Altgeld. We had all been reading his recently published *Autobiography* which made him in his old age, like Dreiser, one of the rediscovered literary heroes of the thirties.

Steffens had been different things at various periods of his life: the patient yet friendly investigator of political bosses and their machines; the municipal reformer incarnate, whose "muck-raking" articles, *The Shame of the Cities* (actually most thoroughly researched), were read by millions of Americans in the 1900's. He had fought to win amnesty for American political and labor prisoners; he had worked for Russian Relief after the last war. After the coming of the Great Crash of 1929 he had gone about questioning his wealthy friends, "the semi-scientific captains of industry," and learned that "they did not know what had happened or what was to be done about it." What else was there, he had asked. There was the example of Russia. Nowadays Steffens called upon our youth to mark well the lessons of the great Russian Revolution. His *Autobiography* was not only a marvelous causerie by a man of wit on the America of half a century past, but also an impressive documentation of the failure of the liberal concept of reform that he himself had so long advocated.

That evening at Dreiser's he nonetheless recommended that we pursue a course of patient petition bearing and peaceful agitation in support of the Harlan miners. He recalled how in the time of the earlier Roosevelt he had campaigned in the press against the corrupt city machines, decrying their business with criminals and prostitutes, until the "better element" in those communities joined in his action. He would then proceed, at the head of a delegation of the silk-stockinged and silk-hatted, to the city hall to lay proposals for reform before the Mayor. As I recall his talk he said:

> We respectable folk would mount the steps of the city hall; the Mayor and his retinue of political heelers would be waiting to receive us, outwardly polite, but secretly laughing at us—we could almost hear their sneering comments—because they despised and hated reformers. Yet those crooked people were only human; and such a visitation as ours, our repeated petitions, made them somehow *uneasy*, and evidently left some little effect, produced some perceptible change for the better. And so I say to you young men, you must go on stubbornly petitioning, though you think it tiresome and useless to do so. But as you persist in making your protests heard, publishing them wherever you can, your words little by little will reach their mark.

It was not only his words that heartened us; to my mind his presence contributed a sense of continuity with the past, linking our present action to earlier movements of Americans of good will.

In that period one of my new friends was John R. Chamberlain, a handsome, rosy-cheeked, curly-haired young man of twenty-seven who had worked as a reporter for *The New York Times* before becoming their daily book reviewer. In his free hours he was then writing an historical account of America's liberal reformers of the preceding generation; the crusading careers of Bryan, Theodore Roosevelt, and La Follette, among others, made up the subject of his book fittingly entitled *Farewell to Reform*, largely inspired by Steffens's *Autobiography*. For long hours John and I, in my barn at Sherman, used to discuss the trials and the failures of those eminent reformers who attempted to "mediate irreconcilables," and we were saying our good-byes to them. In the 1930's we were facing the facts of life. Our nation could not exist "half free, half slave." Were those who were made jobless through no fault of their own better than slaves?

"We must be good agitators, in Emerson's sense of the term," I used to say to Chamberlain. "We must bring steady, unremitting pressure to bear upon the establishment *from the left*." The complaisant and the corrupt might sneer at us, as they had at Steffens and his friends, but in the long run our persistence would wear down the opposition. The communists and their dogmas might seem outlandish in this country, still their fanaticism would help; and aside from theirs we had no organized movement of the left. What was paramount, I wrote in a letter of July 1932, was "to take the side of the extremists, the activists of all kinds, who may shake our inert society to awakening."

John Chamberlain's book, written in the autumn of 1932, ends with a call for "a fighting, organized underdog movement" that would "compel cooperation through its threat of ultimate victory."

III.

I had almost forgotten that we had had a Socialist Party for fifty years or more. Why did not more of us turn to them? Earlier they had shown vigorous growth under the leadership of Eugene V. Debs. But during World War I there had been a split between the pacifist faction and the wartime patriots. Some of the militant socialists had then broken away to form the first underground communist organization. In America our elaborate apparatus of state conventions and primaries does not favor the growth of third or minority parties. In any case, the fatal flaw of the American socialists was their failure to win organized labor. For forty years the AFL had followed the advice of its founder Samuel Gompers that the national labor body support principally one or the other of the two major political parties, "rewarding their friends in office, punishing their enemies." Thus our American socialists, unlike their brothers in Europe, had no mass following of laborers save for some of the foreign-language groups in some big cities. Professional people, teachers, and also churchmen were very prominent among the socialists, and Norman Thomas, their presidential candidate in 1928, typified them; but he gathered in only 400,000 votes, the socialists' lowest ebb in twenty years.

I was curious nevertheless about Thomas and his party's prospects in 1932, and so I arranged to interview him.

Popular prejudice in America can assume a terrible force. Edward Bellamy, writing his socialistic utopia in 1888, named his party "Nationalists" because, as he said, the word socialism was associated with the Devil and brimstone. In time the leadership of the Socialist Party in this country had devolved upon a man who people said "was not like a socialist at all," an eloquent Protestant minister who appealed to the humane and Christian sentiments of his public instead of to class hatred. The doctrinaires of his party objected to his socialism as being "without benefit of Marx." But others approved of it because it was "not without benefit of clergy."

George Soule described his friend Thomas as "a minister who had begun to deliver his sermons out in the street, instead of from the pulpit; but while there are some listeners in the front pews of his outdoor church, the galleries are almost empty." I wrote in *The New Republic*: "The money-changers and their wives go as if to the temple to hear him; or they read reports of his speeches in *The New York Times*. (Mr. Thomas, at all events, is 'news fit to print.') Hearing him . . . they wish a little they could be as decent as he; then go about their business as usual."

With his tall figure, fine head, handsome features, and blue eyes Thomas was by all odds the most personable of radical leaders and fashioned to be an ornament of our public life. He was and is a courageous, a muscular Christian. He had left his rich congregation first to serve a parish of the East Harlem slums among the desperately poor; then in 1917, as an ardent pacifist, he had severed his connection with the church and worked to aid the conscientious objectors—one of whom, his beloved friend Roger Baldwin, was in jail. After the war he had founded together with Baldwin the American Civil Liberties Union, and he also set up the League for Industrial Democracy, which spread among the colleges and was directed by professors and writers of the Fabian socialist type. He had been a crusading socialist in an ugly period of wartime hysteria. And yet, like other angry intellectuals of the thirties, I felt disappointment in him and his program and a stubborn prejudice against him as a "do-gooder."

It would have been pleasant to be able to arrange for a peaceful transition from capitalism to socialism such as Marx sometimes thought might be possible in strongly democratic nations like England and the United States. However, as one of Thomas's intimate associates complained in private, the socialist leader "wasted a lot of his time trying to win over sections of the middle class." That was why Sidney Hillman used to tease his socialist friend Charles W. Ervin by asking him: "Charley, when are you socialists going to *do something?*"

Thomas himself, out of innate honesty, spoke to me of the socialists' failures in fairly pessimistic terms: "There is the possibility of a powerful political force in our party," he said, "but I tell you candidly we have been glacially slow; our party has been in a terrible state these last four years. There are many reasons: the false prosperity of the Coolidge era; then the communist split . . . and the patrioteering of some socialist leaders in the past." I had heard that there were also jealous factions creating dissension within his party, and Thomas admitted as much, remarking sadly that "a sort of inferiority complex" had fixed itself upon the socialists. Its mainly white-collar membership seldom undertook any militant demonstrations and apparently wanted only to carry on educational propaganda for parliamentary socialism.

I asked Mr. Thomas what he thought of the communists, who

at any rate were working diligently to organize the unemployed and were also trying to build up a trade union base. In a disinterested spirit he remarked that "the communists, with their dogmatic passion and fanatical energy might go far some day, despite their weakness in numbers and their blunders." As opportunists they "injected themselves swiftly into labor conflicts, wherever they developed, and preempted those situations for themselves." He went on to say: "It is logical also that they should try to clear the way for themselves by destroying the Socialist Party, whom they regard as 'rival operators.'" But the Socialist Party meant to hang on, he said, and might wear down the other in the long run.

Though Thomas was convinced that "capitalism was dying" he still favored measures of gradual change. If we came to a revolutionary crisis, he argued, what social gain would there be in trying to bring about a complete smashup of the present order with all the suffering that would entail? The Russians had borne terrible privations for fifteen years only to build up a large-scale industrial plant such as America already possessed. "Now the communists preach violence and class struggle; they seek to destroy in order to rebuild. I too am betting on a debacle for capitalism, but hold that the transition should be worked out with a minimum of disorder. My instincts lead me to fight against disaster. Who knows what convulsions the end of capitalism may bring? What will replace it?"

He paused; in the moment of silence it was as if we both stared into an abyss—the unimaginable future—for we knew that the crisis was growing and yet feared that men of good will, socialists or liberals, might be powerless to do anything.

His smile seemed a little sad as he went on: "I'm afraid I have sounded fatalistic or pessimistic. At any rate we have in our party a social philosophy which the two major political parties entirely lack." Then in a challenging tone he added: "What we socialists need is boldness, audacity. We need the flaming passion of a Mazzini."

But there were no Mazzinis either in the socialist parties of Europe that were giving way to fascism or in America's Socialist Party, which had only Norman Thomas.

Though I found Mr. Thomas a most sympathetic personality—

how staunch he has proved in all these years as a keeper of the public conscience—I steeled myself to write of him and his party in the spirit of satire. It was still the Socialist Party of our grand-daddies who played at being socialists without interesting the great public in America. These advocates of piecemeal collectivism seemed a disappointing lot compared with the hardy communists who risked their skins to organize the miners or the Southern tenant farmers and Negroes and stirred up mass demonstrations of the unemployed. Whereas the communists, believing in direct action, gave themselves to full-time agitation and lived in a sort of revolutionary ferment, the socialists practiced adjustment to the present order and gave only a few leisure hours to the attempt to change society by peaceful persuasion.[3]

A closing passage of my profile of presidential candidate Thomas treated with irony an incident in his career in which (as it was later explained to me) he had actually behaved with much courage.

> In 1919, while giving help in the Paterson textile workers' strike, Norman Thomas made a speech to the union men. . . . Suddenly the police entered the hall and cut off all the lights. Not only was crusading forbidden, but the authorities seemed bent on stopping the strikers' meeting by plunging the place in darkness. Thomas became indignant. . . . The trouble, to his mind of an ardent uplifter, was the darkness; the darkness was allied to violence and injustice; besides, it was plainly unconstitutional. . . . Thomas longed to bring light, to persuade the wicked police authorities to behave, to recall them to the spirit in which our forefathers conceived this government of liberty and private property. Boldly arming himself with a candle he read to the strikers as well as to the police officers the Declaration of Independence. The strike one recalls was beaten; but Norman Thomas has been carrying a candle all about the country ever since.[4]

---

[3] Where the socialists had strong local leadership, as in Chicago and Seattle, they brought much help to the unemployed.

[4] "Socialism and Candle-sticks," *The New Republic* (August 17, 1932).

I V .

Even the rich, or at least the well-to-do among our acquaintances were filled with unrest in those days, for their income was falling sharply. One of my friends, D., an artist of talent and intelligence, had recently married a woman of independent means, so that he survived in good style though selling few pictures. For some years these friends had been living in a charmingly decorated house in the East Fifties, where Mrs. D. continued to give large dinners and musicales as she had before the Crash. Her husband's friendships were with artists of the contemporary American school, and also with writers of the left.

As we were about to leave at the end of one of those very agreeable dinner parties which Mrs. D. managed so well, she herself arose and made an almost formal little speech of farewell. This dinner, she said, was to be her last party in New York. Her income from stocks and bonds had been reduced by 25 per cent. She wound up: "We are going away to live in a simple country house"—here she paused, held her head high, and looked very brave and grave, measuring her words—"*and to wait there for The Revolution!*" Everyone laughed nervously. But in 1932 and 1933 rich people sometimes sounded like Marie Antoinette being driven from the Palace of Versailles.

Another of our favorite hostesses of that period was Leonie Knoedler, the heiress of one of the leading art galleries of New York that long catered to collectors of old masters. At her home on Park Avenue Leonie, by preference, collected modern artifacts, Cubist paintings by Braque or a sculpture or two by Brancusi such as you would never have seen in her family's galleries. Such things were still novel here; but at that time no one talked of Brancusi or the Cubists. Instead the talk was all of politics, and Esther Murphy's voice led all the rest.

You could hardly miss Esther Murphy, for she was almost six feet tall, an Amazon with a fine big head and a squint. She dressed with a mannish elegance, and talked withal in an endless stream. I had sometimes seen her in her former habitat, which was Paris, and knew of her as the sister of the Gerald Murphy of Cap

(121)

d'Antibes who was Scott Fitzgerald's long-enduring friend and host. The Murphys were the descendants of an Irish-born merchant prince of Boston and New York (founder of the Mark Cross shops) and also of New England Yankees, Esther's grandfather having been the Civil War General Ben Butler, once governor of Massachusetts.

During her travels abroad Esther Murphy in 1929 had met and married John Strachey, the young British writer on economic affairs. Soon afterward he was elected to Parliament under the Labor Party banner, with his American bride stumping for him in that campaign. They were now separated and about to be divorced, though Esther spoke affectionately of Strachey, whose book *The Coming Struggle for Power*, published here in the autumn of 1932, made a profound impression on the American intelligentsia.

Esther used to hold forth good-humoredly in torrential monologues made up of anecdotes of persons living or dead (often well told) and studded with curious bits of literary and historical erudition. For she knew everybody in the literary world, as she knew the people in New York's Blue Book; the names of Edith Wharton and Virginia Woolf were mingled with those of Mrs. Cornelius Vanderbilt or Mrs. James Potter, and her items of gossip about them, if embroidered or exaggerated, rang true. Now Esther too was deep in politics; she was much exercised over the effects of the economic crisis on Americans, and especially on her friends in Long Island society. At one moment, rising from her chair and slapping her thigh for emphasis, she exclaimed with a roar of laughter: "Why, they say that all Southampton has gone Red!"

She herself was just then reading a biography of Mussolini at the instance of one of her friends, Lawrence P. Dennis, who was an admirer of fascism. But the next we heard of Esther, a year later, she had bounced off to California, married again, and gone to live in some queer colony of utopians in the sand dunes near San Francisco.

Decidedly the old rentier class was growing uneasy. Even Mrs. John D. Rockefeller, Jr., I heard, was waiting for the tumbrils to roll—though meanwhile serving as the generous patron of several young American artists who were in straits. In the spring of 1932 I went to meet Ben Shahn and wrote an affirmative review of his first one-man show at the Downtown Gallery. This included his brilliant series of color drawings in gouache of the leading characters in the Sacco-Vanzetti Case, and also a group of portraits illustrating the Dreyfus Affair—which he said was inspired by reading my book on Emile Zola.

Ben Shahn—now so well fleshed in the ripeness of age and success, then a lean and hungry fellow—informed me cheerfully that Mrs. Rockefeller had purchased a number of his pictures and hung them up in her bedroom, together with some of William Gropper's canvases, remarking: "Come the Revolution, they will find I have some Groppers and Ben Shahn's pictures of Sacco and Vanzetti in my house, and they will perhaps spare me."

From Boston I heard that our eccentric Brahmin, the poet John Brooks Wheelwright, sometimes marched in the processions of the unemployed and on occasion addressed them from a soapbox in Boston Commons. A mutual friend related that he would appear among the unemployed wearing his molted old raccoon coat and a bowler hat, looking quite the decayed dandy. When his radical colleagues pointed out that his costume, fur coat and tuxedo, was inappropriate he expostulated: "But I *have* to keep warm."

I can only imagine how odd must have been his outdoor speeches, given in the name of the Christian Socialism he now professed—could this have been a one-man party?—and delivered in his nasal tone and upper-class Boston accent. He himself reported to me that at one such street rally he was heckled by an angry man with a marked Irish brogue, who cried: "Ah, What are you, a dancer, a waiter? Why don't ye' go back where ye' came from?" And Jack replied quickly: "I am a bourgeois, and I've just been to a dinner party."

Our Jack could not help clowning, it was his rebellious form of humor; but he was also a man of courage and stiff-necked independence. He was then writing in his highly individual and almost cacophonous style his political poems, which were published in obscure journals or in little brochures he gave away. There were not

many authentic political or "social" poems written during the de-
pressed thirties, and his are among the few. In rereading them I feel
the deep breath and passion of Wheelwright's voice and believe
they will be remembered for that, as well as for their glimpses of the
drab street scene of the thirties in Boston and their reflections of
the political emotions of that time. (Because of his early death in
1940, Wheelwright's very curious and sparse writings have already
become the objects of the collector's attention.)

§ § §

At Edmund Wilson's apartment, then in West Fifty-eighth
Street, the discussion of human affairs and of revolutionary strategy
was in full spate. "W. Z. Foster made a very fine impression by his
talk at E. W.'s home last week," I reported in a letter to a friend at
the end of May 1932. I was referring to the Communist Party's
candidate for President of the United States.

A fairly large group of intellectuals had come to Wilson's that
evening to meet the guest of honor, William Z. Foster. Dos Passos
was there, also young Corliss Lamont, son of the chairman of J. P.
Morgan and Company, who shunned banking and taught philosophy at Columbia.

Foster, a working-class type dressed in unfashionable though
well-brushed clothes, stood in marked contrast to the Ivy League
radicals in that living room. He was a tall, bony Irish-American of
about fifty, with thinning red hair, lined face, and blue eyes, who
had gone to work at age ten in a Philadelphia type foundry. In
early youth he had been a member of the IWW and had risen
to leadership of its industrial unions; during World War I he had
gone over to the AFL, and, as an organizer, headed some of the
largest union campaigns of that period. After the defeat of the
steel workers in the 1919 strike, which was under Foster's direction,
the AFL dropped him and he moved on to the Communist Party.

Talking in a cool and logical manner, he seemed wholly unlike
the conventional image of a communist fire-eater. One of my
friends who observed the great steel strike of 1919 once described
him as being "something like General Ludendorff," a master of
organization and supply, who directed his industrial battles with

very close attention to detail. He was not the man to magnetize crowds.

Though Foster showed signs of considerable self-education, he seemed rather wary of intellectual radicals. They were too given to lengthy debate in a competitive or egoistic spirit, he implied, while the way of communists was to discuss things purposively then, "having made their decision, cut out talk and go into action." The bourgeois recruits would have a good deal to learn, he held. Asked why he would not work with the socialists, he answered vehemently that they really strove to preserve the present order: "The socialists see more in capitalism than the capitalists; they see socialism in it." Someone questioned him about the conservative political tendencies of most American workingmen, and he remarked that while they often showed "a petty bourgeois consciousness, objective conditions can turn one hundred per cent Americans into Marxists."

The communists' program, he maintained, sought to create mass demonstrations of a peaceful character; it was the owning class that would turn to violence against the unarmed people. "The situation itself would bring on the revolutionary outcome." As for those who feared for liberty under a dictatorship, he argued: "There is no liberty for the workers; only the bourgeois have a little of it—when there is no Depression."

After the formal part of his talk was over, I got Foster into a corner and asked him: "Why have the communists not made more progress under such favoring circumstances as the present in America? We have been passing through the greatest Depression in our history; are not the results disappointing?"

Foster said deliberately: "But, man, think what a tremendously powerful bourgeoisie we are up against; they have the richest and strongest capitalist state in the world." He sounded almost doleful. He at least was not deceiving himself about the difficulties ahead.

At this point Dos Passos came up and began an animated discussion with Foster about the need to "Americanize" the Communist Party; Dos gesticulated a good deal with his arms as he spoke, while Foster backed up in a corner of the room against a grand piano. A little earlier Margaret Wilson had sent her husband

for refreshments, and Wilson just at that moment returned bearing
about thirty little glasses filled with liquid on a large tray which he
tried to lift clear of the piano. Suddenly the near-sighted Dos Passos,
his back to Wilson, made a grand sweeping gesture with his arm
and overturned the whole tray, sending all the glasses to the floor
with a great crash. We were aghast; in those days even bathtub gin
was not easy to come by. Dos Passos looked almost tearful. But
Wilson, good humored, went off for more glasses and more liquid.

The upshot of the argument seemed to be that Foster wasn't
going to let the Party be "taken over" by a few literary fellows.

V.

Meeting Foster suggested the idea of my doing
an article on him for *The New Yorker*—he seemed like another
presidential impossibility. Although Harold Ross disliked pieces
about "do-gooders"—for thus he regarded the communists—in this
case he gave his approval, stipulating that I should write it in the
form of a reporter's visit with the communists.

A short walk of a few blocks from the room I occupied when
working in the city brought me to Union Square. This dilapidated
little park had acquired a reputation as New York's Red Square.
Here we were in the very vortex of revolutionary activities, the
communists using the place regularly as their outdoor forum for
periodic mass protests—against the expulsion of the Bonus Army
from Washington or the "massacre" at Ford's in Dearborn—as well
as for celebration of fixed holidays on their calendar such as May
Day or Russian Revolution Day in October. In May 1930 there had
been a violent collision here between the police and the communists some of whose speakers, including Foster himself, had
been beaten and arrested; again on May Day of 1932 there had been
great tension when some sixty thousand gathered in Union Square
and the police, out in force, placed machine guns on the roofs of
buildings surrounding the square.

Now the square was rather quiet; knots of people who looked
like workers from the nearby garment shops were standing about

listening to some speakers mounted on little portable platforms decked with American flags. Soapboxers were going on in routine fashion: "*Garbage!* That's what the bosses give the American workers," one of them shouted suddenly. His small audience responded with a roar of laughter, some of them waving placards with slogans such as "Jobs—Not Charity."

A few steps away at 50 East Thirteenth Street was my destination, the national headquarters of the Communist Party, U.S.A. The bleak nine-story loft was now entirely filled by the Party's apparatus, employing about three hundred staff workers. The former small-business occupants of the place had fled in terror when the communists first arrived. There was a cafeteria on the street floor ornamented with pictures of Marx, Lenin, Stalin, and Foster, and adjacent to it was the Workers' Bookshop. In the building were schoolrooms and union offices for such foreign-language groups as the Finnish-American Workers' Association; several whole floors were occupied by the presses and editorial rooms of *The Daily Worker*; above, on the ninth floor, were the offices of the Communist Executive Committee. It was the very beehive of revolutionary activity that was so much talked about, so dreaded in respectable circles.

Outside the pace of life, even vehicular traffic in the street was rather quiet. Here in the communists' headquarters hatless and tieless people went rushing in and out of offices jostling me. Business must be humming, I judged.

A gigantic, stern-looking Negro conducted me in the crowded red-painted elevator cage up to the ninth floor. There I made my way along a corridor jammed with bundles of pamphlets toward a telephone switchboard and its operator. En route I squeezed with difficulty past a large packing case, charged with violent propaganda no doubt, upon which sat a plump young woman and an unshaven, dark-complexioned young man in blue denims. They whispered to each other cheek to cheek, oblivious to all else around them. ("Ah, love among the communists," I said under my breath.) The telephonist to whom I showed my letter of introduction led me to a door at the end of the hallway, and I found myself in a bare, sparsely furnished office with a single grimy window looking north over the cluttered landscape of Union Square, toward the huge new Empire State Building, filling the Manhattan sky.

I waited five minutes, staring at the Empire State Building with all its 110 stories. It was beautifully engineered but artistically disappointing, and after having opened for business a year ago it now stood almost empty. The newly completed Waldorf Astoria, called the world's greatest luxury hotel, was also nearly empty and bankrupt. Builders were now blasting and excavating for Rockefeller Center, a community of business palaces which I suspected would also remain mostly unused. Some were saying these would be the last structural dinosaurs of our era. What a grotesque economic system, I reflected. It was not surprising that the prospects of the communists looked bright.

Earl Browder, whom I had heard of as the Party's new secretary and "strong man," came in first. He was about forty, sandy-haired and blue-eyed, with a long chin; a native of Kansas, he looked as if he might have been a schoolteacher, but he had actually been a bookkeeper. According to current gossip the Communist Party, though tiny, had suffered from more than its share of factional strife. During a drastic reorganization several years earlier Jay Lovestone, then the executive head, had been brusquely ousted at the order of the Comintern, which meant really Stalin's order, and replaced by Earl Browder as executive secretary with Foster as the Party's titular head. Unwittingly I addressed my host as "Mr. Browder," and smiling he corrected me, saying he was "Comrade Browder."

"Oh, my mistake!" I said. "You see I have bourgeois habits and am unused to your conventions. 'Comrade' is after all a convention like 'mister,' is it not?"

"A convention, yes, but one which abolishes all distinctions," he replied firmly.

"But in using it do you not make distinctions against those who are not comrades?"

"Yes, but we invite them all to join us."

I was aware that both Browder and Foster had made long sojourns in Moscow and that Browder had sometimes been assigned by the Third International to various foreign missions; in

1927 he had journeyed to China which he talked of with much interest. But for the rest, at least to an interviewer, he seemed much given to Party-line clichés.

An instinct told me that I would do better not to cross-examine these comrades (for Foster soon joined us) about when and how they proposed to stage the social revolution. I knew from working with Harold Ross of *The New Yorker* that he was extremely curious about "how people did their stuff," whether in Wall Street or in Union Square, and what their day-by-day tasks were like. But there were secrets in every trade; these fellows it seemed to me would probably give me only handouts if I asked them probing questions. Better, I thought, to maintain a light and worldly tone of conversation and try to study their characters and motives as far as possible.

Earl Browder in 1932 I judged a man of average abilities, though he seemed to grow in stature while suffering reverses in his later career, which saw him expelled from the Party in 1946. Foster, the older man, had more of the common touch that appealed to the workingman.

In his matter-of-fact way Foster told me how he came to radical labor and then communism: "because I always hated the *wastefulness* of the capitalist system." In Washington, in Wall Street, in the steel and coal mining centers, all was waste to him. "It is said we suffer in America from 'overproduction,' so-called, of food, machinery, and housing. Well, we communists seek to be scientific. Instead of dissipating the riches of the country we would distribute them all around—that is, when we have established the United Soviet States of America."

I pointed to the Empire State Building and asked what they would do about such a problem.

"Why, we could take charge of the Empire State all right and fill it up to the top," Foster said with a twinkle in his eye. Earl Browder referred to the many luxury apartment buildings on Park Avenue, said to be empty now, and observed with a hard laugh: "We could find more occupants for those places than the realtors ever dream of."

Our talk became at times rather hilarious, and the two men entered into the spirit of it, being not without wit. I pretended that

I must ask them, for the sake of my readers, if they were prepared to recommend that a young man about to start at the bottom of the ladder in business should take up, instead, a career in communism. Grinning wickedly, Foster answered that communism offered "a bright future for the young man of today," something much more adventurous than going to work as a bond salesman or a junior executive in a bank.

"Tell your readers that communism is a good investment for the future," he went on. "Tell them that once there was a Philadelphia soap manufacturer who during the war loaned the Russian Bolshevik Party five thousand pounds sterling on a note signed by the executive committee of the Party. Years later, when he had died, his heirs presented the note to the Soviets and were repaid in full with 6 per cent interest."

In more serious vein Foster went on to say that they were now in an expansive phase, the cardholding membership having gone up recently to fifteen thousand. I was surprised at the smallness of the numbers as given officially. There had been much talk of "hundreds of thousands" being affiliated with the Party through auxiliary bodies all around the country, these reports emanating from a committee of Congress headed by Representative Hamilton Fish of New York—the forerunner of the House Un-American Activities Committee.

The Communist Party, Foster went on, preferred to remain small in numbers, to act as a spearhead of trained organizers penetrating the labor movement and trying to form Red trade unions. Operating as members of a nucleus or cell of three or four fellows, the Party's organizers now tried to wean away locals of the conservative AFL unions or build new locals where there were none. This new policy involved the unpleasant business of breaking up existing labor organizations and creating dual unions, thus provoking dissension among the workers, a method Foster himself had previously opposed. Now he held that this tactic was justified because the AFL people ran "do-nothing unions" or were "traitors." (Admittedly the going was hard: the Party's labor department was small.)

Earl Browder reviewed the work being done by the Party's

missionaries among the Negroes, who were the first to be dismissed from jobs and last to be favored with relief payments. The communists just then were also hard at work trying to save the Scottsboro boys, nine very young Negroes imprisoned in Alabama under sentence of death on charges of assault against two white women. That their trial had been a mockery of justice and the charges false was indicated by the eventual release of the prisoners in 1934, an outcome largely credited to the persistent agitation of the communists. Meanwhile the Party had named as its vice-presidential candidate James Ford, a young college-educated Negro.

Most important of all, the Party, as Browder pointed out, was organizing the unemployed and teaching them to help themselves. Their members were the ringleaders of the new Unemployed Councils in many cities. When penniless families were evicted from their flats the Red "rent fighters" often came hurrying to the scene and helped restore both furniture and tenants to their homes.

Now an election year was upon us; Browder spoke of their hope for "a million votes." They were fated, however, to win only a tenth of that number.

I then asked what were the daily duties and devotions of a good communist (always for the benefit of my imaginary young reader in search of a career open to talent). His life, I was told, would be arduous at the very least. If he worked in a shop or factory he must be on the lookout for employees' grievances that could be turned to account, perhaps also publish a mimeographed shop paper for covert distribution. If there were no union in his factory he must work to organize his fellows, sometimes at considerable physical risk. Meanwhile his evenings were to be devoted to Party committee meetings or to study of the fundamentals of Marxism or trade union strategy in courses given at the Workers' School on Thirteenth Street. Finally he must pay dues of 2 per cent of his weekly earnings, if any, as well as dues to his union local.

If by chance he rose to the eminence of a paid staff worker or field worker attached to national headquarters or some other large city branch, his schedule was one of frenzied activity. He might be obliged to rise at dawn to hand out leaflets before factory gates. Returning to headquarters he would put in a busy day with interruptions only to give stump speeches in Union Square or some other outdoor forum. After having undergone training he might be dispatched on a less than peaceful errand to the Harlan County coal fields. In return for these Spartan labors the proper comrade might receive as wages no more than thirty-five dollars a week, generally paid him on alternate weeks. And if he fell by the wayside, the Party's disciplinarians would denounce him or expel him from membership, branding him as a weakling and publishing his face and name as such in *The Daily Worker.*

The manners and morals of these people were fairly free, though not more so than those of our middle class; that is, they were usually modernists in sex relations despite the stories that Stalin was now forcing the Russians to be puritanical. There was in fact a "togetherness" among the loyal communists that greatly solaced lonely souls whose life had no direction or purpose. But drinking to the point of intoxication was severely censured and could lead to expulsion.

Off the record Earl Browder said to me that he was aware of the significant trend of intellectuals toward the Communist Party. "We are making a special effort to interest writers and artists" he remarked, adding that former radical movements had been wrong to show contempt for such adherents. But, he warned, the Communist Party did not pretend to be able to "solve their problems for them," or help them "find salvation." If they joined, they must be prepared to "come in at our terms" and submit to party discipline.

A most important department of the communists' tactics was concerned with their regularly recurring "spontaneous demonstrations" in the streets. The technique of the big parade was as vital to the men of Union Square as it was to West Point. On the eve of communist holidays headquarters and all branch offices throbbed with excitement: placards, flags, floats, and effigies were made ready; plans and maps were drawn up carefully; all units were contacted for pledges of attendance and money for expenses; the messages flew back and forth until marching orders were given.

The May Day meeting of 1932, which gathered sixty thousand in Union Square and was followed by an imposing procession through the city with massed red banners and challenging placards, was one of the high points of that period in New York. The Young Communist League members were out in force, singing in shrill voice their insurrectionary songs like "Solidarity" or "Red Flag" and giving concerted yells much like collegians or school boys:

> Are we in it, well I guess!
> Communists, Communists, yes, yes, yes!

They even sang the Yale College tune of "Boola-Boola" to communist verses.

A few days after my interview with Foster and Browder I happened to observe an impromptu protest meeting in Union Square. Some four thousand of the working population and the unemployed of the neighborhood were on hand, and among them were the communists, tirelessly on the job, speaker after speaker coming to the stand to deliver minutemen talks. At the end of the meeting the crowd, mostly jobless, began to sing the plaintive old IWW chant "Hallelujah, I'm a bum," whose chorus ends:

> Hallelujah, give us a handout
> To revive us again!

I was standing at the rear chatting with one of New York's finest, a stalwart patrolman six feet tall, swinging his nightstick with nervous energy, glowering at the crowd, and sometimes snorting at some remark that was more provocative than usual. What did he make of the things these people were saying, I asked him. At length, after appraising my white collar and conventional dress, he exclaimed with an expression of supreme contempt: "Oh, hell, I have to listen to 'em day and night. Give us a handout! *Handout!* That's all they're after, the slobs. They want to take away the money that you and I make by using our brains! Eh?"

§   §   §

I hoped that my candid report on the communists as they were would help to dispel romantic myths about them. A good many people believed they might actually be capable of setting off at any moment a sort of slave's revolt of the unemployed. In my judgment their operations were small scale and their resources limited. Several years later, after some recovery in employment and the passage of New Deal labor legislation, their position became much stronger. But in 1932 I reported Foster as sounding "almost melancholy" on his Party's prospects. Was the Revolution many years away, after all?

Like other writers I sometimes had my troubles with Harold Ross, that impetuous man with forelock always falling over his face, a worrier over tremendous trifles and a mighty grumbler yet with a kind heart. While going over one of my recent articles he had exclaimed over a passage I had written: "My God, Mr. Josephson, you must be a socialist!"

In these articles for a popular magazine I worked as if I were pitting my wits against a censor always invisibly present, as I supposed Chekhov and company must have written under the czar. Sometimes in setting forth the little true facts I would use the tactic of distributing praise or blame *for the wrong reason.* I would adopt a rather bland tone in describing the stratagems of some Wall Street pirate who could cut people's throats skillfully, as if that were the most natural thing in the world. While knowing this might increase his business for a while, I hoped, nevertheless, that an exact description of such tricks might draw upon him the attentions of a committee of Congress that would be interested in drafting laws to curb such men. In the same way, when writing of the communists I made the point that they were ill fed, ill dressed, and worked in untidy quarters and under trying conditions. I even pretended to chide them for their "inverted psychology, their never trying to make money, welcoming poverty and adversity, and courting still greater adversity in order that the little CP might, one day, ride into power." In other words, I used terms that would lead Harold Ross and his mythical *New Yorker* clubman Cadwallader, and the Wall Street or Madison Avenue reader alike, to find the communists uncouth. My article quite evidently was not designed to cause a stampede of bourgeois readers into the Party's rank and file; and Ross himself appeared satisfied on that point.

On the other hand, I hoped that the intelligent part of my public, even if a minority, would be able to read between the lines and judge the facts for themselves. That the comrades were men in baggy trousers would mean little to them; but I hoped some appreciation of their dedicated spirit, of their courage and derring-do would spread about. The intelligent reader would be led to see what a mixture of evangelism and freemasonry there was in this movement. The communists would say: "We are small now, but we have the right idea. At least we are doing something, not just waiting." What did it matter if one were ill paid or occasionally slugged by a patrolman's billy, so long as one was doing his part to "change the world."

Harold Ross raised only one serious objection to what I had written, and that on quite unexpected grounds which he explained in a little note: "One conspicuous thing about communists is that their women are noted for their ugliness. Any reporter in New York will testify that he never saw one good-looking communist woman. They seem to attract the ugly. That is perhaps the secret of many memberships; people go into communism because they don't fit into the existing scheme of things. They can't make money so they say we're not out to make money, etc."

We had a shouting match over this point, during which I contended that I had seen a number of female communists who were attractive enough and appeared to be having a high old time. Ross fumed at me; I said I would never work for him again, whereupon he rushed out of the office where I was correcting proofs. The next morning while I was still checking the article he came in, all confusion and embarrassment, and made the most sweeping apologies to me. He also gave me a generous bonus check beyond what I had been promised in payment. This sort of thing happened more than once.

The Communist Party higher-ups never complained, so far as I knew, at the half-serious, half-spoofing treatment I had given them in *The New Yorker*. What was my surprise however to receive a communication from a friend of mine, James Rorty—then an enraptured fellow traveler—which revealed that a group of the severe and humorless breed of communists had planned to denounce me in public with the following statement: "We the undersigned demand that Matthew Josephson explain the purpose of his writing the scurrilous and supercilious article entitled 'The Red House' published recently in *The New Yorker.* We feel that an acknowledgment of his error and a public apology for it is the least that can be expected."

This was my first exposure to the stringent moral conformity some of the communists professed, and it gave me pause. A very genial communist around that time asked me if I did not feel I ought to join the Party. I said to him: "Heavens, I know I'm not virtuous enough to be a communist."

Chapter Seven

❦

Commitments

AS THE CRISIS deepened the distress of my friends who were writers and artists became always more evident, though they were not disposed to complain but often made light of their misfortune. In this country those who worked seriously at the arts—as opposed to purveyors of commercial entertainment— had long accustomed themselves to living in poverty, but not to a destitution without hope. The painters had always been peculiarly dependent on the very rich, who now generally postponed purchases of luxuries.

My neighbor Peter Blume, who had come to live in Sherman in 1929 when he was in his early twenties, had gained a considerable gallery success. A year later his gallery went bankrupt, just as he had embarked on a huge symbolic surrealist canvas entitled "South of Scranton." It was a prodigious fantasy on the American industrial landscape and designed for some museum. But he had a wife and not even the means to pay for their shelter, let alone a studio adequate for a canvas of large proportions. For a period in the winter of 1932 he was installed with his gargantuan picture in my low-ceilinged house while we were away in New York; other friends, especially Malcolm and Muriel Cowley, helped him generously. At length Mrs. John D. Rockefeller ordered a few drawings of him, and the Guggenheim Foundation awarded him a traveling fellowship in 1932.

But who would buy that epic painting to which this ambitious young artist gave five years of intense labor? (Nearly a decade more elapsed before it was purchased by the Metropolitan Museum of Art.)

For many years I had come to prefer the friendship of artists to that of all but a few writers; their aesthetic anxieties were similar to those of writers, while their professional jealousies did not disturb me. During the twenties I sometimes took my vacations at the thriving art colony of Woodstock, New York, often and enjoyably stopping with Henry and Gladys Billings. Revisiting Woodstock in the summer of 1932 I found a great blight had fallen on the place. The sculptor Paul Fiene, younger brother of the painter Ernest Fiene, whom I had met several years earlier, was still working at his "unknown masterpiece," a huge reclining female nude in plaster that was about twenty-five feet in length and proportionately broad. One had to climb a ladder to a high balcony in his barn in order to view the colossal sculpture, which Fiene's confreres laughingly named "Big Bertha." But Bertha was completely unmarketable; Fiene and his wife, Rosella Hartmann, herself a talented artist, were therefore on very short rations, sometimes helped by friends who had only a little more than they. My memory of the depression in the art world is forever associated with the image of a young artist working incessantly on such a project as "Big Bertha"— though none would buy it. Who knows whatever became of that giantess in plaster? Her creator died young.

Arnold Blanch, a somewhat older Woodstock artist who had known success earlier, said at the time with great bitterness: "I have given my whole life to my chosen work but now I feel as if I will never paint another picture again."

Some artists survived by panhandling or borrowing from their relatives or friends. Ben Shahn told me long afterward that he once stole a few rolls to bring to his wife and two children. In 1932 several artists who had gone on the relief rolls in New York were at last given assignments for the decoration of public buildings and a few theaters by the "Gibson Committee."

§　§　§

Our young writers were also down at the heels, though some worked as schoolteachers or found occasional jobs at newspapers.

Others made for such storm shelters as they could find. Katherine Anne Porter, for example, stayed in Mexico, because of her health, and also for economy's sake, in an enforced isolation from her friends in New York. "New York seems so far away," she wrote in a letter at the time. "It seems unreasonable to think I shall not see it again for long and long. . . . It baffles me that I have never been able to live there, when I love the place so much."

One of the most engaging of our young friends, the budding novelist Hamilton Basso of New Orleans, who worked in an advertising agency, described in letters conditions in the South as even worse than in the North. At twenty-seven Basso already had to his credit a highly regarded first novel, *Relics and Angels* (1929), and a second that was accepted for publication but remained unprinted because the publishers reported that no books of any kind were selling. He was nevertheless preparing a biography treating of the Civil War and Reconstruction that he promised would be more realistic than those of the myth-making Southern Regionalists "with their queer worship of the South of Before-the-War." As this would demand a full year for the writing, Basso waged a stern campaign to save part of his salary during a year or two, after which he proposed to resign from his job and go all out for writing: "If only I could get away from the business of increasing the sale of soap, sugar, and salad oil."

Then things began to happen: the advertising agency to which his talents had been "pledged for several years" went on the rocks, he was separated from his job in a way he felt premature, and he had recently been married. The first effect was "a fine feeling of emancipation." Now at last he was blessed with leisure. But he added wryly, "I would have preferred to have achieved it myself instead of having it thrust upon me. Where do we go from here?"

In those days if you lost a job it was forever.

Basso had been corresponding with Sherwood Anderson, whom he had met several years earlier in New Orleans. The older novelist had lately established himself in the small town of Marion, Virginia, where he found publishing a weekly newspaper a pleasant way of life, and he now recommended that Basso go and do likewise. An opportunity had arisen, Anderson reported, to buy another country weekly for a thousand dollars down, in the town of Abingdon, about twenty miles from Anderson's home. Ham promptly set out for the place, but on July 4, 1932, he wrote me calamitous news: "My arrival in Virginia was greeted by a flock of bank failures which well-nigh ended the town of Abingdon." To have bought a country gazette under those circumstances would have meant certain failure. The Bassos then retreated to a small cottage in the mountains outside Asheville, North Carolina, where Ham gave himself to writing as a last resort, even though publication of his books was being delayed. He also earned $35 a month by tutoring, while his young wife worked in the summertime as counsellor in a girls' camp.

In one of his letters he inquired about my own situation. I replied that I was now working as "two men" for fear that we might lose possession of our home. The Depression was a challenge to us, but also a sore trial. Basso wrote: "I should say you stand up extremely well," and urged that I continue to send him my "documents of hope and good cheer."

§   §   §

One morning in December 1931 Erskine Caldwell dropped in at *The New Republic* to ask for some writing assignment at their low space rates. He had already published several youthful books. He told Malcolm Cowley and me that he had hitchhiked from Maine, where he lived, to New York, with the idea of obtaining a small advance from his publisher on his next book.

Caldwell was a tall, red-headed young man of athletic frame and laconic speech—in contrast to his prose, which was fluent enough. Though born in a small village of Georgia he was not a typical Southerner, his father having been a traveling Methodist minister from the North. The young Caldwell had evidently liked to run away from home to wander about the country alone, riding the rails, and sometimes earning his way by anything from cotton picking to semi-professional football. Recently he had been somewhat immobilized, as he had a wife and three young children in Maine.

Of his present straits he talked in the most offhand manner. With a shy grin he admitted that he had reached New York the evening before with only ten cents in his pocket. There had been a heavy snowfall that night and he appeared with only a thin rain-coat—or perhaps without any overcoat at all. I asked him where he had spent the night. He explained that as he knew no one in New York he had walked about a long time and finally entered a luxurious apartment hotel on lower Fifth Avenue, where with the permission of a liveried doorman he had curled up in an easy chair in the lobby. Thus he had passed the stormy night in most comfortable style.

Malcolm Cowley had had the kindly thought of setting up what he called the Indigent Book Reviewers' Fund at *The New Republic* out of a little surplus cash realized from the sales of books received for review but not given any notice. When hungry writers applied to him for more reviewing assignments than he had to give he would hand them, instead, a few dollars from his small relief fund. Thus with Caldwell, whom we also invited to join us for a square lunch.

I had been reading him with no little enjoyment. His sketches of brutish Southern hillbillies and their women, and of Negroes, were done with broad comic strokes and a kind of sportive brutality. Recently he had published in *The New Masses* a short story called "Kneel to the Rising Sun," an account of a lynching-bee in Georgia that was all economy and power and ended on a note of fantastic horror—Caldwell's version of "proletarian literature." That his was a fresh and authentic talent was also evident in *Tobacco Road,* issued by Scribner's early in 1932. This genre novel of the Deep South, oddly enough, was at first read with appreciation only by a select literary audience. When one first came upon Caldwell's primitive folk they were decidedly entertaining in their grotesque way; their behavior had the fantasy of the unexpected. Sexual license can be pleasing when it is comic or poetic, so long as it is not solemnly done. As a consequence, a few months after I met him in 1932, I included a critical appreciation of Erskine Caldwell in an essay on "The Young American Novelists" published in *The Virginia Quarterly*. In it I ranked him with a group of talented young

authors such as Katherine Anne Porter, Kay Boyle, Robert Cantwell, and the then little read William Faulkner.

Caldwell told me that *Tobacco Road* sold only fifteen hundred
copies and had not been reprinted. Was it possible that even
licentious novels did not sell in these hard days? I promised Caldwell that I would speak to Alfred Harcourt, to whom he had
submitted his new manuscript.

When I saw Harcourt a few days later I warmly recommended
Caldwell's work and mentioned his urgent need of a small advance
of $100 against the newly completed novel, *God's Little Acre*.
Though he had a temporary option on this book Harcourt told me
flatly that he had decided to reject it, adding in the rasping tone he
sometimes assumed: "Well, I can't support all the young writers in
Greenwich Village."

"Not Greenwich Village—he comes from Georgia and now lives
in Maine," I put in.

"It doesn't matter, new novelists aren't selling nowadays."

Alfred Harcourt was generally a man of shrewd judgment, but
just then he was determinedly trimming sail. Unfortunately for
Harcourt, Brace, when Caldwell's *God's Little Acre* was finally
issued by Scribner's in 1933 it became a *succès de scandale* and
drew attention to *Tobacco Road*, which also became a best-seller,
particularly after it was adapted as a play and presented by many
road companies all around the country during the thirties. Caldwell's clownish hillbillies became a national legend in that decade
and may have shamed our government into doing something for
the tenant farmers. Their author, having become enriched, took to
writing according to the same successful formula in later years;
cheap editions of his novels sold in the millions, but their quality
was much diluted.

§ § §

The budding writers now leaving school or college and setting off
from all parts of the country for the great literary center of New
York arrived just in time to encounter the Depression era at its
worst. As literary editor of *The New Republic* Malcolm Cowley
was in a strategic position to make a collection of these young

talents, who applied to him for writing assignments. I remember John Cheever as a small, fair-haired youth of seventeen who had run away from his prep school in New England and written for *The New Republic* with astonishing maturity and power an autobiographical sketch of that experience. James T. Farrell was also on the scene, having come from Chicago via Paris. Nathanael West, returning to the States after an apprentice year or two in Paris, was in New York working as a room clerk in a half-empty hotel. Leane Zugsmith, with her oval face and great brown eyes, arrived around that time from Atlantic City, New Jersey, to make her career in the republic of letters. Several of these were to be my good friends through the thirties and afterward.

One of the most attractive of these new men was Robert Cantwell, who looked scarcely old enough to vote. A native of the State of Washington who had come to New York via New Orleans, Cantwell was small, thin, and blond, and possessed of a quick intelligence and uncommon facility of expression. His first novel, *Laugh and Lie Down*, published in New York by John Farrar in 1931, had had few readers but received high praise for its style and for its picture of West Coast youth at the end of the twenties. Like his hero, Cantwell was able to attend college for only a short time; then, to help his family, he went to work in a veneer factory and was employed there for four years. At twenty-three he was already married to a girl from Louisiana—who herself looked like a child but was expecting a baby—and he was deep in a second novel fittingly entitled *The Land of Plenty*.

For young men like Caldwell youth ended early when the Depression era began and care weighed upon their narrow shoulders. At least those of us who were ten years older, born around the turn of the century, had known the stability of an America still given to nineteenth-century ways before World War I; we had managed to complete our schooling and college training without much trouble and even enjoyed some foreign travel at a period when nobody worried much about money or finding jobs, even if, as for Scott Fitzgerald, it was at first only an advertising agency job. But the typical young writers who began their careers during the slump, such as Erskine Caldwell, Bob Cantwell, Jimmie Farrell, and Kenneth Patchen, had only a limited formal education; they lived in constant insecurity, took odd jobs at filling stations or as waiters or clerks, and had to educate themselves or try to write in hours after work. These children of the Depression were in most cases sons of the middle class who were *déclassés*, but Cantwell was of working-class origin with Western radicals of the I.W.W. in his family background.

Bob Cantwell had winning ways and we all were eager to help him. Malcolm Cowley aided him with book review assignments; I found similar work for him through the literary editors of two New York newspapers, so that at least he and his family had $12 a week to eat with, as he wrote me. But he lived in daily dread of the gas man's visit, when light and heat might be cut off from his small Greenwich Village flat. New York for him was vibrant with all sorts of earthquake tremors. He observed with passionate interest the growing tumult of the unemployed marchers led by the communists. One day he wrote me of his fear that the very newspapers he wrote for, the *Post* and the *World-Telegram*, might soon cease publication.

We had talked of finding the Cantwells a small cottage in the country near my house, where they could live with almost no rent to pay. But Cantwell decided that he would rather not leave the city. New York, with its open air meetings, was going to be a wonderfully hectic place during the coming winter, he surmised, and if he were in the country he would be "in an awful stew worrying about what was happening—like being out of sight of some enormous fire and wondering if your house is burning with the rest." Almost without exception these young writers who had come of age in the thirties were waiting impatiently for the Revolution to arrive! On one occasion Bob Cantwell reported the great city as showing a calm, a quietude that seemed to him sinister: "Today the town looks the way you imagine it should during a great depression; no smoke from the chimneys, no elevated trains, no cars or trucks, only a few children playing in perfect safety in the middle of the streets."

Another friend told me later that in Pittsburgh, where in years of normal business you could never see the sun in the daytime nor distinguish clearly the streetlamps overhead at night because of the dense fog of soot from the steel mills, people walked up to the hills to look out at the river valley below in the summer of 1932 under such a blue sky and brilliant sunlight as they did not remember seeing there in all their lives.

II.

American writers had formerly thought little about "affairs of state"; now, in 1932, when we thought of them it was in the prevailing mood of indignation. The nation seemed only half alive—how long could things go on in this way?

Was it principally our economic circumstances that whipped us to anger, I asked myself afterward. Certainly the feeling of insecurity lay always in back of our minds. Yet most of us had jobs or work to do, and even those who were in much worse state, such as Cantwell and Caldwell, managed at least to eat. But we were suffering the shock of complete loss of faith in our social system; all our sentiments based on more or less conscious acceptance of the American and democratic way of life—adding up to an ideological superstructure of sorts—were outraged. Émile Zola, at the period of the Dreyfus Case in France, had spoken of "living in a state of indignation"; although the fate of the Jewish officer Dreyfus did not affect him materially, Zola had felt himself overcome with anger every morning when he read his newspaper. We too in the early thirties lived in a state of sustained indignation.

It was as if arrears of social consciousness had accumulated in us, because for a long period we had acted in the belief that artists could ignore the condition of society. Now we asked ourselves continually: What is to be done? How can we be useful in these times?

In July 1932 I wrote down some phrases that afterward seemed to me overwrought yet reflected well the temper of that season: "I believe the chapter of democracy is ended. This crisis, this depression has assumed a massive and implacable character that demands tactics very different from those of the reformers. My anger, my disgust leads me to the side of the extremists, the activists. . . ."

Some of the young writers spoke of the crisis of conscience they underwent in terms of a religious experience. It was in such a state of exaltation that Sidney Hook summoned us to join those who were willing to change the world, "those who are prepared to struggle for their ideals even unto death, those who pit their intelligence and strength against remediable evils, who scorn the Philistine worldliness which will risk nothing of its fleshpots, as well as the religious otherworldliness which foresakes the most precious of human virtues—intelligence and courage."

Similarly Granville Hicks wrote at about the same period of the inspiration that had come to him from contemplating the example of John Reed, the American journalist who had witnessed the October 1917 Revolution in Russia and wholeheartedly committed himself to it in his book *Ten Days that Shook the World.* The intellectuals of today could serve the good cause in some measure by their talents for writing, music, and painting, but there was another way too: "They must also be prepared to undertake whatever assignments are given them . . . for the revolutionary cause. Reed threw himself into that cause and in it found his greatest fulfillment and the fruition of his talents."

In the past literary genius had enlisted in ever renewed struggles against man's intolerance and injustice to man: there had been Milton and Locke in the seventeenth century, and in the next Voltaire, Rousseau, and the Encyclopedists with their great pamphlets against the infamy of crown and church. After them Tom Paine, Byron, and Shelley. And in America, as Newton Arvin now reminded us, Emerson and Thoreau had served as agitators in the struggle of the Abolitionists against slavery. We too must be "good agitators" in Emerson's sense of the term. It was surely a time for polemicists and pamphleteers, I often reflected.

When it came to the matter of taking action in favor of sweeping social change we naturally turned to the people on the left as possible allies. In the United States, to be sure, neither the socialists nor communists had any real mass organizations such as they had in Europe. I myself had written in 1931 that the Communist Party here was but a feeble instrument. And yet there seemed no other recourse but to build up pressure from the left by giving them our help.

It was not without some hesitation and doubt that I approached cooperation with them. I remember Professor Wolman saying to me with vehemence: "The communists will get nowhere in this country. There will be no Revolution as in Russia. Go ahead and try the communists if you like; I'm sure it will lead only to disappointment."

It must be remembered that persons classed as literary men, and even worse as intellectuals, had virtually no contact with the rich who supported the two major political parties, or the politicians who directed those parties. One might say that the professionals of politics ostracized us. Governor Roosevelt had lately engaged two or three Columbia University professors to help write his campaign speeches, but at first very little was said about them and for a while Roosevelt kept them fairly well hidden.

There was only one of my literary acquaintances of that time who had any connection with the moneymen and the politicians: he was the poet Archibald MacLeish, who had originally prepared himself at Yale and Harvard Law School for the bar. After several years of law practice in Boston however he had decided (on the strength of an inheritance) to give up that career and had gone to live in a small chateau in France where he devoted himself wholly to writing poetry. He first published some poetry that was conventional in style and after that poems in the manner of the avant-garde that appeared in the little review *transition*. But after the Crash of 1929 he had come home and gone to work in New York as an editor of Henry Luce's new publication *Fortune*, the magazine that was supposed to glorify big business in America.

MacLeish at any rate was one writer who was not going left but into the center of things. In January 1932 his "Open Letter to the Young Men of Wall Street," a leading article in *The Saturday Review of Literature*, had created a brief stir. On the one hand, he accused our "gross and materialistic" financiers of having "abdicated" their right to leadership and lost the respect of forward-looking Americans; on the other hand, he found nothing wrong with the economy itself, but called on the old capitalists to make way for young and enlightened men who would deal fairly with the problem of poverty in the U.S.A. Otherwise, he warned, we faced the unpleasant prospect of a coercive state, either fascist or communist. At the same time MacLeish vigorously slated those writers who planned to devote their attention to radical propaganda or to questions of economics, instead of continuing to pursue their "pure" art with minds detached from all mundane things. This Open Letter, a most curious performance that elicited no response from the young or old men of Wall Street, constituted MacLeish's effort to deal in his own middle way with the issues of our time.

In the spring of that year we had lunch together and MacLeish, a keen-looking man, proved to be a fine talker given to sallies of wit and also puns. He was in good humor because his *Conquistador,* the narrative poem of Cortez, had just won the Pulitzer Prize. Our talk ranged over poetry, high finance, and high politics. I remarked that there was the probability that Congress would soon enact sweeping reform legislation and that in times of crisis such measures were usually supported by both major parties, as there was really no difference between them. MacLeish then went on to say that he had recently been invited by a Republican Party bigwig to work at publicity and campaign literature for the Young Republicans; and he asked me what I thought of the idea. I remarked: "Why don't you go for it? Politics is going to be very important in the years ahead, and you might learn a few things." MacLeish agreed that he ought to consider the Young Republicans seriously. The prospects for their Party however soon became quite dim, and MacLeish turned into a Roosevelt Democrat.

Although he held that political questions were not properly the subjects for writers and poets, MacLeish wrote political poems himself, in satirical vein, in which he girded at those who had taken their stand with the Marxists. In "Invitation to the Social Muse" he defined poets as being essentially

> ... Whores ... persons of
> Known vocation, following troops; they must sleep with
> Stragglers from either prince. ...
> They must avoid raising flags.

Besides, Tovarisch, how to embrace an army?
How take to one's chamber a million souls?
How to conceive in the name of a column of marchers?
The poet must go on alone, create alone.
Is it just to demand of us also to bear arms?

In the series of poems entitled "Frescoes for Rockefeller City" MacLeish continued to make sport of the friends of the unemployed in lines that sometimes echoed the anti-Semitic tone of Ezra Pound:

Len! Millennium! Lennium!
Also Comrade Levine who writes of America . . .
Aint you read in d'books you are brudders?
D'glassic historical objective broves you are brudders.
You and d'Wops and d'Chinks you are brudders
Haind't you got it d'same ideology?

MacLeish received many a verbal thrashing in letters to *The New Republic*, which had published his "Invitation to the Social Muse" in 1932; *The New Masses* of course denounced him as "an incipient fascist." In reprinting "Frescoes for Rockefeller City" in book form in 1933 the poet found it expedient to change the name of Comrade Levine to Devine. Several years afterward, in 1935, MacLeish in another about-face (which will be described later) was to make his *amende honorable* to the left.

§   §   §

During the summer of 1932 I heard through some of my friends of a proposal to form an ad hoc committee of independent writers and intellectuals in support of the Communist Party candidates during the current election campaign. Edmund Wilson's several manifestoes in *The New Republic* had pointed to such an action, which was then of course entirely lawful. The plan was discussed at a dinner gathering of about a dozen writers in New York. Malcolm Cowley was among those present; Louis Adamic, the celebrated immigrant from Yugoslavia who wrote so well in English, was one of us; also present were Sidney Hook, Elliott Cohen (later the editor of *Commentary*), Newton Arvin, Meyer

Schapiro, then a Columbia instructor in art history, and James Rorty, a free-lance writer.

The voice of the Communist Party on that occasion was Joseph Freeman, a genial, highly articulate man who had been an active left-wing journalist for many years and also wrote poetry. I had known Freeman a little at Columbia College but had lost track of him. A socialist in his teens, he had joined the communists in the twenties and was a founder and editor of *The New Masses*. He appeared even then as a man of moderate views and, acting as the Party's "cultural front," maintained friendly contacts with many liberals. In behalf of the Communist Party Freeman offered us a vehicle, even a press through which we could ventilate our discontents. There was talk of printing millions of copies of a manifesto or pamphlet in which we would attack the old regime and come out for economic planning and socialism. This would create surprise and shock and, we hoped, might do some good. Certainly some of us then enjoyed very much the idea of "stunning the bourgeois."

James Rorty became the secretary pro tem of our Independent Committee. As he lived only a half hour's drive from my place in Connecticut we met several times at his or my home and worked together on a pamphlet in favor of Foster and Ford. Indeed most of the writing of the pamphlet devolved upon Rorty and me.

A thin, curly-haired, peppery man of thirty-five, James Rorty was a refugee from Madison Avenue's advertising agencies. One day he had walked out or got himself fired and thereafter, having quit the "rat race," lived as a free soul on his few poor acres in the country. After having spent years glorifying the products of American industry, he now wrote articles criticizing those goods from the consumers' point of view. But since these writings earned him little or nothing, Rorty and his wife and baby barely survived. He used to declare that only through returning to the land and living on "iron rations" could American writers function again as free men. In short Jim Rorty was a disciple of Thoreau; in my opinion he had not a Marxist hair in his head. Such, in most cases, were the other members of the group that then brought support to the Communist Party's national ticket for 1932.

In the light of later recantations and "revelations" by some of the persons involved in the left-wing activities here described, and their later claims that it was part of a vast underground "conspiracy" to use writers and scholars as "dupes" who would deliver the people into the hands of the Bolshevists, I should like to deny all such allegations with all my heart. I cannot for the life of me recall anything partaking of the nature of a conspiracy.

A national election contest was under way; a perfectly lawful party (registered in many states) that espoused a militant form of socialism was attempting to bring about change by peaceful electioneering. In effect a group of independent writers had resolved that they were fed up with the Tweedledums and Tweedledees of politics and would, in protest, make a public demonstration in favor of the communists' slate—in full knowledge that that party had not a chance in a million of being elected to office. In undertaking such action these writers hoped to call attention to the severity of the crisis.

"For many of those writers, who were by temperament highly egotistical, it was practically the first time they ever thought about anyone but themselves," was a trenchant comment made afterward by my friend Slater Brown.

In those days, many years before it became unlawful to teach or advocate anything later than Adam Smith's or John Adams's ideas of political economy, people volunteered their services or lent their names freely to such action as we undertook. Dreiser, Steffens, and Anderson were men of some age and experience; I saw no evidence that they or the younger men were deceived, driven, or duped into taking the stand they did in September 1932.

As for the two or three representatives of the Communist Party who were in contact with our Independent Committee, they were so artless as to entrust the writing of an important campaign pamphlet mainly to Jim Rorty and myself, for the reason that there seemed to be no one else who would get it done. Our brochure was to be entitled "Culture and the Crisis," and it would argue for the long-run interest of artists and professional workers in joining the movement of the working class toward socialism. To be sure the pamphlet was to be supervised, in effect censored by the Com-

munist Party's experts in ideology, as we were plainly given to
understand. But the Republicans and Democrats imposed similar
restrictions, I found, upon writers of their own campaign literature.
Our ad hoc committee was named by agreement the League of
Professional Groups for Foster and Ford, and it was always a quite
loosely knit affair.

I remember attending two or three meetings at someone's
apartment in downtown Manhattan at which a dozen to fifteen
persons were present, most of them impecunious young writers or
college teachers, like Sidney Hook or Newton Arvin, and only two
or three of them sounding like pious members of the John Reed
Club, affiliated with the communists. Often Sidney Hook held the
floor; he was most tenacious in argument, and it was not easy to
get a word in. Sometimes our meeting would become a talkfest and
the Party-line fellows would cut in, calling us to get on with the
business in hand.

Certain communists were mistrustful of their new intellectual
allies, as in the case of Mike Gold, the embattled columnist of *The
Daily Worker* who held that only about 10 per cent of the literary
critics, teachers, or ballet masters—who had formerly held a "favored servant status" under capitalism—could be relied upon once
the crisis was over. Gold used to play the Party bulldog, scowling
and growling at those who were only parlor pinks—but then his
gold-toothed smile would come out and we would laugh at him.
The Party's secretary Earl Browder, however, expressed himself as
highly pleased because "the cream of the intellectual life of this
country" had come to the aid of the workers' movement. Their
action was significant he said, not only because of the prominent
names involved, but also because it indicated a real change of heart
going on among many thinking Americans.

§   §   §

Jim Rorty and I sat down in my barn in the country one Sunday,
worked up a draft of our pamphlet of about thirty pages, and sent
it on to the higher authorities in New York. It came back the next
week with a preamble written in heavy Marxist jargon, replete with

all the old canting phrases about the "struggling masses" and the "class-conscious, revolutionary proletarians." This preamble, we were told, must be incorporated into our text at all cost; we were also expected to remind our readers that the Soviet Union alone was carrying out a socialist program. The main sections of the pamphlet, which we had written, were in tolerably clear English and intended to interest literary and professional people.

Both of us suffered a certain mental distress in completing this assignment. I felt that no one would be able to get through the preamble the Party pedants had supplied, and urged that we make a strong complaint to the ideological authorities, whoever they were. Rorty fully agreed with my view, but he pointed out that we were late for the printer and surmised that our objections very likely would go unheeded. In the end Malcolm Cowley undertook to rewrite the preamble and managed very well.

The main section of our pamphlet sounded as if it were conceived under the inspiration of Veblen rather than Marx or Lenin. We argued that the house of capitalism was falling apart; the same people who had so grossly mismanaged affairs were still in command and no one thought of introducing anything but minor repairs. Meanwhile the disinterested counsels of men of learning and technical knowledge were ignored. Not only were the nation's manpower and machinery being wasted but its brains and talent as well. Therefore writers, artists, and technical people were urged to make common cause with the leaders of the working class who hoped some day to establish a new society based on economic democracy, public ownership of national resources, and on human values instead of private profit seeking. The pamphlet wound up: "We claim the right to live and function. It is our business to think and we shall not permit irresponsible business men to teach us our business. We have aligned ourselves with the Party of the workers. . . . We believe the only way to protest against the chaos, the appalling wastefulness and the misery inherent in the present economic system is to vote for the Communist Party candidates."

The Communist Party platform for 1932, it should be noted, was a moderate welfare state program calling for relief of the

unemployed workers and farmers, social security, and nationaliza-
tion of banks. These measures, except for the takeover of banks,
were all passed by Congress within the five years following 1933.

The signers of the pamphlet, entitled "An Open Letter to
Writers, Artists, Teachers, Engineers, Scientists, and other Professional Workers," stated moreover that they had given their endorse-
ment of the communist candidates as an act of protest. I pointed
this out in an interview with the metropolitan newspapers at the
time, adding that nearly all of us were noncommunists.[1]

Our manifesto, surely one of the more estimable pieces of campaign literature that season, was reported only in brief stories in
the back pages of the newspapers, some of which like *Time* dismissed the "Intellectuals' Left Turn" as only a passing fashion. In
liberal circles however the affair was seriously discussed, and many
expressions of approval reached us. But there was no hysteria or
terror for the public safety such as was felt over political nonconformity later, in the years of the Cold War from 1947 to 1960.
The climate of opinion in the United States of those days was far
more favorable to freedom of thought than it is nowadays. I continued to meet with friends who held conservative opinions and
we aired our differences like men of reason.

Our group of fellow travelers were in the highest spirits as they
sallied out together to attend several election rallies that autumn.
The communists among us, though having few real victories to
rejoice over, were as jubilant as a lodge of Elks as they boasted of
their hazardous missionary work among farm strikers or Unemployed Councils. Certain of the young writers who had "joined
for the duration," some of them sons of the middle class or even,
like the writer John Hermann, of well-to-do capitalists, found new
adventure in manning picket lines, directing hunger marches, or
organizing the tenant farmers of the South. In a sense it could be
said they found escape from the miseries of our disintegrating
society. In October 1932 a very successful meeting was held under
the auspices of the writers' group at Cooper Union Hall in New
York; more than two thousand were in attendance and many more
stood in the street outside. I remember thinking to myself that in

[1] *The New York Times* (September 14, 1932).

1864 Lincoln had spoken in the same beautiful old auditorium where now a group of writers held the platform in a new crusade.

As we left the hall warmed by our strong words, our generous emotions, and the cheering crowd, I went off with Jim Rorty, who had been in charge of the box office, and we walked along Third Avenue, New York's Skid Row. A bum reeled against Rorty, who was carrying a brown paper bag. Rorty gripped that bag tightly, muttering that he was worried about spending the night in the cheap furnished room he had engaged. "There's nine hundred dollars in this bag; somebody might murder me for it," he remarked. I accompanied him to his door and said as I left: "Make as if you are just carrying some old clothes in it. Take the money to bed with you, sleep on it, and you'll be all right."

III.

Thus the abysmal year 1932 became for many of us a time of hope. Was it only utopian hope? Virtually all the social inventions that had come into use in other societies in the name of human welfare or progress had been denounced in former times because they were based on intelligent calculations of the probable or the possible. Many people were now aware of the inherent contradictions within the society that were pressing with intolerable force against the bonds of the old order; that in these days the busy workers of our cities were being turned into idle and hungry louts while our once patriotic farmers became increasingly rebels and lawbreakers; and now they were confident that our people would soon say as with one voice that they could no longer live in a world where such things can be.

Here I would like to cross my heart and deny that the mood of the intelligentsia of the 1930's was in any way as melancholy or grim as later revisionists of our literary history, such as Alfred Kazin and others have represented it. (In his most recent reminiscences, Mr. Kazin has described his experiences as an unemployed literary critic, attached to the WPA Writers' Project, under the heading: "The Grim Thirties.")

Edmund Wilson has repeatedly attested that the 1930's formed
the most stimulating period he had known up to then. American
intellectuals were never busier or happier. In this country they had
always suffered from their detachment, one might say their alienation from the life of ordinary people, from the hewers of wood and
drawers of water, as from the world's makers and shakers. Now the
formerly self-centered bookworms or blue stockings left their little
studies and came out into the world; newly converted radicals or
insurgents, they deeply enjoyed their crusading. Those who engaged
themselves in some common action that they hoped would contribute in the long run to setting the world aright were far more
cheerful than if they had merely sat and waited until their last
dollars were gone. I remember one of my friends, a man of decidedly bookish habits who for a while under orders of the communists regularly rose at dawn and went off to distribute leaflets
before the gates of factories in the city's industrial suburbs. It was a
dreary, fatiguing routine, yet one that he mentioned with a smile
radiant as if he were an Early Christian. Others welcomed assignments of a more adventurous sort: picketing with the unemployed
and enduring sometimes beatings and arrest by police. Then in the
evenings they would sometimes go off together to sing and make
merry among the jazz-intoxicated crowds of Harlem's taxi dance
halls, whose denizens regarded the white-skinned radicals as their
true friends.

In notes of a journal I kept under the heading "Valley of
Depression," I wrote in the autumn of 1932:

Americans much more democratic nowadays—very humane and
hospitable. People kinder to each other. . . .

The depression more real than prosperity; the true norm is
wretchedness and endurance. . . . The evils of our system stare at us.
The social question dominates us again.

How the great are brought low; the cowardly flee (Sam Insull);
the rich made somewhat poorer. In such terms Ralph Waldo Emerson also rejoiced at the panic of 1837, as his journal of a century ago
shows.

Men are made to think; brazenness, complacency is routed; inflated minds punctured. Intelligence, true science appears again more potent.

Some twenty years later, when a McCarthovingian darkness reigned over our public life, the "New Conservatives" and the repentant or disillusioned radicals combined to rewrite the history of the 1930's. In their reinterpretations of that era younger men writing from the perspective of the fifties—Daniel Bell, author of *The End of Ideology*, Leslie Fiedler, who wrote *The End of Innocence*, and Peter Viereck in *The Shame and Glory of the Intellectuals*—have managed to represent the nonconformists of 1932 as innocents and dupes who allowed themselves to be manipulated by a few red Machiavellis. Thus they were men who "desired good but also did much evil," as Mr. Viereck charges. Indeed Fielder and Viereck go so far as to accuse the radicals of the thirties of betraying their liberal American heritage. A complicating element in our history (which I shall take up later) also developed from the fact that some of the leading figures among the intelligentsia of the left later became entirely disillusioned with their former action and joined with the New Conservatives in denouncing themselves!

How in the world could we have been both "innocent" and "traitorous" at the same time? If what is meant is that the fellow travelers were so politically naive as to count upon the early arrival of a utopian society in America, then such allegations are very wide of the mark. There were persons of all sorts among us, including some exalted evangelists. But John Dos Passos was not really as innocent as he has pretended in afterthought. Malcolm Cowley wrote realistically of the intellectuals' left turn in 1932 that while it was a momentous affair, it was not "the express train of the revolution" they had boarded, but only a "left bound local." Malcolm used to say at the time that we had no big left movement as did France and England, that the Communist Party here was small but looked as if it might grow. I believed that by making common cause with the communists, American intellectuals might develop a sort of ginger group on the left that could, in years to come, make its weight felt in our politics. Even Dos Passos, who was then angrier, being more emotive, than Cowley or I, wrote in 1932 that

(157)

capitalism looked as if it might survive for a good many years but that "if enough people shake the tree the plums may fall." We wanted to help the people shake the tree.

As a fellow traveler in that period I was by temperament relatively detached, and I have tended to justify the spirit of detachment that was embodied in men of much greater vision than mine, such as Jefferson and the poet Shelley living through the crisis years and the aftermath of the French Revolution. While men like Wordsworth and Coleridge recoiled from their own radical past and turned to support the great reaction in England against revolutionary France, Shelley held to his belief in the good works wrought by the Revolution, despite its excesses. Our American *philosophe* Jefferson, in his own way, also retained his long view and bothered little about repenting.

For my part, while busy exerting my small pressures to the left I was very much aware of the staunchly capitalist spirit that still possessed the great middle class in America. I could see a million worthy storekeepers at the crossroads competing desperately with the low-price supermarkets in their sections by the methods of the astute tradesman. They were caught in the millrace and I felt for them. Capitalism appeared thoroughly "sick," I wrote in 1932, but

> Americans have been sold on the most attractive and profitable form of capitalism in all the world; they still have hope for it. When will that hope be destroyed?
>
> Power in the U.S. lies with several large banking and industrial corporations and . . . the political machines they control—though some pieces are breaking away. Against those entrenched interests the power of progressives, socialists, and communists is nearly zero.

We "sympathizers" were nevertheless much irritated by the dogmatic and intolerant manners of some of the communists around us—mere epigoni, imitators of the Russian Marxists, whose ready-made notions of how to address the working class in America and how to build up the left movement here often struck me as inept. In old letters of the early thirties written to my friend Kenneth Burke I find a good many caustic references to the

"Marxian simpletons" we roundly condemned. One of the most authoritarian of the literary communists was the recent convert Granville Hicks, who while improvising a manual for the "Marxian method of criticism" drew up a sort of *index expurgatorius* of "antisocial authors" ranging from Henry James to William Faulkner and Ernest Hemingway. I continued to read and recommend the authors I liked and paid no attention to the so-called "literary commissar of *The New Masses*."

§ § §

All that year we were hagridden with fear for the fate of Germany, still a republic in form but under pressure of the Nazis and the Nationalists drifting steadily toward authoritarian rule. The first trickle of refugees, Aryan as well as Jewish, began to arrive here in the year before Hitler seized power. Among them was the great German artist George Grosz, whom I had last seen at the Romanisches Café in Berlin ten years earlier. I listened eagerly to Grosz's account of the mounting turbulence in his country, for I remembered him as a man of acute mind.

In earlier years he had been both a Dadaist and a communist; his powerful caricatures with their steel-like drawing, which were widely reproduced, made him for years the battering ram of the left press. His anger derived from his wartime experience, during which he nearly became deranged, and was reflected in his celebrated drawings of the "Face of the Ruling Class" with its army officers, capitalists, and prostitutes. For our age this graphic artist was Goya and Daumier in one.

Grosz, a handsome, solidly built Prussian, had much charm of address; his personal amiability contrasted with the brutal force of such pictures as his Christ in gas mask and Wellington boots entangled in barbed wire. He explained: "I only wanted to show that Christ would have been tortured again by the Christians of today."

When I pressed him on the subject of Germany he could speak only of the boundless relief he felt at having arrived at last, with his family, in the safe refuge of this country. He had been an aficionado of things American years ago; in Berlin he used to dress in cowboy costume and a sombrero and read our newspaper comic strips with delight. As for Germany, he said he for his part was sick of both the Nazis and the communists, who were fighting in the streets every day. The Nazis had repeatedly promised that on taking power one of the first men they would torture and kill would be "the corrupter of German youth," George Grosz.

"Now I am also against scientific communism," he asserted. "I have seen the 'new order of things' in Soviet Russia; I understand it with my reason, but not with my feelings. As an artist I need room to turn around; I need my 'petty bourgeois' liberties, even if I must laugh at myself for it."

In America he meant to enjoy life, to give up his brutal style of satire and paint henceforth lyrical pictures of nudes and landscapes. The revolutionary period was over for him. "On the whole I am pessimistic about our modern civilization, though not about enjoying what is left of life at thirty-eight. There is a glass on the table. I am going to drink it up and nothing anyone says can stop me from drinking it."

For Germany, he said, the prospect was utterly black. The Nazis would take over in six months, he predicted, and they would make life miserable not only for those formerly associated with the left, but also for the Jews.

I appreciated what George Grosz had to tell us about the inconveniences one might suffer under both fascist and communist "coordinators"; but at the same time I felt sadly disappointed in him. He was a good soldier suffering from battle fatigue, now going to the rear.

As for myself I was certainly not going to forget about the Nazis. Like Italy's fascists they were often described by political theorists of the left as constituting "the last desperate resort of capitalism." This no longer appeals to us as an adequate definition of fascism, but inasmuch as their movement called for rearmament and war it had a partial truth. The Weimar Republic, with its six millions on the dole, appeared to be in a state of collapse; the Nazis were crying for *Lebensraum* and a war of revenge.

At the beginning of 1933, after Hitler took power, the American

Committee against Fascist Oppression in Germany was formed as an ad hoc committee to disseminate literature and gather relief funds for political refugees. Its sponsors were liberals such as Jane Addams, John Dewey, Senator Burton K. Wheeler, William Allen White, Oswald G. Villard, and the Reverend John Haynes Holmes. The acting treasurer, however, turned out to be Kyle Crichton, a big hulking young fellow, very good-humored too, who was an editor of *Collier's Weekly* but also wrote satirical pieces for *The New Masses* under the pseudonym of "Robert Forsythe." Crichton, the college-educated son of a Pennsylvania coal miner, was quite openly a fellow traveler; this apparently gave no concern to the distinguished sponsors of his committee, which may well have been one of the transient fronts devised by the communists but supported by liberals.

I had already contemplated writing on the Brown Shirts and the terror they had introduced in Germany when Crichton and Joe Freeman came to me with the proposal that I do a pamphlet on the subject as quickly as possible for the Committee against Fascist Oppression. Freeman also promised that the Communist Party would see to it that hundreds of thousands of copies were printed and distributed in this country. I agreed, obtained a copy of Hitler's *Mein Kampf* (which was not yet available in English), together with some recent literature on political developments in Germany, and set to work in great haste. In a week or ten days I had written a six-thousand-word article titled "Nazi Culture; or the Brown Darkness over Germany" and rushed it to Freeman.

Weeks went by and nothing happened. Since they had told me that I must make all possible haste, I had given my nights as well as days to this unpaid labor at a time when I needed money. Now, though I pursued them by telephone, I could reach neither Freeman nor Crichton. At last Crichton came to the surface and reported that he had managed to wrest my manuscript away from our difficult communist friends, who had finally decided not to help us. They had lost us six weeks' time; but the John Day Company, a "bourgeois" publisher, undertook to issue the piece quickly in their series of twenty-five-cent pamphlets. Crichton wrote me a letter apologizing for the delay.

July 19, 1933

. . . I understand you are angry at me too. . . .

There are many things not right in the radical movement and I think fellows such as us will have to be patient with them. I mean there is inefficiency and often irresponsibility, but that is to be expected. Everybody works under pressure, and with little or no compensation, and the wonder is that anything ever gets done. . . . I'm a communist sympathizer because I believe in it and I'm not going to be put off just because individuals or policies—I mean minor policies, such as we may have in this German committee—don't please me.

I was curious, however, and persisted in my efforts to learn why the Communist Party had decided to avoid sponsoring my pamphlet. Finally I was able to corner the amiable Joe Freeman, and I learned that the Party's ideological experts found what I had written not in accord with their directives. I had neither stressed the immense efforts made by the "heroic workers" of Germany to win their fight nor made it plain that their ultimate triumph was *foreordained*.[2] Freeman went on to say that he personally regretted the decision of his superiors because he thought so highly of the pamphlet himself. His differences with his superiors later led to his resignation from the Party in 1939.

This episode marked the end of my brief efforts at direct collaboration with the communists. I had learned the lesson that if I undertook any polemical writing I could do so only in accordance with my own beliefs. The Communist Party leaders in America might not know from one season to another what their direction would be next; obviously they received their inspiration from the

[2] Far from showing themselves heroic in the crisis of January 1933, the German communists had gone underground, at orders from above, without striking a blow in self-defense. Later charges were made by ex-communists like Arthur Koestler that the German workers were betrayed by their communist leaders or by Stalin. This view seems to me *simpliste*. Moreover the socialists also abjectly surrendered the largest labor organization in Europe. Kurt Meinecke, the old dean of German historians, related in one of his last writings, *Die Deutsche Katastrophe* (1946), that the Reichswehr chief of staff and the Berlin chief of police during the crisis days of 1932–3 assured him that the communists had no real power to stage an insurrection in the face of the Army and the Brown Shirt hordes. Though they had many unemployed followers, their "threat" was illusory but much exploited for propaganda purposes by the nationalists.

Comintern, which meant waiting upon the deliberations of a far-off
bureaucratic group.

§ § §

Though we might differ in opinions, and some of us were aware
of the inconveniences of working with the American Communist
Party, our group of fellow travelers turned up on October 13, 1932,
at two campaign meetings held simultaneously at different halls in
downtown Manhattan. Sidney Hook presided at one of the meetings, opened it with a spirited address, then called on me as the first
speaker.

Our meeting place was a dreary hall used for neighborhood
dances and union meetings; the audience of about eight hundred
consisted of members of several Red trade unions with a sprinkling
of teachers and intellectuals. I had given no thought to how one
should speak to such a mixed group.

My main theme was still the crisis in our cultural activities.
The workers in the arts and the sciences, I argued, were coming to
a dead end under the old regime. Their hope resided now in joining
the progressive element of the working class in the fight to build a
new society controlled not by mercenary but by human values and
the needs of the general welfare; thus engineers and scientific researchers would enjoy the fullest scope in seeking to advance technology, while writers and artists would also be free to achieve the
highest expression of man in art form. (I am setting down in sim-
plified form what I believed then; certainly I had not appraised
carefully the restrictions or the censorships which regimented
socialist societies also tend to impose on education, the press, the
arts, and even the sciences.)

In any case I spoke in a low-keyed way—for I was no platform
artist—and fully suspected that I was talking over the heads of my
audience. Fortunately Mike Gold, a born stump orator, followed
me and gave the capitalists hell and damnation, waved the red flag,
and brought volleys of applause. Hearing him I reflected soberly
that the job of galvanizing the multitudes at street corners or
meeting halls was best left to those equipped for it.

As we left the hall I apologized to Hook for my dull performance and remarked that Mike Gold, a whole circus in himself, had easily made up for my deficiencies. Hook observed: "What you had to say was really much more valid and important than the old soapbox cant Mike gave them, and it will make good reading when printed—but the communist leaders don't realize that."

We strolled in the street for a while, and Sidney Hook burst forth in a sudden tirade against the "stupid leadership" of the Communist Party. In his view they were ignorant fellows who knew nothing about Marxism. He went on to say that it was high time for "some younger fellows with brains" to throw them out and get into the saddle themselves. I had no idea that he was so displeased with his communist associates; it seemed that he too, like Edmund Wilson, wanted to "take communism away from the communists." For my part I was disposed to refuse any share in such an enterprise.

§   §   §

The elections were a disappointment to those who had counted on winning more than the hundred thousand votes given the communist ticket. No one was surprised however at the landslide vote for Franklin D. Roosevelt.

In 1932 Roosevelt was underestimated both by conservative commentators like Walter Lippmann and by those on the left, like Edmund Wilson, who described him as a good deal of a "boy scout." In that contest Roosevelt veered about a good deal, speaking as a progressive in California and a conservative in New Jersey. He could be very moving when he appealed to us to think of the Forgotten Man; yet in his next appearance he might plump for greater economies in the federal budget than Hoover had managed.

Some of the professional politicians advising Roosevelt are on record as having urged that he "could not be radical enough" in these days. Yet he held his hand, knowing that the people would vote "ag'in" the Depression and the party in office. James M. Burns, one of his biographers, wrote of the 1932 contest: "There was no call to action, no summons to a crusade. Roosevelt had no program to offer. . . . For a nation caught in economic crisis it was a curious campaign." Roosevelt's eldest son James afterward recalled that the crowds that year, compared with those of later presidential contests, were not enthusiastic but "strangely silent."

Leo Wolman, however, who was to join the "Brain Trust" early in 1933, reported to me that "Roosevelt was going to make the fur fly"; there would be much reform legislation he said, but in the long run it would change things for the labor movement and the unemployed "only a little bit."

§   §   §

After the election the Independent Committee for Foster and Ford—that is, its active group of a dozen members—called one more meeting, the last I attended. This gathering had some important agenda to discuss: proposals to set up a writers' association with chapters in other cities, to issue a periodical publication, and to organize lecture tours by members.

Soon it became plain that the larger than usual gathering of that November evening—there were fully two dozen on hand—was divided into two hostile factions who were at each others' throats from the start. As I lived far out of town and seldom came to these meetings I had not known that serious trouble was brewing.

Radical groups are very different from conventional political bodies: in the latter, conflicts over doctrine and method are always tempered and resolved, because of the tendency of the leading figures to compromise in order to hold on to office and power. But in an organization of radicals, eternally out of office and with no stake in practical power politics, disputes over theory could go on unconfined, each faction claiming that its members alone could "save the world" because they alone held the true doctrine. So at this meeting we had two camps of implacable opponents who each hated the other without limit. On the one side were the regular Party-line fellows; on the other were the dissidents led by Sidney Hook and Lewis Corey.

The meeting soon became a sort of Donnybrook. Each side used all its lung power. Never in my life had I heard such vituperation without attendant fisticuffs or bloodshed. I heard Hook's faction being denounced as "Trotskyites," a comparatively new epithet. I myself had lately written in admiration of Trotsky both

as revolutionary leader and historian, but it never occurred to me
that the differences over Soviet policy between a Stalin and a
Trotsky should concern us in any immediate way in the United
States.

A good deal of pure egoism came to the surface. The fast-
talking Hook shouted invective at his opponents. Both groups
were bent on assassinating each others' character. At length I
jumped up and as peacemaker urged that we seek agreement by
mutual concessions and get on with our business. Both sides turned
on me in rage, crying out that I knew nothing about the issues
involved.

The Party-line people, wielding their bludgeon, behaved like
harsh bureaucrats. They had come down in sufficient strength to
defeat the Trotskyites and kept pressing the others to come to a
vote; their evident purpose was to throw out the opposition. Sidney
Hook and his allies tried to delay things. They threatened to walk
out in a body if they could not wrest control of the committee and
the proposed writers' organization from the orthodox Party supporters. They were voted down. After they had gone the Independent Committee folded up and was not supplanted until 1935 by
the left-oriented League of American Writers.

Sidney Hook, Herbert Solow, Lewis Corey, Meyer Schapiro,
Jim Rorty, *et al.* had a perfect right to withdraw from the committee on grounds of conscience and give their support to Trotsky's
heretical faction or any other. My impression was that they were
able young men in search of careers open to talents and caught in
the midst of a Great Depression. Several of them moreover were
Jews, and despite brilliant university records they found advancement in their professions seriously delayed by the tacit racial
discrimination then widely practiced. After the economic crisis
moderated most of them found their way to adequate posts in the
academic and journalistic fields, and they ceased to function as
political radicals.

Hook became especially prominent several years later as the
most implacable of anticommunists and eventually as an ardent
defender of the capitalistic establishment. I was certainly not pre-

pared to see him turn upon his former communist associates with such extreme intolerance as he showed, as if in vengeance or in expiation of his own past "guilt." [3] During the time of Senator McCarthy's "terror," Hook, having risen to a post of influence at his university and in our educational world, publicly advocated the dismissal of various teachers (even of mathematics or music) who in past times had been members of the Communist Party but otherwise had done nothing considered wrongful prior to the enforcement of the Smith Act of 1940. Thus Hook would have blighted the careers of persons who, like himself, had once been young rebels or "good agitators," all aflame to set the world aright, as young men so often are. In other words the later Hook would have ruined the youthful Hook and thus deprived society of a popular teacher of philosophy and one of the most determined intellectual defenders of the status quo.

I should never have believed that the time would come, twenty years later, in 1952, when mild Jim Rorty would willingly appear before Senator McCarthy's committee and confess that for a year or two he had been a sympathizer with the communists, had been seduced and "violated" by them, and now was eager to inform McCarthy about his activities and those of his friends. Nor that the earnest Granville Hicks would at the same period make similar recantations and confessions before the inquisitors of the House Committee on Un-American Activities.

Disliking the quarrels of fanatics, and longing to remain as far as possible *au dessus de la mêlée*, I quietly removed myself from the scene of radical agitation and thereafter dealt with the orthodox communists and the heretics alike at arm's length. In 1936 Hook

[3] The English historian Isaac Deutscher has recently written a most penetrating essay on "The Ex-Communist's Conscience." In it he comments on the prevailing disposition of the ex-communists to become extremists in extirpating the heresies they themselves formerly embraced and in the end show themselves the most immitigable and narrow-minded defenders of capitalism itself. In a word, they remain as fanatical, as sectarian as they were before, seeing the world in simple black and white; only the colors are distributed differently. They pretend that ex-communists alone know how to deal with the "grand illusion" of communism; they become in essence demonologists fighting "total evil" all about us and playing a part that is utterly negative and intellectually barren. Isaac Deutscher: *Russia in Transition, and Other Essays* (New York: Grove Press; 1957), pp. 205–13.

and two other friends of his made a journey to my farm in Connecticut. He appealed to me to join a committee to defend Trotsky against official charges of the Stalinist regime in Russia. "You are really one of us and belong with us," Hook said at the time. "A plague o' both your houses," I replied.

Chapter Eight

❧

A Soiree with
Whittaker Chambers

THE FOURTH WINTER of the Great Depression found the Josephson family well dug in at Twin Willow Farm, and, what with sleds, skates, and skis, equipped for year-round living in the country. In the shed leaning against our house was a good store of cordwood cut from my own woodlot, with which we fueled the kitchen range; in our cellar there was coal for our furnace and preserves and vegetables my wife had canned with great labor; and in addition to that an oaken barrel with five gallons of apple brandy. Our illumination was by oil lamps, but a gravity spring on the hill across the road served us with an abundance of running water so that we enjoyed nearly all the conveniences known to rural Americans.

It was a patriarchal life, simple and frugal, enriched by the sense of physical well-being we drew from the air and space of our country situation. I was able to concentrate most of the day on the book I was writing, yet leave part of the afternoon for two hours of vigorous labor out of doors. The cutting of brush and saplings on the knoll above the big brook occupied me for a long while; thus I opened up a panoramic view of our steep-sided valley. Our enlarged kitchen garden required heavy labor to pulverize clods of coarse grass. At such tasks, as well as at household chores, the whole family worked together with a team spirit not easily developed in city apartments. My eldest son, a sturdy fellow of eight,

walked or rode a bicycle to the one-room village schoolhouse two
miles away, then he joined me at clearing the ground while the two
smaller children weeded the garden beds—or played at it. My wife
meanwhile had put aside her own capabilities for editing, scholarship, and writing to work over house and children with all her
heart. She managed also, when housework permitted, to collaborate
with me on research tasks; at night I would consult her, and she
read and edited my manuscripts. In the face of hundreds of weari-
some tasks in household and garden and care of children her joy
of life seemed invincible; the harmony that ruled in our rural
family existence, the hopefulness with which we sometimes faced
adversity, was owing most of all to her.

We saw much of our neighbor Charles Beard at the time I was
writing my study of America's nineteenth-century moneylords, *The
Robber Barons*. Beard and his wife used to rise at six each morning
to begin work on the history textbooks and general books they were
producing. By lunchtime they would have done a good day's stint,
then would drive about ten miles out to a dairy farm Charles
owned and whose business he supervised. At sixty both were robust
and spent part of their afternoons clearing their meadows with
scythe and brush hook. Returning home they would often detour
to our place, and Charles would sit on the porch, stretch out his
long legs, and talk.

This honest and forthright man was greatly exercised over the
scandals about our financial leaders just then being reported in the
newspapers. His was a nature often swept by gusts of moral passion;
at such moments his blue eyes would blaze up, he would flail his arms
wildly and launch into a truly purple passage of vituperation. "Oh!
those *respectable* ones—oh! their *temples* of respectability—how I
detest them, how I would love to pull them all down!" he cried
out one day. It was like the old days of battle in 1917 with Nicholas
Butler and the Columbia University trustees for academic freedom
in wartime. And Mary Beard would exclaim in anxiety: "Hush,
hush, Charles, you mustn't go on like that. You frighten people."

I remarked at the time: "I have often found myself in the precincts of those temples and have always felt myself an infidel
there."

What was eating "Uncle Charlie" was also troubling the entire middle class of America. He had worked long and hard, had prospered and saved something tidy for his old age, and now all of it, the railroad bonds and the real estate mortgages, was melting away. Under our rules the thriftiest of the bourgeois could win no security.

Beard stared at the wide meadow north of my house, where my neighbor's cattle browsed, and said with a grin: "That reminds me: we have just bought another farm." By disposing of some of his weak securities he had bought a two hundred-acre dairy farm at one of the best locations in Sherman township. In the intellectual Beard there was an admixture of the forehanded Yankee trader.

"I bought the farm because I have learned to mistrust all forms of *paper wealth*," he went on. What was the use, he said, of sitting and watching helplessly while your bonds and stocks went down? He pointed to my neighbor's cows in our meadow and said: "I like to be able to see my investments with my own eyes, and if the Depression goes on, if worst comes to worst, at least I can *eat* my investments too."

I wrote to a friend during the winter: "Please cheer up. Out here in the country there has been a roaring bull market for three days; the ground is nearly warmed up, and this is important."

At the end of February 1933 the meadows turned a soft green, the heifers came dancing out of the barns, the brooks gurgled, the earth laughed. But beyond the rim of our valley, throughout the nation an immense panic ruled over our people during the four months' interregnum between incoming and outgoing Presidents. A chain reaction of bank failures was spreading everywhere.

From his mountainside cottage in North Carolina Hamilton Basso wrote that the bank panic was in full progress in the South. "Does this not mark the climax of our confusion?" It was like living in a new age, he observed. "We are waiting for the Fall— Here's to the New Deal—the New Era too. It can't come too soon to suit me." A week later, on March 7, he reported that his last reserve of $150 was gone when a New Orleans bank closed its doors.

In the first week in March two friends arrived with the news that Acting Governor Herbert Lehman of New York had just issued a decree closing all banks in that state as of Monday, March 6. We had heard snatches of President Roosevelt's Inaugural Address on our weak radio, but we had no foreknowledge of the coming bank holiday.

My own funds in two New York banks were blocked, and I had only $10 in cash. We six at the farm could survive for a while on credit; I decided, however, to go down to the city and try to borrow a little additional cash for the emergency.

Well, we had passed another milestone in our history, I said to myself: our land of the almighty dollar has run out of dollars! New York at this moment would be worth seeing.

II.

As I rode toward New York on the suburban train that Sunday night that seemed to many like the evening before the end of the world, I cudgeled my brain to think of what might come next. Would there be more disorder, I wondered.

Throughout the year 1932 there had been a drain of gold from this country to Europe; in defensive action the Federal Reserve had reversed its program of expanding bank money, which now was made scarcer. Meanwhile depositors had taken to standing in long lines before the banks to demand not only green folding money but gold as well. The newspapers were full of pictures of people in queues with valises, paper bags, or brief cases in which to carry away gold coin or bars from the "Fed" in New York and other Reserve Bank cities.

The great run on banks was accompanied by some episodes of rioting, especially in the Midwestern cities. There was also news of unemployed men on looting forays, of farmers gathering in armed bands to halt foreclosures, of homeless Negroes in Chicago invading unused lofts or condemned tenements to take up residence there without rent, of unemployed miners in Pennsylvania digging coal in mines long closed and bootlegging it. There were also reports of 300,000 homeless boys wandering about the country. In the "dead" period between Roosevelt's coming to office with full power and Mr. Hoover's waiting and being unwilling to act, the public drew out several billions in currency and gold bullion that went into hiding in mattresses, cellars, and chimneys.

In all our history our democratic institutions had seldom suffered greater stress. But taken all together the American people were remarkably patient, even submissive. They reflected that fatalism of the multitude that Lord Bryce saw in the 1890's when he wrote *The American Commonwealth*. They had voted at the polls and now waited quietly for the incoming President to "do something."

The new chief magistrate, I surmised, would be forced to take drastic action, such as decreeing a nationwide bank holiday, for you could not have a moratorium in one state with banks open across the river. Then the national government would have to issue additional currency of some kind—any sort of script or "shinplaster" would do—in order to replace temporarily the billions that had gone out of circulation. This would mean that the dollar would be taken off the gold standard; that is the currency unit would be given a reduced gold exchange value or, in other words, inflated. I had seen the Germans doing with purely paper money after World War I, and when the Bank of England devalued the pound sterling in 1931 life went on. Prominent American businessmen who made up the Committee for the Nation had lately been calling for inflation of the dollar.

Judging by official reports the big banks in the principal financial centers had generally made themselves highly liquid in the past year or so by building up cash reserves. The big New York City banks actually opposed the governor's decree of the bank holiday, but they were forced to yield. Other reports of business conditions showed that severe shortages of goods had developed lately in many consumer trades. The studies I was just then pursuing in the history of American capitalism during the nineteenth century showed one business cycle succeeding another, with phases of depression and money panic followed by renewed credit inflation and recovery that sometimes turned into a boom.

For my part I disliked the idea of hoarding money. If the whole system smashed up then not only bank savings but insurance policies and the last few government bonds I had hung on to as the fragments of an inheritance would be worthless. At the weekend the New York Stock Exchange announced that it would remain closed during the bank holiday. Stock prices were then at incredibly low levels such as we had not seen in forty years. I made a mental note that when the market reopened I would be wise to invest in a few gilt-edged common stocks as a hedge against inflation.

Meanwhile our billion horsepower nation, with more motors, engines, electric power, telephones, and railroads than all the rest of the world, had run out of chips needed to stay in the game. And here was I, an honest bourgeois and paterfamilias, owning some acres of rocky land, a house, and in addition a few thousands in bank funds and bonds, forced to go scrounging about borrowing cash from a few friends who had had the foresight to hide money in mattresses or in holes in the ground. What an insane economic "system" we lived under! If there was to be a debacle, I thought, let it come quickly; the most agonizing thing is to live in continued uncertainty.

§ § §

Full of apprehension and absorbed by my troubling thoughts I walked west on Tenth Street in the Village, almost to the docks, where I had rented a small room at Robert Cantwell's apartment for my weekly visits to the city.

The Cantwells were most affectionate friends and always at home at night because of their infant; on my arrival they would appear quickly and greet me with warmth. This time as I knocked at the door no one came to open it, though as I approached I had heard voices inside. Now all was silent. I knocked again, and after a few moments, hearing some slight movements inside, I called out, giving my name. At last I heard Bob Cantwell say to someone: "Oh, it's perfectly all right. It's Matty Josephson. You can come out"—and at the same time he opened the door and let me in. Betsy was with him in the living room; then a man I did not know came out of the hall bedroom I usually occupied. He looked embarrassed, even sheepish; he seemed to have come out of hiding.

While I had waited outside he had evidently retreated in fear of being surprised by some visitor he did not care to see. He was a stocky young man with a round, bumpy face, unkempt sandy hair, and rather pale blue eyes. His rumpled clothes looked as if he had been sleeping in them. Cantwell introduced him as Whittaker Chambers.

I recognized the name as one Bob had mentioned once or twice: a down-at-heel young writer he had met in New Orleans who occasionally had published pieces in *The New Masses* that I had read without much interest. Cantwell had also told me some curious things about Chambers: that he either fancied himself or actually was "a communist secret agent attached to the Russian GPU" (as Bob put it) and that he lived an underground life full of real or imaginary dangers, always under cover or on the run. It also came back to me that Bob had mentioned that Chambers usually carried a revolver with him.

Why should he have felt the need of a revolver? I had asked at the time. "Oh, he's sure he's being trailed by the FBI night and day," Bob had explained with a laugh, adding, "He's probably a bit nutty, too." I had certainly assumed he was either a clown or an eccentric. Now Bob told me apologetically that Chambers had come to New York a few days ago and, since he "had no place to stay" the Cantwells had put him up, during my absence, in the room I used periodically.

We sat down to talk over a nearly empty bottle of bootleg whisky (which Chambers must have contributed) and were soon engaged in a heated discussion of the situation such as went on everywhere at that period. The two younger men asked me at once what I thought of the bank closings; according to Chambers they marked the climactic phase of the economic crisis. I remember his saying: "Isn't this the great debacle of the American financial system—with all the banks closing their doors?—it's the final breakdown, finish for them." He was highly excited and his voice rose to a falsetto pitch.

I disagreed, arguing that some form of money inflation would probably be introduced to set the banking machinery running again. I also mentioned what I had heard about plans of the new

President for relief and expanded public works, and I made the inference that a cyclical recovery in trade might follow as people speculated on prices rising with the inflation of the currency. I had just lately been reading accounts of the money panics of 1893 and 1907—the latter J. P. Morgan "solved" by issuing bank scrip when green money had disappeared from circulation. I argued that the possibility that our business system might be saved for a while must be seriously considered.

At this Chambers exploded with excitement—though only a little whisky had been served—and fairly screamed at me, "Why man, you're crazy! With no money, no work, no food, everything stopped, there's going to be a revolution here right now! This is it— the big smashup. There'll be barricades the end of this week in Union Square, I tell you!" Chambers's calendar for the final class struggle in America was certainly set far ahead of anything Comrade "Bill" Foster had conceived of.

I repeated patiently that no real insurrection seemed to be in sight. "Even without bank money for a period the trains will continue to run on time, the milkman will make his rounds as usual." I stressed the regimented character of our people, caught as they were in the automatism of an industrial society whose machinery drove them along in the routine of every day. As for money the newspapers had already announced that the large semi-public business organizations, such as the gas and telephone companies and railroads, would issue payroll scrip temporarily to workers.

I had been trying to keep to the tone of cool reason, but Chambers's shouting angered me and I too raised my voice. In most positive terms I predicted that some measure of business recovery was at hand and that as soon as the Stock Exchange re-opened the market would rise. Chambers appeared outraged at the very idea and kept bellowing at me phrases that were taken from some old-fashioned communist tracts.

"We must be objective, whatever our hopes, we must not deceive ourselves," I exclaimed. Did Chambers really know his Marx? Well, on reading reports of the great gold strike in California in 1849 Karl Marx had announced that the proletarian Revolution would now be postponed for twenty years. In his view the added gold would inflate the world's currency. Nowadays inflation worked in the same way, at least for the short term.

My citing of Marx in what seemed to me a crushing argument put Chambers into an even greater rage than before. My cool dismissal of his so passionately desired Revolution, his "baby" as it were, on which all his hopes were pinned, was like an unbearable affront. In a voice choked with tears he cried out something about "all the sacrifices" he had been making for years for the sake of the Revolution.[1] Possibly Whittaker Chambers, living in his fantasies, saw himself playing a hero's role in a revolutionary holocaust, riding up to his bridles in blood—and there I was waving the whole image away.

Now Chambers was seized by an access of hysteria. Red-faced, with eyes almost popping out of his head, he began to abuse me, yelling imprecations at the top of his voice, using epithets such as "bourgeois stooge," or "tool of the capitalists"—even at one moment calling me a "spy." Incredibly he implied that for all he knew I might be spying on him!

Impulsively I pushed back my chair and stood up, saying I would not endure such insults from anyone, and, doubling my fists, challenged him to put up his hands. But Bob Cantwell and his wife came between us and asked Chambers to leave. He tore off without another word.

I was quite shaken and it took me a while to cool down. Cantwell apologized for his friend's bad manners, remarking that he seemed almost crazed tonight. He supposed it was because of the strain of the sort of hunted life Chambers led, or thought he led.

What a strange meeting it was—one that left a most unpleasant aftertaste—and since it occurred on the night before the banks closed I often reconstructed it afterward. At the time I simply could not take Whittaker Chambers seriously as a secret agent of anything; rather I thought of him as one of those Bohemian neurotic rebels one sometimes meets in Greenwich Village or

[1] Many communists had the idea that the mass demonstrations of the unemployed would soon build up to a great popular explosion which the devoted comrades would somehow turn to account. "We need a compact well-organized party capable of aggrandizing a series of . . . struggles into a real bid for power," wrote one such doctrinaire of that time in *The New Masses*.

Montparnasse, all emotion and noise and nonsense. The only cause such fellows really cared about was that of their own ill-adjusted personalities. Chambers, I remarked to Cantwell, was only "a half-baked revolutionary" but evidently a thoroughgoing paranoiac. If the communists had many more like him I thought they would not get very far.

And how absurd that the man should be carrying a revolver. Was it not really because he was under a delusion about being *persecuted?* Cantwell thought it was because he was actually working as "a spy for the Russian GPU." I snorted in disbelief.[2]

Cantwell replied however that there were times when he found Chambers "fascinating." He said this as if with the clinical interest of a writer bent on observing singular characters. I gathered that he thought of using the tormented personality of his friend for that of a fictive communist secret agent in one of his "proletarian" novels. The charming Cantwell himself was quite a tense and nervous type. Indeed in Cantwell's second novel, *The Land of Plenty* (1934), which is the story of a strike in a lumber mill on the West Coast, there is a good deal of intriguing and spying.

Cantwell himself used to talk as if he expected the Revolution to break forth almost any hour. After working on the staff of *The New Republic* for a year or so, and later for Lincoln Steffens, he became book review editor of *Time* magazine in 1937. "Well, I'm going to enjoy the fleshpots too," he said to me then. There his radicalism, his fellow traveling, abruptly ended.

I heard no more of Whittaker Chambers until 1938 when I learned that he too had got a job on the staff of *Time*, thanks to his friend Cantwell. I also heard from Cantwell that Chambers had quit the communists and turned completely, bitterly, against them. It did not surprise me at all that he had changed his colors;

[2] Joseph Freeman has often told a story of spending an evening drinking with Whittaker Chambers and the poet Keene Wallis at about the same period, probably late in 1931. Chambers was described as becoming suspicious of Wallis, a rather quiet sort of man, and in a sudden drunken rage drawing a knife and threatening him. Later that night, arriving at Freeman's apartment in Brooklyn, they met Freeman's sister at the door and Chambers fell to his knees and kissed the hem of her skirt, though he had never seen her before. That evening also Chambers used his knife to scratch Freeman's wrist and his own, thus performing the "blood brother" ritual. Freeman thought Chambers "lived in a Dostoevski novel."

that was the way of the rebel without a cause. *Time* was then anti-Roosevelt and much given to angry, slanted reviews of books by writers considered liberal or radical. In 1940 Chambers telephoned me at my home in Connecticut to inform me that he was reviewing a book of mine just published, and sought information about me which I gave with some reserve. In his "Machiavellian" approach to me he used terms of the most arrant flattery. His unsigned review of my book *The President Makers; 1896–1919*, a study of progressive politics in America, appeared in *Time* (October 21, 1940) as one of their typical sneering articles. In it Chambers denounced me as if *I* were a complaisant agent of the Russians(!), a charge no more true than what he had said to me in March 1933. Then he had assailed me as an agent of the capitalists; now he attacked me for the opposite reason. On the first occasion he was a fanatic, and on the later one he was still the same fanatic in the conservative cause.

What did the truth matter to a Whittaker Chambers? In his autobiography *Witness* (1952), in which he tells of how he worked to ruin Alger Hiss and others who had befriended him, he writes as one driven by his fears and hates, all absorbed by his "mission," with which his self-love was identified. His mission by then was not merely to destroy his old comrades the communists, but also the liberals, the New Dealers, and the Fair Dealers, who were all united, as he assures us, in "persecuting" him.

In those years when he was safely established in the Luce organization with his salary mounting steadily—he himself calls them "the golden years"—he grew fat; but he learned by practice to write with more competence than before. It is not precluded that a man in great measure neurotic should not one day become an accomplished writer. I found *Witness* a Dostoevskian fiction full of passion and bombast, at once self-revealing and self-deluded, and imbued with a kind of mad intensity, much like *The Possessed*, whose antisocial hero, Stavrogin, was Chambers's favorite character.

In the light of the public fame that attached to Chambers at the time of the sensational Hiss trial, fifteen years after I met him, I often thought of him again and wondered what sort of a spy he

could really have been. Why did he show his revolver to young
Bob Cantwell and Betsy and confess to them that he was a secret
agent of the Russians? Why did he talk so much about his dangerous business with so many loquacious literary people—even shouting for revolution in my presence. The Cantwells gossiped about
his "espionage" and his gun. I talked about it; others babbled about
it. Chambers was by all odds the best-advertised secret agent I
ever heard of; several score persons in New York and Connecticut
and in the "legal" Communist Party also knew about Chambers's
spying for the Russians and fleeing from the FBI every night. If
the Russian secret service hired him as he avows, then they were
being very clumsy. They should have chosen some solid, respectable-
looking fellow, not a literary Bohemian. Moreover it was a time of
peace, when we had only a tiny military force and there was
scarcely any need for a secret intelligence agent. In those days
members of Congress and executives of federal bureaus regularly
leaked as many official secrets as anyone could desire to any newspaper reporter.

It occurred to me long afterward that Chambers waited seven
years to wreak a petty "vengeance" upon me, whom he scarcely
knew, because I had engaged in dispute with him. His later attack
upon Alger Hiss, the former friend who had dropped him, was a
repetition of such vengeance-taking, though on a far greater and
more terrible scale. Anyone of us might have become the victim of
this psychopath whom the new-born conservatives of the Mc-
Carthian era adopted as their "saint."

§   §   §

And so on March 7, 1933, the catastrophe everyone had dreaded
came to pass. In the morning I set off to borrow a little ready cash
from my friends Henry and Gladys Billings; Gladys, a provident
woman, went to one of her bookshelves, took out a novel of Henry
James, and drew out several twenty dollar bills, one of which she
kindly offered me. At the offices of Harcourt, Brace, Alfred Harcourt received me kindly enough. He showed me his firm's check-
book, indicating that they had $250,000 in cash locked up at the
Guaranty Trust Company and were ostensibly in the same plight as

A Soiree with Whittaker Chambers

I. Then this Madison Avenue country boy winked at me shrewdly, went to a little safe near his desk, drew out a one hundred dollar bill from his petty cash, and handed it to me (charging it to my royalty account). He also gave me a good cigar that he had in his ornate Louis XV desk, while he himself rolled a Bull Durham with all the skill of a motion picture cowboy. Harcourt had no fear about the banks, most of which he thought would reopen in a week or so. I went off feeling rich.

In this hour of universal misfortune people were not only unaccountably cheerful, they were positively kind. The voice of the new President came over the radio very clear, very calm, telling what was happening and why. One heard pleasantries being exchanged about all of us being flat. Many shops had signs in the windows saying they would accept postdated checks. At the Grand Central Terminal I paid for my railroad ticket by check. The trains were running on time.

Chapter Nine

~

The Money Changers
Expelled and Reinstated

IT WAS WHILE I was reporting on the bulls
and bears of Wall Street for *The New Yorker* early in 1932 that
the idea came to me of writing a history of their great forebears, the
legendary captains of industry and financiers who flourished in our
country during the latter half of the nineteenth century and gave
their special character to the period aptly named by Mark Twain
"The Gilded Age."

During the twenties when I had worked in the financial district
some of the ancient moneylords were still alive, and a few of them
such as George F. Baker, Sr., then approaching ninety, were pointed
out to me in the street. More recently I had been interviewing
certain of the veteran stock brokers who had taken part in historic
market conflicts of long ago. Those ruthless old men whom the
young President Theodore Roosevelt had called "malefactors of
great wealth," and whose monopolistic drives he vainly tried to
curb in the courts, were a law unto themselves, creating booms or
panics as they pleased. They embodied power without responsibility. Before "the power of the mighty industrial overlords . . . the
government [was] practically impotent," Roosevelt observed at the
time of the Northern Pacific panic in 1901. These men, he said,
promised America only "the most vulgar form of tyranny . . . the
tyranny of mere wealth, the tyranny of a plutocracy."

In writing the history of those late nineteenth-century capitalists, in reenacting their drama as it were, I hoped to answer this question: How did we as a nation come to such a pass as we found ourselves in? The answer imposed itself forcibly; we had continued the regime of power without responsibility down to 1933. The reader of today in this era of giant government can scarcely conceive how much the administration in Washington and the Congress was then a do-nothing affair.

"What do I care about the law? Hain't I got the power?" old Commodore Vanderbilt used to say in the 1860's.

Our classical American authors had long ago protested our materialistic civilization, from which they felt themselves alienated; but they had seldom examined it closely. Only in more recent times had a few writers tried to locate the centers of real power; notable among these were Thorstein Veblen and Charles A. Beard.[1] Veblen had judged our business society as unscientific as well as irresponsible. Beard had offered more recently his social history of the American people, with a brief account of their developing customs, arts, and industries, in which the highest importance was attached to the role of the men of fortune and the great family dynasties they founded. I proposed to make a large gallery of historical portraits of the men who had put their stamp on our society. My point of departure would be the post-Civil War era in which they thrived, when America was the paradise of the freebooting entrepreneurs.

The self-appointed captains of industries were to be shown building up the half-empty continent while enriching themselves; they provided the plant and machinery that would be needed and the vast railway net that would span its continental distances. They labored in haste and without plan yet served as "agents of progress," as even Marx observed. Among our citizens they were the most aggressive and acquisitive ones who, adopting Herbert Spencer's utilitarian philosophy in vulgarized form, judged that they represented "the survival of the fittest." The essential drama of the age of the Robber Barons was the drive toward concentration in industry and banking that culminated in the giant trusts.

[1] Gustavus Myers's *History of the Great American Fortunes* (1910) was a lengthy and painstaking compilation; however, it omitted many of the leading figures of the period I studied.

How much panache those old American moneylords had! With their regal chateaux in imitation Renaissance or Gothic style, their palace cars on rails, and their pleasure yachts, one of which Morgan defiantly christened *The Corsair*. In effect they conducted themselves like the robber knights of feudal times who used to operate in such regions as the Rhine Valley; here too the overlords of transport seized upon the strategic mountain passes or valley roads, those "narrows" through which commerce must flow, and levied their toll. The protesting farmers of the Middle West used to petition Congress unweariedly for relief from such extortion, and it was in one of their antimonopoly pamphlets of 1880 that I found the name Robber Barons applied to the masters of railroads.

The Robber Barons was written during the Great Slump of 1932–3. It was my design to include in objective spirit and without anger extended observations on the manners and morals of our industrial dynasts, as well as an account of how they got the money. At a time when money seemed to be disappearing on every hand I found it an amusing distraction to describe how quickly and skillfully our Robber Barons accumulated their boodle. In my searches for material I had the good fortune to come upon old correspondence of men like C. P. Huntington and Jay Gould, as revealed in trial records or in legislative inquiries. For the most part such persons either destroyed or kept the records of their corporations secret, as they have remained in the case of the big railroads to this very day. Some of the most interesting revelations about the business methods of my moneymen I found in the numerous works of hagiography which they had ordered written about themselves by naive sycophants. My neighbor Charles Beard noticed this and asked me: "How in the world did you have the patience to read those dreary old books about those awful people?" The fact was I enjoyed writing about my "scoundrels" and dissecting their frauds or mystifications.

I was moreover in a very happy mood while working on the history of *The Robber Barons*, for I had stopped all writing of magazine articles for the time and was my own editor. In the case of one of my recent *New Yorker* profiles of the old stock broker Harry Content, Harold Ross had forbidden me to use many of the historical reminiscences Content had provided, though he did invite me to do my own cutting. Ross showed a prickly independence in running his magazine, but he was an old-fashioned conservative at heart. At his office, all around him, I saw in imagination signs reading: *Keep off the Grass*. At any rate, in writing my own book I worked with the fullest freedom. When Harold Ross read it he said to me with a wicked grin: "It's a fine book, but, dammit, if only I had had a chance to do a little editing on it!—"

Throughout 1932 and during the early months of the new Roosevelt administration several committees of Congress held scathing inquiries into the operations of America's latter-day leaders in finance, and thus day by day the scandals of the twenties were exposed to the public on the front pages of their newspapers. When my book appeared, early in 1934, the readers of that period turned to it with lively interest, for in my account of the old capitalists of the preceding generations they recognized the progenitors of the new financial breed, our architects of national disaster. For a season or two *The Robber Barons* was required reading for the New Deal's reformers. The title became a part of everyday American speech.[2]

II.

Let us return meanwhile to the Ides of March in 1933 when we endured the fateful banking moratorium and waited for it to end. Few of us understood then why or how such a complete breakdown of America's financial system had come about, though we suspected there had been some colossal blundering. It was several years after those events that I learned some surprising things about the recriminations and dissensions that raged in high financial and government circles during the winter of 1933, prior to the proclamation of the bank holiday by the incoming Presi-

[2] A young man just out of college was reported to have applied to Kuhn, Loeb and Company for a job. On being asked what qualifications he thought he possessed for such work, he said: "I have read a book called *The Robber Barons* and I have decided I would like to be one of them."

dent. In the awkward changeover period at the White House, Mr. Hoover refused to take any action to improve the situation so long as he could not have the agreement of the President-elect to share his responsibility. In the meantime depositors' runs were spreading again that winter, especially in the Midwest. There, as I learned afterward, one obdurate old magnate alone, Henry Ford, helped precipitate a great banking crisis in Michigan whose effects quickly spread into neighboring states with a force that seemed irresistible.

We have enjoyed some great successes in the course of our history, but our national disasters have been truly spectacular. In the early days of February 1933 one of the two largest banks in Detroit, the Guardian Trust, reported privately to the RFC that it could not meet demands for withdrawals unless it obtained a loan of $50 million. Treasury Department officials and Federal Reserve Banks then shared authority for approval of RFC loans; they learned that such a proposed loan would exceed by a good deal the maximum value of collateral security the bank might be able to turn over. The only way to save this large popular bank under existing rules was to have its biggest depositor, also one of its stockholders, the Ford Motor Company, subordinate its deposit claims to the extent of $7.5 million.

Henry Ford, however, declared himself unwilling to go along with this plan. Whereupon emissaries from the White House, the Treasury Department, and the RFC hastened to Detroit to reason with the old man and try to bring him around. One of them was Undersecretary of the Treasury Arthur A. Ballantine, a prominent New York corporation lawyer who later gave me his account of the affair. What Ballantine feared was that the fall of the Guardian would break the other big Detroit bank chain, the First National, and then runs would occur all over the country. But Ford stubbornly refused to subordinate his claims, saying he was determined to draw on the Guardian Bank for all his deposits and also threatening to call on the other big bank, the First National of Detroit, for $25 million he had there—which would eliminate all the ready money left in that city. Let the government and its RFC carry the burden, Ford insisted; he had helped the banks as long as he could. The other automobile giants, General Motors and Chrysler, had cooperated by subordinating their large claims against the Guardian Bank.

President Hoover's emissaries appealed to Ford earnestly in the name of his President and his country, pointing out that the RFC had appraised the bank's collateral at optimum value and could not lawfully go beyond this. Ford was warned that widespread distress among small depositors would be created by his refusal of cooperation and even that "serious social disorders might follow" not only in Michigan but in neighboring states. But Henry Ford set his face like flint, saying, "If the crash has to come, let it come"; he felt young and would start in business all over again! The whole country needed a good "cleaning up" he held. Moreover he aired suspicions that the effort to use him in rescuing the big Detroit banks was part of a "plot" against him directed by mysterious enemies he would not name.

Thus one ignorant and stubborn old man thwarted the government's rescue party. In former times Henry Ford, one of America's most creative industrialists, had contributed much to the country's real wealth. Now in the panic days of the 1930's he dismissed 80 per cent of his 250,000 workers and maintained a private army of 1,000 thugs "to guard his grandchildren," as he said, against the riotous unemployed.

When the interview between Ford and the group from Washington was over the governor of Michigan declared a temporary bank holiday throughout the state. Bank runs then spread to Illinois, Indiana, and Ohio, and there was the devil to pay.

In behalf of the Federal Reserve George Harrison now urged President Hoover to declare a national bank moratorium as of February 17, two weeks before Inauguration Day. But Hoover said he "did not want his last official act to be the closing of all the banks." The irresponsible behavior of Ford had helped to feed the panic. The stubbornness of Hoover added to the inconvenience and loss suffered by the public in the final stages of the bank crisis.

§ § §

The denouement of the banking crisis was given all the greater dramatic force by the delays and blunders that preceded it. Roosevelt's first Inaugural Address, in contrast with his campaign speeches, was delivered at a time when despair convulsed our business community and Europe was in tumult over the advent of Hitler to power. That address was a masterly affair and had to our American ears a perceptibly authoritarian tone.

"This nation asks for action," he said in his high and penetrating voice. He would act swiftly; if need be he would employ wartime authority to carry out emergency measures and put people to work again. Using an aphorism from Thoreau to the effect that "we have nothing to fear but fear itself," he sought to inspire courage in the public. "The money changers have fled from their high seats in the temple" was another of the resounding phrases we heard that day. Almost immediately thereafter he decreed the closing of banks and the embargo on shipments of gold (taking the dollar off the gold standard), and issued a call for a special session of Congress to convene March 9 and enact emergency laws. Some of these were immediately passed, virtually without debate, as in the case of the Emergency Banking Act of March 9, 1933.

The new banking act authorized the Reserve Banks to give credit *at their discretion* to member banks against *all assets*, instead of requiring collateral such as government bonds and high grade commercial loans as hitherto; Reserve Bank notes were simply to be issued, as Harrison said, "against all kinds of junk, even the brass spittoons in old-fashioned country banks." The government's banking experts were shocked at what they themselves were doing.

Harrison's memorandum at the time stated:

The first thing we realized was that we were actually out of money. Money in circulation, that is hoarded money mostly, had jumped to the record figure of six billions by March, 1933. We had closed in the midst of a great bank run, and as far as we knew would reopen under the same condition. Should the panic continue for some time there was every possibility that there would not be enough Federal Reserve notes, secured by 40 per cent gold under existing law, to meet all demands. This time it was decided that we not use Clearing-House scrip, as in previous crises, but real currency.

The Money Changers Expelled and Reinstated

No reform of our topsy-turvy banking structure was attempted and no change of ownership was effected, but the government pumped paper money into all banks that were reopened with the approval of Federal Reserve examiners. Many important banks that were on the margin of insolvency were bailed out by the government and survived, though about 4,500 (mainly country town) banks were closed down.

Thus after having castigated the money changers, President Roosevelt hastily reinstated them in their high places. Among Roosevelt's advisers were several men with advanced ideas who believed that the President, in that hour of crisis, could have nationalized the banking system without serious opposition. Rexford Tugwell proposed using the Postal Savings Banks as popular depositories while setting up another government institution to administer commercial credits. Senator Bronson Cutting, Progressive Republican of New Mexico and a personal friend of the President, held that something drastic should have been done about reorganizing the whole banking structure and that Roosevelt's failure to do so at the start of his term was his greatest mistake. Tugwell wrote in his diary at the time that the President seemed to have "missed a trick."

Roosevelt to be sure was active on many fronts, carrying out various emergency measures with dispatch: unemployment relief was expanded; a larger public works program was initiated; the Agricultural Adjustment Act, providing for aid to the farmers through government price supports, bounties for crop curtailment, and currency inflation was hurriedly drafted and sent to Congress for enactment. (If these things were not done promptly, Roosevelt had warned, ". . . we will have an agrarian revolution.") National economic planning of industry was also attempted for the first time, under the National Industrial Recovery Act. In the crisis of the first hundred days the rather calculating politician of Albany was transformed into a supremely confident and courageous leader. At last the national government had taken cognizance of the needs of the people and had acted to help them under the general welfare clause of the Constitution.

President Roosevelt's first Sunday evening "fireside chat" by radio on the subject of the money crisis was considered by experts of the banking business, such as Harrison, a superb performance for the purpose in view: to allay fear, to assure the public that only sound banks would be licensed for reopening, and that the country would henceforth be blessed with ample currency "backed by actual good assets." As a result depositors came back with a rush in the next week, and most of the $6 billion in hoarded currency returned to circulation. The stock market, on resuming business, entered on a boom period. The reopening of the banks was made festive when Roosevelt, obtaining quick action from Congress, managed to give the people beer around the same time.

Chapter Ten

~

Russian Journey

IT HAS ALWAYS given me a marvelous sense
of release, after the fatigues of a long book were done with, to take
a sea voyage. Like the narrator of *Moby Dick*, whenever I felt
myself "growing grim about the mouth . . . and drizzly November
in my soul," I thought it high time to leave the shore and see the
watery world outside. Thus, in late autumn 1933 I was on board
ship in the blue waters of the Atlantic, the waves pounding at our
sides and the salt wind blowing weariness away.

Formerly I should have proceeded directly to Paris, which I,
like so many of my generation, held to be the fountainhead of
West Europe's literary culture. But this time I made a long
northerly detour, changing ship at London and sailing up the
Baltic to Leningrad, then going on by train to Moscow for a
month's stay before going back to France. (By arrangement with
the Guggenheim Foundation, which had awarded me a fellowship,
I was to spend part of a year at literary research in Paris.)

Why Russia? The Soviets had been in high fashion since the
end of the twenties, and Moscow was the Mecca of Americans
young and old. History was being made there! After the years of
armed intervention by the Allies, and the *cordon sanitaire*, Russia
had managed to raise herself from her ruins and begin reconstruction upon a grand scale. While the capitalist nations of the West
floundered in depression and Italy and Germany turned to fascism,
socialist Russia, furiously engaged in raising up new cities, plants,
and power sites, seemed like the hope of the world—the only large
nation run by men of reason.

At alternating periods in her history, Russia, as Arnold Toynbee has written, had drawn upon the ideas of the West and also recoiled against them, later returning to make her own original contribution. Since 1927 the Soviets' Five Year Plans had aroused immense interest in the world outside. Several of *The New Republic*'s writers on economic questions, namely Rexford Tugwell, Stuart Chase, and George Soule, had gone there to report on Russia's progress. The idea of socialism was, of course, drawn from the West, and that of national economic planning as well. But the Russians were actually applying these ideas under peacetime conditions and in a big way. A few days before my departure, as if to signify the increasingly friendly interest of the world outside, the United States government under Roosevelt officially recognized the Soviet regime—after sixteen years of nonrecognition.

At the London docks I boarded a little five-thousand-ton Soviet freighter, the S.S. *Siberia*. Stevedores and sailors were completing stowage, the decks were all noise and confusion. A stocky little Russian sailor, clad in the worst rags I had ever seen, darted out to take my suitcases and lead me up to my cabin on the bridge deck. I took out some silver to tip him, but the man only looked at me with a strange smile, refusing to take the money, shaking his head. I was dumfounded; never in my life had anyone handling my luggage refused a gratuity. It came to me that my bourgeois habits were deeply rooted; I must certainly try to curb them during my sojourn in the socialist Fatherland. It was my first lesson in Bolshevik pride, administered by a man in tatters. I encountered him later, all shaven and cleanly dressed, presiding as secretary of the sailors' soviet on the ship.

The sea voyage was unduly long, eleven days instead of the usual four. Yet winter travel in these waters, though I had expected it to be only cold and dreary, had its special beauties. The sub-Arctic nights were long; by the time we reached Finland our ship was handsomely sheathed in ice and snow.

We passengers constituted a cross section of international commerce in the Depression years. A Mr. C., an American engineer of Russian descent, was bound for a tractor plant in Kharkov. A sprightly Mr. E. was a fur buyer for a firm of London and New

York. At Rotterdam a tall Hollander, aged forty, with waxed mustaches and wearing a dark suit, celluloid collar, and stock tie, climbed on board, bringing with him a dozen crates with 500,000 tulip bulbs for export to Russia. Mr. L. was a Catholic and conservative in politics, he said, but looked forward with pleasure to visiting the Russians as he had done before the war. "Under the skin they have not changed much," he remarked, adding: "You will find they are a very good sort of people, amiable and lively in society, and good scientists." Very different from the commercial travelers were two youthful Irishmen of working-class type, who confided to me that they had got into some trouble in Belfast and skipped the country. They were to seek work in Russia, but both sounded already a little homesick for Ireland.

One passenger who interested me was Hans H., a stocky German of about twenty-five, a native of the working-class quarter in Munich who had emigrated to America in 1930. A photographer by trade, he had drifted all about the States for several years, finding work only occasionally. He could not go home, for his people were Reds who had often brawled with the Nazi streetfighters in Munich. "The Nazis would torture and kill me," he said. The future of Germany was dark; the workers, he reported, were flocking like sheep to the camp of the Nazis. As for the Russians, he thought them inferior in every way to the Germans, and he also evinced a strong disgust for America. "How terrible the way the American government treated the unemployed," he exclaimed; "even the Nazis have maintained the dole." And so he was for Russia as a last resort.

The S.S. *Siberia* was a part of Russia and her people were wary. Nevertheless, I wanted to explore the ship and meet the crew. With the permission of the captain I went below deck accompanied by the engineer's mate. He was a tow-headed young fellow with blue eyes who had worked for two years in the oil fields under an American engineer, and so he talked American English with a Western accent. "Russians get along fine with Americans," he shouted to me above the roar of the diesel engines.

To one of the sailors, a huge, stout fellow who had served in British merchant vessels, I put some questions about working con-

ditions on board. I had already been told that the crews of the
Sovflot (Shipping Trust) were elite workers and fervent communists who enjoyed pay and food superior to that received by
most workers on the mainland. In cockney English that abounded
with phrases and slogans of the new day in Russia my fat sailor
assured me that life on the S.S. Siberia was far better than that on
British vessels. The sailors slept in cabins instead of forecastle
bunks, and they received incentive wages—following the plan of
"socialist competition" (which was certainly not pure communism). They had their local council, or soviet, and elected their
own secretary, but their soviet confined itself to social, educational, and propaganda business.

"On the capitalist ships," the Russian sailor declared, "the more
you cringe, the more you suck their arses, the better they treat you.
Here on our Soviet ship we are all comrades. The captain is in
command because of his training, his ability, not because he be-
longs to a superior class. When he comes in here, we do not lower
our eyes as sailors do before their *masters* under other flags. He is
one of us—here it's all for one and one for all!"

He went on: "The State gives us security. You must go and
see the workers' cooperatives in our country; and the theaters,
cinemas, and libraries at factories. And where do your workers go
for their amusement? To *public houses!*"

The last words were uttered with explosive scorn. Who had
ever heard of a sailor, and an old sailor at that, running down
public houses!

The secretary of the ship's soviet, the same who had refused
my tip, then invited me to come back the next evening and have a
talk with the sailors during their "culture hour." I came, and
Mr. C., the Russian-American engineer, interpreted for me. During
our discussion I remarked that while Americans had built up the
largest industrial machine in the world, they were now running it
at about 50 per cent of capacity. My little audience of twenty
sailors found such conduct highly "irrational," and "antisocial."
They also thought it was madness to allow a *few individuals* to
reap vast profits for merely performing "necessary services for the
society." The young engineer's mate remarked: "We too have our

difficulties in building up new industries or railroads, but we build in a socialist way without allowing capitalists to rob our people." If America's conventional wisdom found the Russians benighted slaves, the Russians for their part found American ways "backward."

I felt, at any rate, that I had enjoyed real communication with these men, though I had spoken with moderation about the difficulties of my own country and without pretending to be an orthodox Marxist. At that time I was in no mood to leap to the defense of our capitalist system. (If I had, I would have been promptly corrected, no doubt!)

For two days, toward the end of the journey, our ship had been moving at a snail's pace and with much vibration through three-inch ice. At last, at sundown, we ground to a halt in a frozen wilderness twenty miles out of Leningrad harbor. In line before us were six merchant vessels, fast in the ice, and as many behind, all of them signalling each other with searchlights that made a brilliant holiday illumination over the ice fields. Meanwhile two stout icebreakers circled around a whole day long, slowly grinding up a trail before the ships, which were escorted, one after another, like chicks led by a hen. "You cannot hurry things in Russia," my Dutch friend said.

II.

The numerous armed guards at the docks of Leningrad, in their preposterously long winter coats and peaked helmets with red star, were the first people I saw in Russia; they looked like no other soldiers I had ever known, and gave me quite a turn. My first impression in Leningrad as in Moscow was of many soldiers all about, so that Soviet Russia in peacetime had the appearance, as in the past, of a nation in arms. (Stalin can do whatever he pleases with me, I remember reflecting, and I had better behave.)

Leningrad, Czar Peter's winter capital, with its huge plazas and palaces, was one of the most beautiful baroque cities of Europe.

But the façades of its handsome buildings were dilapidated; many shops that had been the repair of fashion were boarded up; at others crowds of ill-clad people stood in line in the bitter cold to buy food on rations. Here the tempo of life appeared slow.

The first moments in Moscow, however, were overpowering; even to a city-bred American the volume of noise was prodigious, and the crowds spilling off the curbs into the middle of the boulevards in the central quarter seemed enormous. These people, apparently belonging to every one of Russia's seventy races, were roughly dressed in old furs or leather greatcoats and high boots; the women wore shawls and quantities of padding, for the air was shockingly cold. By comparison with decaying Leningrad most of Russia's energy seemed centered in Moscow, whose population had recently doubled and whose continuing construction boom was accompanied by a hammering and riveting that was enough to split one's eardrums. Jerry-built skyscrapers reared themselves incongruously beside old Russian cathedrals and medieval palaces, making Moscow an architectural hodgepodge. Much of the uproar, punctuated by periodic sounds of blasting, came from the subway then being constructed under our feet. The hurrying crowds of Moscow gave the city a dynamic style reminiscent of New York or Chicago in boom times.

The contrasts here leaped to the eye: the vehicles threading their way through the crowds ranged from smart Lincoln sedans carrying government officials to horse-drawn droshkys, or carts pulled by troikas. Ragged old women hopped between the vehicles to sweep up the dry snow. In the "open stores" people almost trampled each other to buy scarce goods that were of inferior quality. That same winter in London and Paris I saw almost no customers in the shops; half a dozen sales clerks would leap up to bring you a single pair of gloves.

Everywhere in Moscow I saw huge red banners with diverse legends hung above the street and colored posters on all the hoardings at the site of the future subway stations. These bill posters, however, were not selling any toiletries, cigarettes, or chewing gum. What was being advertised so insistently was the progress of production on factory and farm. One of those huge banners pointed with pride to the fact that the "Red Heroes' Cable and Wire Factory Exceeded its Quota by 21 per cent," winning a citation from Stalin. Thus the pulse of industrial-technological progress under the Second Five Year Program was taken and reported day by day or broadcast by radio at the street corners. Here propaganda replaced our omnipresent commercial advertising in America and was as ubiquitous. Often it was used to "sell" social welfare; some of the big street signs urged the public to improve their personal hygiene: "Brush Your Teeth with Toothbrush and Powder"; or: "Fight Syphilis." Thus the all-seeing and paternal regime exhorted and prodded the people to become both more sanitary and more productive. And apparently they needed prodding: only a decade ago the Russians were about 80 per cent illiterate; now the advance of education had reversed these proportions.

The industrialization of the country was going forward rapidly; but I could see that in a backward country pursuing the socialist program, without ready capital, it could be a terribly costly and arduous business. Heavy sacrifices were demanded of the people: they must create savings to provide for future growth by postponing present convenience, by enduring shortages of food, clothing, and consumer goods. Thus a good part of their labor and primary produce was set aside to be "invested" in new machines, factories, railways, and power sites. Hence the Soviet regime borrowed American methods of mass publicity to popularize the over-all economic program. These reflections about the *Massemensch* in Russia came to me as I prowled about Moscow alone.

I often tried to evade the earnest little bureaucrats of the Intourist Service who were supposed to chaperone me, for I enjoyed wandering off course and mingling with ordinary Moscow crowds in the street or in those old cellar cafés reeking of stale beer and *kvas*, where I was sure I saw characters out of the pre-Revolutionary days of Dostoevsky and Chekhov.

Late one night I took supper at the old Savoy Hotel, whose dining room was decorated in nineteenth-century gimcrack style, even boasting a gilded fountain with carp swimming in it. Three Army officers sat guzzling Georgian champagne at a table near me. At one point they all arose and went fishing in the fountain basin, using a little net provided for the purpose. Each in turn tried with unsteady hands to net a fish but kept losing it. I joined them, got their permission to try my luck, and in a moment drew up a fine big carp.

The officers were delighted with me and insisted that I join them to drink some bubbly wine in honor of Soviet-American friendship. Imperiously they called the head waiter to sit down with us and act as interpreter. Our three-way conversation became a hilarious affair.

"I am commandant of the fortress of Chabarovsk in the Maritime Province of Siberia," said one in the uniform of a colonel. "You are a good fisherman and an excellent fellow. You must come and be my guest. All that your heart desires will be yours, the best food and drink. You can stay as long as you please."

"But I'm a married man and must go to Paris in a few weeks to meet my wife," I explained. "What would I do without the company of a woman?"

"Oh, *nichevo!* We have the most beautiful women in Siberia, and you can have all you like!" the Colonel said.

They were typical red-faced old wardogs, swapping stories about their exploits in the Civil War. The Red Army people were well treated in Soviet Russia, and they supported the dictator. But then Russia, with her too-accessible borders, had always been a sort of *place d'armes*. I wrote in a letter from Moscow: "Soldiers everywhere, marching in good order, young, cheerful, warm in their greatcoats that sweep the snow, and singing in fine ensemble."

§   §   §

Amid the dislocations of the Revolution what had become, I wondered, of the old upper class? I had met some disconsolate exiles in Paris and New York, even admirals and generals. Here they were not easy to find. But in my hotel the thin, tired-looking chambermaid who cleaned my room proved to be a woman of aristocratic origin.

Putting aside her mops she approached me and whispered: *"Qu'est-ce que vous pensez, monsieur, de ce sort de société qu'ils font en Russie?"* She went on: "If you could only know how we have suffered. I was a governess in a noble family of Moscow, and am myself of an old family. Now I am but a charwoman!"

I said something commiserating about my hope that the new regime in time would moderate its severities and know how to be just to all the people. The lower classes, I remarked, had suffered much under the old czarist order. The woman looked angry and, with some exclamation of discontent, flounced out of the room.

How many hundreds of thousands of the *déclassés* and dispossessed were there in Russia, I wondered. This society had not yet found peace within itself. The American newspaper correspondents I met in Moscow reported that there was widespread unrest among the peasants forced into the collective farms.

I now exerted myself to get about and observe things on my own. With a fellow American, the excellent Charles Emhart, then a roving correspondent for the Baltimore *Sun* who had his own interpreter, I was able to go on several journeys that were planned according to our own ideas. Another American, a Midwesterner of Slavic descent who spoke Russian, kindly volunteered to serve as my guide on tours of factories in the Moscow region. I could go where I wanted, he promised, and ask any questions I pleased.

We rode out to the biggest steel plant in the vicinity, the Hammer and Sickle Works; it employed twelve thousand men to turn out finished steel products and structural shapes. Formerly an ammunition factory, it looked old-fashioned and untidy compared to our mills in Pittsburgh or Detroit. The director, a short, swarthy man with huge mustaches and wearing a brightly colored tunic, proved to be well worth knowing. He answered my questions with wit and showed political sense.

"I am one of the old Bolsheviks," Comrade Murashev said with pride. He spoke apologetically about his old-fashioned plant, observing that completely modern steel works had been built recently in the Don Basin and the Trans-Ural country. But still some improvements had been introduced here too. When he had first come to work here as a young man the hours had been twelve per day, and the hired hands slept in a rude dormitory within the factory compound. Now, under the Bolsheviks, hours had been cut to seven per day, and the men lived in a new cooperative housing development outside the plant.

As I left the director's office to tour the place he said to me, with a grin and a twinkle in his eye: "You will be at liberty to inspect any part of our factory—even the *toilets*. Perhaps you may not find everything suited to your American taste; we are still in the midst of changing things. But we have a Russian proverb: 'A person's home should not be judged by the condition of its watercloset.'"

I burst out laughing when this remark was translated to me. It was exactly the antithesis of our American credo, advertised in all our family magazines, that a person's home *is* to be judged by the immaculateness of its bathroom. I had seen in our own factories lavatories that, as late as 1929, would not bear close inspection. The dark cloacae of the Hammer and Sickle Works, however, were in a class by themselves, as the knowing director had forewarned.

This steel plant proved to be a perfect mixture of obsolete and modern machinery—a mirror of Soviet Russia's stage of transition. In some departments the pace of production seemed slow; in others automatic machinery, such as I had seen in America, stamped out steel rods or wire at high speed, the men merely manipulating the red-hot shapes with long tongs into conveyors. These machine workers told us they were "Stakhanovites" earning high wages for rapid output at the piecework scale. The socialist ideal of giving to "each according to his needs" was thus discarded in favor of incentive methods.

Director Murashev had laid great stress in his talk with me on the leadership exercised by cadres of communists in each department of his factory. Constituting about 10 per cent of the personnel they guided and supervised their fellow workers; after hours they also carried on a busy program of "social work" in the factory club and housing development. The comrades could put the fear of the devil into wayward workers. On the other hand some aspects of their activity appeared evangelistic: if a fellow got into trouble, or beat his wife, or drank too much, a committee of his communist shopmates would visit him and say: "Cheer up! We wish to help you." No man must be left alone, even if he enjoyed his private misery. It was not so much that Big Brother watched you (as Orwell would write later in 1984), but that a lot of Party brethren tried to look after you constantly, which could be consoling but also an irksome form of regimentation.

Soviet socialism, in short, was anything but utopian; it was made to work, under the command of the iron-willed Stalin, though obviously at great cost. There were no secrets of industrial technology that these Russians could not master. After World War II great masses of the formerly "backward," now awakened, Asians and Africans would be attracted to the arduous Soviet program of self-development.

In the thirties the way of socialism evolving from a capitalism in a state of collapse, or girding for war, strongly appealed to many of us as a "higher" though more difficult form of organization. As I wrote in retrospect, after returning from Russia:

> To speak truthfully, the socialist revolution for most men always has been the *hardest way*, and as much of its appeal to human courage and ingenuity may reside in its difficulty as in its promise of justice; while capitalism seems the "easiest way," the way of profit. The one system demands a self-denial, self-sacrifice, responsibility without commensurate rewards, new habits of cooperation and discipline; the other stamps its price upon every human quality, hiring and firing men or ideas according to the criteria of the market place.

With the coming of industrial technology, to be sure, man everywhere suffers loss of freedom and lives under the tyranny of the factory whistle. This thought came to me in 1933, and was borne in upon me again in 1949 when I was visiting Czechoslovakia, behind the Iron Curtain. I was stopping in an ultra-modern hotel, overlooking a beautiful planned city in a mountain valley, a city built around a single industry: it was that of Bata, the largest shoe factory in the world, now nationalized. After much fatiguing talk with visitors to a late hour, I had dropped into a sleep troubled by fear dreams when suddenly—after only a few minutes, it seemed—I was awakened by a mighty howling and sobbing sound that filled all the region around me with its tremendous flood of decibels. A powerful siren had gone off, and the surrounding mountain walls magnified the sound. I leaped up and ran to the window to look out. We were then at a stage of the Cold War tense with expectation of atomic disaster. Was this some fateful signal I heard? In the gray light I could see large crowds of people marching along, but quite calmly; they were going to work at the huge factory, whose siren had sent forth its first call at 6:30 a.m.

I was distraught and angry at this rude awakening. But in that community of thirty thousand souls people had to live with that fearful siren every day of their lives. Whether capitalist or socialist, a factory whistle is a factory whistle.

III.

After some ten days had passed in Moscow I began to feel let down. The food was dull, and I could not have my uncomfortable hotel room changed for another. I felt also some discouragement at my poor attempts to learn all about this enormous country in a few weeks without knowing the language. To be sure, I gathered some intelligence by joining the group of foreign correspondents at their cocktail hour; but that was not enough.

My hope had been to meet Russians of my own sort with whom I could establish myself on a friendly footing. To this end I had brought a few letters of introduction, signed by a leading communist writer for the foreign language press in America who had shown some interest in my books. One of these letters was addressed to VOKS, the organization that maintained international cultural relations; but at their headquarters a dignified woman official told me—rather coolly, I thought—that I would hear from them "in due course." Two or three letters addressed to contemporary Russian authors I had forwarded promptly on my arrival; but I had neither replies nor telephone messages at my hotel.

Then I recalled that those letters (whose writer had translated them for me) described me as a "liberal bourgeois intellectual." This was candid and proper; but I began to wonder if that appellation "bourgeois intellectual" hadn't spoiled everything for me. Would any respectable Soviet Comrade dare to invite me around?

One evening I left the newspaper men whom I used to join at the bar of the National Hotel to go to eat in its ornate old dining room. Here I tried to order supper in my dictionary Russian, but the waiter could make nothing of what I said. A man with a neat Van Dyke beard and a rather sensitive face, dining at an adjacent table, then addressed me in faultless English, asking if he could help me with my orders. I assented, thanked him, and he invited me to join him at his table.

He gave me his name as Mirsky; later I learned that he was the Prince D. S. Mirsky who with his White Russian family had gone into exile in England more than fifteen years ago. He had lectured as an authority on Russian literature at Oxford University and published books in English. A year before our meeting he had decided to return to his native land and pledge his loyalty to the Soviet regime. Mirsky was dressed in clothes of good English cut and, though somewhat reserved in manner, had much charm.

He wanted to hear of recent developments in American literature; I spoke of my desire to meet Russian writers, saying I thought I could learn a good deal about life in Russia through persons of my own calling whom I could meet on common ground. I also alluded to the fact that no one had replied to the letters I had sent, mentioning two or three names.

"Some may be away, but that one is certainly in Moscow now, and I am sure he would enjoy meeting you," Mirsky exclaimed. "If you like, I'll telephone him and some others and ask them here."

Thus Prince Mirsky broke the ice for me; within a quarter of an hour a novelist I had written to and a couple of poets came to join us at the hotel. After that I was never without the company of Russians.

One of those I met through Mirsky was Bruno Yashensky, a slender, dark-eyed man of Polish descent, vibrant with nervous energy and very fluent in speech, who was then a successful author of the new Soviet breed. In his youth he had lived in Paris among the Surrealists, and we found we had old friends in common, especially Louis Aragon.

(203)

It was exciting to discover that, although we had grown up thousands of miles apart, we had undergone much the same orientation. In youth we had been for all that was experimental and of the avant-garde; but, at the end of the twenties, we had each turned away from Surrealism to face the growing crisis of our time. I believe that, despite differences in national origin, we enjoyed the sense of a perfect meeting of minds and of sharing a common cultural heritage.

At our first encounter Bruno Yashensky said to me in his forthright way: "We like each other! As long as you are in Moscow you must come to my house every night without fail and dine with my wife and me and our friends." The food, he promised, would be better for me than the fare in Moscow's restaurants. When in return I invited him and other Russian writers to dine out with me, they all politely refused. I then realized that, as communists, they did not care to be seen at hotels or other public places frequented by foreign tourists, black-market profiteers, and other "criminal types."

At his apartment Bruno and his wife, who was also a writer, habitually entertained from a dozen to twenty guests with the old easygoing Russian hospitality. His latest novel, a study of the cotton-farming region in the south of Russia, had sold six million copies, not unusual for Soviet authors, and so he was spending all his royalties. "Who wants to save money?" he exclaimed.

Thanks to my new-found friends it was quickly arranged that I should go to the theater every night as a guest of the Theater Club of Moscow, accompanied by an interpreter. In a word, life in Moscow was opening up for me.

In a letter of January 1934 I wrote:

During several evening gatherings at Y . . .'s, where the conversation, for my benefit, was largely carried on in French, I found the talk very good and the animation of literary life as I had known it before only in Paris in the early twenties. Moscow, vibrant, crowded metropolis, with its sixty professional theatres, its numberless publications, its restless brains, and late hours, Moscow now becomes the *ville lumière* which was Paris. Moreover the swarm of distinguished exiles driven here by the proconsuls of barbarism in Germany gives to society in Moscow a pronounced international character, which is in itself of the highest interest. I have found the Russians charming and very outgoing in their social life. They are not only an intelligent people, but they know how to amuse themselves.

IV.

The questions I addressed to my new acquaintances in Moscow were: How did writers, artists, and theater workers adjust themselves to the altered social values of the Soviet regime? And was it true that they were "artists in uniform" writing only propaganda in the form of Marxist fictions?

It was quite evident to me that there had been a powerful official campaign to align all writers in support of the regime. According to the manifestoes of the Russian authors' organization all literary work was to be judged in accordance with its tendency to negate or affirm the Revolution. The whole prewar school, typified by the émigrés Ivan Bunin and Alexander Kuprin, had been condemned as "pessimistic" and "antisocial." The poet Boris Pasternak was not banned, but I hardly ever heard him mentioned, though he had become known abroad. Books by such people tended to disappear from circulation, and so life became somewhat difficult for their authors, though they were not otherwise molested.

The tendency novels I was reading, at the time in French or German translations, told the stories of new factories or collective farms; or the "hero" might be a hydroelectric station! While a few authors of eminence, such as Sholokhov, still wrote historical fiction treating of the recent Civil War after the literary method of Tolstoy, most of the current literature about the age of Stalin, with its heroic tractor drivers or plant managers, seemed as mediocre and as much given to sentimental optimism as our own "bourgeois" *Saturday Evening Post* fiction of yesterday.

From Serge Tretiakov, who was then a leading figure in the school of Socialist Realism, I heard the official view stated in somewhat exaggerated terms that I found unwittingly funny. As novelist and playwright Tretiakov then enjoyed an international reputation,

(205)

his drama *Roar China* having been produced with success by the Theatre Guild in New York in 1930. Like Mirsky he was of the upper class; after years of expatriation in China, however, he too returned to Russia and embraced the communist faith.

Tretiakov was an odd figure of a man, then about forty years of age, six feet tall, fair complexioned and blue-eyed, with his long pate so closely cropped that it gave the effect of a piece of ivory from which hung two large ears. Clad in English tweeds, he affected rather novel zipper-lined pockets that he pulled open and shut as he talked. His apartment, in a new building, was decorated in the aseptic international style; he was, in a word, a man of the modern fashion and his literary views reflected this.

"In my youth," he told me, "I wrote twenty-five hundred poems about fairy princes, roses, and sunsets, all of which I took out of my head. The Revolution changed me. Now I write about facts, *Facts*, FACTS. Henceforth all literature must be based on facts, and nothing may be invented out of a writer's fancy."

At that time Tretiakov was writing about the *kolkhoz;* he traveled all about visiting the new agricultural "factories," reporting on their progress and also establishing local newspapers in those rural communes, since the demand for reading matter of all kinds was overwhelming. He pointed to a formidable pile of books, plays, and pamphlets on his table, all completed in the last two or three years.

I ventured an objection: such subjects as the development of the poultry trust (one of his topics) seemed appropriate material for reportage. Yet I doubted whether journalism could permanently supplant the appeal of creative literature in all its range. I wound up: "When you have done the histories of forty factories or a hundred *kolkhozes,* what then? What about the rest of life, the human drama, *l'homme moyen sensuel* and his little pleasures and sorrows?" In a word, I was thoroughly skeptical about planning for literature to support the communist establishment. I also expressed doubt that the reading public in the West would be interested in such topical novels. In America as in western Europe many writers, far from welcoming the advance of mechanization, deplored it.

Tretiakov replied: "In your bourgeois countries industrial technology is a dull or distasteful subject, since its products are intended only for capitalist gain." But in the Soviet view every significant achievement by socialist workers and engineers was *"eine Sache der Ehre"*—an affair of honor or glory. Theirs was like the religious passion that possessed the crowds of artisans who built the cathedral of Chartres in the thirteenth century.

It was in the capitalist nations that the majority were really kept at "forced labor" (!) from which they could derive neither interest nor hope for the future, while only a minority drew the lion's share. At a time when there was much propaganda about forced labor in Russia, Tretiakov tried to turn the tables on us.

"Your typical bourgeois citizen," he went on, "dreams only of a millennium in which he will have enough money to work two hours a day and leave twenty-two hours for his hobbies. But to the Bolshevik work is creative, purposeful, unselfish."

Decidedly Tretiakov was long on wit and paradox. I learned from others that he was not a member of the Communist Party but only a recent convert who was trying to work his passage by appearing "more Bolshevik than the Bolshevists." (In the end, it did not save him.)

The excitement in Russia over the Five Year Plans recalled the days in America after the Civil War when our people migrated to the frontiers, built new cities, and spanned the continent with railways. During my stay in Moscow I heard much of a big project being rushed through by a team of writers, commanded by none other than Maxim Gorky, who undertook to compose in short order a documentary history of the building of the great Bielnostroy Canal. This new sea-level channel, 225 kilometers in length, was dug in only twenty months' time by 100,000 prisoners of the *Cheka,* or secret police, the prisoners being mainly thieves and vagabonds, but also rebellious peasants. The regime offered criminals or political prisoners hope of early release and restoration to citizenship if they labored well. The writers traveled about the big canal interviewing thousands of the forced laborers and also studying the records kept by the police. Yashensky spoke of the affair as "a great romance of the masses," a victory for the Soviet method of penology. "Think of it!" he exclaimed, "thousands upon thousands of former criminals, outcasts of society, made useful, redeemed."

The Russians boasted exuberantly of their new Dnieperstroys ("the largest power dam") and their new industrial cities, much as pioneering Americans in the nineteenth century boasted of new Californias and railways at our "festivals of the Golden Spike." Our own constructions too often became the subject of gross public scandals, but the Soviet writers had no misgivings about their "empire builders." I wished them well, though I expressed reservations about this literature.

In the United States many writers worked willingly under the "collar" of the mass circulation magazines; such writers were well paid, while the nonconformists lived from hand to mouth. Under a socialist dictatorship literature came under more severe restriction, and the question gave me more and more concern (as will be seen). My own heroes of letters were the great nonconformists, and their lot had not been easy under any regime.

In articles I published on my return to America in 1934 I reported that the young Russian writers seemed mad with enthusiasm over the conquest of their frontiers, their "Wild West" in Siberia; but I added that the celebrants of these modern miracles limited themselves mainly to reportage in fictional form, which, as literature, seemed much inferior both to the work of their own older generation and that of our modern school of writers in America. A period of revolutionary upheaval is seldom favorable to great art, as witness the years of the French Revolution and the Empire.

V.

During my second week in Moscow one of my new acquaintances took me to see Serge Eisenstein, whom I regarded as the world's leading exponent of the modern art of the film. The spacious, old-fashioned apartment he occupied, near the Bolshoi Theatre Square, had at one time been the home of Dostoevsky. Its living room had been turned by Eisenstein into a library filled with books in free-standing rows of shelves.

Eisenstein, a small, stocky man with keen eyes and a huge domed forehead—half of him seemed head—came trotting out to greet me in good English, and said: "But I know your writing very well. One moment—" He then went to one of his book shelves and, to my surprise, came back with a copy of my *Zola and His Time*. During his stay in America two years earlier, he told me, he had had the idea of doing a film on Zola and the Dreyfus Case and had written a script based on the narrative of my book. "I wanted terribly to make that film," he said. But the Paramount Company had finally rejected the project; Eistenstein left Hollywood and went off to work on a film in Mexico.[1]

Serge Eisenstein was not only a fine talker bristling with ideas; he was a man of uncommon versatility who brought many skills to his art. He conceived of the film as an extension of the theater, breaking out of its frame into a larger space thanks to the mobility of the camera. Having been trained for theatrical production, he brought to his films the modern Russian theater's "pictorial" style of stage architecture and choreography. The film, moreover, presented to his mind opportunities for heightened pictorial effects by the use of montage, or by dividing the screen into separate panels—"as in the paintings of the old Flemish artist Memling," he remarked.

How did he compose his film dramas? I asked. Eisenstein said he began by saturating himself in long studies of the settings and the people chosen as his material. For the film *S.S. Potemkin* he lived for many weeks among sailors on a Soviet warship; for a film about a village he settled for a while among peasants—much like Robert Flaherty preparing his documentary drama of the Eskimos, *Nanook of the North*.

Eisenstein's search for new depths of realism in the film were inspired, he told me, by Zola's novels. "Zola got marvelous physical effects of atmosphere into his pages, even the very smell of things. He used to become ecstatic over garbage, even excrement." Eisen-

---

[1] Several years later an excellent film, *The Story of Émile Zola*, was made in Hollywood after my book, by the well-known director William Dieterle; however, I would have given much to see what Eisenstein would have done with the same subject.

stein's ruling idea was, by exposure to and study of life itself, "to search constantly for the deeper political and social meanings reflected in a given social stratum or group of people—for I believe implicitly in the philosophy of Marx." Out of such studies some simple dramatic theme eventually emerged from the situation itself.

More recently Eisenstein had become interested in James Joyce's *Ulysses* and its stream of consciousness method; the Joycean interior monologue, he thought, offered fascinating possibilities for film treatment. It was obvious that Eisenstein only toyed with the idea of such experiments, for he was quite aware of the censorship overhanging film directors. Though a Marxist, it was plain from what he said that he had no use for propaganda in literal form.

I spoke of my own distaste for the topical plays and films I had already seen, each carrying its oft-repeated political lesson, and I candidly mentioned the views of foreign commentators on Russia's "artists in uniform." Eisenstein remarked that the situation was "parallel to that of the early Italian artists who were obliged to paint New Testament subjects, crucifixion scenes, or portraits of the Virgin Mary, over and over again as propaganda for the church, yet performed their task with effects of infinite variety and beauty."

Through the Moscow grapevine, I had learned that Eisenstein was out of favor just then with the managers of the Soviet film trust, and possibly with Stalin himself. This genius among film directors was therefore not being assigned to the production of any films at present but limited to teaching. He had incurred official displeasure because during years of travel he had come back with empty hands, following disputes with the "vulgar" Hollywood magnates, and afterward with Upton Sinclair's group, which had backed his project in Mexico. His political stock sometimes fell, but it also rose again. It was said that he feared no man, not even Number One, and was as strong willed.

I asked Eisenstein what pictures he planned for the future. He answered deliberately: "I am working up a historical film, a biography, so to speak, of a great city through the ages, in fact Moscow—from the time of Ivan the Terrible to—" he hesitated.

"To the time of Josef Stalin?" I interjected.

Eisenstein turned on me, glared, and, suddenly raising his voice to a theatrical shout, cried: *"How dare you couple those names together in my presence!* There is no connection between them whatsoever, I tell you. The subject of my picture is from the time of Czar Ivan to a recent period, perhaps 1917."

I was momentarily astonished at his sudden change of tone; then caught my cue, and said in a loud voice: "I apologize. I expressed myself inadvertently, merely to indicate the span of time."

Was it possible, I wondered, that this renowned artist was held under surveillance? Did the walls have ears? He had certainly spoken "for the record."

His manner changed abruptly again; very much the actor, he was grinning amiably as I left. I thought that in the hour I had spent with him he had surpassed in clarity of thought and range of interest anyone I had ever met in the field of the dramatic or plastic arts. In wartime he was to rise again with his historical film dramas. After World War II he was reported to be in disfavor again and living in retirement; he died of a heart attack in 1951.

§   §   §

At last, after having been absent on a journey, my old friend the artist Elie Lissitsky, whom I had known well years ago in Germany, turned up at my hotel and we embraced each other like long lost brothers.

Lissitsky, now in his forties, was a small man of slight figure, with a beautiful round head, delicate features, and brilliant eyes— a quite remarkable Russian-Jewish type, all integrity and idealism. I always felt surprised at the contrast between his composed manner and low voice and the dynamic power of his "classic-abstract" paintings; they were architectural engineering inventions functioning along clean lines of force.

During the 1917 Revolution Lissitsky had served as a partisan of the Bolshevists and later taught art at the Academy of Leningrad. In the terrible winters of the Civil War he had contracted tuberculosis and gone to Germany to be cured. In the twenties he enjoyed an international repute as one of the school of Constructivist painters. As he was a thoroughly Westernized Russian and we had been warm friends "outside," I counted on learning much from him about the actual situation of artists in this society.

The news of himself was that he had been married a few years earlier, and his wife, a German woman, had borne him a son. Because of his health he lived in the country, and he invited me for the following weekend to his house at Schodnia, twenty-five miles out of Moscow.

On the appointed day I managed to make my way to the October Station and climbed into the little branch-line train running to his village in the steppes. The train was so crowded that most of the passengers lay on the floor or dozed on top of their luggage; they seemed the most cheerful, patient, and friendly ragamuffins in the world. When I could see out through the frosted windows there was a marvelous sunlit landscape of snow-covered steppes cut by strips of deep woods, mostly of evergreen and white birch. It was like riding through Wisconsin in winter.

At Schodnia, Lissitsky was on hand with his infant son, and we trudged a half-mile over the packed snow to his place. Lissitsky's house was a simple rustic structure heated by great porcelain stoves. Its living room had a section set apart as his studio.

What of Lissitsky's art? He told me frankly that four or five years earlier he had given up painting entirely. Since then he had been fully occupied as technical director of Red Army publications, charged with the designing of books and magazines and their illustration.

What a great loss this was, I thought to myself. Ten years ago, when we were together in the liberal German Republic, Lissitsky was inspired by his mission as artist. I also felt that his Constructivist pictures, organized around machine symbols, had qualities of prophecy—the engineer's dream of industrial design, of the good art of the future. Like the Bauhaus Dessau group under Walter Gropius, with whom Lissitsky had close ties, he seemed bent on "saving the world through art." Perhaps their dream was too functional, too mechanically neat and aseptic to be true. Yet the rising socialist society badly needed the new architectonics, the modern artifacts that men like Lissitsky might invent. I had recently seen some shows of contemporary artists and found them wretched imitations of the nineteenth-century academic. Lissitsky admitted that the approved style of painting was retrograde.

"But how could you bring yourself to give up your painting?" I protested. I was not the only one who regarded Lissitsky as one of the foremost abstract artists of his era.

"No, the time for all that has gone by," he said with his fine sad little smile. "Perhaps some day, after I am gone, we will come back to it." Meanwhile he had enlisted with all his artistic equipment in the battle for Soviet Russia's survival.

"It is as if we are at war now," he continued gloomily. "A great war is certainly coming." He foresaw a rearmed Germany under Hitler invading Russia. Therefore he had put aside all "individual interests"; his talents were now nationalized. "This has been a period of self-sacrifice which many of us have voluntarily accepted, because we know it is necessary and worth while. We know what price we are paying."

This was the last time I saw my friend. In the winter of 1941, when the invading German armies approached Moscow, Lissitsky and his family migrated eastward during the great stampede from the Moscow region; he, an invalid with only one lung, did not survive the rigors of that tragic time.

§ § §

I was now a somewhat pampered foreign visitor, going to the theater every night as the guest of the Moscow Theater Club, accompanied as a rule by a woman interpreter speaking English or French. The curtain would rise at six or seven. With some discomfort I adjusted myself to the odd Muscovite schedule of late hours fixed by their short days in winter. The women interpreters were very polite, though reserved. I felt aware that they observed certain conventions, established not only by public opinion but by the omnipresent secret police, and tried to be as discreet as possible.

One evening at the theater my interpreter happened to be a tall, pleasant-looking blond woman of about thirty, with a Russian name, yet speaking faultless English. She was in fact an American from Philadelphia, of Quaker background; she had come to Russia a few years earlier and married a Russian theater director. Comrade

(213)

Anna B., a blue-stocking type, assured me that her happy domestic life was not very different from that of the average Philadelphian.

That evening we were also invited to a banquet and concert at the Theater Club. It was held toward midnight at the marble mansion of a former merchant prince whose ballroom was arranged like a private theater. The whole Moscow film and theater community as well as the foreign press corps were there; and, as usual at such functions, the Russians did themselves proud. Though the masses might live on slim rations, we enjoyed Gargantuan portions of Russian salad and vodka before sitting down to a groaning board for supper. Serge Eisenstein presided in his liveliest vein as master of ceremonies, alternately speaking English and Russian. I had Comrade Anna to my right; on her right sat a big swarthy Russian, whom she presented to me as the commissar of the theatrical industry; in other words, as she whispered, the big boss himself. I was impressed and thought I must try to be as diplomatic as possible, smiling at him occasionally; when he smiled it looked as if he were scowling.

We ate and drank copiously. As for the commissar, the more he drank the more gallant he became to Comrade Anna sitting between us. He held her hand; I asked her what fond things he was saying. She murmured in English that he was very drunk and insisted that she go home and sleep with him, which she refused to do.

"But are you permitted to refuse such an important personage?" I asked. Perhaps he considered he had seigneural rights, and her job as well as that of her husband—who was on tour—depended on the commissar. But Comrade Anna said with resolution that she was going home, come what may, and she wished that I would see her home.

We rose to go. The commissar also stood up and threw his arms around my interpreter as if to detain her. I forgot all my good resolutions, put my palm to his chest, and shoved him back. The commissar looked astonished, turned red in the face, and really scowled at me. There were people all around us, and I was afraid we were going to have a public tussle. It would mean, I feared, that I would be clapped into that old Lubianka Prison someone had pointed out to me the other day. But my opponent, with some angry expression, turned on his heels and went tottering off. Walking the streets of Moscow at 33 degrees below zero we nearly froze before we found one of the scarce all-night taxis, with which I delivered my charge safely to her home.

The next morning I worried a bit about that commissar being vengeful and setting the police on my trail. But all such anxieties were set at rest by a carefree young American named Ed Williams, whom I met around that time. Williams was a hardy young Yankee—one of the new breed now migrating to Moscow instead of to Paris—who could outwit any Russian bureaucrat. Within a few months he had learned to speak their language, and he knew all the ropes. Despite the housing shortage he boasted a comfortable apartment that he stocked with scarce food, wines, and liquors. It was through him, I am sorry to say, that I learned to ride about Moscow by jumping on and off the rear steps of crowded street cars, without fighting my way through the mobs of "pregnant" women inside—and without paying fare, as bad boys used to do in Brooklyn.

"But the police will surely arrest us," I said. "The GPU 'knows all, hears all, sees all.' "

"*Nichevo*," Williams laughed. "Stalin doesn't bother about small fry. It's easy to get along in Russia if you have the know-how."

Williams, a student at Eisenstein's cinema school, had made many friends among Russians of his own age, and as I expressed eagerness to meet such persons he arranged a party for my benefit, the other guests being theater and cinema people. On that occasion I met several members of the younger generation with charming manners, but singled out for special attention an enchanting-looking young film actress. I was in the susceptible condition of a lonely traveler who had not seen many pretty faces lately and now found myself happily dancing with a golden-haired lass named Tanya or Natasha. We had been eating a very mixed *salade russe* with vodka and wine; with every nip I invented fresh compliments for my partner. In other words, I pressed the siege from the start.

In the gentlest way in the world the lovely young thing rejected my advances, informing me that she had a fiancé she loved. "I am a

Komsomol," she wound up with an air of great earnestness. "We young communists are more serious than our people used to be: we believe in love, we marry, we stay married." And with these words she made her departure, pleading an engagement.

I was all broken up; I thought nothing could console me after the departure of this Tanya, or was it Natasha? At that very moment another and much older woman stepped before me and began speaking in rapid French. She had been introduced to me earlier as a singer in the Moscow Opera Company; with her large frame, poor complexion, and long nose she appeared rather frightening to one in my condition (lamenting Tanya). Meanwhile she impulsively seized me in her arms and began to whirl me round and round in a rapid waltz—played by an accordion—and I soon began to feel rather faint. While she danced me about she kept crying out with dramatic emphasis: "*Vous êtes mon type, je vous aime bien!*" She insisted she must see me often during my stay in Moscow, in fact, that very night.

Decidedly she was not *my* type. The wine, vodka, and smorgasbord, and the mad dance with this aging chanteuse as well, all seemed too much for my poor head. I remember asking myself what an inoffensive American could do to escape the clutches of an excited Russian diva. At that point I simply passed out. When I came to it was three in the morning, all the guests had left, I was in Williams's bed, and he had removed my shoes. That kindly young man then took me for a walk in the snowy streets and we had some food in a nearby café.

VI.

Playgoing in Moscow proved rewarding, not only because the Russians seemed born actors, but also because the contemporary theater, far better than official guides or newspapers, furnished me with insights into the actual morals and manners of the Soviet people.

Their "classical" theater exemplified by Stanislavsky's company and the equally famous productions of Meyerhold, to be sure,

avoided baldly propagandistic material. I was invited to attend a
rehearsal directed by Meyerhold of a play by Ostrowski depicting
Russian society of the 1860's; it was treated by him as a sharp
satire of the old ruling class. He had his actors miming everything
in mannered, almost rhythmic style. There would be the scene of
a country squire wooing a rich Moscow lady; periodically their
dialogue would be interrupted by having the curtain descend and
a lantern-slide projection thrown upon it with a printed legend
representing what the suitor was actually thinking of: for instance,
the amount of marriage dowry he expected. Meyerhold explained
to me that this innovation was adapted from the subtitles of silent
films and constituted an experiment in conveying interior monologue.

At the Theater of the Revolution, however, I saw the work of
younger directors who gave themselves entirely to topical or
propagandistic plays. We witnessed all the trials of a young factory
director, his plant in continued crisis, needing money and new
machinery. At the Wachtangov Playhouse, devised as a theater-in-
the-square, I attended a play whose subject was the violent conflict
over the introduction of collective farms among the Don Cossacks.
The play about the factory had interlarded with its political scenes
some episodes of sheer entertainment: the wives, in a chorus,
pining for their husbands who were forced to work all night, singing a Russian version of the "Empty-Bed Blues." So in the play
about the rebellious peasants, there were comic episodes of singing
and dancing in which the players fairly "stopped" the play.

Arriving at the Wachtangov with a new interpreter, a small
Russian woman, I found the foyer completely filled with a crowd
of young factory workers whose club had subscribed to the performance. For a full hour the play was delayed, while these young
people carried on an impromptu concert and dance in a spirit of
almost hysterical gaiety. I had never seen so much high jinks in all
my life as these reputed "slave laborers" carried on.

As we were leaving that theater there was a terrible crush at
the exit. The corridors were very narrow and became thoroughly
blocked at the site of the two small cloakrooms. Several hundred
persons began to push and shout, while trying to collect their outer

clothing. The cement floor was slippery; as the people in the crowd kept shoving each other a whole mass of them fell down, their legs waving in air. By main force, and in the nick of time, I just managed to pull my companion out of the crush to a safe corner.

Little Varvara, my interpreter, a pale intellectual type, suddenly drew herself up to her full five feet and began to cry out in a tone of command: *"Ne Sovietsky! Ne Sovietsky!"* and shouted orders to the crowd. She explained to me afterward that she had protested because they were behaving in a manner "unworthy of Soviet citizens" and had threatened to call the militia. Those burly factory workers sheepishly arose and formed into line. Children of peasants, they had not lived in cities very long nor gone to the theater often. The scene of panic gave me food for thought about the problems of controlling such masses and the way the communists among them imposed order.

Meanwhile, Varvara was full of expressions of gratitude because I had saved her from possible injury in that stampede; formerly reserved in manner, she unbent and became quite friendly. Some of the best talk I heard about the actual situation in Russia came from her, as she was both informed and intelligent. On the night before my departure she agreed to dine with me and appeared at my hotel in a silk dinner dress of prewar vintage. Finding me, however, thoroughly sick to my stomach and in no condition to go out, she stayed to help me, ordering medicine and seeing to my comfort.

I sat up in bed drinking tea and tried to sum up for her the impressions I had received: I felt happy to have seen something of "the great social experiment of our time," and had no doubt that the people of the Soviets would one day fill up their country with big machines and even skyscrapers. But I had my reservations: under the regimented Soviet order one felt large arrears in human amenities; private life was unfortunately circumscribed, allowing too little room for individual variation and the play of the creative; in the name of *raison d'état* everyone was assigned to his post and there was little free choice. After all, our interest in economic reorganization lay in securing sufficient food and shelter so that some day we might *stop thinking in terms of economics*. The material improvements the Soviet people pursued, for which they made heavy sacrifices, were only means to an end, a proximate social justice. But the thinkers of the Renaissance and the Enlightenment had held that the great end was that "men should be as gods," liberated by their knowledge of universal nature and achieving their highest fulfillment in the language of the arts and science.

Varvara, a product of Russia's educated middle class, understood very well what I meant when I spoke of having missed in Russia "the old amenities of individual life" enjoyed in the West. Nevertheless, she declared that the advantages I described must necessarily be sacrificed for the present "in order to change the world." Everyone sensed that war impended, she said gravely; "Later, perhaps, we will enjoy the 'freedoms' of which you speak."

The Popular Front was emerging in 1934. The Soviets, then making overtures to the League of Nations, were aligning themselves with peace-loving men and gave promise of serving as a strong bulwark against the fascists. Many then shared the views of Sidney and Beatrice Webb that in the new Soviet society reposed "the hope of civilization."

I had certainly been made aware of the harsh bureaucratic discipline imposed upon the whole country. Students of Russia with whom I talked after returning to the United States were then agreed that a strong, centralized government seemed highly necessary in order to hold that huge nation together in these threatening times. But in the years that followed, the Stalin regime, instead of relaxing its severities, became ever more rigorous.

When I had returned home I wrote to several persons I had met in Moscow who had befriended me. To my surprise no one ever replied to my letters, not even my old friend Lissitsky. In November 1934 occurred the mysterious assassination of S. M. Kirov, commissar of Leningrad and one of Stalin's principal aides. After that the climate of the U.S.S.R., which had been almost tolerant, completely changed. During the Purge Trials that came two years later, accompanied by many secret arrests and executions, nearly all the persons who had received me hospitably in Russia— Borodine, Yashensky, Tretiakov, Meyerhold, and Mirsky—disappeared.

Chapter Eleven

~

France and Spain: The Republics in Danger

THE INTERNATIONAL TRAIN from Moscow to Paris not only traversed the map of Europe but, at almost each border, carried the traveler into a different stage of history. From the area of planned socialism under harsh conditions of life in Russia you passed the next morning into the country of poor farm villages and slattern ghettoes at the Polish frontier. Warsaw was a handsome city, but its streets seemed filled with beggars (eliminated in the U.S.S.R.). Crossing into Germany you came to another era: the neat countryside and cities reflected a higher standard of living than East Europe's, but the political regime was of the fifteenth century. Where were the *gemütliche* Germans, the "good Europeans" I had admired in former years? Though warned not to do so, I would have liked to stop over in Berlin; but whom could I talk with? A few months later, when I chanced to visit Italy, I had the same dismal thought: the people looked as genial as ever, but there seemed to be none I could really communicate with. Marinetti, the Futurist poet who once amused us, was now writing such bloody nonsense as: "War is beautiful because it creates new architectures, such as the heavy tank . . . the airplane, the spiral smoke of burning villages, the passion-orchids of machine-gun fire. War is beautiful because it serves the greatness of great Fascist Italy."

After an absence of five years I could measure how much

Europe had changed. Whole populations were now ruled by the new "Machiavellis of the masses." Journeying through those countries was like attending an outdoor university where one learned the theory and practice of crisis politics.

To arrive in Paris again was to return to my "second country," and its old gray houses and palaces were as gracious as ever to the eye. I felt, nevertheless, disenchanted; the ancient city of the arts, the "capital of literature" which had inspired us in our youth, had somehow, like France herself, shrunk in my estimation. Her citizens seemed too self-regarding and unaware of what went on outside their small world. I found it hard to speak to them of the arduous adventures that the hungry Russians were undertaking, or even of my own muddled America where national problems were at least being attacked on a big scale. The Parisian had always the laughter of indifference; even the catastrophic changes in neighboring Germany seemed "desperate but not serious."

Each time I returned to Paris I used to ask myself if I could ever be as happy as in my youth here, when I sometimes had to live on two meals a day. After World War I the twenties in France were a time of hope. Now I felt that a malaise hung over the capital, as if emanating from the soft rain clouds overhead.

When I asked the poet Philippe Soupault how he would define the difference between our Paris of yesterday and the Paris of the present, he ventured: "When you first came here soon after the long 'stupid' war ended, we were full of joy; it was as if we had won a reprieve from a death sentence. We were interested in everything, we wanted to be *alive* above all, and we were. Paris was international and also pro-American. Now she has gone back to her old ways, to being entirely French, even provincial!"

To call Paris provincial was the supreme insult. But Soupault went on: "Paris is dead, dead, dead. In France we have gone back to being a small, petty-bourgeois country ruled by narrow ideas. But in Russia, as in America, things are done on a continental scale, and the people of both have a large view of things." Soupault had recently published a novel bearing the Cassandra-like title: *The Last Nights of Paris.*

Other old friends I found again one by one: Tristan Tzara, the

first among the Dadaists, was at the same table in the same café.
The Surrealist painters André Masson and Max Ernst were working
in new styles of their own invention. The poet Robert Desnos,
looking a bit drugged and with great pouches under his protuberant
eyes, had quit the camp of the Surrealists; his divertingly licentious
and "Sadistic" verses were now chanted in night clubs and broadcast by radio. (Desnos, however, had reserves of courage, and was
fated to die as a martyr of the Resistance Movement in 1945.)
Roger Vitrac continued his experiments as he had for ten years in
the "theater of the absurd," in which he was the precursor of his
friend Jean Anouilh. However, the experiments which once fascinated me seemed to have no point in this time of deepening
crisis.

Some of these old acquaintances met in the cafés had a way of
shaking my hand with the utmost languor while their eyes looked
beyond me to admire themselves in the mirrors on the walls. Those
hands sometimes felt like the appendages of Egyptian mummies.

The Parisian carries his boredom like an invisible cross to be
borne in this world; he is perpetually unsurprised to see you or any
one else turn up again at the same café after a long absence; and
he dispels enthusiasm by laughing deprecatingly at himself or
politely at you. The prevailing mood of my old Paris friends could
be described in one word: indifference.

Ten days after my return, my wife arrived by boat. I had looked
forward eagerly to our reunion here, for she had not only been the
undaunted companion of the difficult early years, but had also
shared fully our intellectual adventures of that time. I wanted to
go about everywhere with her, retracing our steps together.

"Why is Paris so sad for us now?" we kept asking each other.

The truth was that our friends of years past, the persons who
had made life here good for us, had changed and were divided into
quarreling factions. In the late twenties the rump of the Surrealist
School led by André Breton had determined that it was not enough
to undertake—for the sake of art and literature—to change men's
minds, but they must henceforth join the Marxists in trying to
"change the world." Breton and his followers had therefore tried
to make common cause with the Left. The high Communist Party

officials, however, had proven inhospitable to these literary "snobs," whom they considered antisocial. Breton ended by giving up the Stalinists and aligning his group with the exiled Leon Trotsky. As this was a very limited minority movement, the action of *"la Révolution Surréaliste"* remained fairly Platonic—except in the case of Louis Aragon.

Aragon, who had shared with Breton the leadership of the Surrealists, toward 1930 had become a devoted member of the French Communist Party and one of its leading lights, now serving as managing editor of their daily newspaper, *Humanité*. However, most other members of the Surrealist group opposed affiliation with any political party at the time. The choleric Breton denounced his old friend Aragon as "a traitor to the human spirit"; Aragon in turn attacked Breton and company. In short, it was a free-for-all in which everyone "excommunicated" everybody else—one of those "wars of art" that Paris had often known. Under the circumstances I found it expedient to see only one faction at a time; then I would go and listen to their adversaries. It was all very solemn and also absurd.

I was curious about the sudden conversion of Aragon, my oldest friend in Paris, and went around to his newspaper office to hear his story. When I had last seen him, several years earlier, he had been the literary secretary of the millionaire couturier and art patron Jacques Doucet, enjoying a sinecure that was cut off when Aragon turned communist. He told me that his change of heart dated from the time in the autumn of 1928 when he had met the celebrated Russian poet Vladimir Maiakovsky in a Paris café. That tempestuous Russian was accompanied by his wife and also her sister Elsa (Kagon) Triolet, formerly married to a Frenchman. Aragon was not only deeply impressed by Maiakovsky and his "collectivist" poetry, but was even more affected by meeting Elsa Triolet, whom he married not long afterward.

With Elsa, Aragon traveled to Russia to attend the Revolutionary Writers' Congress of 1930; it was his intention to persuade the official communist movement to accept his French group, the Surrealists, as their allies. But he ended by reversing himself and announcing his full adherence to the Communist Party "line." The thought had come to him that he had hitherto occupied himself only with aesthetic revolt, and had been a kind of verbal nihilist engaged only with "words, words, words" and "saying nothing beautifully, with the utmost freedom of expression." Now at last he saw the true path—and Elsa's influence had counted for much—though it meant a complete break with old friends such as Breton. In testifying to his new faith Aragon published a long poem, *Front Rouge*, denouncing his government, its Army, and its police, and calling upon his own people to emulate the men of 1917.

Front Rouge was a pure revolutionary act, and it was also poetry in the declamatory style of Maiakovsky (very different from Aragon's later classical lyrics of the Resistance period). Its lines of inspired invective were rendered into English by none other than E. E. Cummings. In Paris, meanwhile, the Minister of the Interior in 1931 proceeded to have Aragon indicted and tried for sedition and for defamation of the Army. The trial itself became an occasion for some typical French theatrics: the tall, handsome poet sat proudly in the dock looking like a fallen angel, asking none for mercy, though if convicted he was liable to ten years in prison. As I read of his trial in the newspapers I could not help seeing the parallel with the case of the rebellious Julien Sorel, in Stendhal's *The Red and the Black*. (It was the book Aragon had given me to read in 1921, when I asked him what the young men believed.)

During the trial two hundred of France's leading scientists, scholars, and writers—and Maurice Chevalier too—signed petitions or testified in behalf of the poet and against "the persecution of a poetic text." The judges found Aragon guilty, but they suspended sentence. He walked out a hero of the left.

Aragon's whole way of life changed: the young dandy of former years had lived in poverty for a time; then he turned into the responsible editor of a large newspaper. I found him much occupied by detail, often interrupted by telephone calls, and yet—as if his mind were compartmented—able to give me a connected narration of all that had taken place in the years since we had last met. Nowadays he had to travel off to meetings of miners in the north and read them his poems, or join in the communists' street demonstrations in Paris. In a word, he was no longer addicted to "mere literature" but was a public figure, one of the big wheels of what was becoming the largest political party in France. Consequently I felt a new kind of constraint in speaking with him; his was now the voice of an organization; the old easy exchange of confidences was no longer possible. I was (and am) extremely fond of him, and I honored him for his public spirit; but I saw that I could not, like him, surrender myself wholly to the discipline of any political body.

II.

During our first walks together in the last days of January, my wife and I repeatedly found ourselves caught in the midst of street riots that started up unexpectedly in the St. Germain quarter, adjacent to the Chamber of Deputies. By pulling up the iron grills over the gutters or around trees and taking up street benches, the rioters would soon have a little barricade set up; a few minutes later the police would arrive and charge the crowd blocking the boulevard. Or a young man would heave a brickbat at a street lamp and there would be a crash of splintered glass followed by the screaming of police sirens. Riot squads would leap from their vans and begin pushing the passersby along the curb, shouting: *"Circulez! Circulez!"* On several occasions we were caught between the fists of the demonstrators and the batons of the police and had to extricate ourselves as nimbly as we could. In one scuffle we were driven into a doorway together with a stout, respectable-looking old citizen who barked at the police: "Circulate yourself! I'm standing at the door of my own house, why should I move?" It was funny to see how offhand typical Parisians could be with their police.

At first it all seemed good clean sport. But after a while we realized that a rather sinister sort of farce was being played in the streets; the principal actors were not unemployed persons but extreme rightists inspired by the royalists, or proto-fascists, known as the *Camelots du Roi,* joined by groups of veterans who had begun to imitate Hitler's bully boys. These people were calling for the overthrow of the Republic.

For about a year the public had been all stirred up over the Stavisky Case, an affair of government construction contracts in which some government officials had been accused of accepting bribes from Stavisky, a Frenchman of Polish descent, who, faced with indictment, had committed suicide. A formal judicial investigation was now being pursued. The whole business involved but a few million dollars filched from the Treasury, but extravagant charges were being aired in the press that the entire Chamber of Deputies was guilty of bribe-taking, and people were shouting and fighting over the issue in the streets, and even, oddly enough, in the theaters of Paris.

On my arrival in Paris from Moscow I had noticed men scuffling outside the Comédie-Française, in the Palais Royal quarter, and being led away by police. They were playing Shakespeare's *Coriolanus* in a new and free French translation, and to my astonishment the audience emerging from the theater seemed to be engaged in fisticuffs over Will Shakespeare, three centuries in his grave! Shakespeare's tragedy of a Roman autocrat in conflict with the democratic crowd had been done over by a tendentious translator-playwright who took liberties with the text in order to discredit parliamentary institutions. Some passages in French seemed even to bear directly on the Stavisky scandal: "Well, then, are you willing to sell the consulship—how much?" Thus day after day people brawled violently in the classic theater of the Avenue de l'Opéra or outside its doors; the faction of the left shouted for suppression of the play while the royalists vociferously defended the antidemocratic translation. No such fracas over Shakespeare had been seen here since 1823, when the anti-British passions of the crowd caused Stendhal to write: *"La politique est une pierre attachée au cou de la littérature."*

In that season of vexation almost any issue, even old Shakespeare, could be made cause for a riot. Meanwhile the middle-road ministry carried on with its usual policies, raising taxes and cutting the salaries of 800,000 federal employees.

My wife and I then frequented the Café des Deux Magots on the Boulevard St. Germain, usually the rendezvous of writers and editors working in that quarter. Now the place became the focal point of the royalist-fascist rioters, a crowd of fancy men with sharp clothes and pomaded hair. They were loud-mouthed nationalists who looked and talked of their dislike for foreigners, especially Americans; as they drank and rolled their dice on the tables they boasted of the riots they were going to stage, so that not only we could hear them, but also the plainclothes policemen detailed to follow them around.

The royalists had not ten thousand adherents in all Paris, yet they stirred up the whole city. Moreover, the police "suppressed" them so gently that one could have said they picked up those young men's hats for them while taking them into custody. When, however, the restive communist crowds gathered in force on the other side of town, the same police faced them with drawn revolvers. M. Chiappé, called the "fascist" Chief of Police of Paris, was widely accused of being the cause of this partiality for the right-wing agitators. He came frequently to the Deux Magots, where both his detectives and the royalists were congregated, to check up on things. At his entrance the royalists cried out their welcome: "*Chic pour le Commissaire de Police—Hurrah!*"

Within thirty days France saw two Premiers resign. The current ministry, that of Edouard Daladier, pressed by the left-of-center parties to dismiss Chiappé, finally did so on February 5, 1934.

Underneath all the confused emotions lay a deep anxiety about the future relations of France and Germany. The French were sharply divided along class lines; but the majority dreaded a new war with Germany. At little bars all over France I heard mechanics, clerks, or peasants saying "We'd as lief go to a madhouse as go to the front again!" The cost of victory in 1914–18 had come too high.

I had completed arrangements to start on a long journey by car to southern Spain, beginning February 6, with the intention of both resting and working there. That morning my wife and I drove by the Palais Bourbon where about a thousand policemen were drawn up to protect the Deputies within. At the Pont de la Concorde I could see crowds of people assembled, just standing about. Traffic at that point was thick, but the police allowed us to go through. Many people on foot were hurrying along to cross the bridge and join the crowd on the other side. I felt a sense of excitement and strain in people and policemen, but drove on. The rest of the city was quiet, and I continued south on the road to Chartres. There, at nightfall, we heard over the radio reports of the bloody rioting in the Place de la Concorde and at the bridge leading from it to the Chamber of Deputies. Some adventurous individuals among the groups of veterans had turned up with arms (a short time after I had driven by) and the shooting began. The Paris crowd, which had swelled to enormous proportions, went berserk; several were killed and scores of persons were wounded.

Driving down all the length of France toward Spain during the next three days I found people jammed in the central squares or the Grande Rue of the towns, listening to the radio and arguing heatedly, but keeping order. At cafés or garages along our route, shopkeepers and mechanics said to us in outspoken fashion: "You have come from Paris—eh? What games are they up to there? Fascists?—We'll take care of them all right!"

In the crisis days of February 1934, France seemed on the verge of a fascist coup d'état but quickly recoiled. The vast majority was then on the democratic side, while the imitators of the Nazis proved wholly unequal to carrying the country. Moreover the CGT, the nation's trade union body of five million, held a general strike of one day throughout the country as a mass demonstration against the native fascists. On that day, February 10, my wife and I marched in the big trade union parade at Bayonne near the Spanish border. A new coalition ministry was soon formed and used emergency powers, but it respected the democratic sentiments of the people. In the next year the government was swung toward the Popular Front led by the socialist Léon Blum. The rallying movement in defense of democracy prevailed for a while before the onset of war. But in the dark days of 1934 we, who still clung to our idea of the French as the people of the great Revolution, were tormented by our doubts and our fears.

III.

During five years after 1933 I could not shake off
the foreboding that a second world war was being prepared in
Europe, and that America would become involved in it. (In the
sixth year, that of the Munich Pact, the foreboding became a
certainty.) In those days we toured about with the feeling that we
were taking last lingering looks at the old Europe, and therefore we
cared less to examine old monuments or ruins of the past than to
observe history in the making and, in some measure, to read the
future.

In Spain the Revolution of 1931 had reversed the trend to
dictatorship and seemed a good augury. The Spanish had thrown
out Primo de Rivera and their King Alfonso as well, bringing
forth their new liberal republic. Thus we drove down the French
coast eager to see a "renascent" Spain.

Although the provincial towns of France had looked shabby
compared with metropolitan Paris, our hearts really sank as we
crossed the border, rode through the back streets of Irun and saw
its dark slums, its beggars, its children with diseased eyes, its ragged
women still carrying water on their heads. The moment one crossed
into this arid region one felt a steep drop in the standard of living,
so that even the south of France seemed by comparison a rich and
green land.

Of course we encountered the antique Spain of shepherds,
shepherdesses, and muleteers; on the road toward Castile there
were walled villages, romanesque churches, and all the ruined
castles you could ask for—always set at the crest of the red clay
hills, against the hard blue sky. Entering the single long street of
Tolosa, a large Basque village, we found a carnival in progress and
the narrow way blocked by crowds in native dress, for it was Mi-
Carême. These peasant people bore themselves with pride; when
they smiled all their teeth flashed. Soon a little crowd, laughing
and singing, surrounded us. Our way forward was barred by a large
painted cariole, decorated with paper flowers and bunting; musicians mounted on it played guitars and accordions. A young woman
in mask and domino sprang down from the vehicle, ran to my car,

threw her arms about me and kissed me. I returned her kiss and threw some coins to the band, after which we were permitted to drive on.

Our old French car kept breaking down repeatedly, so that, seeking help, we were thrown upon the mercies of the plain people of the hills. Sometimes a bullock driver came to the rescue; on one occasion a young schoolmaster bore me away on the handlebar of his thundering motorcycle to fetch a mechanic ten miles distant, and all the while we carried on a shouted conversation about the state of the republic. The Guardia Civil, those armed men in green uniforms and shiny patent leather hats, stopped us frequently to search our car for contraband arms, explaining that bandits, anarchists, and Reds were all about, and that "semi-martial law" had been proclaimed. Life in this republic was not as simple as it appeared on the surface.

At last we threaded our way into the central quarter of Madrid (where people were holding carnival in the streets), and stopped at a hotel in the Puerto del Sol. I had a letter of introduction from Louis Aragon to Rafael Alberti, one of the leading poets of Spain, and sent my message along the next morning. Promptly that afternoon came a pale, thin young man, the journalist Emilio Delgado, who extended to us Alberti's welcome and brought us to his home for tea.

To our surprise the young poet and his wife were quartered in a modern penthouse apartment in one of the most elegant sections of town, its terraces offering grand views over the Western Park and the surrounding mountain ranges. Alberti, the most winning of men, received us with great warmth. He was a native of Cadiz, then thirty-two, short but of athletic figure, with brilliant dark eyes and handsome and regular features, looking so much the glamorous young poet that one wondered if it could be true, as I had heard, that he had won all the prizes and was accepted as the peer of men like García Lorca and Antonio Machado and a leader of the young generation in Spain. But when I heard him read his work, and managed with no little labor to read and translate a few of his poems for myself, I was impressed by one whose language carried so much authority.

A group of a dozen young painters and writers were on hand that evening, the respectful disciples of the *chef d'école*. After meeting them we were presented to the poet's wife, Maria Theresa León, who was just then suffering from arthritis and so reclined on a chaise longue. She was a dark-eyed Castilian beauty with a mass of golden hair, fair complexion, and the finely modeled features of some antique Roman matron. Maria Theresa was also an accomplished author.

One of the first things Maria Theresa said to my wife and me was that as long as we stayed in Madrid we were to come to her home every day at the same hour and "meet everybody." She also commanded two of her young courtiers to conduct us about the city and show us all its treasures, as well as its working-class quarters which, she said, we would find uncommonly amusing. Thereafter Dario Carmona, an artist, and Emilio Delgado (who was a native of Puerto Rico) became our daily companions and guides.

The young men of Alberti's circle were of the middle class, but they represented a cross section of Madrid's left intelligentsia. I had not met a more attractive group in any of the capitals of Europe since the time of our twenties in Paris. All of them had what I came to think of as the Spaniard's art of friendship; they were infinitely hospitable and thoughtful of us, and without affectation in being so; they had in their talk a romantic vein, and also a special humor deriving from Madrid and its people, at once genial and astringent.

We walked about the city with our young companions, questioning and being instructed. Thus we caught some of the feeling of the times and of the history of this old city so often touched with tragedy. We saw the azure sky of Madrid through the roofs of burnt-out churches; and that was history made visible. Our friends also gave us their account of the 1931 Revolution.

Following years of depression and popular agitation against Spain's retrograde government the monarchy had apparently disintegrated out of pure weakness. On April 14, 1931, the Republic was proclaimed; the common people, exultant, came out into the streets (as so often before), while the rich drew down the iron curtains of their shops or hid themselves. Leaders of Spain's extremely conservative Catholic Church had spoken out in a provocative way against the popular revolution, and in anger the anarchists had sacked and burned churches here and there.

One could hardly find a country more divided by class feeling. The workers and peasants had a long account to settle with the big landowners and the church people who were large landowners; the capitalist class also showed much animus and fear. Since the 1870's the syndicalist teachings of Bakunin had become deeply rooted in large sections of the workers and peasants, who carried on the class war by direct action. Yet the Revolution of 1931 passed off virtually without violence and, in the view of my young Spanish friends, almost as comic opera. Within a day or two everyone was back at his job, and the liberal republic began its shaky career under Manuel Azana *et al.*

"In Spain," one of the young men said to us with the Madrileno's irony, "an insurrection may begin on a Friday; the people may fight in the streets all day and perhaps the next; but Sunday is a day of rest and, by tradition, the revolution stops. The women go to church; the men go to the bull ring, the bordello, and afterward to the café."

Emilio and Dario pointed out that the conservative classes had been thrown into a panic by the Constitution of 1931-2, which disestablished the Church, and they had formed a coalition of extreme right parties. In 1932 the Army generals had made a bungling attempt at a coup d'état, easily crushed by Premier Azana. The military plotters were let off too lightly and survived to try again in 1936. The recent elections in November 1933, however, when women voted for the first time, had proved disappointing, for the conservatives gained seats in the Cortes in numbers disproportionate to their total vote. A center group of ministers now governed Spain, but turned more and more for support to the Catholic-conservative bloc.

The left groups were now said to be moving toward a united front of the liberal parties with the two labor organizations, the Socialists and the Anarcho-Syndicalists—though these too were old rivals. The Anarchists' labor body, the Confederacion Nacional del Trabajo, or CNT, with 1,500,000 adherents, however, still refused to participate in the government. There was now much fear that the present ministry might bring the implacable "Jesuit" Gil Robles into the cabinet; and Largo Caballero, the socialists' leader, had threatened that in that event all the workers of Spain "would come out in the streets as one man." Meanwhile nothing was settled; reforms were postponed. Small fascist groups, imitating Mussolini's Black Shirts, showed themselves bolder in street brawling with every day that passed.

Returning to the Albertis we heard the poet declare that the Republic of 1931 had utterly failed to carry out its promised social reforms, especially the division of land among the peasants. What Spain needed was economic planning and a thoroughgoing reconstruction. In his highly rational view, there was nothing romantic or mystical about the poverty and underdevelopment of Spain. Alberti was angered by those who believed that his people could just go on living as whimsical Don Quixotes. During a journey to Soviet Russia a few months earlier the Albertis had met Maxim Gorky, and they protested that too many visitors to Spain, including some Russians, saw in their country "only a picturesque old land full of Sancho Panzas mounted on their little asses." Whereupon Gorky had commented: "But we have a great many little asses in Soviet Russia too!"

"There is surely going to be a blood bath in Spain," Alberti said with an air of finality. I was incredulous; I too had the foreign visitor's initial impression that among the Spanish there would be much talk but little of getting down to business. However the leading Madrid newspaper was publishing news stories of food riots, payroll and bank robberies occurring in different parts of the country, under the standing head: *Los Conflictos Sociales.* These repeated incidents were interpreted as part of a systematic campaign against the establishment directed by the Anarcho-Syndicalists.

Meanwhile the charming young men in the Albertis' drawing room could be heard almost any day talking in debonair tones of political assassinations committed (or threatened), or of how they proposed to arm themselves when the need arose. They smiled, they talked of such matters as regrettable but unavoidable. The lovely Maria Theresa remarked in the same offhand manner: "Things are growing serious for us here; the stupid police have been paying us visits, searching for incriminating papers, finding nothing." These young people confidently expected that they would soon have to go into the streets to face the enemy.

"And you too?" I asked the golden-haired Maria Theresa. "Will you go out into the streets to fight?" She replied calmly, but with resolution: "Yes, I too, so far as my strength will permit."

But the well-born Maria Theresa, I reflected, was made to ornament a salon, and the glamorous Rafael to read verses in his fine baritone, as a lion of the lecture halls. Were my Spanish friends pulling my foot, I wondered? In Paris in the twenties the Surrealists resorted to some ghoulish conversational humor, in the style of Sade, and we used to laugh over it. So, at first, I refused to believe that the Madrilenos' revolutionary talk was to be taken seriously. But in truth my incredulity was unjustified; Spain had been addicted to civil strife, especially in the form of separatist rebellions, throughout her history.

One afternoon a young man rushed into the Albertis' drawing room with news just off the press wires that the Austrian workers in Vienna had risen against their government. The Catholic fascist Dollfus had attempted to disarm the socialists, but they were defending themselves with desperate courage against regular Army forces. Rafael quickly turned on the radio for late news of the battle at the Karl Marx Hof. As more and more people arrived, Alberti got up on a chair to address them with an impassioned speech accompanied by marvelous gestures. The workers at last had begun to fight, he exclaimed, instead of yielding themselves passively to the fascists. Could not Vienna be the flame that would ignite all Europe? Everyone cheered for the embattled socialists, and as Alberti turned on a record of the *Internationale* they began to sing. A wave of joyous emotion swept that small band.

A day or two later came news of the defeat of the Austrian workers, and my friends' joy turned to mourning. The lights of popular government in Europe seemed to be going out: Italy, Germany, and now Austria. "It must not happen here!" the youthful Madrilenos said with somber resolution. They seemed to me romantic, given to fine gestures and florid speech. I relished their enthusiasm; but only after more time had passed did I begin to see how dark was the prospect for them. As an American, accustomed to a well-policed nation, I felt aware of the tension of class hatred and the disorders afflicting their society. To them it was an old story. And now, as in past epochs, Spain was waiting for the hour of conflict.

Visiting the magnificent Prado Museum, we had before us the images of Spain's past which, to our minds, projected themselves into the present and merged with it. On another occasion the El Grecos, which made the very walls palpitate with their violence, would have been the high point of our visit. However, what I had really come for this time was Goya.

We were now permitted to view the paintings of Goya's old age, those of the "dark period" of his nightmare visions—long hidden from the public—of a Spain at war with the invading armies of Napoleon from 1807 to 1812. These were funereal and "expressionist" canvasses of immense size rendered in a prevailing black— sometimes even black on black. They were frightening, in contrast with the brightly colored pictures of his earlier days we had seen in other rooms of the gallery, the merry carnivals, the bullfights, the dancing gypsies. For the aged Goya there were only the "disasters of war," massacres and debauches, humans with the forms of fiends. Such were the last thoughts of the lonely and rebellious genius filled with an undying hatred of Church and monarchy. Would not these black chimeras appear again over Europe, we wondered?

One morning our friends Emilio and Dario took us to visit the Cuatros Caminos, the teeming quarter of Madrid's proletarians and the repair of the anarchists, which had often been the city's focal point of unrest. We found it a district of homely tenements, but inhabited by a smiling people who seemed to live outdoors in the sunlight that drenched their grimy courtyards and alleys. Entering one of the local cafés our friends inquired for certain anarchists they were acquainted with.

Many of the poor workers had conceived a fanatical faith in the anarchists because they really put the fear of the devil into employers and landowners. In Spain the moneyed class had long enjoyed royal and clerical patronage and had been defended by an elaborate military bureaucracy with more generals than could ever be used; the poor could have no redress from them. They had also seen how successive governments of liberal or conservative politicians deceived them; but the anarchists' methods of direct action seemed to bring relief. The militant anarchists believed in proletarian revolt as their religion; they also found romantic excitement in operating through their secret order, the Federacion Anarquista Iberica, or FAI. It was not surprising that the syndicalist movement exerted a more powerful appeal in Spain than in any other country.

Dario, as a member of the Socialist Youth, told us that he disapproved of the anarchists, who rejected social realities in favor of their ideal of "communal" socialism in factory and farm. Yet he worked to effect a united front with them, adding: "They are sincere, they are brave fighters, but they are also romantic children. We must be patient with them and try to wean them from their acts of violence."

At last we found the two ringleaders we were looking for: one was a sturdy young fellow in striped jersey shirt, the other a wrinkled but wiry old man with bent back, dressed in a soiled smock and a beret. The older man was in authority here; he was described to me as a noted street fighter, quick with gun and knife. He talked with an insouciance characteristic of his breed, while his dark eyes danced. "When are you going to make a revolution in America? If you need help I have some machine guns hidden away." In or out of prison the man evidently enjoyed himself.

In reply to questions put by our friends, the two anarchists admitted that a little excitement was being planned in the district that very morning and that the rendezvous of their followers had been fixed for eleven o'clock in this square. If we returned in three quarters of an hour we would see some action. We agreed to return, and my wife insisted on staying with us.

After a walk in the neighborhood, we came back at the appointed hour and found our two genial anarchists stationed at the same café terrace fronting the square of the Cuatros Caminos. They pointed silently toward a little knot of people gathered at the opposite side of the square in front of some food shops. We walked across the plaza toward that spot and noticed several men filtering through the crowd and passing out mimeographed sheets of paper bearing instructions (as Dario explained). Then, at a given signal, the men at the head of the crowd, now greatly increased in numbers, heaved big stones at the shop windows. There was a loud crash; everyone began milling about, some pulling away the splintered glass while others reached for the food in the window or ran in and looted the shop, then took to their heels.

Dario now thought it wise to take us back to the shelter of a stairway leading down to a subway station, from which my wife and I could observe what was to follow with our heads at about street level. Our two anarchists rejoined us and explained the routine. There was an interval, a minute or two of complete stillness—like a slow-motion film—during which the crowd thinned out a great deal.

"Now everybody is watching out for the police—let them come!" whispered the older anarchist. Suddenly we heard an explosive sound in the distance beyond the square and ducked our heads; it was only a truck backfiring as it started off. After that three big police vans came roaring up with their cutouts open, then stopped. In the hard sunlight we could see police with carbines come out slowly, questioning a few persons, detaining one or two, everyone behaving as if nothing out of the ordinary had happened.

It was the first time I had ever seen, by special appointment, a planned disturbance of the peace. For the anarchists it was an everyday affair; bread riots were going on at points scattered all over Spain, marking the steady disintegration of public order. Thus, when we journeyed on to Andalusia we found our hotels carefully locked and bolted behind their walled gardens, and at their gates an armed guard pacing back and forth all night.

IV.

We drove southward to dazzling Granada high in the Sierras, with temperature at freezing, and then down to the Mediterranean shore. That journey over the mountains was made during the last relatively peaceful days of the Republic. The civil guards continued to search us for arms; one of their officers said in explanation: "The socialists and the other leftists are getting ready to revolt. Soon we will be shooting it out with them. Why? The left seeks control—they are very *bad* people."

On the contrary, we found the ragged peasants and shepherds of Andalusia, with few exceptions, charming. When our faint-hearted old chariot gave way on some remote part of the mountain road, someone would always come to our help or guide us to those who could. At last, spiraling down the steep southern face of the Sierra Nevada, we felt ourselves bathed in a flood of warm air; we came to the orchards and gardens at sea level, the land where the lemons bloomed, and also palms and banana trees and hedges of giant geraniums. Here we were in another climate, the subtropics, with the African shore visible across the straits of the Mediterranean. Spain is not one nation, but at least half a dozen separate regions divided from the others by the high *cordilleras*.

During two months that winter we were quartered in a small hotel at the eastern edge of Malaga, where our rooms overlooked a lush garden and the sea. Here I caught up with mail and some cablegrams that had been following me around Europe. Alfred Harcourt wired that a large book club edition of my last work could be arranged if I would consent to change its title, *The Robber Barons*, to some milder appellation. I replied that I preferred to keep the title as it was. In any case the book club edition was put through quickly, with the title left unchanged. This was cheering news, as our old French automobile had been eating up the funds of my traveling fellowship.

The morning after our arrival, a car driven by a chauffeur stopped at the gate and delivered a huge bunch of red roses for my wife, with a card of greeting from one of the persons to whom our friends in Madrid had written of our coming. Thereafter fresh-cut flowers arrived almost every morning of our stay. Their gallant donor soon presented himself in person and took us in hand as his particular guests and friends. He was Ramon, a handsome, olive-skinned Andalusian, turned out in smart sports costume. As the son of one of Malaga's leading manufacturers he looked just the sort of charming and wealthy young Spaniard women of the North often dream about. Withal, he was a serious fellow, devoting time and money to avant-garde literature and radical politics. His parents, he confided, were pious in their religion and fascist in politics; but he was fed up with the old order.

Through Ramon we came to know Malaga's gilded youth: journalists, teachers, musicians, and would-be writers, most of whom were without employment of any kind. They would meet in the forenoon and afternoon at the corner café near the waterfront that was their rendezvous and sit there over a coffee hoping that some friendly soul would arrive to pay for it. One of the nicest things about Ramon was the unobtrusive manner in which he always picked up his friends' checks.

In this moribund provincial society there were no careers open to talent. One of these young men, a large, stout man named Domingo, having won a place on the staff of the leading newspaper in town a year ago, had married but soon afterward lost his job, so that he and his wife had been forced to live with his mother ever since. Another named José worked for a small socialist newspaper but was paid almost nothing. A third was a professor at the lycée, teaching French and English literature; he was blessed with a fiancée, but never with enough money to marry her. I sometimes strolled with that lively young scholar in the beautiful public gardens by the port. About two paces behind us his little fiancée trotted along, and with her a younger sister and an aged duenna. The virgins of old Andalusia were still closely guarded, and with reason.

A life of unchanging boredom and idleness faced these provincial intellectuals without a future. Spain lacked both the enterprise of the United States and the dynamism of Soviet Russia. And so these young men sat in a group of five or six or more every day, "doing penance" at the café table, as they termed it; or they walked the same streets they had known all their lives, especially at nightfall, when all Malaga came out to promenade the main street of town and greet each other before turning in for their late supper. The only excitement for them was an occasional visit to the cinema or to the ancient music hall of Malaga down by the port, noted for its bawdy shows and frequented by prostitutes. The young professor who was waiting to be married—judging from his own reports—

(239)

evidently used his few pesetas for that resort, thus by his self-indulgence postponing further the time of married bliss. The conventional sort of Spaniard—though not the radicals—looked forward eagerly to the opening of the bullfighting season, a signal event in Malaga.

As for Ramon, that forward-looking young man of fortune, the "old Spanish customs" were out; he was then waging a stubborn campaign against the authority of his parents, who opposed his intended marriage to the woman he loved. This was Quinina, a young widow with a child, who worked in a business office as a secretary in order to support herself and so was the "wrong woman" in every way to Ramon's father. (That devoted pair were finally married, and even managed to survive the Civil War.)

One of the more eccentric figures among the local intelligentsia, who came to their café only at rare intervals, was the Andalusian poet Emilio Prados, a dark, slender man then in his early thirties and rather deaf. His talk was edged with a mordant humor. Though his poetry had been widely published and much praised, Prados assured me that it earned him almost nothing, and that he barely managed to subsist by writing occasional prose sketches for the newspapers. In the presence of our young blades, Prados said roundly that he hated the life of the town intellectuals. "They just sit in cafés and talk politics; or go home to torment their mothers and sisters and curse life; but they are lazy and never get anything done."

He lived alone, without family or women, in a hut on the beach at the village of Palo nearby. An evangelistic sort of Marxist, Prados occupied himself in helping the fishermen and instructing their children without pay. He invited me to visit him the next day and see how the poor folk lived there.

I came by an old bus to that tiny hamlet. It was situated in some sandstone cliffs, along a ravine that led down to the sea, and was made up entirely of caves hollowed out of the cliffs by the natives. In its desolate way the place was rather pretty. Going into some of the caves with Prados, I found that they consisted usually of one bedroom and a kitchen placed at the entrance. A family of eight or ten might live in such a cave, with only two beds between them, and yet pay a small rent to a landlord. The fishermen, while pulling in their nets, told me that on lucky days they earned five pesetas (then sixty cents) and on average far less.

A thin, sad-faced mother with a brood of children in her cave (which was quite clean) said to me: "The Republic might give us better homes to live in; it is the same as under the King. All we ask is something to eat." The children seldom attended school after the age of ten, but went out to help with the catch. I had never in my life seen such poverty as I saw here (save for a few other corners of Spain), and at this lovely, sunlit shore of white sand.

Prados whistled and a group of small boys came running to him and made a circle in the sand. They were half naked in their rags, their bodies covered with sores, their eyes diseased. Though several of them were ten or twelve, he said, most were illiterate; not only was he teaching them to read, but also to swim, for they scarcely ever bathed. Soon he had them singing; then he began reading stories to them. It was a highly informal class conducted in the open air, the sort Rousseau would have approved of.

I never saw this accomplished and profoundly unhappy poet again. Emilio Prados died in exile in Mexico City in 1962, not long after I happened to visit that city. I tried to call on him, but he was deaf and did not respond to my knock at the door.

I had seldom before lived in daily contact with the members of a provincial community, certainly in no place like Andalusia, whose natives assured me they were by descent a mixture of Goths, Moors, and Jews. Their different personalities all remained sharply etched in my memory, so that I might well have written a documented regional novel about them. Two years later their lives were completely shaken up by the collective tragedy of the Civil War. Some would play their part in the war as heroes, the others would behave ignobly, as I could have foreseen in each instance.

V.

We were not to leave without paying our respects to the bull ring. The spring bullfighting season opened on a Sunday in March with a great fiesta at which Spain's most noted matadors began their annual tourney in balmy Malaga before going north. Like all the poor and rich of the region, with faces washed and in Sunday clothes, we came to the oval-shaped arena of yellow sand and took our places at a good location in the center, close to the barrier. Domingo, one of the café intellectuals and a former journalist, acting as our mentor, kindly explained all the fine points of the action.

After the brassy musical overture, and the ritualistic procession of toreros and attendant picadors, the opening performance of the mounted toreador, El Algebeno, caught our eye more than anything else that followed. He was a tall horseman riding a great prancing steed; with his lance, afterward exchanged for a short sword, he overcame a rather indifferent, even puzzled-looking bull. After that decorous execution El Algebeno doffed his broad-brimmed hat and walked all about the ring, acknowledging the crowd's ovations, accompanied by a shower of ladies' fans, handkerchiefs, flowers, and men's hats. There was gore to see even at this mild curtain raiser; but El Algebeno was to provide us with far more excitement than we had expected.

After him came the more serious matadors, fighting on foot against more spirited animals and working very close to their deadly horns. Though knowing nothing about the art, I found myself helplessly fascinated by this deadly play. The bloodletting, the sense of danger, the pantherlike grace of the matadors, whose snug costumes displayed hips, calves, and torso in dancelike movement, all contributed to the pleasure of the spectators. The women and men alike ogled those supple gladiators.

Afterward I summed up my impressions of the *correos* as a kind of crowd orgasm, a priapic orgy in which transference of the sex impulse occurs amid a setting of violence and bloodshed. I calculated that many of the spectators must have spent the preceding Saturday night in bordellos, or with their wives, then attended church in the morning, and after having eaten and drunk heartily had wound up with the voyeurism of the bull ring, making quite a well-rounded program for all the senses. I was by no means the first to see the *correos* as a sexual rite; the left intelligentsia held it to be worse than any other opium of the people.

The mounted torero El Algebeno happened to leave the place before the last fight, just as my wife and I rose to go. He came up to our tier to salute friends, then moved on with long strides, a magnificent figure in his costume of gray and black.

We walked homeward along the sea, happy to be away from the bull ring. Across the street from our hotel was the big Caleta Palace Hotel where the bull fighters stopped. I had the thought of drinking some good sherry at their bar before dinner, and so we turned in at the entrance gate. Just as we arrived there we found a little knot of people in the driveway, all buzzing with excitement and among them several policemen and civil guards. They were talking of some accident; we heard the word "*muerta*" repeated. As we reached the door of the hotel itself we saw two litters being carried into an ambulance waiting there, the occupants being completely covered. The barman told us what had happened.

About ten minutes before, El Algebeno, who had taken the precaution of leaving the ring before the great crowd, entered his big Hispano limousine and, with his brother at the wheel, drove to the Caleta Palace. As the car reached the gate several men standing there with submachine guns opened fire. El Algebeno's brother was instantly killed and the torero himself was wounded, though he recovered afterward.

I learned that evening that El Algebeno maintained a big cattle ranch near Seville. Some months earlier a poor farmhand in the neighborhood, who had previously been accused of poaching, had stolen a sheep. El Algebeno himself happened to catch the man in the act and shot him dead. At his trial he pleaded self-defense and was acquitted. "But the anarchists' secret tribunal judged him, found him guilty and condemned him to death," my informant related.

At dinner that night a little bespectacled old lady from Belfast coolly told us of having witnessed the whole scene from her third-floor window. She had been looking toward the Caleta just as the limousine drove up, then saw the men waiting by the gate open fire and go running off. "I said to myself: somebody is being assassinated again. I saw it all with my own eyes," she wound up.

"And how did you feel when you saw it?" I asked solicitously.

"How did I feel? Why, I simply thought I was back in Ireland."

Chapter Twelve

~

The Washington Scene, 1934; The New Dealers

SPRING WAS IN FULL TIDE when I reached New York again and a pleasing change in the social climate of the United States was also noticeable. In the autumn of 1933, as I left the country, Roosevelt's expenditures for relief had just begun to take effect; the citizens had scarcely roused themselves from their state of funk. Now I could have sworn that the people in the street looked positively cheerful. Even if all was not as smiling as it appeared on the surface, the rate of business activity had risen about 50 per cent above the abysmal depths of January 1933; though there were still ten million unemployed, many had gone back to jobs and most of the rest were on regular relief rolls.

A friend had written me a few weeks before my arrival: "When you get back you'll hardly recognize your old country. You would be interested to know that the President seized all the Federal Reserve gold and got only a two-column head in *The New York Times*. . . ."

No President in our history had exhibited so much derring-do in trying out various schemes for expanding employment; none had ever dreamed of attempting central planning of the nation's industry and agriculture as the bold-handed Roosevelt was doing. And at every step of his program he tried, like a fatherly teacher, in fireside chats over the radio, to spread understanding of his program among the people; the new plans or slogans devised by the New Dealers,

(245)

such as "pump-priming," or "commodity dollars," or "crop allotment," became terms of everyday speech. So much direct intervention by the federal government in our economic life was unheard of,
and yet was managed as a sort of peaceful revolution. After having
seen something of Europe coming under the spell of the new
condottierri, Mussolini and Hitler, I found the America of 1934
led by its "gay reformer" a most heartening scene—at least at first
blush.

One effect of the crisis years was that the people were doing "a
heap of thinking" and, judging from their reading of books, felt
deeply critical of our capitalist system itself. They were just then
reading *The Coming Struggle for Power*, by John Strachey, in which
a doom was pronounced upon the free market economy; in *The
Merchants of Death*, by F. C. Hanighen and H. C. Engelbrecht,
they were learning all about the international arms traffic; and in
surprisingly large number they were also reading my own slice of
recent American social history. I found people on trains and buses
not only reading *The Robber Barons* but sometimes nodding themselves to sleep over it. To witness that was one of the privileges of
fame.

§ § §

Shortly after my return I was called to the office of *The New Yorker*
and commissioned to write a profile in three installments of General
Hugh S. Johnson, one of the President's chief lieutenants, then
much publicized as the "dictator" of the National Recovery Administration. *The New Yorker* had never previously printed anything on
a political subject save in jest, and hardly ever on anyone whose life
was not centered in the metropolis on the banks of the Hudson.
But now the existence of a New Deal was fully recognized even by
Harold Ross, though he declared its methods were beyond his com-
prehension. What was wanted was not only a portrait of Johnson,
but also a clarifying account of the actual working of the new government bureau he headed.

Nothing could have pleased me more than to go and post myself
in Washington for several weeks and see the new men and the new
methods of the Roosevelt administration. The NRA was evidently

its key operation, as Roosevelt had declared. We had also heard the most contradictory reports about the New Deal "revolution" since the excitement of the first hundred days of 1933 had subsided. Some said that it did violence to our free institutions, others that really nothing much was changed or not enough was being done. Still other reports held that the planning of Roosevelt and his aides for a partnership between government, capital, and labor was simply one hell of a confusion. But I wanted to compare whatever it was with what I had seen of total planning in Russia and with what I had learned in Europe of National Socialism.

Notable changes had taken place since my last visit to the capital city in 1929; the *personae* were strikingly different too. Then the place had been a dull provincial town; you could still see the old-style courthouse politicians who were on the federal payroll sitting around brass spittoons in hotel lobbies downtown and smoking their cigars in leisurely fashion. Now the capital was crowded with a bustling sort of people, most of them young; the city hummed with excited talk of big events soon to be announced, of new ideas that were to be tried out.

A sort of mass migration of university-trained intellectuals had been going on since Roosevelt's inauguration a year ago; the new men were lawyers, economists, social workers, engineers, journalists, and still more lawyers. In the past when there had been a change of parties a crowd of spoilsmen attached to the winning candidate usually descended upon Washington to feed at the public trough. That was the plan for the public service introduced in 1828 by Andrew Jackson, who had replaced office-holding Bostonians and Virginians with men of his own band. The advent of civil service reform in the 1880's had only moderated the political spoils system. But under Roosevelt the new breed of federal job holders was different, and it included a surprisingly large number of my own acquaintances, the sort of persons I used to see at *The New Republic* and even men and women of the literary profession.

There was for example my old friend and college classmate Miles L. Colean, a native of Peoria, Illinois, employed as assistant director of the new Federal Housing Administration. Colean had pointed for writing and published one novel, though with indifferent results, then turned to architecture. As building activity was all but halted, he had wound up in Washington. I also found Catherine K. Bauer, a tall and vivacious young woman formerly of the staff of Harcourt, Brace, now acting as a consultant to the Public Works Administration. Miss Bauer, under the inspiration of Lewis Mumford's writings, had lately become a student of modern housing. The book on that subject she was then completing in her spare time was to become a modern classic. One of my Connecticut friends, Robert Wohlforth, a graduate of West Point who had resigned his Army commission and published a novel, *Tin Soldier*, an angry satire of the military profession, was now using his military knowledge to assist Senator Gerald P. Nye's special committee investigating the munitions industry. Another young writer named Malcolm Ross, who would later publish *The Life and Death of a Yale Man* (1939), one of the earlier exposés of the advertising profession, was just then directing public relations for Senator La Follette's subcommittee on labor. Indeed a whole host of formerly impecunious literary men and unemployed journalists was now assisting one or another of the New Deal bigwigs or ghostwriting speeches for them. Washington brimmed over with youth, beauty, and talent, all living for the while in a state of euphoria.

Almost every evening there were cocktail gatherings where my friends the new bureaucrats met to talk shop and exchange notes on the progress of America's "peaceful revolution." These friends, each deeply engaged in his or her sector of the New Deal battlefront, eagerly gave account of their activities, their exploits, or their disappointments, and so helped me to understand what was going on here.

The Washington they described was even then a jungle of wirepullers, intriguers, and their lawyers. After a year of the New Deal, plenty of opposition had developed; the conservative "enemy" lay within the gates, directing the noisiest lobbies against current reform measures and dispensing quantities of money, whisky, and cigars for the entertainment (or bewilderment) of lawmakers. The New Deal's advocates, however, like little heroes were forever rushing to put their fingers in the dike at points where it threatened to give way. They would go to any lengths, as they related, to reach Frances

Perkins, or Harold Ickes, or Harry Hopkins, or Eleanor Roosevelt, or even—at the last moment—the President himself in order to squash some piece of skullduggery by the conservative opposition. The upshot would be a blast from some accredited aide of Roosevelt or a powerful speech in the Senate by the young La Follette or Robert Wagner of New York—of course planned and ghostwritten by my young friends—and the day would be saved.

Only the year before it seemed intellectuals of their type had been awaiting (like Whittaker Chambers) a revolution of violence, generated by riotous farmers and unemployed mobs. Now they appeared reconciled to the peaceful transformation managed by Roosevelt. They could not fail to see that the President was much given to the arts of compromise, yet they showed an abiding faith in him. "Sometimes we must wait a good while for our turn, but in the long run he comes back to us," one of the young government economists, Isador Lubin of the Labor Department, said to me. And another expressed what seemed to be the consensus of what the young zealots then felt: "Well, here in Washington, at least we are trying to *do something* about the Depression instead of just looking on."

The striking change in the whole complexion of the government bureaucracy has been remarked upon by historians as important in itself, though there has been little agreement on how it was brought about. Roosevelt as governor counted largely on the political professionals in his entourage, such as Louis Howe and James Farley. But he also used several university professors, such as Rexford Tugwell, Raymond Moley, and A. A. Berle, to help write his campaign speeches in 1932. After the election, Tugwell has related, the President-elect—to Tugwell's great surprise—asked him, Moley, and others to stay in his service and arranged to place them in relatively high federal offices. This in itself was something of an innovation. To be sure Roosevelt appointed a number of party hacks and donors of campaign funds as members of his Cabinet or ambassadors, but he included among them liberal Republicans like Harold Ickes and Henry A. Wallace. Then too he had called Professor Felix Frankfurter of the Harvard Law School to Hyde Park a few weeks before the Inauguration, consulted him at great length, and offered him the high post of U. S. Solicitor General in the Department of Justice.

Though Frankfurter had not been a member of the 1932 Brain Trust he had known Roosevelt since 1913, when he was Assistant Secretary of the Navy, and had corresponded with him after he became governor of New York. Among the group of university professors I used to meet at *The New Republic* in 1931 and 1932 Frankfurter and Tugwell, in contrast to the "wild young literary men" in that circle (including myself), had pinned their hopes on the regular Democratic presidential candidate.

On that occasion when the President-elect had Frankfurter with him at Hyde Park, he had kept him up until 2 a.m. asking him all sorts of questions about regulative commissions and banking and railroad reorganization and about revising the antitrust act. Frankfurter had had much experience in antitrust work under President Theodore Roosevelt and also as government lawyer under Taft and Wilson. Thereafter during many years at Harvard he had been a popular teacher of constitutional or public law. Frankfurter's wife, who was present with Eleanor Roosevelt at that conference, recalled that her husband, though very respectfully, had talked to the President "like a teacher to his pupil." But the President had enjoyed it. Though some had the impression that Roosevelt was shallow minded, he liked people with verve who threw ideas at him, and he often played by ear. Felix Frankfurter moreover was not only a man of resourceful mind, he also had an engaging warmth of manner and was disinterested in the advice he gave. Roosevelt wanted him near him in Washington, and hinted that he might end up as a Justice of the Supreme Court. Frankfurter however refused the Solicitor Generalship, and it would appear that his declination raised him in the President's esteem. He said he could be of more help to the President at Harvard Law School than in Washington and would be at his beck and call at all times.

The President freely used his services thereafter as an unsalaried volunteer and as one of his confidants. Roosevelt especially needed his advice in selecting competent or, occasionally, expert persons for new federal tasks; and here the professor proved most useful since he had long been a sort of talent scout, sending his law school graduates to jobs with eminent law firms or recommending them for government posts; his outstanding pupils were elected to be law clerks to his friends Supreme Court Justices Holmes and Brandeis. During long years after 1933 Frankfurter regularly commuted between Harvard University and Washington, entering the White House by the back door, staying there often as a guest, and sometimes by invitation listening in on important conferences. Roosevelt found in him a loyal friend who knew how to keep his mouth buttoned. Felix Frankfurter, for his part, deeply enjoyed being a "secret adviser" to the most powerful of modern Presidents.

For many years there had been President makers among us, often men of wealth linked with party machines, like W. C. Whitney and Mark Hanna. But more recently the role of the presidential adviser had assumed increasing importance. Colonel Edward House, Wilson's self-effacing confidant, had been one of this type. Something of a parlor socialist in earlier years, House had evidently been much influenced by reading H. G. Wells's novel *The New Machiavelli*, whose hero persistently seeks to become the intimate of men of power and to lead them toward Fabian socialism. Colonel House himself privately published a novel he wrote entitled *Dru*, in which he prophesied his own future role as the adviser of a President who, by stern reform measures, saves the country in a time of revolutionary crisis.

Toward 1914, when Frankfurter served as a law officer in the War Department, he had been the ringleader of a band of young intellectuals in Washington who, while dining and wining together every night, talked up all sorts of burning issues and in an effort to influence national policy tried to set new reform ideas in circulation. At that time his friend in court was Justice Louis D. Brandeis, who also acted as a confidential adviser to President Wilson. It was my feeling when later I came to write of Frankfurter's career and his elevation to the Supreme Court in 1939 that he hoped to serve vis-à-vis Franklin Roosevelt in the role of Colonel House or Brandeis in Wilsonian days.

Colonel House eventually found that President Wilson listened to him only some of the time. Frankfurter, it turned out, had only part of the presidential ear and was one of a dozen others, each of whom was made by Roosevelt to believe that he was the President's most trusted confidant. Some observers thought that Frankfurter really played "Jiminy Cricket" to Roosevelt's "Pinocchio," acting as the President's conscience. Even so the newspaper men noticed Frankfurter's quiet comings and goings and made him a Man of Mystery in the press, which he also enjoyed.

Stendhal, foreseeing the coming of age of constitutional republics toward 1830, also prophesied that "the next century would belong to the lawyers." Felix Frankfurter had been an inspiring teacher to a whole generation of students upon whom he had left the stamp of his "modernist" faith. An admirer of the British tradition of civil service, he had also urged his bright young men to go to work for the government and help raise its standard of service. The New Deal, with its many hastily improvised administrative bureaus and its untried reform legislation, desperately needed good lawyers. Wherever a report or ruling touched on agreements between government and private interests a lawyer, even a whole staff of lawyers, was required to give counsel or write such rulings in precise legal form. Those men, as Frankfurter used to say, would no longer be fighting merely for their clients' dollars but as "lawyers for the community," like Brandeis in former years and Frankfurter too. One of Frankfurter's pupils at Harvard recalled: "Felix used to tell us that the new federal commissions regulating banking, commerce, and agriculture, would soon be running the whole country, and so we thought that, instead of going to some office in Wall Street which was *kaput*, we would take jobs in Washington."

One of Frankfurter's earlier gifts to the federal government had been his lively pupil Thomas G. Corcoran, who in 1932, under President Hoover had become assistant to the chairman of the RFC and was later moved over to the White House as a presidential assistant to Roosevelt. Corcoran soon had the assignment of finding lawyers to fill the new government posts, and often he selected them after a telephone consultation with Frankfurter (though not all of them were from Harvard). "Tommy" Corcoran told me afterward that during the first year of Roosevelt's term some three hundred law school graduates were hired by him. Eventually Corcoran collided with Postmaster General Farley, who wielded most of the power of patronage for the Democratic Party. According to Corcoran, "Farley wanted the usual old Party hacks appointed to jobs. But it was too late to use such mediocrities. The times had changed."

Swelling with pride, Corcoran wound up saying: "We, Felix and I, helped to bring about a great transformation of the whole federal service, which under Roosevelt assumed something like the high standards of the British public service."

It is to the glory of Felix Frankfurter that he helped to inspire the migration of young lawyers and professors to Washington at the time of the national crisis. The capitalists and their political friends, it must be remembered, had lost hope and faith and were then in a defeatist mood. But Frankfurter said at the time in a public speech in February 1933: "Despite our present plight, we have it more than ever within our power to be masters of our fate . . . if only we have the will to translate knowledge into action. . . ." While the moneymen had been abdicating the troop of young professors and lawyers acted as if they had nothing to lose, and they showed themselves full of courage, hope, and faith in the nation's future. The new men became a leavening force within the government. Despite the muddle of politics going on, the old regime in America was changing as the government extended its power over industry and agriculture, finance and labor. And at every step the government's lawyers met with stubborn resistance provided by their brother lawyers from Harvard, Yale, or Columbia who were defending private corporate interests; and so the battle of the lawyers raged on.

At the time when I came to Washington in 1934 the conservative elements and their allies in Congress had somewhat recovered their aplomb and begun a vigorous defensive action. A great hue and cry was raised in the press about an alleged cabal of Reds or pinks among Roosevelt's advisers who aimed to take over the federal government and bend it to their sinister purposes. Most often the finger of suspicion was pointed at Professor Felix Frankfurter, described as the Svengali of the White House, and sometimes at his young protégé Tommy Corcoran. Other alleged "plotters" were Rex Tugwell, then Assistant Secretary of Agriculture, and Harry Hopkins, directing the Federal Relief Administration. As Roosevelt was enormously popular, the strategy of the opposition was to avoid direct attack on him and to represent him as an innocent beguiled by wicked schemers. Certainly it seems time that the old myths about Frankfurter's radical influence should be laid to rest.

To be sure Frankfurter had sometimes in the past been deeply swayed by his humane sentiments and his passion for justice, as in the Sacco-Vanzetti Case, and earlier while serving as chairman of the War Labor Board under President Wilson. But aside from his conviction that the federal government could legally intervene in the economic crisis under the general welfare clause of the Constitution, he never had any fixed social program, least of all a radical one. The concept of change Frankfurter absorbed from his older friends Brandeis and Holmes was pragmatic and evolutionary. In fact he strongly advised against the collectivist plans of the NRA to drop antitrust surveillance, although Roosevelt for several years ignored such advice. In essence he was a Brandeisian-Wilsonian liberal of the 1912 vintage.

I remember meeting Frankfurter at a cocktail party in Connecticut given by his old friends the Beards. It was a few months before his (expected) appointment to the Supreme Court. He buttonholed me at once, as if he had known me all his life, exclaiming impetuously: "Mr. Josephson, why must you young men be so impatient and seek to change everything all at once? Don't you realize that these things *take time,* that it is far better to move slowly, without doing violence to democratic tradition?" It was in this spirit that Felix had worked with leaders of the establishment such as Henry L. Stimson and Eugene Meyers, ever pinning his hopes upon the better element.

II.

I was gathering in a good deal of the folklore already accumulating around the New Deal while preparing my articles on General Johnson and the NRA. It was my method in such investigations to try to permeate a situation rather than start at the front office, where I might receive only publicity handouts. Instead I busied myself compiling my own dossier from the newspaper morgues, and with the advice of certain Washington correspondents.

The National Industrial Recovery Act, like the Agricultural Adjustment Act, was one of the omnibus bills that had been hurriedly passed by Congress as emergency legislation in 1933. It called for planning and control of virtually all the country's manufacturing industry and commerce, with a view to expanding employment by reducing hours of labor. Over-all planning for the different industries was to be established by agreements, or "codes" so-called, accepted by the members of trade associations (sometimes with the cooperation of labor unions in their fields) and authorized by the President. The scheme involved fixing not only wages and hours but also prices and production schedules. This constituted a historic breakaway from the free market capitalism traditional to America and, in fact, a violation of the Anti-Trust Act of 1890 forbidding monopolistic combinations in restraint of trade. The President however undertook to hold signers of the NRA codes immune to prosecution by the Department of Justice, on the grounds of national emergency.

The NRA was the New Deal's major effort to stimulate recovery; it appeared to me to be an unusually complex scheme for imposing nationwide controls, and also to have been based on the experience of the War Industries Board during World War I. Americans, however, had no tradition in their everyday business life of absolute obedience to a central government authority, as did the Russians and above all the Germans—who were just then carrying on a reemployment program very effectively under Hitler and Finance Minister Schacht. The most conflicting reports on the NRA came to me: that it performed good works on the one hand and on the other threatened to set up a despotic bureaucracy.

Franklin Roosevelt, as Rex Tugwell said afterward, knew nothing about economics. He had been convinced however, by the end of 1932, that the Great Depression was different from earlier ones and would not just go away as many hoped. Just before he took office Roosevelt had hinted in private conversation that it might be necessary for the while to experiment with some socialistic measures such as were being tried "on the other side" (Europe).

In reality the recovery program became a mixed bag of various schemes proposed by different interest groups. The American Federation of Labor had been agitating for a bill that would spread work through imposing the thirty-hour week; such a measure, sponsored by Senator Hugo Black, was near passage by Congress in April 1933. A group of big business leaders headed by Gerard Swope of General Electric and H. I. Harriman of the U. S. Chamber of Commerce was at the same time backing an alternate proposal, the "Swope Plan," which called for industrywide agreements on prices and production.

The harried Roosevelt had assigned to Raymond Moley the task of shaping a viable scheme out of these conflicting proposals as well as those of his own economic advisers such as Tugwell, who urged a "collectivist" program. Professor Moley then brought in General Hugh S. Johnson, a research assistant of the financier Bernard M. Baruch whom Baruch had loaned to Roosevelt's Brain Trust during the 1932 election campaign. Johnson had previously had some experience as one of the representatives of the Army in planning arms production under the old War Industries Board, of which Baruch was chairman. Johnson then undertook to write a bill for a recovery program that would combine the various proposals. There were at least three different committees or teams (each authorized by Roosevelt to advise him on a recovery plan), but Johnson took all their various proposals, locked himself in a hotel room with a couple of bottles of whisky, and emerged twenty-four hours later with a draft of the law in brief form—according to his own account.

A different story was told me, however, by the well-known Chicago lawyer Donald R. Richberg, who was general counsel and deputy administrator of the NRA. There had been sharp conflict between those who urged a weak or "voluntary" program and those who favored a bill with stern enforcement provisions. Tugwell thought that Johnson did not care about any planning except by business associations. "Roosevelt then ordered us all to get into a room and 'weave' the whole bill together," Richberg said. What came out was a compromise bill that was weak on enforcement.

(256)

At conferences in the White House Roosevelt found Johnson at any rate highly enthusiastic and imaginative about the whole project. Acting quickly on one of his hunches, Roosevelt appointed him administrator of the momentous National Recovery Act. While the President often called upon professors and experts for aid, he also tried to strike a balance by choosing some of his officials from among the "Baruch School" so-called, of men who were supposed to know the ways of practical business.

One provision of the bill that was vaguely written but destined to have an enormous effect on the fortunes of the entire working class was the famous Section 7(a), the so-called "charter for labor" through which the government required collective bargaining between employers and workers represented by unions of their free choice. The business leaders advising Roosevelt, Gerard Swope and H. I. Harriman, strongly opposed this clause. Roosevelt left the decision to the tug-of-war among his advisers. It was in fact given as a consolation prize to the AFL and liberal Senators Black and Wagner, who thereupon agreed to drop their thirty-hour-week bill.

As soon as the bill was passed, in June 1933, Johnson began to tear about the country in an Army plane, visiting the industrial centers of the Midwest and trying to hurry through negotiations for NRA codes with several of the large manufacturing groups. From the start the burly, red-faced general assumed a resolute military air calculated to impress the public. "The Roosevelt Plan," he promised, would "lead the people in a great pilgrimage . . . away from the horrors of depression." Working hours would be regulated, unfair competition in business would be suppressed. "Nothing could be simpler," he cried. "We're gonna put millions back to work and pay them living wages." In radio speeches he called on labor to refrain from strikes and on capital to postpone profits. His hoarse, bass voice went rolling into homes, pool parlors, and filling stations throughout the land, now cajoling, now threatening those who resisted the proposed controls with "the pistol I have in my hip pocket." He referred to the President's presumed emergency authority to force corporations or individuals into line, and he let it be known that much of that power had been delegated to him. But was there ever such authority legally? Afterward Johnson himself explained that he used overemphatic expressions to rouse public opinion in support of the NRA.

For about a year General Johnson enjoyed more attention in the press than any member of the new Cabinet, almost as much as the President himself. To the newspaper columnists he was "America's most powerful man after Roosevelt," and "of the stuff dictators are made of." He gave all the appearance of a New Deal autocrat brow-beating corporations and workers alike; and for a season or two he was celebrated as "Crack-Down" Johnson—also "Iron-Pants" John-son in deference to his cavalryman's style of speech. Yet all that I learned by my own inquiries indicated that Johnson's methods were largely bluster and bluff. From the start there had been serious delay in lining up industries for the government-sponsored codes; some of the largest employers simply consulted their lawyers and then flatly refused to comply. I also came upon reports of skullduggery in those very agreements on market prices, trade standards, and labor relations.

Now in his early fifties, Johnson, as I learned, was born in Kansas, the son of a small-town lawyer, and had attended West Point where he received a commission in 1903 as a second lieutenant of cavalry. Though he had had boyhood dreams of martial adven-tures, the nearest he came to fulfilling them was his part in Persh-ing's inglorious expedition to Mexico in 1916 in pursuit of Villa. Johnson's tentmate of that campaign, Colonel George S. Patton, told me that because of his loud voice and gruff manner he earned at that time the cognomen of "Tuffy" Johnson.

During long years of idleness at Army posts in the West Johnson had taken up writing, and he succeeded in publishing some "west-erns" in popular fiction magazines like *The Sunset,* also dime novels for juveniles. There was certainly a romantic nature under that crust. Thereafter his ambitions led him to the study of law, and so he moved into the Judge Advocate's department. In 1916, on the eve of war with Germany, he was called to General Enoch Crowder's staff in Washington, where he helped write and plan the administra-tion of the draft act. As a desk soldier he had also seen service on the War Industries Board and at the end of the war attained the rank of Brevet Brigadier General. Resigning from the Army in 1919,

Johnson entered business in partnership with another of Baruch's young men of the War Industries Board, George N. Peek, who had specialized in problems relating to agriculture. Baruch told me that he had placed the pair of them in charge of a plow manufacturing company which needed reorganization but which eventually in 1926 went into receivership. Though he had not been lucky in business, Johnson thereafter was given a job by Baruch as an assistant on his Wall Street staff, where he gathered business intelligence for the famous stock market plunger and wrote statistical reports.

Early in the Depression Johnson came up with sundry schemes (though hardly original) for halting the decline of business: one of them was set forth in a privately circulated pamphlet entitled "Muscle-Inny," advocating the deportation of Congress and setting up of an economic dictatorship in these states like that of Italy. He also carried on some studies in ways of remodeling our government by means of a constitutional convention. Though apparently imbued with some alien, or Mussolinian, notions he willingly boarded the campaign train of the liberal Roosevelt in the summer of 1932 and joined his Brain Trust. That was done at the suggestion of Johnson's employer Baruch, who had not supported the nomination of Roosevelt at the 1932 Democratic Convention, but when he won out had offered him advice, money donations, and his research assistant Johnson.

For many years the canny old Baruch had found it both diverting and useful to serve as patron to various Democratic Party politicians. I wondered a good deal why Roosevelt had not chosen the reputedly brilliant financier himself to head the NRA, instead of the former desk general and dime novelist who had been a failure at business. Pondering such questions I went to see Baruch himself, and I found him approachable, garrulous, and also disingenuous. In those days he did not yet enjoy the repute of an elder statesman blessed with infallible wisdom about our national affairs, but rather of a clever stock gambler who directed large syndicate or pool manipulations. He was credited with having better access to inside intelligence than almost anyone else in his business: some of this was said to have derived from his intimacy with leading political figures and had led to his being harshly investigated by a senate committee in

1917 for alleged stock market manipulation—prior to his taking office in President Wilson's wartime government. The high post he had then occupied had left him with an itch to fill some important public office again.

It was not surprising therefore that from the moment Roosevelt had won the Democratic nomination the multimillionaire hovered about him. Indeed Roosevelt, according to Raymond Moley, had allowed Baruch and another Democratic Party donor, Joseph P. Kennedy, to read the draft of his acceptance speech in advance. Roosevelt needed the help of wealthy Democrats, and he tactfully courted their advice. They in turn were not unwilling to infiltrate the new Roosevelt administration. Baruch himself moved down to Washington where he entertained political cronies with much hospitality. Herbert Bayard Swope, former newspaper editor and brother of Gerard Swope, acted as his publicity man while Arthur Krock of *The New York Times* Washington Bureau also helped the growth of the Baruch legend. (For a man of modest talents to become established as the perennial adviser of Presidents much publicity was needed.)

There were always eyes and ears around so powerful a President as Roosevelt, always hands ready to give and even more ready to take. The odd thing was that Roosevelt instinctively distrusted Baruch. But still he often reminded such aides as Tugwell to consult with Baruch and be "nice" to him. Tugwell wrote in his diary for February 21, 1933, just before the Inauguration, "So much Baruch money has been spread around—as campaign contributions and otherwise—that it never does to criticize him publicly. But FDR is well aware of it and cautions us about it."

Tugwell, following talks with Baruch on the gold question, observed privately: "He has an immense sense of his ability . . . but in this case not much knowledge." Roosevelt in the end failed to appoint Baruch to his Cabinet; but his naming of Johnson and Peek, as head of the NRA and AAA respectively, was supposed to reflect Baruch's behind-the-scenes influence.

At sixty-four Baruch was a tall, slender, and quite personable man with blue eyes and white hair. With some touches of pique he made it plain that he was discontented with what he termed the ill-digested plans of the New Deal. As for Hugh Johnson, Baruch expressed no high opinion of him; he had only loaned him to Roosevelt, but afterward, he remarked with a laugh, "Roosevelt appointed him administrator of the NRA without asking my permission." Despite his reputation for wizardry Baruch talked in the commonplace terms of an economic conservative: the Roosevelt government should try to cut expenses, balance the budget, and at the same time raise taxes (during a depression!) to provide for poor relief. Moreover he himself had no faith in national economic planning.

"Humph," he wound up. "Roosevelt's men are a bunch of Young Turks. They forget that Rome wasn't built in one day."

III.

The original working plan for the NRA was to establish codes for a score of the largest industries, embracing the bulk of manufacturing labor, and thus begin quickly to reduce hours and spread work. Many of the smaller trade groups, however, saw a splendid profit picture in having competition regulated and being able to fix prices with governmental sanction. Therefore, when the NRA opened for business there was a perfect stampede to Washington by small businessmen and representatives of the trade associations (about seven hundred in all) covering everything from babies' jiffy pants to widgets and zippers. With these numerous business groups came their lawyers, who were determined to get the best possible terms for their clients before the NRA codes were drawn up and approved. When General Johnson found that everybody wanted NRA codes of some kind he undertook to give them what they wanted. He loved excitement and soon found himself in the midst of a confused mass of people debating over proposed agreements night and day. The scene at the headquarters of the NRA in the Commerce Building was that of a wartime boom; crowds of business representatives remained camped there or held forth at meetings that overflowed into the banquet halls of various downtown hotels.

Capital and labor were supposed to lie down together like the lion and the lamb; they proceeded however to haggle and wrangle interminably. One code alone, that for cotton textiles, required six weeks of hearings. At this rate the government-approved plans were subject to intolerable delays. Johnson fumed and stormed: "Speed the codes," he cried. Nothing availed. Before the employers' groups would agree to reduce hours and hire more workers at increased wages they demanded the right to increase the price of their products enough, often more than enough, to cover added production costs. In expectation that the government would sanction such price raising, many manufacturing firms hastened to pile up inventories of various materials and so beat the codes, which would authorize higher prices. A little speculative boom accompanied the start of the NRA in the summer of 1933. But the tempo of the "Roosevelt recovery" soon slowed down. Meanwhile the actual establishment of codes in the most important industries was badly stalled as large employers like Henry Ford and the steel manufacturer Ernest Weir absolutely refused compliance with the government's program and would have no truck with any labor unions—except company unions managed by themselves.

Johnson thereupon bethought himself of a new stratagem: it was to have many thousands of business concerns throughout the country sign a blanket agreement with President Roosevelt by which they pledged themselves to increase employment and reduce hours *voluntarily*, pending arrangements for definitive codes. In return General Johnson would issue to them placards certifying their compliance with the NRA and bearing a blue eagle emblem along with the legend "NRA: WE DO OUR PART." The idea derived from the 1918 War Industries Board, which employed mass advertising to win compliance with its plans for storing up scrap iron or saving sugar.

Raising the banner of the Blue Eagle Johnson took the field and toured the country in the autumn of 1933. A crowd of deputies and volunteers also traveled about addressing Rotary clubs and chambers of commerce in hundreds of towns and cities. Monster parades and torchlight processions were organized in honor of the Blue Eagle. In New York Johnson spoke before a crowd of ten thousand at Madison Square Garden; with characteristic vehemence he denounced those who opposed the New Deal, "those corporals of disaster who . . . yesterday were gorged with paper profits and . . . reveled in a fool's paradise." Johnson promised everything: sales for the salesman, work for the laborer, and profits for the employer. His Blue Eagle would certainly lay the golden egg by creating six million jobs!

The next afternoon a million people turned out to watch New York's NRA parade, in which a quarter of a million others marched, cheered, and sang until midnight. There were theatrical floats, jazz orchestras, police bands playing "The Yanks are Coming," and shapely chorus girls representing Miss NRA in bathing costume. Tons of confetti rained down upon this scene of patriotic carnival, and seventy-three airplanes soared above. When it was over the confetti and the soiled Blue Eagle placards and sandwich signs were all swept away, and people went back to face the facts of life.

No miracles followed, despite so much incantation, advertising, and radio sound. Neither in Wall Street nor in Washington did informed people take the Recovery Administration seriously. It was noticeable that General Johnson, in his "tough guy" style, regularly attacked both capitalists who refused cooperation with the NRA and labor unions that rejected his rulings. However, in his eagerness to gain shorter hours and spread work, Johnson approved of codes by which large corporations settled questions of hours and wages by negotiating with company unions under their own control. There was a flurry of strikes as a consequence; but Johnson moved quickly to hold back labor in the steel, automobile, and textile fields. In vehement public statements he declared that strikes were "unnecessary" and "unpatriotic"—because the NRA stood ready to adjudicate all labor disputes. Liberal publications, such as *The New Republic*, now assailed General Johnson as a "fascist," who would deprive labor of its historic right of self-defense and prepare the way for a "corporative state."

§ § §

A powerful revival of the long-dormant labor movement was one of the unexpected by-products of the NRA. National and local leaders alert to the opportunities for increasing union membership under Section 7(a) now agitated vigorously for improved wages and work-

ing conditions or called strikes for union recognition. The United
Mine Workers in the summer of 1933, under John L. Lewis, carried
out a spectacular membership campaign. His organizers went about
crying "President Roosevelt *wants* you to join your union," and
"John L. Lewis has been eating ham and eggs with the President in
the White House."

Formerly one of the most retrograde of the AFL leaders, a
changed Lewis now spoke with immense pride of the advance of the
miners' union. He said to me: "We went into Pennsylvania towns
long run by the companies' Coal and Iron Police, where for many
years no union agents had dared show themselves; and we organized; and as we organized, the AFL teamsters followed after us and
expanded; and then the building workers and the clothing workers
came in also."

Once having reestablished the economic power of the unions in
their fields, heads of strong unions such as Lewis and Sidney Hillman were able to bargain on equal terms with employers before the
NRA code authorities. However, where the unions were weak or
nonexistent, as in textiles, the NRA's administrator permitted trade
agreements calling for wages as low as $12 to $13 a week.

Assuming the air of some grand panjandrum, Johnson would
announce at a press conference in his gruffest tones that he had
issued an ultimatum to the magnates of the oil industry, demanding
that they "come in the next morning at 10 a.m. and sign on the
dotted line" a code he had prepared for them. His publicity agents
represented Johnson as a "man of elemental force" who feared no
oil kings, and who might well become "the actual functioning head
of the government." But the oil interests, represented by men like
Harry Sinclair and W. C. Teagle of Standard Oil of New Jersey,
obtained highly satisfactory terms, and there was no nonsense about
bargaining with bona fide labor unions. President Roosevelt was informed about his lieutenant's methods, but in the early stages of the
NRA he chose to look the other way.

§ § §

By the time I came to Washington in June 1934 I found Johnson had assembled a bureaucratic army of about three thousand

assistants, including big business executives, lawyers, and field agents to enforce compliance with codes. As in the wartime planning board subdivisions had been set up to represent the different interests of management, labor, and the consuming public.

Rambling about the NRA headquarters I perceived that an impressive contingent of big business volunteers—recalling the dollar-a-year men of 1918—was installed here. Members of the NRA's Industrial and Labor Advisory Board included Walter C. Teagle of Standard Oil, S. Clay Williams of Reynolds Tobacco, Gerard Swope, and Pierre S. Dupont. In another office down the hall I encountered John J. Raskob, Mr. Dupont's confrere at General Motors. Johnson made no secret of the fact that he relied in the main on the planning of hard-boiled businessmen and mistrusted academicians. However, labor's William Green and John L. Lewis sat in council nowadays with those eminent capitalists while my old friend of *New Republic* days, Professor Leo Wolman, presided over their board as a presumably impartial chairman acting for the President.

A great free-for-all raged in Washington around the NRA, with everyone shouting as loud as he pleased his objections to whatever was being done. As I had recently spent some time in Soviet Russia, where men spoke as if the walls had ears, I thoroughly enjoyed the utter freedom with which political differences in America were being aired. Many actually accused President Roosevelt of being a blithering "dictator," yet no one arrested them.

On Capitol Hill certain senators, including the Progressive Republicans William E. Borah and Gerald P. Nye, regularly assailed Johnson and the NRA as fostering unlawful monopolies. Johnson in reply stigmatized these statesmen as mere "croakers and demagogues." Citing those insulting terms, Senator Nye, on the occasion when I interviewed him, went into a grand tirade against the autocrat of the NRA, calling him "a Nero who rants and roars while the country burns." Indeed the senator was so agitated and spoke so forcefully that, while sitting with him in his office, I involuntarily glanced over my shoulder to see if there were an audience of ten thousand he was addressing.

At the centrally located Hotel Willard where I stopped, some of the banquet rooms downstairs were being used for overflow meetings of industry-labor groups still working out codes. In one of those banquet rooms I found, oddly enough, the aged "people's lawyer" Clarence Darrow presiding as chairman of the National Recovery Review Board (most of whose members were appointed by Senator Nye), which was subjecting the NRA and all its works to a severe investigation. A large man with a big head, a deeply lined face, and twinkling eyes, Darrow was dressed in sober black, wore a string tie, and looked like an American worthy of olden times. He kept wheezing and laughing as he described what he conceived as the fraudulent and monopolistic practices of leading industrial groups. "Your Robber Barons are all coming back," he exclaimed, laughing, "and under the so-called New Deal!" His committee had been accumulating the complaints of many consumers and small businessmen. Their report had been ready for some time, but its release to the public was being delayed for several weeks by Johnson and Roosevelt until Johnson could make a suitable reply.

In actual practice a powerful minority (generally the largest manufacturers) in each industry negotiated the terms covering fair trade practices, prices, and wages on a profitable basis—in return for shortening the hours of labor. Thereafter the representatives of those cartelized industries (such as steel, oil, motors) often remained with the NRA staff as volunteers, enforcing the codes or themselves acting as the government's code authorities!

In another of the ornate old banquet rooms in the Willard I found a meeting of the hatters' trade in progress and happened to notice there an old acquaintance of mine, a New York lawyer who was representing the labor union in the field, The Hat, Cap and Millinery Workers, AFL. He recognized me, left the meeting, and walked about with me describing frankly the crooked deals that the manufacturers' association in the business had tried to pull off.

"We in the union got wind of the scheme," he said, "and came down to Washington and called on Assistant Secretary of Labor Edward McGrady to lodge our protest. [McGrady had formerly been secretary of the AFL.] He told us that he 'happened' just then to be reading a draft of the proposed hatters' code in behalf of Miss Perkins. He then said to our delegation: 'Gentlemen, I have an important engagement at the White House with Mr. Roosevelt; I must leave now and will be gone for only thirty minutes. Will you please wait here and entertain yourselves in any way you please until I return.' The draft of that code was left there on his desk, and though of course we were not explicitly given permission to do so we took the occasion to read it all through carefully and saw that the labor provisions were scandalous. We had arrived just before the agreement was to be signed by Johnson, and we raised hell at the NRA and before Congress, so that the case was reopened. We are now working out wages and hours we consider acceptable."

There was also the Consumers' Advisory Board for the protection of the public; one of its officials was Leon Henderson, formerly an economist for the Russell Sage Foundation of New York and for a while something of a technocrat too. Sidney Hillman had brought him down to Washington to testify as an independent expert at hearings on a proposed code for woolens, and Henderson had produced figures showing its wage scales too low and hours of work too high to help reemployment. Johnson as presiding officer yelled and pounded the table. Henderson, adopting the same style, bellowed his replies at the top of his voice and, like Johnson, got off some hearty oaths too. Impressed by the young man's lung power Johnson offered him a paid position on the Consumers' Advisory Board, which he accepted.

The most genteel of professors, lawyers, or economists who came to Washington in those early years of the New Deal soon took to hollering and table-pounding like old-fashioned politicians as a way of impressing the public, the press, and members of Congress.

Henderson was then chubby and rosy-cheeked, very much the youthful social worker. In discussing with me the problems of the NRA he pointed out that in many instances prices of merchandise had been raised out of all proportion to advances in wages. The Southern textile manufacturers were allowed minimum wages as low as $12 a week. That, Henderson pointed out, was no way to cure the country's depressed buying power. He had made strong protests against certain industry codes, but General Johnson had exclaimed: "Who the hell cares what the Consumers' Board thinks!"

Henderson remarked that Johnson had "bravely" cracked down on some shopkeepers in the cleaning and dyeing trade for code violations—a tailor in New Jersey was actually jailed for a few days—but the General avoided engagements with big corporations whose delinquencies were far more serious.

§   §   §

Hugh Johnson's biggest headaches nowadays came from labor. Inspired by the hopeful auguries of NRA's labor clause, union leaders and workers in 1933 undertook some hasty organizing in industries where collective bargaining was almost nonexistent. With the support of the AFL, efforts were made to revive a long defunct union in the steel trade. In Detroit a first, highly enthusiastic organizing drive enlisted 150,000 auto workers in a temporary "federal local" of the AFL and posed the threat of a large strike for union recognition. In ruling on the application of Section 7(a) Johnson declared that while he did not favor company unions, the new law must not be used as an instrument guaranteeing the closed union shop. This Solomon-like judgment proved to be a signal for manufacturing employers to throw together numerous company unions.

I went to see Sidney Hillman about the inconsistencies that had developed in the NRA's labor policy. He was one of the most enthusiastic adherents of the New Deal; while speaking softly, he worked with much tenacity to advance bona fide unionism and improve some of the worst of the earlier codes. By fairly hounding Secretary Perkins and the President during a whole year he brought about a revision of the labor schedule in the sweated cotton textile industry, Roosevelt brusquely overruling Johnson and ordering wages (moderately) raised and hours cut.

"President Roosevelt has proved the greatest friend labor ever had in the White House," Hillman insisted. "We have under Section 7(a) all the rights and privileges we have long dreamed of—provided we go out and organize people ourselves. We cannot expect Roosevelt to do it for us. But now at last we are wiping out child labor, and have the possibility of eliminating sweatshops."

At the threat of a big strike of auto workers Roosevelt himself intervened and imposed arbitration of the dispute—over company unions versus independent unions—through a specially appointed Automobile Labor Board, with Leo Wolman as its supposedly impartial chairman. To everyone's surprise the Board, in the autumn of 1934, decided in favor of recognizing the company unions—Professor Wolman casting the deciding vote. "A traitor to labor!" Hillman called him. That set back real unionism for the auto workers almost three years.

I had recently seen Wolman in Washington and learned with surprise that he had taken to dining out with men like Alfred Sloan of General Motors and W. C. Teagle of Standard Oil, whom he described to me as "a most charming gentleman." Not long afterward, having been induced to resign from Roosevelt's service, Wolman turned against the New Deal and became an immitigable conservative, for which he was rewarded with directorships in banks and insurance companies. (Thus some of the New Dealers passed over to the opposition at an early stage.)

Among trade unionists the opinion prevailed that Roosevelt's view of the labor question shifted in accordance with the pressures brought to bear on him. One New Deal official, Jerome Frank, then General Counsel of the AAA, said to me with a wicked grin: "Roosevelt knows nothing whatsoever about labor or trade unions. They say in Washington that the only contacts he ever had with the working class were with chorus girls he met when he went to Harvard."

The series of "palace wars" that raged within the New Deal at the time was one of the features of the period that none could ignore. The different boards and committees that Roosevelt habitually appointed to deal with fresh contingencies in the public domain often came into conflict with each other. In particular the AAA, the important new bureau established within the Department of Agriculture to plan for economic recovery on the farms, was engaged in a bitter contest with General Johnson's agency. As fast as the AAA curtailed crops and raised bounty payments to farmers, the NRA seemed to work even faster to raise the prices of articles the farmers consumed, such as barbed wire, rubber boots, and farm tools. The planners in the Department of Agriculture, Henry Wallace and Rex Tugwell, strongly petitioned the President to remove from Johnson's jurisdiction certain food and other products used by farmers; this Roosevelt finally did by executive order. The General vented his rage at "the professors who wear the heaviest of horn-rimmed glasses." But Jerome Frank was exultant because the AAA had taken Johnson's scalp, and he quipped: "General Johnson is only a sheep in wolf's clothing."

In emergencies Johnson used to rush in upon the President and would rant, make scenes, or even burst into tears, which distressed Roosevelt.

On several occasions I consulted Donald R. Richberg, the NRA's general counsel and deputy administrator, and I found his style of operation quite different from the General's. Richberg was a large man with a bald head, very big ears, and small shrewd eyes; he smoked enormous cigars. Formerly a labor lawyer of progressive tendencies and highly regarded in Chicago, he seemed much more given now to the arts of compromise. Meanwhile this clever and well-spoken man, evidently working somewhat at cross purposes with Johnson, moved himself as close to the throne of Roosevelt as possible, so that the newspapers sometimes named him "Mr. Assistant President." In the autumn of 1934 when Roosevelt reorganized the NRA, Richberg was chosen as its chairman, Johnson having finally resigned.

§　　§　　§

The NRA, for all its muddle, was an ambitious, precedent-breaking adventure in national economic planning, relying mainly on the voluntary cooperation of employers who, however, had no tradition of such discipline. Moreover they were predominantly skeptical about the whole scheme, since the country's leading corporation lawyers assured them that it would soon be nullified by the Supreme Court as unconstitutional. Then the persons administering the program had no experience of the techniques of government industrial planning in peacetime. They had not even compiled adequate statistics to measure the effect of the codes on prices, output, and buying power. To be sure the industrial cartels lent themselves to the program for the time being, since it changed in no way their dominant market positions nor the institutional structure of the business system.

Some gains were recorded nevertheless: the President's Reemployment Agreement of September 1933 reduced hours moderately and returned about 2.4 million workers to jobs. It was simply not enough, since five times as many were left dependent on relief.

The NRA was supposed to move in step with enlarged public works expenditures and relief payments to the unemployed. Although Harry Hopkins administered relief with tremendous speed, the Public Works Authority under "Honest Harold" Ickes moved slowly; it required time-consuming plans and blueprints, none of which were ready. For these various reasons, as one financial expert, the Utah banker Marriner Eccles, remarked, poor General Johnson's "trumpets, placards, and parades" were all to no avail. Eccles, then an adviser to the Treasury Department, held that the NRA permitted business men "to get higher prices, but no markets; and labor higher wages, but few jobs. . . . It did not provide the necessary consumer purchasing power which alone could . . . sustain recovery." [1]

A vigorous recovery set in by contrast in western Europe, especially in Germany under Hitler and the guidance of the financial wizard Hjalmar Schacht. The program of public works, rearmament, and fiscal controls harshly imposed by dictatorial power brought the country quickly to full employment. The Reich expanded its budget by about 300 per cent during 1933 to 1938 (from about eight to thirty-two billion marks), operating at an enormous deficit, yet neither bankruptcy nor paper money inflation resulted. Federal spending in the United States was by comparison stingy, amounting to only about 33 per cent more than under Hoover. (To be sure the economic "miracle" of Germany was directed to the ends of war—we too performed miracles of spending in World War II—but the vast budgetary deficits of wartime could just as well have been used for a War against Poverty.)

John Maynard Keynes, the leading English exponent of govern-

[1] Marriner S. Eccles: *Beckoning Frontiers* (New York: Alfred A. Knopf; 1951), p. 126.

ment deficit spending during depression cycles, arrived in this country in 1934 and conferred with President Roosevelt. Keynes himself, before writing his *General Theory of Employment*, was then learning what he could about planning and managed capitalism, and had already expressed high approval of President Roosevelt's intuitive approach to this problem. Keynes however was somewhat taken aback at finding the President in no way literate in economics.

In talking with Roosevelt's advisers, such as Tugwell, Keynes made the point that the country's deficit spending was niggardly, a mere $2.5 billion a year. Were it doubled in scale it might have spread employment rapidly and ensured recovery.

Yet Roosevelt was much influenced also by such conservative advisers as Lewis Douglas, Director of the Budget, and Henry J. Morgenthau, Secretary of the Treasury, who continued to warn him that the deluge of inflation would be upon us any day—"the end of civilization"—unless he approached a balancing of the budget. Powerful conservatives in the Senate also pressed such views upon him, and so he continued to be relatively parsimonious.

IV.

The first birthday of the NRA was being celebrated as I came in to see General Johnson. (In my articles published in August 1934 I hinted that the first birthday anniversary of the NRA might well prove to be its last.) Frances Robbins, Johnson's amiable and lively secretary, was directing the festivities in the reception room and had set out a huge cake decorated with the letters NRA and the Blue Eagle. A number of Johnson's deputies were on hand, mostly business executives and Army officers, to whom he had given jobs.

It was an open secret in Washington that the red-headed Miss Robbins, or Robbie, ran a goodly part of the NRA organization and was "more than a secretary," as Johnson himself said off the record. When disappointments multiplied or tensions became too much, it was rumored, Johnson would disappear for two days on a bender and Robbie would tend shop.

I was reflecting that Hugh Johnson was certainly a dead duck, when he himself came rolling in. He was a man in his fifties, of medium height, stocky and beer-bellied; while no great beauty, with his bulbous red nose, rough complexion, and wide jaw, his voice nevertheless was low and pleasant, his manner almost shy. When he chose, he could be good-humored, and even ingratiating.

In answer to my questions about his work on the industrial codes he said ruefully: "There's always a lot of hot water boiling around here." In pensive mood he reflected upon all the built-in resistances within the three branches of government and within the society itself that made industrial planning so difficult. The NRA was supposed to eliminate unfair business competition yet see to it that no monopolies were fostered; it must raise prices yet avoid burdening the consumer; it must increase wages for labor yet leave the employer his profit; and the administrator was expected to discipline violators of the codes yet avoid a showdown in the courts. (Frankfurter and Richberg had warned that the National Recovery Act would be found unconstitutional by the Supreme Court. The fateful suit which was being prosecuted by the Administration against a dealer in chickens was just then pending in the courts.)

Johnson reviewed some of these problems in ironic vein then said: "Anyway the NRA has been a great education for American business and government; their working in partnership has left its mark upon the world."

I asked him whether, in view of the many reports of his differences with high officials in the government, he intended to resign in the near future. Johnson snapped testily: "I'm not leaving until this thing has jelled a lot better than it has thus far." (One of his assistants I talked with at NRA headquarters quoted him as saying, not without signs of megalomania: "After all, next to Franklin Roosevelt, I am the man with the largest personal following in this country; I have to stay here.") Then he softened, smiled, and talked good-humoredly of his earlier career in the Army.

In the entourage of the General I found at least one of his young aides who was frankly an enthusiast for fascism. To this young man I remarked upon the similarities between the NRA scheme of partnership and the corporative state; and he exclaimed joyously that there would be more similarities in the future. Recurrences of depression and growing labor disorder (as in the San Francisco general strike of July 1934) would create the need for a Mussolini. "Labor is driving for socialism in five years, and Roosevelt is a *weak* leader," the young man went on brightly, "and that means crisis. Then General Johnson will have a really big part to play! And that is why I am stringing along with him."

I listened as blandly as I could, drawing the young man out, and remarked: "Then General Johnson is regarded as a possible Man on Horseback by some people? To be sure, he was once a cavalry officer." The young man nodded assent; he was definitely hitching his wagon to Johnson's horse.

Around that time there was recurrent gossip about some native American fascists plotting to overthrow the President and supplant him with a military leader. In November 1934, the retired Major General Smedley D. Butler, of the Marine Corps, a sort of maverick among soldiers, gave sensational testimony before Congress charging that a Wall Street group, together with various Army officers, were talking of raising up a force of 500,000 men to capture Washington. Butler stated that he had been approached by such persons, and had heard General Hugh S. Johnson named as one of their first choices as military dictator. Among other alternate choices mentioned was General Douglas MacArthur. Butler declared that he had been outraged by this treasonable talk, and determined to expose the affair—which others ridiculed as a "cocktail *putsch.*" MacArthur denied knowledge of such schemes; and Johnson said he had never heard of them and would have denounced them if he had.

Oddly enough, when Johnson finally left office in mid-October of that year, he made a highly emotional speech to his staff in the auditorium of the Commerce Building, sometimes in his rambling talk paying his respects to the ideas of Mussolini, at other times shedding tears. When his desk was cleaned out, according to rumors at the time, a military map of Washington, with every public building plainly marked, was found in a drawer. These reports were cited to me by Frankfurter, who in his own way was fond of gossip. Why should the administrator of our economic program have bothered to keep a military map of the capital district handy in his desk?

§   §   §

While gathering material on Johnson I was directed to Colonel George S. Patton of the U. S. Army, commandant at Washington, who had known Johnson well in the early days, and I went to call on him at Fort Meyer. He had the repute of a sort of Pukka Sahib of the regular Army and functioned as a social lion at ceremonial dinners at the White House and on other formal occasions. Patton, a Virginian, was well-to-do through marriage to the heiress of a New England textile fortune.

Although he was in his late forties, Patton was a handsome and athletic figure; he had just come in from the polo field, bathed, and changed into white linen fatigue dress. While he spoke of "Tuffy" Johnson in friendly terms, he did not pretend to a high estimate of his abilities.

"What do *you* think," he asked me at one point, "of this New Deal and all those socialist schemes—and all the labor troubles? Where is it all going to lead?"

I was already familiar with this tone and on my guard. "President Roosevelt is a middle-road reformer," I said, "there is really very little of the socialist in him; he is trying to save capitalism."

Patton looked incredulous. "Just two years ago," he said, "I was busy protecting the conservative Republican, President Hoover"— referring to his action in the battle with the Bonus Army—"and now, think of it, here I am supposed to defend President Franklin D. Roosevelt with all the forces at my command!" He laughed, as if there were something wholly incongruous about the position he found himself in, given his particular beliefs.

"Well, anyway, we professional soldiers are supposed to be nonpartisan," he went on. "It is our duty to defend the party in power, whichever it is."

Patton's manners were polite in those days before he came to high command. He produced an excellent whisky, and after a few drinks brought out some of his poems for me to read. They were poor doggerel and had something of the Boy Scout spirit that imbued Hugh Johnson's youthful literature. Patton too wrote poems to distract himself during his years at Army posts. I was reflecting upon how dreary life must be for an Army officer between wars when Colonel Patton directed another question to me: "What do you think of all the fuss over the Hitlers and Mussolinis, and the disturbances in France? Is it anything serious, really?" He had heard from me that I had just returned from a long tour of Europe.

I said it was my feeling that the impetus of the Nazi and fascist movements was very strong and growing stronger, while the western Allies appeared divided and weak. Hitler was sure to win the impending plebiscite on the French-occupied Saar province. If things went on like this, I concluded, "I really believe there will be a second world war in a few years, perhaps four or five."

At these words Colonel Patton's face brightened visibly. He rose, drew himself up, and began to pace back and forth across the room exclaiming, "There's going to be a war, you're sure of it! Every twenty years there is a war. They neglect the Army for twenty years and then *they need us* soldiers. They will need us again!" Patton was absolutely radiant with hope. Not long afterward, as I heard, he gave up his polo horses and had some tanks brought to Fort Meyer for maneuvers.

Chapter Thirteen

◆

The Liberals
Plowed Under

ON ONE of my first evenings in Washington in early June of 1934 I walked up Connecticut Avenue to the Mayflower Hotel (then the center of the capital's social life), and was about to enter the lobby when I saw Rexford Tugwell step out of a taxi in front of the hotel. I had last seen him three years before at a dinner of *The New Republic* in New York. Now he was gotten up smartly in a white linen suit, his face was tanned, his thick graying locks waved in the breeze, and he looked by all odds "the handsomest of the New Deal commissars," as the newspapers described him. I was about to greet him when a little crowd surged forward to shake his hand and pay their respects. It was a spontaneous ovation for one of the heroes of that day. Before the thrust of that little mob of admirers and well-wishers I retreated and went on my way.

Tugwell's fortunes had undergone a marked change, for he now was reputed to be, like Frankfurter, the intimate friend and adviser of the President, and so he was exposed to political attack. At the time of my arrival in Washington the newspapers were reporting Senate Committee hearings on the recent nomination of Tugwell as Undersecretary of the Department of Agriculture. After being questioned closely as to his knowledge of agriculture, the former Columbia professor of economics had defended himself effectively by recalling that he was born in a country village in upstate New

York and was long familiar with the problems of the dirt farmer.

Tugwell's writings as an advocate of central economic planning caused him to be stigmatized in the press as a "statist" and "collectivist" and, as *Newsweek* called him, "the sweetheart of the regimenters." His efforts to draft a modernized Pure Food and Drug Act earned him the undying enmity of the pharmaceutical industry's lobby and of the large newspapers and magazines that printed their voluminous advertisements. When later he tried to have the lead arsenate content of farmers' fruit sprays reduced, the whole chemical industry also began to hate him. Soon the newspaper columnists published everything they could uncover about his past, including some Whitmanesque verses he (too!) had written in youth: ". . . I am sick of propertied Caesars./ I have dreamed my great dreams of their passing./ I shall roll up my sleeves and make America over!"

Meanwhile the young people who came as pilgrims to Washington during the Rooseveltian reformation fairly idolized Tugwell for the enemies he had made and as one who embodied all that was best in the New Deal. In many ways they exaggerated the influence such men enjoyed over the President, and they did not understand then how transitory was their power. From my observation the New Deal "commissars" did not hold office or last very long, except for a few who were opportunistic and had thick hides. At any moment their heads might be cut off, as soon happened to Hugh Johnson and Raymond Moley.

In the early period of their relations, prior to Roosevelt's taking office—as Tugwell describes it in his retrospective writings—the professor thought he had won the President over to his own statist ideas. Being convinced that underconsumption among the masses of people was the principal cause of depression, he urged that the state should intervene and restore buying power by the redistribution of income. Roosevelt at intervals favored deficit spending, also urged by Harry Hopkins and others. Yet he never held to any consistent ideology for long, but kept shifting ground, now showing himself progressive, now conservative. His practice of *Realpolitik* and of the arts of compromise was both fascinating and disconcerting. In afterthought Tugwell made the penetrating observation that Roosevelt was always very well aware of how much he needed the support of conservatives, especially in Congress, but felt that the liberals could be allowed to wait for what they wanted. My own thought was that, after all, the liberals had *nowhere else to go;* they had no one to lean on but Roosevelt.

His want of intellectual consistency has puzzled historians ever since his time, as it troubled many of his own contemporaries. He had a taste for bold experiments but was likely to abandon them hastily when results proved unrewarding. His complete about-face on the issue of monopoly, which he strongly encouraged in his first term under the NRA but prosecuted in his second term, is only one of the more famous examples of Roosevelt's reversing his course. Some have tried to define his beliefs as those of a patrician, a landed squire who was never much occupied with practical business but held by the idea of the noblesse oblige of inherited wealth. Yet the patrician side of him explains nothing; other descendants of old merchant families with far greater wealth showed no sense of obligation to the poor. The intellectuals of the thirties thought of him as essentially the honest broker weighing the claims of opposing interest groups in the society.

Roosevelt at all times was terribly aware of the built-in resistances within our government of divided powers. After the springtime honeymoon of 1933 the senior members of Congress (often Southern Democrats) took the time to read the bills he submitted and practiced the arts of delay as always in the past. He faced powerful resistance also in the Supreme Court. And even in the administrative branch a man like Jesse Jones, who was affiliated with big business and controlled a vast government banking empire in the RFC, could not be dislodged except at great cost. Roosevelt maintained terms of peace, if not of friendship, not only with Jones but with the other old Texas banker, Vice-President Garner, still a power in the Senate.

Though he was obviously partial to the progressives and reformers in his entourage, Roosevelt made it plain to them on a number of occasions that he would not go far out to help them if they got into trouble with the professionals and regional bosses of his party. A man of power often feels lonely, and so Roosevelt enjoyed his relations with advisers such as Tugwell who were loyal and disinterested. After becoming Assistant Secretary of Agriculture, however, Tugwell was soon involved in the dissensions within the AAA. The President therefore thought of kicking him upstairs in 1934 to the office of Undersecretary of his department, at the same time removing him from the controversies in the AAA. However, South Carolina's Senator E. D. ("Cotton Ed") Smith stood in a position to harass the agricultural program and block the promotion of Tugwell. Then Roosevelt learned that Smith wanted a political crony of his, a man with a homicide record, appointed as a U. S. Marshal, and he promptly granted this request. Thereafter he used to jest about having gained Tugwell's confirmation by virtue of a horse-trade for Senator Smith's "favorite murderer." You could probably not find in all the volumes on modern political science a better illustration of Franklin Roosevelt's improvisations in the art of government.

§ § §

While studying the working of the NRA I looked in on the Department of Agriculture in order to learn something of how the planning of our agricultural economy was proceeding. There I found my old acquaintance Jerome N. Frank enthroned in an enormous office as general counsel of the Agricultural Adjustment Authority, then the major activity of his department. The quick, high-spirited Frank operated as Secretary Henry A. Wallace's chief legal counsel, regularly accompanying him to conferences at the White House and serving virtually as head and front of the New Deal contingent in the AAA. Frank looked happy because of the power he wielded. Commanding the large legal staff of the AAA he labored to define that bureau's powers, supervised its administrative work, and enforced its rulings.

I had met Frank in 1928 in Chicago, where he had lived since childhood and practiced law successfully for many years. For a corporation lawyer in that hard-boiled town he was surprisingly bookish and literary; at our first meeting he kept me up all night talking of a bewildering variety of subjects. As a student at the University of Chicago he had first specialized in literature, and by the age of twenty he had completed an autobiographical novel that editors thought brilliant but which was so self-revealing he dared not publish it. His father, however, a man of business who had once been disbarred from the practice of law, urged Jerry so persistently to take up the legal profession in his place that he finally yielded. Jerry passed the bar and soon became a member of a leading Chicago law firm. He also took an active part in the Democratic reform movement that centered on Mayor Dever and Professor Charles E. Merriam. At the same time, having married the accomplished poet Florence Kiper, he enjoyed friendships during the twenties with members of Chicago's remarkable literary group: Carl Sandburg, Sherwood Anderson, Ben Hecht, and others. In 1929 he moved to New York, where he joined the large firm of Chadbourne, Stanchfield, and Levy. Around that time he returned to writing and completed his first, highly original book, *Law and the Modern Mind* (1930), a Freudian study of the psychology of courts, lawyers, and clients.

In his early forties Jerry was a singular-looking individual and, though well-to-do, negligently dressed. He was of medium height and skinny figure, with a sloping forehead, a tousled mop of gray-black hair, a long nose, and eyes that glittered feverishly in their dark bags, the consequence of his chronic insomnia. Lying awake at night he read omniverously. He was a compulsive talker and continually astonished his hearers with his erudition in such different fields as ancient law, or anthropology, or Russian literature, or the latest theories of semantic philosophy. As he was a man of wit, indeed an apt maker of phrases, I found him, as did others, endlessly entertaining if sometimes disconcerting; he was moreover good-humored and gracious in argument. I can think of none who could expound the policies of the New Deal with more insight than he.

When I encountered him in New York in the early thirties he told me he was becoming fed up with his lucrative but "very cynical" corporation practice. In March 1933 he wrote to Felix Frankfurter: "I want to get out of this Wall Street racket. This crisis seems to me the equivalent of a war, and I would like to join up for the duration." Frankfurter, who knew Jerry only by reputa-

tion, recommended his services to Tugwell and Wallace, and so he
was appointed general counsel of the AAA.

A strong attraction grew up at first among the three men. Frank
found Wallace "sincere and simple" (though he proved more complex later on), and he felt a deep kinship with Tugwell. Before their
families could join them in Washington they lived for a while in
adjacent rooms at the Cosmos Club and worked together in high
excitement, day and night, on contracts and enforcement procedures for the AAA program; Jerry also helped Tugwell and Johnson
draft parts of the NRA law (which followed passage of the AAA by
six weeks).

The case history of Jerome Frank has long fascinated me; it is
the story of a brilliant intellectual and lawyer who enlisted for the
New Deal, rapidly became one of Roosevelt's court favorites, and
for a while appeared in a role a big city boy would never have
anticipated for himself, that of benefactor for millions of America's
farmers. The account of the trials endured by him, and also by
Tugwell and Wallace, which Frank gave me seems to illuminate
important aspects of the Roosevelt Era that have not yet been
clearly explained.

Amid the tumult of farmers taking up their shotguns to resist
foreclosures, or overturning milk trucks at scattered points from
New York to Oregon, the AAA was quickly devised as an omnibus
bill offering several alternate methods of farm aid by the government to be employed at the discretion of the President and his
deputies. The law contained provisions for price support, for export
subsidies, for bounty payments to farmers voluntarily reducing their
acreage, even for crop loans at prices above the market; finally, it
called for inflating the currency in terms of gold.

Henry Wallace, son of a former Republican Secretary of Agriculture and a liberal farm journal editor, was an excellent choice
for the director of the program. Associated with him was George N.
Peek, who was named Administrator of the AAA and enjoyed a
more or less autonomous position, much like his friend Johnson in
the NRA. Peek, a former farm implement manufacturer associated
since War Industry Board days with Bernard Baruch, had long been
an active advocate of federal aid for farmers as laid down in the

McNary–Haugen "equalization" bill, which called for export subsidies of farm products. Both Presidents Coolidge and Hoover had opposed the McNary–Haugen scheme, but its provisions were included in the AAA bill with the support of the American Farm Bureau Federation, the conservative farmers' group.

The more forward-looking element in the Department of Agriculture, headed by Professor M. L. Wilson of Montana State College, pinned their hopes for recovery mainly on the newer farm allotment plan for crop and acreage curtailment and government bounty payments in accordance with such reduction. Farm allotment was a bold scheme, chiefly M. L. Wilson's, to control (really to cut) production in the face of colossal surpluses and declining world markets. It required that farmers vote for such a plan in the counties, and where a majority opted for allotment they were to go in with the program.

As the passage of the AAA act in the late spring of 1933 had met with some delay, planting and breeding had already begun and big surpluses were again expected. Government agents therefore hastened to introduce agreements for plowing under a part of the cotton crop and for the slaughter of six million pigs. The farmers were promised not only cash bounties but also rising market prices.

With the launching of the AAA (as with the NRA a few weeks later) the federal government went into business in a big way. It attempted to control the entire food raising economy by converting abundance into scarcity. (For then too our national problem was affluence in farm commodities.) To raise some $500 million in benefits the farm allotment plan required that processors of farm products, meat packers, tobacco firms, dairying concerns, and cotton manufacturers pay a processing tax on the increased wholesale price of their goods that would be passed on to the consumers. In short the government entered into collusion with the industrialists of the food processing trade to permit price increases and then taxed away part of such increases to pay farmers for acreage production.

Peek, a bluff, red-faced, pugnacious man of about sixty, disliked the farm allotment scheme favored by Wallace and Tugwell, but he went along with them for the while—hoping the plan would fail and that the government would then fall back on his own recipe of marketing agreements and export subsidies. To this end he urged using only mild controls over producing farmers and processors. Jerome Frank soon found that in the matter of price agreements the meat packers, milk distributors, and cotton and tobacco manufacturers, acting in combination, were trying to put over the largest possible increases in wholesale prices of finished products. This was bound to happen when government became the active partner of industry and protected it from prosecution. Frank therefore, with the support of Wallace and Tugwell, worked for strict control of the processors in order to prevent gouging of the public.

The AAA had also a consumers' council for the protection of the public. Its chief was Frederic C. Howe, the aging liberal lawyer and author; his principal assistant was Gardner Jackson, a former resident of Boston and a protégé of Frankfurter who had been involved in the long fight to save Sacco and Vanzetti. The impetuous Jackson, a convivial figure in Washington society of that day, was by inheritance a man of independent means but an emotional radical. He carried on a loud and forceful agitation against Peek's policies, which he held favored the big farmers and food industrialists. Millions were on relief and needed milk for their children, he protested, yet prices were being drastically increased to the highest levels in years.

In the AAA, as in the NRA, big business codes were constantly under negotiation with government officials, and internal conflicts over policy quickly developed and were freely aired in public. Peek would be off somewhere making deals with packers or cigarette manufacturers, while Tugwell, in a public speech, would deliver a blast at those same interests. In one instance Tugwell, in Wallace's absence (but with his evident approval), cut off funds marked by Peek for certain export "dumping" agreements. In this dispute over authority Peek lodged his protests before Roosevelt. Conservatives in Congress raised an outcry against the "Reds" and "city lawyers" in the AAA who were "ignorant" of farm problems. Roosevelt had to compose, as best he could, these quarrels among his aides and avoid hostile action in Congress by Southern Democrats. On this occasion he upheld the Wallace-Tugwell-Frank faction and invited Peek to resign and go on a foreign mission to study export markets for farm commodities. In December 1933 Chester C. Davis, a Western farm editor who had been Peek's chief assistant, replaced him as administrator of the AAA.

During our talks in Washington Frank leaked a good deal of information to me (off the record) about the warfare raging between the AAA's legal division and the pork barons, tobacco kings, and their like. Whenever his department ruled that price-raising agreements were to be revised downward, "all hell would break loose," Jerry said. The food and tobacco manufacturing companies embodied some of the world's greatest corporate fortunes, and their lawyers and lobbyists were well equipped to give battle to the liberals. It was the sort of legal-political struggle that Frank fairly reveled in.

Frank said that he had been repeatedly asked to sanction agreements arranged by Peek and his aides that he found to be "infamous bargains" and so "shameful" that he refused to sign them for the AAA. On the contrary he insisted that the food and tobacco processors open their books and records to the government's lawyers so that, by standard accounting practice, agreements might be reached that would be fair both to the public and the industrialists. But the companies were up in arms at the very idea of showing their books. Frank pointed out that they were ready to accept the government's aid in forming combinations to control output and raise prices, but they would not move to cooperate in the public's interest. Since Peek's faction and the legal division were deadlocked, Frank with the help of Tugwell had brought about a showdown the previous winter between the conservative group in AAA and Secretary Wallace. Frank had a grin as big as the Cheshire cat's in relating how Peek (who had tried to remove him) had himself been ousted, largely because of Rex Tugwell's powerful pleading before Roosevelt.

Still there was no peace on the agricultural front. The press cried scandal at the slaughter of millions of pigs in a time of world hunger. Wallace defended this course as an emergency action made necessary by the failure of the old regime to deal with the farm surpluses. No one made moral protests, he pointed out, when manufacturers closed down plants to kill output and adjust to lowered demand.

The drought in 1934 gave temporary help to the AAA's scarcity program. But in time it became clear that the acreage reduction plan worsened the plight of poor tenant farmers and share-croppers and benefited mainly the big commercial farms. These were signed up for the AAA allotment contracts and received cash benefits; in curtailing acreage they generally cut out marginal land, most often rented to tenants, and raised output on their richer soil with the aid of chemicals and machinery. The five million families and single men on subsistence farms received little or no cash benefits. Many of them were dispossessed, forced to leave their wretched cottages and go on relief or ride off in jalopies, like the Joads in John Steinbeck's novel *The Grapes of Wrath*, toward California to find work as migratory laborers.

At the end of 1933, in an order designed to lessen distress among tenant farmers, the AAA's legal division stipulated that farm owners receiving benefits for acreage reduction pay a proportionate part of such cash to their tenants and share-croppers and allow them to remain in their cabins and on the land they rented. The large Southern cotton farmers angrily protested that such restrictions violated their freedom to manage their own property. Though we tend to idealize our individualistic farmers as the sturdy yeomanry of America, the truth is they were finding ways under the New Deal of robbing tenants of their small share of AAA benefits and dispossessing them by the tens of thousands. It was indeed a difficult task for the government to control the expenditure of cash benefits by cotton farmers all over the Southern states. But the legal division of the AAA showed itself determined to put teeth in the contracts for 1935 so as to safeguard the interests of tenants. As a result the cotton farmers brought great pressure to bear upon the AAA through the Farm Bureau Federation and their friends in Congress.

Throughout 1934 the newspapers carried accounts of demonstrations by mobs of dispossessed share-croppers in Arkansas and other cotton-growing states, and of their being brutally suppressed by the local authorities. In July 1934 the Southern Farm Tenants' Union was organized in Arkansas; its strike activities and some shooting affrays were attributed by owner-farmers to the influence of radical agitators arriving from the North, including the socialist leader Norman Thomas, who was run out of one county. Gardner Jackson made a tour of Arkansas for the AAA staff and brought back grim tales of the share-croppers' misfortunes. But the conservative personnel administering the AAA, now headed by Chester C. Davis, favored "letting things be" and avoiding enforcement measures that might exasperate the commercial farmers. Davis, incidentally, had been advised by his predecessor, Peek, to get rid of Jerome Frank and his "gang" of New Deal lawyers, as well as of Gardner Jackson; and Davis seems to have resolved to undo them at the first good opportunity.

§   §   §

By 1935 a measure of success attended the government's farm program, partly owing to money inflation, partly to the hand of God bringing drought. Within two years farm income had risen by 55 per cent on the average, though it was not yet up to full parity with the revenues of the mid-twenties. Yet many tenant farmers who badly needed buying power seemed worse off than before. Their labor at food raising was becoming redundant. Indeed theirs was the old problem of rural poverty, only now more fully exposed. Meanwhile it seemed that their landlords were being paid by the government to throw them on the relief rolls! After a time the agricultural planners would form new schemes such as the Rural Resettlement Administration, which was initiated in 1935, to rescue a portion of them.

II.

As I left Washington in the summer of 1934 Jerry Frank was riding high, apparently enjoying the full favor of the President. But several months later, in February 1935, I read in the newspapers that this redoubtable man had been suddenly dismissed from office. It happened that I did not see him again until

(287)

we met during the summer at the beach on Martha's Vineyard and he told me his story.

At first he spoke with a reluctance unusual in him. Quite evidently his amour-propre had been sorely wounded. His wife told me later that he had never in his life met with any such reverse, but had always managed to land on his feet. Nor had he cherished any illusions about Roosevelt's methods of *Realpolitik*. What Jerry reproached himself for was not having played his cards at the game of power cleverly enough.

When he was rudely sacked, after two years of devoted labor and while carrying out faithfully the directives of the President and Secretary Wallace, Frank made no complaint to the newspaper reporters who sought an explanation; in fact he made no statement at all. With him a goodly number of the young lawyers of his staff were fired, also several of the officials of the AAA Consumers' Council, including Gardner Jackson. Were they guilty of any wrongdoing? From what Frank told me, and from what I learned elsewhere, it was a brutal purge of the liberal faction in the AAA.

During the latter part of 1934 the deadlock had continued between the executive group under Chester C. Davis and the legal division under Frank. Marketing agreements for the next season's crops were negotiated with the meat packers and other processors by Davis and his aides according to Davis's policies. As far as possible Frank delayed these contracts in the legal division, which had authority to review and, if need be, correct their terms. The millers, packers, and cotton spinners continued to protest that the AAA's lawyers were "socialists" who sought access to their private business records in order to impose a socialistic control over their business. Hitherto Secretary Wallace had given support to the lawyers' group by public statements to the effect that "capitalism takes out too much in the way of profits and does not pay out enough to labor and agriculture."

The conflict grew sharper when it came to dealing with the grievances of the share-croppers. Davis evidently believed that the AAA should not tie in provisions for social reform or for relief of the tenants with its benefit payments. Meanwhile he tried to establish some procedures by which ousted tenants could lodge complaints and seek redress. The legal division, however, considered this method ineffectual, for the share-croppers would be faced with years of litigation in the courts. Thus it pressed for strict agreements by which farm owners would be obliged to retain their tenants.

Quite a remarkable group of lawyers had been recruited by Jerome Frank for the AAA. As many as one hundred and thirty of them at the peak period of AAA activity were engaged in writing or reviewing marketing and acreage contracts or seeing to their enforcement. They constituted undoubtedly a bureaucratic organization of some weight in carrying on the New Deal program, which they believed was intended to aid the poor and the landless as well as the rich farmers. Among them were men like Thurman Arnold, a native of Wyoming and professor at the Yale Law School; Adlai Stevenson, a young member of the Illinois bar; the precocious Abe Fortas, a native of Tennessee, then just out of Yale Law School; and a whole group of Harvard Law School graduates recommended by Felix Frankfurter, including Alger Hiss, Lee Pressman, and Nathan Witt, also John Abt, a graduate of the University of Chicago.

Alger Hiss said in recalling this period: "For the first time in ages, as it seemed, the conjunction of social and economic forces had brought together in Washington a group of dedicated intellectuals who were determined to help change the old order and try new ways of doing things." Another of these law officers said years later: "We came down to Washington like young knights in shining armor, believing that at last we could do something for the people."

But far from being inundated with liberals or radicals, the AAA staff contained a goodly number of executives from food processing companies, like Armour and Swift, in key positions, as well as former managers of corporation farms of 100,000 acres or more. Moreover the hundreds of field agents of the Agricultural Department's Extension Service enforcing the crop control program were long accustomed to working with the local representatives of the Farm Bureau Federation, most of whom considered the share-croppers expendable. One concludes that the New Deal zealots in the AAA were a minority, but a vocal and spirited minority.

Outwardly the New Deal showed a smiling and paternal image; it promised both economic recovery and some redistribution of income. But when you worked on the inside of the new federal agencies and found your government acting in collusion with the industrial cartels, when you saw how the terms of important contracts were actually negotiated with those corporations' lawyers, and when you met with implacable resistance in trying to correct some of the evils introduced into such agreements, then the encounter with these powerful and selfish interests could be a sorely disillusioning experience. Under the circumstances it was not surprising that a few of these young men dreamed of some other and more just form of society. (Several persons on the AAA staff were afterward accused of having been members of the Communist Party.)

Frank's chief assistant in drafting and reviewing agreements was Alger Hiss, who had graduated from the Harvard Law School with high honors and served as secretary to Supreme Court Justice Holmes. Hiss had been recommended for his position by Felix Frankfurter. Another active aide of the general counsel was Lee Pressman, Hiss's classmate at Harvard who had worked under Jerome Frank at his New York law firm. This group decided to draft a "reinterpretation" of Mr. Davis's preliminary cotton contract form so that cash benefits would be reduced to farm owners who dispossessed tenants from acreage taken out of cultivation. Tenants were to be assured of the right of occupation during the period of such contracts. The new version of the agreement was written by Alger Hiss, whom Frank considered objective and prudent, and under Frank's supervision. During Davis's absence from Washington the new forms, after being approved by his deputy administrator, were issued to the AAA's agents.

The cotton planters immediately set up a great cry of anguish; Davis rushed back to Washington in a rage and cancelled the new orders. He then went to Secretary Wallace, denounced the action of the legal division as representing a complete reversal of previous policy, and demanded the outright dismissal of Jerome Frank and company, as well as of certain members of the Consumers' Council, on the ground of insubordination. Being a man of tougher fiber than Peek, Davis made it plain to Wallace that he was delivering an ultimatum: he indicated that the farm bloc would now raise a storm in Congress and Wallace himself might be out of the Department of Agriculture in thirty days.

Henry Wallace was certainly fashioned to be an ornament of our public life. One of the most knowledgeable men in his field, he spoke and wrote with authority and a native eloquence, as one inspired with his mission to restore the health of our agricultural communities. Owing to the initial success of his program he had emerged as one of the plumed knights of the Roosevelt administration and marked for future glory. In a crisis, however, when the clash of powerful interest groups swirled about him, Wallace was likely to behave in the strangest fashion, becoming the most enigmatic of men and sometimes actually doing a vanishing act. Though he had reserves of moral courage after his own fashion, he evidently found the struggle distasteful and longed to be away from it all, under a tree, a mystic or *guru* contemplating the universe. Roosevelt found him a most estimable man, but he called him a "Yoga." Gardner Jackson, who was then close to Wallace, saw him as a "divided soul." But Jerome Frank perceived the presidential urge in him. Nor was Wallace alone among Roosevelt's Cabinet secretaries in entertaining such ambitions: Ickes, Hull, Farley, Hopkins, and others all dreamed about the presidential succession in 1940; and Wallace, by gaining the Vice-Presidency in the unexpected third term, came closer to the throne than the others.

Meanwhile Davis insisted that Jerome Frank and all his crowd of reformers be sacked; he himself would throw them out with Wallace's authorization. But they were Wallace's loyal lieutenants. Later Wallace indicated to Frank that he took the issue to Roosevelt, but the President either could not understand what it was all about (as Frank surmised) or desired to remain above the battle.

In the clash with Peek, a year earlier, Wallace had gone out of town while Tugwell and Frank had forced a showdown. This time, as it happened, Tugwell was absent in Florida recovering from a bout of influenza. The troubled Wallace surrendered to Davis.

That noon, ignorant of the confrontation between Wallace and Davis, Frank and Lee Pressman went out to lunch together; on their return to their offices they found, to their surprise, brief notes of dismissal placed on their desks, signed by Administrator Davis. Frank became highly agitated, finding it inconceivable that Wallace should have authorized his dismissal without a hearing on some claim that he had "exceeded his authority." Government lawyers often reinterpreted or modified directives in accordance with their understanding of the law. "I simply can't believe it!" Frank exclaimed. "And without a hearing!" He had faith in Wallace and insisted that he must see him immediately, but, as often happened, the Secretary had shut himself off from all visitors. The whole legal staff was in tumult that day. Those dismissed included six lawyers assisting the General Counsel, as well as Gardner Jackson of the Consumers' Council; several others were going to resign in protest.

At the end of that afternoon Frank and Alger Hiss, as delegates for the others who were fired, were permitted to see Wallace in his office. (Hiss had not been dismissed, but it was his intention to resign and go to some other government agency.) Wallace showed deep embarrassment. When asked by Frank why he had not gone to them directly with any objections he might have had to their conduct, he admitted that it was because he "could not bear to face them." It was true, he said, that Frank and the other men who were purged had labored well, but he had no choice in the matter. At the time not only Wallace but Roosevelt himself lived in fear of certain senators, including Joseph T. Robinson of Arkansas.

In his press conference announcing the purge of the reformers the next morning Wallace, by way of explanation, remarked flippantly that there had been "too much *New Republic*-Liberal-Socialist spirit" in his Department.[1]

Jerome Frank said nothing in public to defend himself. Even Roosevelt felt apologetic about his dismissal, for he asked his White House assistant, Corcoran, to find a place for Frank as a legal consultant.

Meanwhile Rex Tugwell hastened back to Washington at the weekend in a belated attempt to rescue his allies. His impassioned protests before his "august friend Franklin" (as he called him) were

---

[1] Henry Wallace was to perform some remarkable somersaults in later years, not only writing a political column for *The New Republic* but also, in opposition to the Cold War, running for President on the little Progressive Party ticket in 1948 in alliance with Lee Pressman and Rex Tugwell.

vain. Although Tugwell had been cautioned earlier by the President to avoid further controversy over AAA policy, he now declared roundly that those who fought for the New Deal had been betrayed and that Henry Wallace was "a man of jelly." He ended up by tendering his own resignation. Roosevelt prevailed upon him to remain at his post for the while, which he did out of personal loyalty.

Originally Tugwell had hoped that the AAA would lead Americans to the middle way between socialism and capitalism; our farmers, formerly so narrowly individualistic, would be forced by the crisis and their own self-interest to work collectively for the public good. Writing in retrospect twenty years later, he declared that the AAA benefited the food and cotton corporations mainly and only about 20 per cent, the upper crust, of the farm population.

In a letter of February 1935 Mary Heaton Vorse, then employed in the Indian Bureau, wrote me: "They are saying in Washington that the New Deal is all washed up since the 'purge.'" But the band of immitigable young reformers who had been plowed under made merry over their reverses. Their hoped-for agency of reform had simply become the captive of the great food corporations. The bright young men who were purged or resigned (like Hiss, Witt, and Abt) were promptly invited to take up useful posts in other federal bureaus under Ickes, Hopkins, and Morgenthau, or with Congressional committees like those headed by Nye or La Follette. Two years later President Roosevelt called Frank back to Washington to serve as a member of the Securities and Exchange Commission. After that he was appointed a Justice of the Federal Court of Appeals in the Southern District of New York, one of the country's highest judicial offices. In his years on the bench our ebullient, diverting Jerry performed with greater distinction than he had in any previous role; some of his decisions made legal history. He also enjoyed lecturing at the Yale Law School, and in those days, in his own restless fashion, he seemed truly happy.

To look back, however, at the events of 1935, much was written at that time and in the years that followed of the rise of a "new elite," made up of Roosevelt's administrative lieutenants in charge of powerful federal agencies—the "commissars" of the New Deal.

It was often remarked then that mere unknowns, even former social workers or professors, the sort of people who had "never met a payroll," served as advisers to the President or headed big bureaucratic organizations such as the NRA, the AAA, the WPA, or the TVA. Some experts in public affairs, like Felix Frankfurter, hoped that these developments signified progress toward an improved civil service of career men. Others, however, like James Burnham writing at the end of the thirties, leaped to the conclusion that this extension of the powers of the executive branch of government portended the arrival of a managerial society. At the same time many large corporations were becoming institution-like bureaucracies, controlled not by owner stockholders but by directorates of executive officers (as is well illustrated by A. A. Berle and Gardner Means in *The Corporation and Private Property*). These parallel developments toward institutionalism in government and private industry led Burnham to prophesy with confidence the coming of a "Managerial Revolution" (the title of the book he published in 1940).[2] To Burnham Roosevelt's top administrative assistants, Hopkins, Ickes, Wallace, Tugwell, Frank, and the like, made up an elite group of managers who served as the proconsuls of the new order. The same trend toward managerial control by an elite was detected by him in Communist Russia and National Socialist Germany.

My own observation of the alternations of fortune suffered by such "managerial" fellows as General Johnson or Tugwell was that their power was quite ephemeral. In my periodic visits to Washington I could see how they rose and fell, how their public careers were suddenly and rudely terminated. Such persons constituted no newly emergent power group because their tenure in the New Deal agencies was so uncertain. It depended entirely on the presidential authority, and even the mighty Roosevelt often wavered or came tardily to the support of his lieutenants after their troubles had become acute.

Tugwell wrote in his diary toward 1933 that the power struggles going on behind the scenes in Washington exceeded in ferocity anything he had known in all the years he had studied our political

[2] Burnham, of course, imitates the thinking of Vilfredo Pareto, the old sociologist of fascism who regarded history as a "circulation of elites."

economy. The conflicts involved regional and class forces in politics: the old farm bloc caused Wallace's mind to be changed for him and forced the elimination of men like Tugwell and Frank. Tugwell deeply disliked the secret power struggles; but some "managers" like Ickes, Hopkins, Morgenthau, and even Wallace endured for years by adapting themselves to the President's opportunist tactics and compromising with principle in the hope that good would eventually come of it.

Rex Tugwell's career remains for us an illuminating story of those times. His set of assumptions, to my mind, came down to the idea of a republic ruled by a philosopher king—as in Plato's *Dialogues*. In terms of modern America the President was our elected king; instructed by virtuous counsellors he might use his large powers to reorganize our society as a welfare state, part collectivist, part regulated private enterprise. But the attempt at national planning never worked in real life as neatly as men like Tugwell had hoped; in truth it broke down in many sectors of the economy. Perhaps Tugwell, like others, exaggerated the charisma Franklin Roosevelt acquired during the hundred days of the 1933 crisis. After that the President had to resort not to magic but to the tools of raw power. The upshot was that the original welfare programs worked out on paper were, in practice, modified beyond all recognition. And so Tugwell, one of the most disinterested and idealistic of Roosevelt's advisers, found his grand purpose thwarted, his hopes betrayed.

Detaching himself from Roosevelt, Tugwell later acted as an adviser to two other brilliant politicos with mass appeal for voters: Mayor La Guardia of New York and Munoz Marin of Puerto Rico. Repeatedly he tried to translate his ideas into reality through the agency of those power-conscious leaders. But his efforts usually ended, as he has confessed, in relative or complete failure. For example, when he and Mrs. Roosevelt were helping to resettle landless farmers on subsistence homesteads and in handicrafts jobs, he found that most of them drifted away as soon as they could earn more elsewhere. Some of Tugwell's friends thought him politically naive or weak. But if he met with repeated disappointment he remains nevertheless an appealing figure among the crowds thronging the corridors of power, and study of his failures themselves seems instructive.

§ § §

Walking with Jerry Frank on the beach that night a few months after the "purge" and listening to his story, I thought him one of the most tormented human beings I had ever seen. He had not the faith of a Marxian to sustain him in the hope of predestined improvement, but as a practiced corporation lawyer he considered himself well versed in the Machiavellianism of business or public life. Therefore he reproached himself all the more bitterly for having fallen victim to the power struggle in Washington. He admitted that his head had been turned by the authority he enjoyed as legal policeman for the AAA.

When he had finished his account I remarked: "After all men like you, Tugwell, and others enjoyed only an ephemeral, a transient power through the favor of the great white chief. You court favorites and commissars only *thought* you had power. But the moment his support was removed on grounds of expediency you were out, done for. You may be an able lawyer or economist, but it doesn't matter, because you fellows have no political or geographical constituencies, no mass support behind you."

Organized labor, I pointed out, was now enjoying a remarkable growth in influence. Recently Sidney Hillman, among others, had been able to bring pressure to bear on Roosevelt against General Johnson and against Professor Leo Wolman, the President's arbiter in automobile and steel labor disputes; eventually they were both forced to resign. Hillman was in a position to influence several hundred thousand voters in New York and Chicago by virtue of his strong union, which also had money for election campaigns. John L. Lewis likewise had hundreds of thousands of marching men behind him in Pennsylvania, Ohio, and Illinois, and a war chest. Such men commanded the big battalions that were needed to win battles. "And they will remain on the scene a long time," I wound up, "while you who have no grassroots following come and go at the whim of a clever President."

Jerry Frank laughed ruefully, assenting to my inferences.

III.

On that evening in 1935 when Frank unburdened himself to me he gave no intimation that there had ever been anything questionable about the behavior of the members of his staff. Several of them however, especially Alger Hiss, became highly controversial personages and figured in the famous public cause stirred up thirteen years later, in 1948, by the revelations and accusations of Whittaker Chambers.

To return to Chambers, whom I remembered after our one meeting in 1933 as a sort of conspiratorial clown, it seems that his business as an underground intelligence agent, according to his confessions, brought him to Washington. While posing as a journalist he was able to make contact with certain federal officials in the years 1933 to 1936, among them Alger Hiss, who during part of that time was a legal assistant to the Senate Committee for the Investigation of the Munitions Industry and afterward served in the State Department. In his later guise as an exalted patriot who would save the country by recanting his earlier beliefs and denouncing both himself and his former friends, Chambers made sweeping charges in public that communists had infiltrated the federal bureaus in great number and had established a "cell" in the Department of Agriculture with the purpose of undermining our government.

A number of historians have accepted at face value the charges of a conspiracy in the AAA, and Chambers's assertions that Jerome Frank's legal division harbored an underground group plotting "in shrouded evening meetings . . . to sabotage the New Deal." These people, as Arthur M. Schlesinger, Jr., has concluded, were interested not in helping the farmer but "in using his woes as a lever with which to discredit the system." [3]

After going to work on the staff of *Time*, Chambers enjoyed rapid promotion, rising eventually to the position of senior editor in charge of foreign affairs. I had the impression that Henry Luce, publisher of *Time*, then gave strong encouragement to repentant radicals like Chambers who claimed to be experts in exposing

[3] *The Age of Roosevelt* (Boston: Houghton Mifflin; 1958), II, pp. 52, 54, 59.

Russia and communism. At one time Chambers was even permitted to screen persons applying for jobs in his department of the magazine, asking them such questions as: "Do you believe in God? Do you own property? Anyone who hasn't invested in America's soil cannot be trusted to be loyal." [4]

In September 1939, as war opened in Europe and Soviet Russia appeared now aligned with Nazi Germany, Whittaker Chambers called on Assistant Secretary of State A. A. Berle and made revelations about Communist Party "fractions" within the State Department and other bureaus. Chambers's accusation centered upon Alger Hiss. At the time Mr. Berle, who was in charge of security matters in his department, indicated extreme disbelief that "the Hiss boys and Nat Witt," a handful of young lawyers, were "going to take over the government" and with it the Army and Navy. Chambers then did not claim that these persons were actually engaged in conspiracy, but only that they had formed a Marxist study group in order to prepare for a revolution. Berle, however, felt that he could not proceed against such people as Hiss on the ground that they were accused of studying something or other.

Chambers waited almost a decade longer before returning to the attack in 1948. By then the Cold War was on with its Red scares and its spy hunts. Now Chambers testified in public before the House Un-American Activities Committee, under the wing of Richard M. Nixon, Republican Representative from California, to the effect that Alger Hiss while in federal office had been a communist in close working relations with him, Chambers. There followed the public denials of these allegations by Hiss—then President of the Carnegie Peace Foundation—who also testified voluntarily to the same effect before the House Committee. When Chambers repeated his charges over the radio, without the immunity of a Congressional hearing, Alger Hiss brought civil suit for libel. Before that suit could be tried Chambers came out with his accusations that Hiss had lent himself to espionage by transmitting secret State Department documents to him; then he

[4] Joseph Freeman to author. Freeman also described his interview with Chambers in 1941, on the occasion of his applying for a position on *Time*, in letters to Professor Daniel Aron of Smith College.

brought forth his famous pumpkin with its microfilm and type-written documents, which led to the indictment of Alger Hiss on the charge of perjury.

All this, it will be remembered, took place during an election campaign, under the inspiration of a Committee of Congress dominated then by Mr. Nixon and determined to ruin not only Alger Hiss, but also the reputation of the New Deal and the Fair Deal. I was told that some of Chambers's old friends, who had turned just as violently anticommunist as he, warned him that his course would do great injury to all liberal movements. Chambers would listen to no one: he was utterly convinced that the liberals and New Dealers were "worse" than the communists, and were all "plotting" his destruction—by defending the cause of Hiss. Such expressions have all the signs of paranoia, and I have never understood how men of any intelligence could put much trust in Whittaker Chambers's statements.

On the other hand, many informed persons who have closely studied the labyrinthine Hiss-Chambers Case believe that Chambers, with his disturbed personality, could well have lent himself to a frame-up; and that only an inflamed public opinion judged and sentenced Alger Hiss.

But let us here consider only the allegations of Chambers about the AAA from 1933 to 1935. At the hearings before the Committee and in his autobiography *Witness*, Chambers gives different versions of the alleged conspiracy, but he also declares that the officials he accused were "not primarily an espionage group." Their role, he insists, was however no less important; they were recruiting people for their underground organization and placing them in various government agencies. He adds in summary: "The real power of the Group . . . was a power to influence, from the most strategic positions, the policies of the United States Government, *especially in the labor and welfare fields.* . . . Moreover the Communist Party was in a position to exert a millstone effect both in favor of policies and persons it supported, and against policies and persons it disliked." [5]

This is quite a spider web of intrigue that Chambers depicts for

[5] Whittaker Chambers: *Witness* (New York: Random House; 1952), p. 343.

us. But Lee Pressman, who in 1950, at the time of the Korean War
severed relations with his associates of the left, testified before the
House Un-American Activities Committee that he had been a
member of the Communist Party for about a year, in 1934, and
attended meetings of the group described by Chambers; and he
stated under oath that Alger Hiss had never been one of them.
All of the testimony added together does not yield any evidence
that there ever was a conspiracy to sabotage the AAA farm
program.

In those days the rules of the Department of Agriculture allowed no questioning on Party affiliation in the hiring of personnel,
though it would have been embarrassing to have membership
in the Communist Party generally known. Nor was it surprising that some communists chose to enter the federal service at this
period; as Marxists they hoped the government would one day
control the entire economy, and they desired in the meantime to
familiarize themselves with public administration. To be sure the
government office-holders in overwhelming mass were not communists; moreover the deputies of the big industrial corporations
were present in as great force within the AAA as within the NRA,
and their pressure far exceeded that of the small left groups.

In his posthumous papers Jerome Frank, as I found, had a
good deal to say, though in private—at the time of the Hiss-
Chambers Case—about Chambers's accusations, and also about the
accident of Frank's having engaged a few persons who were afterward charged with being communists. Several years before his
death in 1955 he dictated a long memorandum on the matter of
the alleged conspiracy within his legal division. Of the eighty
lawyers he reckoned that he himself had hired, only five appeared
to have been members of the Communist Party. They had been
recommended as coming not only from preeminent law schools,
like Harvard's, but also, as in the case of Lee Pressman, from important New York law offices. Gardner Jackson, for example, who
was the most rebellious member of the AAA staff, was a man of
independent means, never attracted to communist solutions.

Frank remembered Lee Pressman as having been always correct
in his conduct and "a most resourceful legal mind." He showed

traces of the Marxian "fanatic," Frank recalled, but then he made no secret of his beliefs. Indeed Pressman used to argue vehemently with George Peek about social welfare measures such as establishing low-priced milk stations for the unemployed—which were tried in several municipalities with wide public approval. Pressman had not acted in the way of a conspirator, and had no opportunity to be one.

Finally Frank reviewed his association during two years with Alger Hiss, who had worked always under Frank's supervision. Young Hiss seemed to have been very detached and prudent—"the last man I would have thought of as a communist." Administrator Davis, after dismissing Jerome Frank, had invited Hiss to stay on as his general counsel in place of Frank, which Hiss after some hesitation declined to do. In conclusion Frank declared in his tape-recorded notes that to his knowledge no member of his staff had ever committed any improper or "subversive" action.[6]

Those who knew Alger Hiss in his early years in Washington have described him to me as a gentle soul, reserved and deliberate in manner but capable of strong feelings about situations like that of the tenant farmers. His wife Priscilla was also much affected by the atmosphere of crisis through which the country passed; Jerome Frank called her a "parlor pink." The Hiss couple were also known to be infinitely hospitable to young acquaintances who sometimes descended upon them for help, and shelter too, as did the unhappy Whittaker Chambers. Sometimes the Hiss's small house in Washington was filled with visiting friends who, for lack of space, slept on the floor in the parlor. One receives the impression that it was in innocence that Hiss performed acts of kindness for such a one as Chambers, the pretended journalist, who pursued Hiss with his attentions, tried to learn what he could from him or use him, but in the end brought ruin upon his benefactor.

[6] The tape-recorded interviews given by Jerome Frank are in the Columbia University Oral History Archives. I am indebted to Mrs. Florence K. Frank for permission to use her husband's papers.

Chapter Fourteen

~

"Saving Capitalism"

THE NEW DEAL was not only occupied in the early years with plans for economic recovery, but also with carrying out corrective legislation that would accomplish the reform of a large part of our business system, especially the financial business. There you had the Brandeisian side of the Roosevelt Administration, some of whose new laws stressed *moral reform* above all things, since they required of financial corporations scrupulous regard for their responsibilities to the public and full disclosure of all relevant information to investors in stocks and bonds. The new banking acts of 1933 and 1934 established the very useful Federal Deposit Insurance Agency and separated commercial banks from the securities business; the Securities Exchange Act of 1934 introduced the policing of stock markets by the federal government—after which Roosevelt could say that the nation's financial capital had at last been "removed from Wall Street to Washington."

The spiritual father of all this business reform was the aged Supreme Court Justice Louis D. Brandeis, who earlier in his career had fought many a rousing battle against malefactors in banking, insurance, and railroads. (There was a well-established tradition, dating back twenty years, that Brandeis's powerful attacks in court upon the Morgan-controlled railroad combinations had led the aging J. P. Morgan to get away from it all by journeying as far as Rome, where he died in 1913.)

Two presidential assistants, Thomas Corcoran and Benjamin Cohen, were assigned to the actual drafting of the Securities Exchange bill and to helping secure its passage through Congress. Its provisions generally resembled England's century-old British Companies Act and also derived from our existing state "blue-sky" laws, then but poorly enforced. Roosevelt had pledged sweeping reform of the financial system and supported the SEC bill with great zeal.

President Richard Whitney of the New York Stock Exchange now turned up in Washington at the head of a large Wall Street lobby and a phalanx of corporation lawyers, and he directed a fierce campaign to defeat the bill. Repeatedly he warned Congress that efforts at government control of stock manipulation, and at eliciting information about the transactions of company insiders, would end the free and liquid market so that "grass would grow" in Wall Street. Whitney's arrogant refusal to compromise with the will of Congress was said to have hardened the bill's sponsors, led by Sam Rayburn of Texas, and brought severer regulation than would otherwise have been enacted. But on the morning after the bill was passed Whitney turned about and promised the full cooperation of the Stock Exchange. (How badly the SEC law was needed was well illustrated three years later by the exposure of Whitney's own embezzlements.)

Judging from the furor in the press, generated by the Stock Exchange's publicity men, you would have thought that Corcoran and Cohen were political firebrands carrying bombs in their pockets. I went around to see Ben Cohen and found him entirely different from his public image: he was tall, pale, bespectacled, a gentle-mannered scholar of the law who looked much younger than his forty years. A native of Indiana, educated at the University of Chicago and Harvard Law School, he had not only been successful in private practice but had also acquired some experience in writing public law while counseling the power commissions of Illinois and Wisconsin. Moreover he was knowledgeable enough of investment to have made himself independently wealthy; and now, out of principle, gave his talents to the government. About his work, reputed to be that of a brilliant technician at drafting bills so they would stand tests in court, he could be the most reticent of men. It was with some difficulty that I located him in a tiny office in the vast Interior Building, where he worked nominally under Secretary Ickes but was at the beck and call of the White House. This "solitary bachelor," as he was called, seemed to enjoy seclusion and anonymity.

In conversation he was given to drawing fine legal distinctions and lengthy circumlocutions; yet if one listened patiently one heard him say searching things. I happened to remark that while the SEC was something long needed, it seemed to promise no basic changes; speculation would go on, and boom and busts. Cohen replied that he himself was opposed to drastic planning of everything by the state and hoped that the Roosevelt administration would remain "flexible, experimental, and even not too logical . . . in dealing with the complex character of modern economic life." The federal government, he held, should intervene only where the relations of interdependent groups had broken down, as between banks and their depositors, or stock exchange firms and investors, or industrial management and labor; and it should then intervene only to restore balance, so that the natural forces in society making for change and evolution might come into full play. There, in essence, was the gospel Brandeis had long preached in his famous "socio-logical" briefs and judicial opinions.

The Brandeis school of liberals was strong within the New Deal camp, and as sponsors of true individualism its adherents vigorously dissented from the faction of central planners and controllers. In his first term Roosevelt discreetly called on Brandeis for counsel, though Supreme Court Justices were not supposed to give advice to the executive branch. Tommy Corcoran would run back and forth between the two men. "I was the funnel between the White House and Brandeis—and the ancient Holmes too," he said to me. "And those old men loved to be consulted secretly by the President."

Brandeis's ideal was a Jeffersonian society of public-spirited businessmen working at "more than mere moneymaking" to build a humane, civilized society. His grand design was to improve the ethics of business; and to this end he and his disciples had long ago worked up models of social legislation, covering minimum wages and hours and woman and child labor in various states. From these the New Deal derived many of its ideas. Brandeis was nonetheless a champion of unrestricted competition as the way to progress, and he was a defender of property as well as liberty.

The Justice was not a judicious type but forthright and blunt, sometimes addressing stern admonitions even to Roosevelt on the score of fostering monopoly and price-raising agreements. On such occasions the President merely laughed and called him "old uncle Isaiah."

I tended to believe, with both Karl Marx and Henry Ford, that giant industrial units were an inevitable stage of technological advance, and also that a managed economy might successfully regulate (or own) them some day instead of trying to break up the big ones into little ones. On one occasion when I had been invited to have tea and cookies with Justice Brandeis I hinted at these collectivistic beliefs, and the leonine old man turned so wrathful that he almost blew me out of his parlor. Even at eighty his eyes flashed, his mind was razor sharp, his tongue terrible and swift.

Tommy Corcoran, the curly-haired boy from Rhode Island who became the most famous and uninhibited of presidential assistants, was very different from his partner Ben Cohen: he was shrewd and quick, all Irish gaiety and wit, and there was nothing self-effacing about him. Roosevelt apparently liked such bouncy young men as his aides. But it was not only by drinking whisky with them or playing the guitar for the politicians on the Hill that Corcoran prevailed. As Roosevelt's surrogate he always carried the President's power of patronage as a big stick, usually held in reserve, but sometimes wielded in brutal fashion.

"I'm the sort of half-ass guy," he once said to me, "who can talk with the reformers, then go over to the other camp and sit down and talk to the men of affairs in their own language."

Corcoran too had come out of Frankfurter's class at Harvard to serve as law clerk under Justice Holmes and afterward at the RFC. From 1933 on, as the President's agent trading official patronage for legislative support, he came to glory in the art of the manipulator. While Cohen did the planning and writing, Corcoran did the lobbying. In public hearings in the Senate on the SEC bill in 1934 Corcoran showed a grasp of his subject, and a forcefulness in argument, that astonished financial experts. He recalled this exploit with pride, saying: "I was alone against a whole battery of Wall Street's corporation lawyers, men like John W. Davis and John Foster Dulles—with only Sam Rayburn helping us—and we jammed the bill through."

Did Corcoran hold by any beliefs? He said he tried to be like Roosevelt, "whose strength it was that he had *no* ideology, but improvised from day to day." In the manner of the President, Corcoran looked at the political arena as the site of naked power struggles. The members of Congress who were unchallenged as regional bosses in their states, men like Harry Byrd of Virginia, Huey Long of Louisiana, or Burton Wheeler of Montana, must be treated by the elected "king" as semi-independent political "barons"; their quarrels with each other were to be composed, their demands for federal jobs for their local followers gratified. It was Corcoran's informed opinion that the successive rebellions of men like Long and Wheeler against the Party leader in the White House were provoked by Roosevelt's covert and ruthless maneuvers to strip them of power through the denial of federal patronage.

In these struggles it sometimes fell to Corcoran to carry out "some real dirty work"—so he phrased it—especially during Roosevelt's attempted purge of the Democratic Party's conservatives in 1938. "Some of our finest welfare legislation came to flower out of the slime and dung of low political bargains," he exclaimed in his quite expressive way. In the course of such rough-handed work he acquired lasting enmities "which impaired my usefulness to the President; and so, by 1939, I was expendable and returned to private law."

He told me of all this in 1954. On first coming to Washington he had been as high-minded as any of Frankfurter's honors graduates. But later, when he was out of the government service, during World War II, he used his manipulative skills as advocate and lobbyist for important suppliers of war materials and for pipe lines, shipbuilding companies, and others. "By then," he said, "I wanted to make money and after that more money. A million for each of my six children. After all, there's nothing like dollars to make the wheels go around." He could still speak in a tone of reverence of his saintly friend Ben Cohen, who continued as the idealistic public servant under two Presidents during twenty years, never rightly rewarded, deriving satisfaction only from the performance of his tasks. But in his later years Corcoran himself sounded like a character out of Balzac's *Les Illusions Perdues.*

§   §   §

When Roosevelt appointed Joseph P. Kennedy as chairman of the SEC, which was to enforce the new order in all the nation's securities markets, New Dealers gasped in surprise. Jerome Frank remarked at the time that "putting Joe Kennedy on the SEC is like setting a wolf to guard a flock of sheep." [1] The other four commissioners who surrounded Kennedy were however staunch reformers, including Ferdinand Pecora and James M. Landis. At forty-six the tall, bespectacled, Harvard-educated Joe Kennedy, son of a Boston saloonkeeper and ward boss and son-in-law of Boston's former Mayor John Fitzgerald, was a self-made millionaire and typified some of the newly rich Democrats who hovered about Roosevelt. I remember that Arthur Krock of *The New York Times,* who was often Kennedy's guest at his winter residence in Palm Beach, Florida, described the place as having gold-plated fittings in its bathrooms. Kennedy was not the sort of man who would frighten Wall Street, and in fact he went to great pains to reassure the finance capitalists that the SEC had come to improve Wall Street, not to bury it.

The SEC was soon running smoothly as a federal regulative agency. At its most important branch office, at 120 Broadway, New York, telegraph tickers recording all Stock Exchange transactions, with a clock device stamping their time, were under constant surveillance of the SEC's financial detectives. At the first sign of suspicious activity they would go into action swiftly and begin inquiries. Tips, flashes, and rigged market orders, in fact all the ancient tricks of deception were forbidden; directors of corporations who bought or sold their own stocks were obliged to report such operations publicly and in some circumstances to turn over

[1] As recently as 1933 Kennedy's (then lawful) stock manipulations had been exposed to the public by the Senate Banking Committee.

their profits to their company. Full disclosure of information was required for the flotation of new issues or for their public listing. Violations of the various rules involved penalties of large fines and prison sentences. As Ben Cohen remarked blandly: "Henceforth no big speculators can pretend they were ignorant of what their wives were doing in the market."

Would Wall Street ever be the same again? I asked myself, as I reviewed its changed situation in a magazine article. Certainly Jay Gould would never recognize his old happy hunting grounds. I looked up the old stock market pirate "Sell 'Em Ben" Smith and heard his judgment: "It was high time they regulated the securities markets," he growled; "this was long overdue." As for manipulation, that would go on he prophesied cheerfully, though in more discreet style. "Hell, everybody knows there isn't a stock on the list that doesn't have its 'daddy.' " ("Daddy" was local parlance for financial sponsor or syndicate manager.)

The occasion of the first formal visit of the five Securities and Exchange Commissioners to the New York Stock Exchange caused muffled excitement in the Street. President Whitney, whatever he thought of them, undertook to conduct them on their tour of inspection. It was well known that the floor brokers, then about 150 in number, were given to all sorts of horseplay during market hours; they were equal to slipping a live mouse or a fake gold brick into each other's pockets, or practicing similar crude pranks on the federal commissioners. A die-hard faction among them was said to be so angry over the new law that they would have liked to inflict bodily harm on the SEC delegation. The governors of the Exchange actually threw guards about the trading floor after warning the brokers to be on their good behavior. The brokers stared coldly at the commissioners, but nobody even whistled or thumbed his nose. Meanwhile the market that day almost came to a standstill.

Soon Wall Street took heart again. The SEC carried on its policing work unobtrusively, putting a number of blue-sky and bucket-shop concerns out of business. The element of risk was in no way eliminated, but the ethical standards of the business were perceptibly improved. After some years had passed the manager of one of the largest wire houses said to me: "I don't know how we could have got along without the SEC before this."

II.

The spring and summer of 1934 were memorable for large-scale labor conflicts. Minneapolis witnessed a general strike climaxing the fight of the Teamsters Union for recognition. In San Francisco too, early in June, there was a general strike provoked by the action of police and militia in shooting down striking longshoremen. Legends arose that radical rank-and-file leaders such as Harry Bridges instigated the general strike in the hope of using it as a revolutionary weapon. In reality seasoned leaders of San Francisco's Central Labor Council took command of the affair from the "wild men" of the waterfront; it was they who called out the city's 150,000 workers in every trade in an orderly demonstration of labor power which ended peacefully, as planned, in three days.

During a vacation trip in the late summer I made a little tour of the textile strike front with my friend William Ross, New England organizer for the Ladies Garment Workers, just then on loan to the textile unions in that region. In Massachusetts and Rhode Island the workers were out en masse; their open air meetings, attended by many thousands in the old cities of Providence, New Bedford, and Fall River, had an air of fiesta. Not since the stirring days of 1919 had such crowd movement and enthusiasm been seen here. There had been fighting in the streets, and Ross was often accompanied by armed guards.

At one picnic gathering I heard some grizzled AFL officials addressing the workers in their old-fashioned rhetoric, and I remarked to my friend that the AFL's "Fourth of July orators sounded pretty corny to me." He said: "Never mind that; we are really going places now."

The official American labor body, the AFL, had shown great structural weakness at a time when masses of the unorganized came to join unions, dividing them into different craft unions or throwing them into "federal locals" under officers who knew nothing about their industries. The assembly-line laborers then needed the plant-wide or industrial union, such as the miners and garment workers already had—the "one big union" of the IWW that would soon reappear in modern form. In addition to their troubles with the AFL bureaucrats, the insurgent workers were also vexed by the ambiguous rulings of NRA administrators and the contradictory decisions of Roosevelt himself.

For all the excited palaver in the press about a labor government ruling Washington during the early New Deal, the "friend of the Forgotten Man" appeared not only detached but rather cool to the claims of union labor. Tugwell has related that Roosevelt never really showed the same interest in trade unionism that he did in the farmers. Company unions, recruited it was widely believed by methods of intimidation, continued to expand their numbers in rivalry with free unions. Compliance by management with NRA codes remained voluntary. As a consequence the wave of organizing strikes by textile workers along the whole East Coast in 1934 ended in utter defeat.

To meet the widespread complaints of workers the NRA's Labor Advisory Board was soon replaced by the National Labor Board, which had only vague powers. Its first chairman was Lloyd Garrison, a Wisconsin University professor of law; after his resignation came Francis Biddle of Philadelphia. The Board tried, at first with little success, to bring about compliance with labor codes. Senator Wagner was then led, in the spring of 1934, to propose a labor disputes bill establishing a federal agency fully empowered to supervise shop elections and enforce agreements on union labor conditions. Roosevelt at first was cold to the idea, as was Secretary of Labor Frances Perkins. In an interview in February 1935 the President said: "The federal government cannot, of course, undertake to compel employees and employers to organize. It should be a voluntary organization."

The newly formed American Newspaper Guild, under the high-spirited Heywood Broun, was just then trying to organize the staff of Hearst's newspapers in San Francisco and brought an appeal to the National Labor Board in behalf of a reporter who had been

dismissed for soliciting union members. Chairman Biddle sought
to learn the wishes of the President, who—on the advice of Donald
Richberg—wrote Biddle a letter ordering the Labor Board to stay
out of the case. It was as if to say that the reinstatement of that
reporter would have been "an infringement of the freedom of the
press." At a mass meeting of Newspaper Guild members in New
York Heywood Broun denounced not only the "traitor" Richberg,
but also President Roosevelt, whom he named as "labor's public
enemy number one."

Nevertheless important social gains were slowly and painfully
won: the federal government was being moved gradually to a position where it recognized something like an "inherent right" of
workers to organize for collective bargaining with their employers
in "unions of their own choosing."

The President also appeared divided in his mind about how to
deal with growing public complaint of high prices fixed under NRA
codes. In the late summer of 1934 he issued an executive order
forbidding henceforth all monopolistic price raising and production—curbing agreements under NRA codes. In retrospect Tugwell
said of these confusing procedures: "The economic policy [of the
New Deal] would never have the straightforwardness and simplicity
it should have. And it would never achieve recovery . . . until the
war was imminent—unemployment would never be nearly cured." [2]

§   §   §

Suddenly, all the perplexities of the statesmen and the public about
"national planning" were dissolved on May 27, 1935, when the
Supreme Court handed down its unanimous decision in the "Sick
Chicken Case" (U.S. *vs.* Schechter), declaring the National Recovery Act of 1933 null and void. This sweeping judgment left
Roosevelt and his lieutenants confounded. The High Court ruling,
supported by its liberal minority, allowed no doubt that it held the
labor clause of NRA unconstitutional and that too broad discre-
tionary powers had been delegated by Congress to the President and
his deputies.

[2] R. G. Tugwell: *The Democratic Roosevelt* (New York: Doubleday; 1957), p.
240.

Roosevelt's angry reaction at the moment, and his statement that the Supreme Court would turn back our legal usages to the "horse and buggy days," reflected the sentiment of many Americans. The Court, though with liberals dissenting, had previously struck down several other pieces of New Deal legislation. We had the frightening feeling that the road to the welfare state was barred by our "Nine Old Men." Though the President had won a huge popular mandate in the November 1934 Congressional elections, the aged conservatives of the Court composed an anachronistic institution, a veritable fortress of legal fundamentalism thwarting the will of the majority and their elected representatives. We were forcibly reminded that ours is a "constitutional republic" of divided powers, ruled in accordance with a written charter of long ago that would not lend itself easily to change; in that time of crisis we were not made happier by such reminders.

Chapter Fifteen

❧

Parlor Fascists
and Rabble-Rousers

I STILL ENJOYED friendships formed during the twenties with New Yorkers of the cosmopolitan type, who followed the arts, went to Paris every year, and owned a Picasso or two. But how greatly the subjects of drawing-room conversation had changed! Earlier there would have been talk of the latest capers of Jean Cocteau, or about Joyce's *Finnegans Wake*. Nowadays they spoke of nothing but politics. Some of these young persons, though wealthy, would casually mention on arriving at a cocktail party that they had just come from a picket line somewhere in town. Others purveyed the latest gossip from Washington, gathered through some minor government official or newspaper correspondent; and a knot of eager listeners would gather around the man with inside information.

By the mid 1930's people of the well-to-do class searched anxiously for some alternative to the radicalism of the left. Others called for some crusade that, unlike the Marxists', would "talk American." Such was the campaign of the famous radio priest Father Charles Coughlin, whose panacea was money inflation; that of Upton Sinclair, then leading the EPIC movement (End Poverty in California); and of Senator Huey Long, the boss of Louisiana whose slogan was "Share Our Wealth" and whose rabble-rousing strategems spelled, to many minds, "the coming American fascism."

In the late autumn of 1934, returning from an evening party in midtown Manhattan at the home of a couple who were in the Social Register, I jotted down some random notes of talk I had heard. They suggest the pattern of the conversation that night:

—I tell you this Congress coming in is the wildest bunch of silver money inflationists, know-nothings, and bonus voters there ever was. . . .

—I got it straight from Senator * * * that the farmers in his state are arming themselves. This is *not* a peaceful country. . . .

—As for me, I was for communism from the start, the straight answer, socialism in activist form—but they threw me out, they wouldn't have me because I've got a *petty bourgeois mentality*. . . .

—Give me a corporal's file of engineers, and I could take over and end this Depression in a week.

—Bah! Everybody talks of seizing power or taking over in Washington. But it looks to me as if this country is going to break up into separate regions. The South will go for Huey, the West for Sinclair, and the Middle West for Floyd Olson. . . .

—Capitalism is doomed—that's what this man Lawrence Dennis has been saying everywhere. Unemployment is rising again; the whole system is breaking up under your nose. You might as well get ready for fascism. . . .

—Capitalism dying—capitalism dying is all I hear. [A young man from Wall Street breaks in hysterically at this point.] Won't anybody, won't anybody here say a good word for capitalism? Please!

In such circles I occasionally met again the Amazonian Esther Murphy, all six feet of her, eccentric and yet to me very sympathetic. Esther always sat sidewise, presenting her left profile to conceal her bad eye, and had the air of addressing herself to the room at large as she delivered her monologues in a deep voice that was authoritative and good-humored. She talked sometimes of her first husband, John Strachey, from whom she had been divorced two years earlier. During his first term in Parliament Strachey, she reminded us, had been one of the "angry young men of Labour" led by Sir Oswald Mosley. But Mosley had bolted from his Party in 1931 and launched the British Fascist Party. For a short time

Strachey, Mosley's friend, flirted with fascism, then "turned away in horror."

Recently I had encountered John Strachey also at parties (elsewhere) in New York. He had come to work and lecture in the United States; his book *The Coming Struggle for Power*, published in January 1933, was mostly written during a stay at Cape Cod. I reviewed it with strong approval in *The New Republic*. In that very trenchant essay in Marxian theory (which that season was the favorite reading of American and British intellectuals), he attacked the conventional economics of our time, represented the capitalist order as in dissolution, and prophesied its replacement by dictatorships of the left or the right. During long lecture tours of the United States he expounded Marxism in the style of a brilliant Oxford University debater before respectable audiences, usually at college forums, whose members were left both thrilled and frightened. When staying in New York this large young man kept himself in physical condition for future emergencies by playing soccer football in Central Park every Sunday morning. However the State Department, after several years of this, decided to exclude Strachey from this country, despite the outcry of his many admirers here. After the German-Russian pact and the beginning of war Strachey abjured Marxism and communism, served in the RAF, and in 1945 became a minister in Clement Attlee's Cabinet.

When I saw Esther again in 1934 she appeared with her new husband, Chester Alan Arthur III, grandson of the Republican President whose name he bore. Arthur, who was not yet thirty and whose father was said to be a rather stuffy figure in New York society, had been a young rebel and run away to California on his own, his father having cut him off. There Esther Murphy must have found him literally "on the beach," where many young people had gone to wait out the Depression in a utopia of their own devising in the benign Pacific climate. Theirs was a loosely knit yet fraternal and communal organization—inspired in part by the ideas of Thoreau, in part by Howard Scott.

"I had been living out on the sand dunes on starvation rations with a lot of dead-beat noncomformists," Arthur told me. "Then

the Hearst newspapers began running stories about alleged Reds
on the beach who were plotting to overthrow the government.
Since we were denounced, we came out and held public meetings
for the 'Utopians' in the Los Angeles area and told every one about
our ideas of 'production for use.' Soon after that we heard about
the End Poverty in California crusade of Upton Sinclair and decided to join forces with him. I took the stump for EPIC and
Sinclair. We would always start our meetings by raising the American flag, offering a prayer, and singing 'The Star-Spangled Banner.'
Then an Army officer in uniform would read something from the
scriptures. Yes, the flag and the scriptures meant a lot to millions
of people."

Thus this grandson of a President became one of Upton Sinclair's aides, serving as secretary of the California State Democratic
Committee during Sinclair's campaign for the governorship. As for
Esther, the descendant of merchant princes, she too helped. On
one occasion during a mass meeting at the Olympic Stadium in
Los Angeles the EPIC candidate was late in arriving, and Arthur
told me that Esther, showing unsuspected power as a stump orator,
ad libbed for an hour before a microphone in the center of the
boxing ring, turning to all four sides with sweeping gestures to hold
the audience. When Upton Sinclair finally arrived the crowd
wanted none of him and kept roaring: "We want Esther!"

I had my doubts about the political wisdom of the old socialist
pamphleteer, as well as a sincere admiration for him as author. In
early life he had written novels truly Zolaesque in scale; and then a
stream of eighty volumes of topical fiction, social tracts, and books
of exposure which he had to publish himself. Though he was read
throughout the world, his very real abilities were underestimated in
the United States. In 1933 he had issued his historic pamphlet,
I, Governor of California, and How I Ended Poverty. In the face
of so much misery in the earth's richest region, he had proposed
remedies that were not only simple but all too logical: on being
elected governor he would take over idle shops, factories, and surplus stores and put hundreds of thousands of unemployed to work
processing and manufacturing the food and clothing they themselves so badly needed. Great crowds responded to his message; to

everyone's surprise Sinclair captured California's Democratic Convention in 1934 and was nominated for the governorship.

There was panic in Washington among the professionals over the threat of utopianism within the Democratic Party. There was panic throughout California at the swarming jacquerie attending EPIC's eye-filling rallies. Sinclair and his aides were strong on propaganda and pageantry. At their meetings they presented striking tableaux and skits showing how the poor were saved by going into production-for-use cooperatives. But the opposition employed an even more powerful scare campaign that was broadcast over the radio and appeared in newspapers and motion picture newsreels. The association of motion picture companies, with Louis B. Mayer at its head, threatened to leave California in a body if Sinclair were elected. Shopkeepers, realtors, and the chambers of commerce of small and large towns were terrified by the reemployment scheme and joined in the fight against Sinclair. Films purporting to be documentaries were shown throughout California in which bearded Bolsheviks spoke for EPIC and ragged hoboes were represented as overrunning the fair cities and farms of the state. It is noteworthy that the extensive use of film for propaganda was generated not by crypto-communists, but by the owners of the motion picture companies themselves, convulsed with fear and bent on crushing the half-socialist EPIC movement. It is noteworthy too that they succeeded.

II.

There were many voices in the land, and they came over the loudspeakers into every street. Father Coughlin's rasping voice, edged with hate, had a hypnotic quality. Even in New York I saw overflow crowds in the street outside the huge Hippodrome, simple people wondering doubtless if they would get some "free silver" for themselves by joining the movement for Social Justice. Coughlin's scapegoats were the international bankers, often designated by Jewish names. At first this demagogue of the air waves gave vociferous encouragement to Roosevelt's monetary experiments, though later he turned against the President.

Little bands of native fascists in Silver Shirts or Khaki Shirts made some stir at periods, threatening to march on Washington. "General" Art Smith of the Khaki Shirts, for example, boasted of his "citadel" in Philadelphia filled with arms. Such leaders however often proved to be crooks involved in fraud or even crimes of violence.

Among all the current rabble-rousers the one who was taken most seriously was Senator Huey P. Long, the Kingfish of Louisiana, whom I had seen in Washington strutting about the Senate and displaying his native wit in debate. This powerful regional boss repeatedly denied any interest in foreign doctrines such as fascism. Nevertheless he acted on the belief that his march toward national leadership depended on offering more generous distributions of money or social benefits than any other politician. Hitler gave his people egalitarianism and security, though in military uniform; Long offered the American Dream—his "Share-our-Wealth" platform—in terms the plain people from the hills could understand. Seeing him from close by, as he passed in the corridor of the Senate, I thought his face and eyes to be those of an animal of unusual cunning; I promised myself I would try to see more of him one day.

In New York I heard of a number of pro-fascist intellectuals who considered Long their potential *Duce*. One of these was Lawrence P. Dennis, who, I remembered, had appeared early in 1933 at the home of a friend of mine, Forrest Davis, and taken part in a debate with a socialist scholar in which Dennis espoused fascist doctrines. A former official of the State Department who had held consular offices and for a time had been an agent of international bankers, Dennis had lately published a book entitled *Is Capitalism Doomed?* His diagnosis allowed of no hope for the sick economy. Soon afterward he became an associate editor of *The Awakener*, a fortnightly journal issued in New York by an American fascist group. When out of curiosity I came to their office, located in a midtown skyscraper, to purchase copies of their paper, I found its editors shared space with the so-called Italian Historical Society, a thinly camouflaged propaganda agency of Mussolini's staffed by

Italians. (*The Awakener's* editor in chief, Harold Lord Varney, was formerly a publicity agent for fascist Italy.)

Esther Murphy also told me a good deal about Dennis. Toward 1932 he had been friendly with John Strachey. Because of Dennis's past experience as an agent of American bankers lending money to Latin American governments, he had been able to furnish valuable testimony in 1932 before the Senate Banking Committee on the scandalous practices of those international bankers. Afterward he had explored with John Strachey the merits of communism. He had concluded that communism would take too long to gain acceptance in America. In the autumn of 1932, according to Esther, he saw a great light: Adolf Hitler would soon take power in Germany, he prophesied. He proved right; and soon he himself took the plunge into fascism.

The fascists had the idea of soliciting money for their cause from rich people. Esther Murphy told me that Dennis continued to see her and repeatedly pressed her to introduce him to some of her wealthy friends. A distinguished surgeon who treated me at the time, Dr. John Randolph Page, related that some of his millionaire patients lived in a state of sheer terror, as if expecting a Red revolution at any moment, and they were highly susceptible to appeals for funds from would-be defenders. One of the most frightened of them all was Mrs. Helen Gould Kingdon, daughter of the well-hated robber baron Jay Gould. She not only gave much money to right-wing groups, but also paid for the printing of Elisabeth Dilling's *The Red Network*, a weird compendium listing 1,500 alleged communist conspirators and subversive organizations. It included President Nicholas Murray Butler of Columbia, Eleanor Roosevelt, Frances Perkins, and the present writer.

At length I ran down Dennis at the Harvard Club; we had lunch there, and he spent the afternoon expounding his ideas. I had a tentative plan to write a portrait of a "parlor fascist" and follow it up with an article on Huey Long as a working demagogue.

Dennis proved to be as trenchant in speech and as vivacious as I had been led to expect. Just turning forty, he was a tall man with dark complexion and black hair, handsome in his way, especially when he gave his boyish grin. He told me he had been born in

Georgia, where his father was a successful businessman. He had been sent north to study first at Phillips Exeter, then at schools in England, and he had completed his education at Harvard in 1920. There had been an interruption of a year for war service in France as a second lieutenant of military police. His Harvard classmates remembered him as seeming much older than they, maintaining an air of disillusionment and keeping much to himself, though he was well spoken, especially in college debates. After Harvard he had entered the State Department, serving as secretary of legation in Rumania and in two Central American republics. Promotion in the State Department came too slowly, "except for bluebloods," he thought; and so he had moved on to Wall Street, where in 1926 he was appointed a representative in South America of the old banking firm of J. & W. Seligman and Co.

One of the prime financial scandals of the period was the default of several billions in South American government bonds distributed to American investors by United States bankers who originated those loans. Dennis resigned, but he kept his own records to prove he had warned his employers that the bonds would in most cases go into default. They had ignored his warnings and even loaned fresh funds to the fraudulent dictators in Peru and Venezuela. It was the investment bankers, Dennis said, who really "prepared the way for communism." They played the public for suckers, passing on high-interest foreign bonds, pocketing their big commissions, and allowing the bondholders to be defrauded.

"I have a very low opinion of bankers," he exclaimed. "If only they weren't so smug, so full of their pieties!" The Roosevelt government now followed a middle course, he continued. "But business can't recover; we are going over a cliff into a terrible inflation, in one year." Only an iron-handed dictatorship could impose the absolute control of production needed to rationalize industry and keep the peace. "But Mrs. Roosevelt, Miss Perkins, and the other New Deal advisers look on the U.S.A. as an interesting settlement-house proposition with which intellectual ladies and college professors can divert themselves at the public expense! The New Deal is only a huge muddle—and yet the old trading class, the bankers, the merchants, the politicians, and labor leaders are still in the saddle.

"It just can't go on I tell you, the future is to the extremists," he said with feeling. "I admire the communists' ideas of power: if I were Russian I would be a Bolshevik. But here they haven't a ghost of a chance. The working class—bah! The proletariat rise? Not on your life—it isn't in the beast. The American worker won't even fight for his class. What this country needs is a radical movement that talks American. Our workers not only don't 'get' Marx, they can't even *lift* him.

"Who will fight for power? Why, the frustrated middle classes. The man of the middle class has been slipping pretty badly. He's getting mad; he'll soon be ready to join our Army of the Frustrated." Like the philosopher of fascism, Pareto, he saw history only as a shifting of the base of power. The times, he said, called for "new men, with ability and knowledge . . . men fitted for power." Why were they new and why fit? "Because they know how to take power and hold it, like Mussolini and Hitler." His reasoning about power seemed to me decidedly of the *circulatory* kind; there was no long-range view of anything, and there were accents of a sophomoric cynicism, perhaps cultivated during his years in the diplomatic underworld of the banana republics or as agent for the international bankers.

From press reports of some of his speeches and from what he said to me, I concluded that Dennis regarded human beings as so much raw material to be molded into the forms desired by men of power. It was his habit to heap contempt on those who cherished humane sentiments. In *The Coming American Fascism* (1936), he declared that Americans had been conditioned by press and radio to be the most "standardized, regimented and docile people in the world"; they could be indoctrinated with any set of ideas, and were therefore ripe for fascism. As for their notion of liberty, it was only a catch-word and would doubtless be used by some demagogue to justify the establishment of a fascist dictatorship. Around that time Huey Long was also credited with having made the shrewd observation that if fascism ever came to America it would be in the guise of a nationalist movement to defend democracy and liberty.

At cocktail gatherings in New York, Dennis, in expounding his doctrines, evidently took a boyish delight in sending chills up the spines of his hearers by his blood-curdling talk of coups d'état. He had not only witnessed such actions but had once been under fire during an insurrection in Nicaragua, when he rode about like a young kingmaker in a little car with an American flag between the lines of embattled armies, to negotiate a settlement. When he won State Department recognition of the party he favored it was afterward enforced by five thousand U. S. Marines.

"And how would you make a revolution, Mr. Dennis?" someone asked him on one of these occasions.

"A successful revolution? Perfectly simple. It's like robbing a bank. Only you play for bigger stakes. You have to 'case the joint,' plan the action in every detail—and time it. You'd need only 15,000 men! Then the machine guns would go off"—and Dennis would illustrate, making the sound "put-put-put" and giving his brightest smile.

"And what would you do with me—after you had made your revolution, Mr. Dennis?" put in a pretty young woman who was for Mr. Roosevelt.

"Oh, I wouldn't do anything to you—I'd give you a job," he answered gallantly.

More and more insistently Dennis assumed the air of a prophet of the "coming American fascism," when speaking at public forums or writing for *The Awakener*. A number of wealthy young men, at any rate, were responsive to his appeals to join the fascist elite. One was the same Seward Collins who published *The American Review*. Philip Johnson, a well-heeled young Harvard graduate and architectural student, and his friend Alan Blackburn were among those who wrote articles in *The American Review* championing fascism. They also turned up in San Francisco in 1934 at the height of the general strike, to help the employers quell the workers, but in the confusion of the moment the police fell upon them and threw them into jail for the night. Later these two young men made a pilgrimage to Louisiana to sit at the feet of Huey Long; the Kingfish, however, as I was informed by one of his friends, rebuffed their advances.

In my long conversation with Dennis I am afraid my manner was a little disingenuous; I did not dispute with him, but indicated that I wished "to get at the facts, so that I might make up my own mind."

Dennis had been going on about his prospects like a typical American boomer, when I asked whether men of capital were actually coming forward to help his movement. At this he became a little rueful.

"Oh, the moneyed people don't want fascism—*just yet*," he confided to me, "but they are interested just the same. When the time comes they'll give rather than face socialism or communism. After all, fascism calls for a *nationalist* revolution that leaves property owners in the same social status as before, though it forbids them to do *entirely* as they please with their property. Then, instead of destroying existing skills as would a communist rising, the corporative state would preserve the elite of experts and managers, the people who understand production and can keep the system running. The men who have been earning ten thousand a year have been going down badly. They will follow a good demagogue."

Did he expect that the violent methods of Hitler would come into play in this country, I asked. Most of our businessmen, I suggested, might fear and oppose such a movement.

"Oh, we'd liquidate them if they gave trouble. We have to redistribute *some* of the wealth, you know. After all the military power has the last word. Take Hitler, he uses the industrialists now, but he can shoot them whenever he wants to, as he did Captain Roehm!"

When I asked his opinion of the various "shirt" movements springing up, Dennis spoke of them with scorn. He would have no truck with the brawling groups of native fascists. His mission for the present was to carry on with education and propaganda in peaceful style, before audiences of businessmen and women's clubs. Dennis also intended to avoid the line of religious bigotry and race hatred as propagated by "irresponsibles," holding such doctrines unsuited to our melting-pot society.

(323)

As we left the Harvard Club, an aged member accosted Dennis and exclaimed: "Yes, we all have to stand together and fight for the liberties won by our forefathers who developed the frontier!" The older Harvard men of his type evidently thought they already had a dictator in President Roosevelt.

Dennis replied brusquely: "Remember Mr.——, the frontier is finished; liberty is a dead issue."

The old man gaped at him, mumbled to himself: "Yes, liberty—" and went off.

My last question to Dennis touched on Senator Long, who had lately come out in open revolt against Roosevelt. He remarked with pride, "Long reads my stuff," and added that he had visited him at Baton Rouge. "Huey Long is smarter than Hitler," Dennis said. Long was being cautious about connections with fascist movements, but he had asked Dennis to help him write a book on the redistribution of wealth. Long needed a Brain Trust and effective propagandists, Dennis observed hopefully.

To share the wealth, I remarked, was a kindly thought, and socialistic. The Nazis also talked about that. But of what advantage could Long's proposal for a capital levy be to those who now possessed wealth?

Dennis replied rather shrewdly that the rich really need not fear such men as Long. He might promise gold to the rabble to win their support, but once in power he would quietly put aside the more extreme remedies. Capital would remain much as before "in the hands of those who know how to manage it."

Dennis wound up our talk on a reflective note tinged with melancholy. The road ahead for him involved struggle and sacrifice, perhaps even persecution. But the day of the fascists would surely come. What was needed was a leader, "a man who has been brooding for years over his hatred of the present order, one who believes he is sent on a God-given mission." But Dennis was not that kind of man. His real interest lay in theory and strategy; he would like to be the mind and voice of the "coming American fascism." (Not like Rousseau before the French Revolution, I thought to myself, but Dr. Goebbels.) An odd and clever fellow was Dennis, but with great gaps on the human side.

Meanwhile, what he had told me of Huey Long had whetted my curiosity to meet the great man himself.

III.

That winter I drove south with my wife and two sons, to stay for a few weeks in Florida then go on to New Orleans. En route we halted for a day at Charlottesville, Virginia, putting up at an inn adjoining the lovely old university campus. Two years before I had contributed an essay to *The Virginia Quarterly Review* in which I had expressed high interest in some of the young Southern novelists. The *Review*'s editor, Lawrence Lee, a tall blond young poet and professor of English, received us hospitably. It was most agreeable to stroll with him among Jefferson's charming Georgian buildings, talking of life and letters and the problems of the South.

A native of Montgomery, Alabama, Lawrence Lee was a fervent progressive; his mind was drawn to the rational values of Jefferson, for whom he wrote a memorable elegy in which he avowed this faith. At the moment, in December 1934, he agonized over the Scottsboro Case involving nine young Negro boys falsely accused of rape and long imprisoned in Alabama. Lee held that while the communists exhibited a sort of "mad courage," they made it impossible for the better element to hold the white extremists in check. Meanwhile he freely conceded that the Scottsboro boys had been kept alive in jail only by the determined agitation of communists throughout the world and the exertions of the lawyers they sent down from New York. Acts of racial repression and lynchings of Negroes had in the past aroused only local attention; nowadays such incidents penetrated the nation's conscience. The early thirties saw the real beginning of the Negro's march toward civil rights.

That winter the red clay country through which I rode southward assumed for me the quality of a tragic landscape. In the black ghettoes of mill towns, in the villages of cotton and tobacco growers, people stood idle in the unpaved streets, friendly and cheerful enough. But not even in the poor quarters of old Spain had I seen human beings in worse rags or such wretched dwellings as theirs, unpainted cabins crazily propped on stilts. Much of the Deep South was not only a thousand miles from New York, it was a century distant in time.

Florida had not yet recovered from the blight of hard times. Orange plantations left a good part of their crop to rot, though the country could have increased its consumption of oranges by 200 per cent with benefit to its health. The once teeming hotels were nearly empty in January. At Clearwater I placed my family in a large old-fashioned hotel having the air of a mortuary establishment, then I continued along the Gulf Coast by train and bus to New Orleans.

Arriving in New Orleans, I had the whim to stop at an old-fashioned and crummy hotel in the heart of the French Quarter. The all-powerful Huey Long was said to have cleaned up French Town and closed its well-established houses of prostitution, a source of revenue to his political opponents. Yet at the little bars where I stopped for oysters and a glass of wine women approached me freely to ask for a drink and a dance. By night organized vice wore an amiable visage, quite in the style of old New Orleans. Mr. Long had only driven the Quarter's tarts out of their houses and into the bars.

"I want to know this, what does it feel like to live under a *dictatorship?*" was the question I put to the first resident of New Orleans I met by appointment. He was Monte M. Lemann, a leading member of the Louisiana bar, who had formerly served with distinction as a federal District Attorney under President Wilson. Louisiana was unique among our forty-eight states for its one-man government. Was it like fascist Italy, Nazi Germany, or like one of the Latin American republics?

We were at Antoine's, among the potted palms, partaking of a luncheon of pompano *en papillotte* and Chablis; the good fare, the sense of well-being permeated me; but I was taken aback by the gloomy reports Mr. Lemann communicated. He was a knowledgeable man, judicious in language and unemphatic; and this made what he was saying all the more troubling.

The picture he gave was of a clever, aggressive, and unscrupulous politico commanding a rabble of voters and a band of loyal henchmen, steadily reaching out for more and more power over the life of a whole state and its two million inhabitants. During four years as governor, prior to 1932, Long had made a mockery of the legislature, passing whatever bills he pleased; the elected representatives cast their votes automatically at his command. His successor, the new governor, was a rubber stamp. The state militia, like a Praetorian guard, went marching about with arms as if to cow all opposition. Lately Long had been taking over control of metropolitan New Orleans and its police force, despite the resistance of the mayor, an old guard Democrat and political opponent.

"What we have here," Mr. Lemann said, "is an American duplicate of Mussolini, if not Hitler, in the person of an energetic but crooked political boss—a racketeer in fact—using democratic forms and a popular kind of oratory to impose his personal rule."

Mr. Lemann went on to describe the operations of Senator Long but never mentioned him by name, referring to him only as "he" (in the way people talked of Stalin in Russia). "Everything is done with an air of legality, for *he* is an ingenious lawyer drafting omnibus bills himself so that their clauses often have the effect of bills of attainder aimed at individuals or groups. He controls the boards of assessment and so can punish you by raising your taxes or reward you by lowering them, for the lower courts are under his thumb. He has complete power over all public works, road building, and schools. Through the power to license and tax he can drive any corporation or businessman out of the state. Having reduced the newspapers of New Orleans to submission and even won domination of the Bar Association, he can disbar me or any lawyer opposing him. In fact I am a marked man, because my lifelong partner is his political enemy. It matters little to me. If there is to be no liberty here I may pack up and move to Boston or New York—but what of the others who have no means of doing that?"

Only Louisiana's Supreme Court worked to block, or at least delay, Long's progress toward limitless power. Lemann was then engaged in studying the mass of laws Long had decreed; they embodied delphic clauses, such as those by which the state's public construction was siphoned to private corporations manned by Long's agents or dummies.

Meanwhile Long played Robin Hood to his people. Many of his measures were obviously designed to please the poor, providing new schools, free textbooks, dental clinics, and newly paved roads for the upstate farmers. The old-time Democratic machine had run a plunderbund for its own profit, thus earning the hatred of the people. Long's machine shared some of its graft with the poor and made jobs. "Share Our Graft" was the real meaning of his program.

"But democracy has been strangled in Louisiana," exclaimed Lemann with growing emotion. "People no longer feel themselves free men, dare not talk out loud." The veteran clerk of the intransigent Supreme Court—a key officer in the judicial system—had just been dismissed from his post after forty-two years of service to be replaced by a henchman of Long's, and I had read of this affair in the morning newspaper. I was told also of the case of a student at Louisiana State University who had attacked the Kingfish in the campus newspaper of which he was the editor. The President of the University, a henchman of Long's, had promptly expelled the boy. Then Long had also struck at the boy's father, who was forced to close up his small trucking business. *He* wasn't going to permit a student to write against him "in a university I pay for, or help pay for," Long said. Other opponents had been beaten almost to death by the boss's hoodlums; one local politician had even been kidnapped.

Lemann, who was of an old Louisiana family, remarked that in the old days a man who had been outraged by a Huey Long would have sent him word that he was coming around to see him with a gun. Now the time of duels of honor was over. "But still someone may kill him one day," he mused. The Kingfish himself thought he had good reason to maintain armed guards by his side night and day, for he lived in mortal fear of assassination.

§   §   §

Using only the classical methods of our machine bosses—vote gathering and plundering—Long had set up a home-grown fascist government. Lawrence Dennis wrote that, thanks to his absolute control of Louisiana, Long was in a position to extend his influence throughout the South and eventually to win control of the Democratic Party.

With the help of Clarke Salmon, editor of the New Orleans *Item-Tribune*, I was able to search through that newspaper's clipping files on the Kingfish. It was soon borne in upon me that we had here quite an original.

Born in the sandy pineland of northwestern Louisiana, Long was neither poor white nor hillbilly, though he posed as such. His parents were of the rural middle class, strong for religion and education. Because there were nine children in the family, their life was often necessitous. Huey, the seventh child, was remarked as a schoolboy for cleverness and the spirit of mischief; though he won a scholarship to the state university his parents, then in straits, were unable to help him through college. He wandered off to earn his living as a drummer of cooking oil and patent medicines. At periods he enjoyed flush times, spending his money like a young brassbounder; but part of the time he was unemployed, drifting about like a hobo. Somehow in 1912 he managed a year at Oklahoma State University by working as a printer's devil. A while later, though he had married at an early age, he borrowed money in order to study law at Tulane University. After only eight months of case reading night and day he passed the bar and put up his shingle in his home town of Winnfield.

In the early days Long played the poor man's lawyer. The northern Louisiana folk, in great measure, were native radicals or populists in the manner of William J. Bryan or "Pitchfork" Ben Tillman. Long joined with the upstate politicians in opposing the oligarchy of aristocrats from southern Louisiana and New Orleans who controlled the entire state. Having won some public notice at the age of twenty-five he was elected to the Louisiana Railroad Commission, and thereafter amid loud controversy he exerted himself to regulate the railroad and utility corporations.

After his years as a drummer Long knew how to sell the plain people with his coarse jests and his clowning. Meanwhile the corrupt "Bourbon" machine was vulnerable to attack. Long was a born actor; his passion and his angry style, shown in fantastic personal abuse of his opponents, delighted his redneck public. His rasping Deep South voice came strong over the new radio receivers; the extensive use of the sound truck during his second race for governor in 1928 was something of an innovation. The impoverished farmers and Cajuns pinned their hopes on this bouncy young politician.

Practicing law in Shreveport while still holding office in the state's regulatory commission, Long acquired certain rich corporation clients as well as poor ones. In his gubernatorial campaign of 1928 he admittedly received financial help from one of the large gas companies. John McClure, the poet who had been editor of the New Orleans literary review *The Double-Dealer,* told me that he had known Long at Oklahoma State and remembered his reading Cellini's *Autobiography* with relish. Even then he planned "to use the arts of corruption to advance himself," McClure said.

Very shrewdly Long once remarked that the advocacy of radical ideas was a highly effective way of advancing one's personal interests. "There are all kinds of demagogues," he said. "Some deceive the people in the interests of [their] masters Rockefeller and Morgan. Some of them deceive the people in their own interests." But Long pretended that he kept his promises. He had even lately repealed the poll tax in Louisiana, adding 300,000 to the rolls of voters; and he willingly posed as a friend of the Negroes.

Governor Long's method was entirely different from that of other state bosses. The others used arbitrary power over legislatures to levy tribute upon a state or city, but they did this quietly and under cover, the active boss working behind the scenes through puppets. But Long held both public office and control of the party machine. Openly and unashamed he bragged of his absolute power and found that part of his public was amused by his swaggering.

His attacks on monopolistic corporations were executed with great fanfares and, it was said, were sometimes motivated by the spirit of vengeance. In one of his early attempts to get rich quick he had tried drilling wildcat oil wells; but the Standard Oil Company of Louisiana ruined everything by cutting off purchases of crude oil from independent drillers. One of his first official acts as governor was to initiate a tax of five cents a barrel on refined oil. A determined effort to oust him from office followed but was beaten off. He continued to raise corporation taxes and built public monuments to himself in the form of new roads, bridges, schools, and insane asylums, as well as the Shushan Airport of New Orleans. His dummy corporations received contracts for most of this state business, and their profits were funneled into Huey's war chest. Though he was without scruples of any kind, Long evidently did not use the unaccounted funds for his personal enrichment but for state and nationwide propaganda and for the Share-Our-Wealth League that was to prepare for his march on the White House.

His high-handed procedures in keeping Louisiana's banks open during the panic added greatly to his laurels. In January 1933 two large New Orleans banks were ready to close down, the trouble centering in the Hibernia Bank, whose president was Rudolph C. Hecht, a nationally known financier. Long took charge of the whole affair, sent his armed guards to lock up the bank directors in their board room, and insisted that they stay open. His stentorian calls to the Treasury Department and RFC in Washington and to the Federal Reserve in New York won prompt relief in the form of $20 million in cash. Long also moved state funds about or turned up to harangue panicky depositors in various cities. Louisiana came out of the banking crisis in better shape than most states, and banker Hecht was thereafter Long's firm ally.

His emergency operations to shore up the banks caused Long to believe that the masters of capital were but men of straw; the strong politico could do anything with them. "He really believes the capitalists have been making too much money," one of his longtime acquaintances said to me, "and should and will split part of what they have got with him to redistribute wealth rather than fight such a dangerous brigand as himself. Meanwhile he knows nothing of economics or recks not that a capital levy might breed financial chaos."

Long's style of action seems to have been modeled in part after the new gangster films. His dashing about in a big limousine surrounded by gunmen was calculated to intimidate people; his enjoyment of nightclubs and the fleshpots, like his loud dress, were ostentatious in the way of Hollywood tough guys. On the other hand, he also imitated the totalitarian dictators of Europe in deploying bodies of uniformed troops at points of trouble. He used to jam "emergency" bills through the legislature, saying: "I am the State of Louisiana," and "I am the Constitution."

Around the time of my visit to New Orleans in January 1935 there was a good deal of tension in the air, though this was, in truth, a chronic condition. I heard talk of armed insurrection by Long's opponents. At Baton Rouge several hundred men were actually drilling as if to prepare for an uprising. Then too Huey's relations with Roosevelt had reached the breaking point. More and more openly the Kingfish uttered threats of bolting from the Democratic Party, with his "seven million" followers, in time for the next election contest. Roosevelt turned on Long with a cold anger unusual for him. Later Tommy Corcoran informed me that at that period there had been some furious sessions with Huey in which Roosevelt and Farley refused the Kingfish all federal patronage in Louisiana.

Just then the Louisiana ring's dummy corporations were in default for large federal income tax payments, and Treasury men were probing everywhere for unreported funds. Attempts by Long's agents to reach an accommodation by paying off arrears were rebuffed. The Kingfish was hard pressed and yet at the same time he nursed big plans for the future. It was at this stage in his affairs that I came to see him.

My appointment with Long was arranged by Mr. Salmon of the *Item-Tribune*. His newspaper, like the *Times-Picayune*, had been forced to make its peace with Long. "We couldn't beat him so we joined him," Salmon said ruefully.

I had first to pass muster before the autocrat's "grand chamberlain" so-called—actually his bagman—Seymour Weiss, Colonel of the Louisiana National Guard. Weiss was a director in several ring-controlled corporations and manager of the Hotel Roosevelt, whose royal suite on the top floor Long used as his New Orleans headquarters. The Colonel, a large, pink-complexioned, balding man with the unctuous manners of a maitre d'hotel, had formerly managed the hotel's barber shop. Lately he had gained the honor of being indicted for evasion of federal income taxes to the tune of $176,000.

Weiss warned me that the Kingfish's moods were unpredictable: "He might just tell you to get the hell out."

We went up to the tenth floor anyway; Weiss knocked at the door of the suite as if with a special signal. It was opened slightly, he pushed in, and a man in his waistcoat with two revolvers at his armpits frisked me and then waved me on to the sitting room.

The place was unlike the headquarters of any politicians I had ever visited; it was during a good deal of the time the de facto government center of Louisiana, though there was also Long's puppet, Governor O. K. Allen, and the bicameral legislature at Baton Rouge up the river. A group of more than thirty persons milled about the room waiting for the levée of the Kingfish to begin when he rose at ten o'clock. Among them were several hard-nosed characters bulging with guns, whom I placed as bodyguards. The rest were a mixture of plain, workaday ward heelers with crisp-looking lawyers and men of finance. One of the latter was Harvey C. Couch, head of the Louisiana and Arkansas Railroad and of local electric utilities as well. Another was the banker Rudolph C. Hecht, a past president of the American Bankers' Association. The lawyers on hand represented Standard Oil. Finally there was a pink-faced, youngish-looking man with prematurely gray hair and light blue eyes, a Baptist minister, the Reverend Gerald K. Smith. He was presented to me by Colonel Weiss as "a silver-tongued orator" and "the amazingly successful" director of the Share-Our-Wealth League. I had only lately heard of the Reverend Mr. Smith in these parts. I saw him in retrospect as a man of sweet and earnest manner who was a deadly serious fanatic on fascism and racism, one with whom you could never reason about anything. To all of these persons I was introduced by Colonel Weiss, in impressive style, as a "famous autobiographer"—though I had not yet found time to become that.

For some time we had been hearing the raucous voice of the Kingfish in an adjacent room bellowing orders at assistants. At last he came bouncing into the room, clad in gold-colored pajamas and a bright blue silk dressing gown, and flung himself into a large easy chair, sprawling at full length while we gathered in a circle around him.

He was a droll-looking, homely fellow, of medium height and pudgy figure. His bumpy face and head were round, his nose a ball of putty, his chin receding but wide. His protuberant brown eyes, which were extremely bright, had a sharp, unpleasant stare; they moved about restlessly taking in everyone in the room, fixing on me for a moment as an unfamiliar one. Then he lolled back in his chair almost horizontally while one after another of his petitioners talked; as if having nothing to hide, he answered their requests directly. He relaxed while someone made a proposition, shut his eyes, then opened them wide and, thinking of something wholly unrelated, sprang from his chair and darted into the next room bawling: "Hi-yah-Joe—something else." It concerned the release he was preparing on the Baton Rouge oil business. Then he returned and heard more petitions, a prince holding court.

A tall, dark Cajun who had been caught selling bootlegged un-stamped liquor made his plea. "Mr. Long," he said, "I'm from Shreveport. I must have my liquor license back—I have to make my living. I have nine sons who vote. I'll be your friend all my life. I promise I never do this again. . . ."

Long said coolly: "Did they catch you? You been fined? Lucky you aren't in jail. If I did it they'd put me in jail—ha-ha! Well go on back up there; behave for a month, then we'll see." The man stood there, as if hating to leave without more assurance for the future. Long winked at him, adding in kindlier fashion: "Go and see the supervisor; she's a good-hearted girl, pay your fine." He was amiable with his plain people. I was standing nearby, and Long winked at me too.

Harvey Couch the financier then came forward and whispered his business. Next a New Orleans official consulted him about hiring new deputy clerks for the Assessment Board, and Long, screwing up his face and shutting his eyes, recited from memory a precise list of dozens of names and the different wards they were to be assigned to.

He was in fine fettle. Lately he had overcome whatever opposition remained in the state legislature and now could push through a whole series of Share-Our-Wealth bills, one of which fixed a high tax on crude oil shipped from fields in Texas to the Standard Oil's refinery at Baton Rouge, as a way of favoring local oil drillers. This was what had raised the latest storm; Standard Oil had dismissed a thousand refinery workers at Baton Rouge, and it was they who were preparing to riot against the dictator. An anti-Long group called the Citizens' Committee had gathered some shotguns and joined forces with the oil workers. (A week after my visit, Long rode up to Baton Rouge at the head of a battalion of his steel-helmeted National Guard, put the dissidents to rout without bloodshed, and imposed martial law.)

Meanwhile he proceeded to work out a compromise with the lawyers of Standard Oil that was openly discussed at the gathering I attended. The state would offer a rebate of 80 per cent of the tax on refined products from oil drilled in Louisiana. In response to my query about this measure, Long explained that Standard Oil had been "using my river"—the Mississippi!—"to run barges up to Baton Rouge with oil not only from Texas but from Venezuela." From out-of-state newspapers I learned the news (suppressed in Louisiana) that a ring-controlled syndicate of oil drillers that had concessions of rich acreage from the state would be the chief beneficiary of the new law.

A delegation of refinery workers happened to come into the room, and Long spoke to them in friendly manner, explaining that he was adjusting things. In truth none of the Kingfish's legislation was helpful to mechanical laborers; highway workers were still paid ten cents an hour and child labor survived in Louisiana.

The Kingfish also addressed himself to the reporters on hand, speaking with considerable poise. I remarked that the Standard Oil people had the reputation of being very stubborn in a conflict of this sort.

"Oh, we can make them sick if we fight long enough," Long said cheerfully. "I've made an offer of a concession, but I want something in return. I'm holding up the new terms a few hours until we can hear from their executives at 26 Broadway, New York—but I think we'll manage all right."

Whenever he felt fatigued during that session with so many

persons he simply left his chair and threw himself on a nearby couch, face down. I had never seen a public man so self-indulgent and uninhibited. He yawned, squinted, or burped as he pleased. His rudeness seemed deliberate, a defiance of traditional Louisiana good manners. I can well believe James Farley's story, which I read afterward, of how Long called on President Roosevelt at the White House and kept his hat on throughout their conference.

I left the levée with a feeling of distress. Long easily stood out as the most forceful person in that crowd of petitioners of high or low estate. America's number one "native radical" directed a "crusade," whose only object was advancing himself. In his cynical fashion he was offering a so-called economic program for making "every man a king," a plan inspired, as he said, by the Pentateuch! If we were to have fascism in hillbilly or Bible-belt style then it promised to be a completely thievish affair, and I could not look forward to it with any joy.

Long's Share-Our-Wealth manifestoes proposed a distribution by the federal government of $5,000 per family to provide for a homestead (by means of a capital levy) and a guaranteed income of $2,000 a year. I was told that in support of his ideas he cited learned publications of the Brookings Institution and also a recently published *Survey of America's Product Capacity*, prepared by my old friend Harold A. Loeb, who had turned technocrat and was working with a team of researchers on the staff of Harry Hopkins in Washington. Loeb's survey indicated that at full production we might provide an income of about $3,000 a year per family. Yet no one then knew how to achieve full production and employment without a dictator or a great war. Long's proposed capital levy of about $100 billion seemed to me a debasement of the New Deal program.

Meanwhile the Kingfish talked openly of his plans to launch a third party in 1936 in collaboration with several state organizations of the Deep South, including that of Governor Eugene Talmadge of Georgia. A number of eminent New York financiers seemed to be discreetly encouraging Long's schemes to split off the "solid" South from the Roosevelt Democrats during the next election contest. The Kingfish was observed making a surreptitious visit to New

York to consult with an executive of the Rockefeller-controlled Chase Bank (who happened to be a native of Louisiana). It was not only the rednecks Long attracted, but also some of the moneyed men of the so-called Liberty League who were fighting the New Deal and hoped to exploit Long for their own ends—much as their fellows in Germany had hoped to use Hitler.

But though he had many accomplices, Long had a way of making implacable enemies too. This brilliant neurotic (as he seemed to me) took great joy in wreaking vengeance on opponents and even heaping insults on them after he had got them down. At the same time he was said to be unable to sleep for fear that someone would fall upon him, despite his bodyguards. Throughout 1935 he talked of plots by his enemies to assassinate him, and he qualified remarks on his future plans with the phrase: *"If I live."*

A certain Louisiana judge whom Long had attacked in public (saying his wife had "nigger" blood) had a young son-in-law whose hatred of the homegrown Caesar became an obsession. One day in September 1935 the young man managed to elude Long's guards momentarily in the corridor of the state capital at Baton Rouge; he shot and mortally wounded Long and was then himself promptly murdered by the gunmen nearby. (Some thought the bodyguards also finished off Mr. Long, for there was no autopsy.)

President Roosevelt, who admittedly stood in great fear of Long as one of "the two or three most dangerous men in America," barely managed to conceal his sense of relief at the man's violent death. Five years later, in an off-the-record interview with Max Lerner, he said: "We had the menace of Huey Long, and somehow we were rid of him."

§ § §

All about the country other blatant demagogues were on the march, and their chuckle-headed followers were in ferment. Father Coughlin claimed 817,000 subscribers to his Union of Social Justice; Gerald Winrod generated waves of hatred from Kansas; Dr. Francis Townsend spread the gospel of old age pensions throughout the West. Around 1936 I had occasion to drive through that region. At a filling station somewhere in the Dust Bowl a man serving gasoline, who sounded like a follower of Winrod or Townsend or both, held me up with a long palaver about monetary reform.

"You ought to read about Free Silver," he repeated, and asked me what line I was in.

"I own a farm," I said.

Glancing at my Connecticut license plate, he looked incredulous. "And what do you farm, may I ask?"

"Rocks!" I exclaimed, "that's what we raise—rocks." And I drove off with a grinding of gears, while the man gaped at me.

Chapter Sixteen

❧

A Railroad
Baron: 1937 Model

AMONG THE VARIED ACTIVITIES of that period I find one quixotic affair that engaged me, in spare time, during several years after the autumn of 1934: I served as a member of a small committee of independent investors defending our rights in the case of a bankrupt railroad, a few of whose defaulted bonds we owned. Thereupon we became involved in a head-on conflict with the giant Morgan banking and insurance consortium, the old Money Trust. Of course we were emboldened by the new reform laws governing the securities business. We could bring our complaints into court; we could petition for our rights before Congress. Indeed our action had a far greater impact than we had imagined possible. But first I must describe the circumstances of this legal and political contest.

After the Securities and Exchange Act was passed people in the financial world did a lot of housecleaning, throwing out old rubbish, in the form of securities made worthless as a result of the collapse of various "empires." Probably the most spectacular of the fallen business giants were the two Van Sweringen brothers of Cleveland, who had raised up the Alleghany (sic) Corporation as a mighty pyramid of a holding company controlling six large railroads and affiliated properties valued in 1929 at about three billion dollars. Now the Alleghany Corporation was in default, after having sold $250 millions of debenture notes and preferred stock to the

(339)

public; and half of its subsidiary railroads, among other properties, had gone into receivership. Since 1914 the Van Sweringens had been heavily backed by the House of Morgan, which distributed their railway and holding company securities to the public at a handsome profit but finally wound up holding the bag for about $48 million of the Van Sweringen personal notes. The Morgans had secretly "carried" the Van Sweringens since the Crash of 1929, when they were already insolvent. In September 1934, it was reported that Morgan's and certain affiliated banks were going to dispose of all the Van Sweringen collateral they held, much of it nearly worthless, at forced public sale.

I had once gone to interview the fabulous Van Sweringens at their Cleveland headquarters in the Union Terminal Tower, in their heyday, early in 1929. I knew well their Horatio Alger legend: how they had started as newspaper boys, then become big realtors, acquiring a medium-sized railroad to provide rapid transit for their suburban development, Shaker Heights, outside Cleveland. That first road had been handed them on credit by the Morgan-Vanderbilt interests; thereafter they began to sell securities to the public and buy control of one railway after another. These included the rich coal-carrier, Chesapeake & Ohio, and the Missouri-Pacific in the West, which they linked with the Erie and other trunklines in the East to make up a transcontinental net of 23,000 miles of track (as large as all England's), along with coal mines, terminals, and mercantile properties. From their luxurious thirty-fourth-floor office the Van Sweringens could look down over the whole midland city they had been rebuilding and far out over the plains their roads crisscrossed, while the people looked up at them in awe. I too was suitably impressed by the very scale of their operations, though I found the brothers, like most acquisitive types, outwardly rather commonplace. The elder brother, M. J., reputedly the financial wizard of the two, could never explain in so many words his complex manipulations—based on borrowing and using "other people's money." The education of both men had stopped at grammar school; the very name of their holding company was a misspelling of Allegheny.

Within a few short years their whole "empire" had foundered.

A *Railroad Baron: 1937* Model

The Van Sweringen bankruptcy, one of the best-hidden skeleton closets in Wall Street, became public knowledge.

That historic sale of late September 1934 was held in the dingy auction rooms of Adrian H. Muller & Sons on Vesey Street, New York, a locale full of old furniture, cheap pictures, and bric-a-brac, illuminated by a dirty skylight and some glaring arc lamps. There was quite a distinguished little audience of topflight financiers and corporation lawyers on hand: the handsome, bored-looking George Whitney appeared for Morgan's, together with lawyers from Davis, Polk, Wardwell and Reed; also present was a Midwestern group headed by the pudgy, round-faced O. P. Van Sweringen. In response to the auctioneer's offers, an associate of Van Sweringen's droned out bids for everything that was put under the hammer. The bidder, as it turned out, was really acting for one George A. Ball, an aging glass-jar manufacturer of Muncie, Indiana. Among the securities disposed of at receivership prices was a key parcel of over two million shares of Alleghany common stock carrying voting control of the whole railway system. It went to Mr. Ball at $1.37½ per share, or roughly $3 million. (The same shares had sold at $56 in 1929!) "*Going, going, gone!*" the auctioneer cried; and the whole decrepit railway empire went to the only bidder.

A few days after the auction I happened to visit Charles Beard at New Milford, Connecticut; our friend Max Lowenthal, who had served as an assistant counsel to the Senate Banking Committee during its investigations of recent financial scandals, was also present. As both Beard and I had some souvenirs of the Van Sweringen wreck in the form of a few defaulted railroad bonds, we asked Lowenthal what the forced sale would mean to us. He had long experience in corporate law and had recently published an informative and lucid little book on railroad receiverships.[1]

"The same banking crowd that financed and advised the Alleghany combination of railroads, until it reached its present condition, will stay in control," he explained. "They continue as trustees and 'preferred' bankers to those companies." The new owner, he went on, appeared to be only a dummy who had given the Van Sweringen brothers an option to buy it all back within a stated

---

[1] Max Lowenthal: *The Investor Pays* (New York: Alfred A. Knopf; 1933).

number of years; and they were to continue as executive officers. Meanwhile the same bankers who had helped burden those companies with debt would put through a reorganization plan for Alleghany and its insolvent railroads by which mortgage debt would be reduced, and the value of equity shares (carrying control) would be increased. Thus Beard, as holder of five Missouri–Pacific bonds, and I as owner of one, now worth only about fifteen cents on the dollar, would have to take our losses, while the bankers would get big fees for managing the reorganization.

Beard and I looked at each other and laughed. "Why, we chuckle-headed investors are being trimmed again!" Beard exclaimed.

Lowenthal's marked sense of humor, at once bland and ironical, came into play as he described the typical banker operations in such affairs: "Think of it, the Morgan partners and their associated banks believed that the more money the Van Sweringens lost for them the more they were obliged to lend them. And when it got so they owed more than they could ever repay, nearly fifty millions, then the Morgans decided to be more careful of the Van Sweringens than ever. They provided the insolvent brothers with a salary of $150,000 a year, to keep them in the style they were accustomed to—for the bankers were so *kind*, so sorry for them, they truly believed in throwing good money after bad!" Lowenthal had us rocking with laughter, though the fun was partly at our expense.

"Now the same crowd who helped manage the rise and fall of the Alleghany System are already actively promoting their plan to reorganize the financial structure of those bankrupt railroads, supposedly for the benefit of the 'widow-and-orphan' investors. After some years, to be sure, there may be new receiverships—for which they will again exact millions in banking fees."

It was the same old sucker game. Beard proposed that we lodge some protest before Congress. This led to the impromptu formation of our Missouri–Pacific Railroad Independent Bondholders' Committee, for it is always better to have a committee bring petitions. I agreed to be a member and nominated Charles Beard as chairman. Lowenthal recalled that the Amalgamated Bank of New York, founded by the ACWA union, owned a few M.P. bonds.

We induced the bank's president, James Murray, to join our committee. Lowenthal had recently become counsel to the Senate Subcommittee on Interstate Commerce, headed by Senator Burton K. Wheeler, which was then preparing railroad legislation. The fact that we would have a sympathetic hearing before the Wheeler Committee contributed to our decision to start an insurgent investors' movement. Reorganization plans were already being presented before the federal judge in charge of the M.P. receivership, the one with the most important sponsorship being that of Morgan, Guaranty Trust and New York Life Insurance Company, who were acting in concert. Nevertheless we intended to throw a spanner into the works by presenting testimony about the unhappy results of those same bankers' financial control of the Van Sweringen railroads before the Senate, the RFC, and in federal court.

Everything favored our enterprise; certain eminent New Dealers, including Felix Frankfurter, advised us informally; the lawyers for the Amalgamated Bank served as our counsel; and Senator Wheeler and Lowenthal gave us all the time and publicity we needed at their public forum in Washington.

Beard, moreover, was an impressive witness at the Senate hearings. He charged that the Van Sweringens had "milked" the Missouri–Pacific's treasury of many millions and falsified its records; in a desperate effort to support the declining market in their Alleghany shares, they had unloaded weak properties on "our" railway with resultant losses. Now the same mismanagers and their favorite bankers were bent on putting over their own reorganization plan, which would leave them in full charge again. In the name of our little Committee of Independent Bondholders, Beard called on the Senate to investigate the fraudulent transactions carried on by Missouri–Pacific and other railroad officials under the Van Sweringen orders.

Our committee's testimony had a bombshell effect; its releases received a surprising amount of attention in the national press. We were a David assaulting the financial Goliath. The Wheeler committee proceeded to carry out a searching probe of the Van Sweringen and other railroad affairs; meanwhile lawyers for other protesting bondholders filed injunction suits in court in opposition to the "Morgan plan." In the course of these extended inquests and suits, O. P. Van Sweringen died in 1935 of a sudden illness; in the next year his elder brother M. J. also expired of a heart attack while riding in his private train. The railway bankers actually showed themselves discouraged.

Around that time the Alleghany's titular owner, Mr. Ball, who was seventy and knew nothing about railroads, decided to sell out his holdings to an independent group of capitalists for a modest profit. Thus, in 1937, an unknown from Texas, Robert R. Young, gained control of the entire Alleghany Corporation for a bagatelle, and announced to the world that he was going to manage its railroads in the interest of the public.

Here was an unexpected outcome made possible only by the regulation of the bankers under the New Deal, the Senate's inquiries, and also, in some measure—as I liked to believe—by the agitation of our own little Independent Bondholders Committee. In fact we had all helped to bring forth a tycoon of a "new breed."

R. R. Young flashed across the newspaper headlines like a comet, making a blazing tail for a number of years. Still in his thirties then, he was, for the press, "the daring young man from Texas," one of a new generation of financiers who had risen under the hard conditions of the thirties. Having taken over that huge railway combination (largely on credit), he called a press conference at his small apartment on Park Avenue, gaily dispensed cocktails to all who came, and promised that he would be a faithful shepherd to the flocks of poor investors.

The son of a country town banker, Young was a small, thin man with pale blue eyes and prematurely whitened hair; not a pretty boy, but keen-looking, with a quick Scottish brain. His education at the University of Virginia had been interrupted by an early marriage and a spell at "cutting powder" in the Dupont Works during World War I. Then he had gone to the auditing department of Dupont, trained himself as an accountant, and moved on to General Motors, as a junior executive assisting John J. Raskob. In the late twenties, disliking the routine of "all those committees at GM," he had struck out for himself as a broker on the New York Stock Exchange. He had survived the Great Crash of 1929, as he afterward claimed, by "predicting" it and selling short actively. During the Depression he found that there were opportunities aplenty for sharp-eyed bargain hunters to pick up not only private yachts or diamond sunbursts, but also dilapidated railway empires. Together with an "angel," who possessed inherited wealth, Allen Kirby, Young had been buying blocks of depreciated securities of potential value, and in 1937 he acquired control of the common stock of Alleghany from Ball. A New York banker at the time said: "Anyone who would buy into Alleghany should have his head examined." The next day Young's head was literally being examined by the formidable Senator Wheeler and his counsel Lowenthal, who had called him to a hearing in Washington.

Was he just another shoestring speculator, the senator asked? Was it not true that he had used only $254,000 of his own money to buy control of Alleghany? Young admitted this was true. He and his silent partner had gone into it on the buy-now-pay-later plan.

> Senator Wheeler: There is the possibility, with the control of three billion dollars' worth of railroads . . . as you well know, to make money in a hundred different ways. For one man to have power of life and death over such a combination, and subject to so much temptation is surely a bad thing.
>
> R. R. Young: Yes, it is a bad thing.[2]

Wheeler then reminded Young of some of the wrongdoings of the railroads' bankers, and asked what he could do about that. Young avowed that he "would do a better job of reform than the government. . . . We are going to beat you to it. I have nothing to conceal." Questioned as to plans for future financing, he replied in momentous words: "It is our intention to open things to competitive bidding. We expect to shop around and sell our bonds in the best possible market."

This declaration of fiscal independence caused a seismic shock throughout the nation's financial community. The big railroads had long maintained "preferred" or insider's relations with certain large investment banks such as Morgan's, or Kuhn, Loeb and Company,

[2] Matthew Josephson: "The Daring Young Man from Wall St." *The Saturday Evening Post* (August 11, 18, 25, 1945).

which were regularly favored with the "gravy" of their financing business. But now Young promised that he would eliminate such business favoritism, and "snap the old Van Sweringen chain." Lowenthal remarked to Wheeler at the time: "This man Young seems just like an evangelist—perhaps a self-deceived evangelist." Then he added: "But it's the evangelists who are making all the money nowadays!"

I felt the keenest curiosity about Young as a self-declared reformer of the old regime; I began to study reports of his activities, and made plans to write about what happened to him. It seemed ludicrous that our vital transport net should be run by bankers interested mainly in their financing fees, or by market plungers like Young. Why in heaven's name, I asked Max Lowenthal, should anyone fight for control of a debt-ridden, bankrupt railroad system, and he replied: "Man, think of all the *perquisites* that go with it. After all, the roads must run their thousands of cars every day, spend millions on coal, steel rails, wooden ties, and paint. Even insolvent, a road like the 'Miserable-Pacific' maintains large deposits in banks, and wields business and political influence in thirteen states."

With his accountant's eye for special situations where "sick" companies could be reorganized with much profit for the insiders, Young had calculated nicely the potential asset value and "leverage" character of the cheap Alleghany shares—in the event of business recovery. But he soon found that taking command of this holding company was like riding a tiger. There were endless law suits; there were prolonged contests with the trustee banks, such as Guaranty Trust, which held the Alleghany's collateral to cover its bonded debt. The autumn stock market crash in 1937 caused Young tremendous paper losses at a time when he had large personal debts to meet. All through the next year he was furiously engaged in litigation with powerful adversaries, and in stockholders' contests, during which he expected from day to day that he might lose control of the railway system. While at his home in Newport, Rhode Island, Young, who had become intensely despondent, made a first attempt at suicide, as I was told later by a member of his family. His neighbor, Robert L. Stettinius, happened to come through the garden into his library to visit him, found Young at his desk with a revolver in hand, and wrested it from him.

Somehow he hung on thereafter. He bombarded his financial opponents with pamphlets and proxy-soliciting literature in which he stigmatized them before the country as a "monopolistic banking clique" that exploited the railroads, the shippers and public. Wall Street called him a "raider" and a "demagogue." The officers of Morgan, plainly embarrassed by this adverse publicity in the newspapers, warned Young to cut out the propaganda. But he sent word that he considered publicity the most effective weapon he had and would continue to use it. In the autumn of 1938 he won a decisive stockholders' contest for control of the Chesapeake & Ohio, of which he became chairman. Thereafter he harried the railroad bankers by opening up new bond issues to competitive bidding, distributing them at lower cost through independent financial groups such as Halsey, Stuart of Chicago, and Cyrus K. Eaton's firm of Otis and Company. He also won a famous law suit for damages against the George Ball interests—which had been engaged in unlawful manipulation of the market in Alleghany stocks. The onset of the war in Europe the following year created a booming demand for coal and freight of all sorts, and even the most waterlogged railroads, including the Alleghany group, all became prosperous.

That R. R. Young had made a veritable New Deal crusade out of his battle for financial survival aroused my sympathetic interest, and I wrote him a letter to this effect. He responded cordially; we met and talked frequently, and I arranged to write a series of articles (in *The Saturday Evening Post*) about his much-bruited contests with the railway bankers. These he described to me with great frankness, as he did also in public testimony before various committees of Congress. Young opened all his papers to me, including his private diary covering the principal events of his career. Thus I came to know him more intimately than I did any other capitalist of eminence in those times. Some things that he revealed to me I could never have learned from any text on the working of the financial system.

For example he said that when he first took over the Alleghany

Corporation, Thomas W. Lamont, chairman of J. P. Morgan's, invited him to lunch. At first Young indicated that he regarded such a meeting as "politically embarrassing," but he was warned by his lawyers that it was a royal command, and he came. Lamont, then in his sixties, and usually a smooth old fellow, Young related, "raked me over the coals for developing a consolidation plan without discussing it first with Morgan's." They and Guaranty Trust had been working with those roads for sixty years, and "wanted to be informed" about everything that was done. Young allowed that "Morgan and Guaranty Trust were Rome, and all roads led there." Lamont's warning signified: "Don't do this again, or else!—" But Young followed an independent course. Thus he became celebrated as "the man who defied J. P. Morgan's and still lived."

To my mind Young's greatest invention was his method of combining an evangelistic vocabulary with shrewd calculations of how to realize cash on frozen assets. While he applied some mild restoratives to the Alleghany group of roads, his own personal investment of $254,000, within five years, increased thirty-fold, to about seven or eight million dollars.

I found this "new" finance capitalist a man of quick mind and quite sophisticated about the politics of reform, which he adapted for his own use. He was also aggressive, even bull-headed, and ready to litigate at the drop of a hat. Ambition racked him, in fact, sickened him; for he suffered from hypertension. At times I felt he enjoyed confiding in me as a sympathetic outsider; at other times I thought he was deceiving me about some things, and sought only to use me for favorable publicity.

One day Young invited me—as I was preparing my articles—to accompany him on one of his periodic journeys by private train to Cleveland to attend a quarterly directors' meeting of the C & O. I was delighted to go, as representatives of the press were almost never allowed to witness such meetings, especially in the case of one of our largest railroads. With Young and several of his associates I went to Jersey City to board a train whose old-fashioned luxury recalled the gas-lit era of the old Robber Barons. We were well dined and wined and quartered in spacious bedrooms instead of berths. With us was the C & O's President Carl Newton, a young partner in the law firm of General William J. Donavan, whom Young had put in office though he was no railroad man. Allen W. Kirby, a shy gentleman farmer, then Young's very silent partner, also came on board. Another member of the party was Joseph P. Routh, a burly man of lively and outgoing ways, who operated coal mines and truck companies. Finally there was a former professional football player, Raymond Morfa, Young's private secretary, who ran his proxy-soliciting crews. The small financier, dwarfed by these tall men, carried himself with a sort of fierce dignity.

I noticed that Mr. Routh, after we had had our cocktails, attacked his dinner like a wolf; and I remarked: "You must have a good conscience, Mr. Routh, for you eat hearty."

He exploded in laughter: "Hell, I haven't got any conscience. You can't afford one of those things with these boys around here." And he grinned at Young.

Young gave a rather cold prim smile at this sally, remarking: "Joe Routh always sounds off; you mustn't take him seriously." Whereupon Routh rejoined: "Yes, I'm impulsive and Irish, while Bob Young always thinks before he speaks." He was the jester in the group; but I was beginning to wonder what kind of reformers these men were.

In Cleveland I used part of the morning to drive off to the outskirts and look over the immense real estate properties developed by the Van Sweringens, now being sold off against debt. Among several parcels at Shaker Heights was the Van Sweringen estate, Daisy Hill, a seven-hundred-acre farm that nobody could buy since it was wartime and residential construction was halted. To see it now was an experience; the brothers had built themselves a monstrous Swiss chalet out of an oversized dairy barn, to which they attached other buildings as wings, until the crazy structure had the area of a city block. On the main floor was a huge ballroom designed like the interior of a ship, where no one had ever danced because it was only completed in 1930, a bad year for the Van Sweringens. Below the ballroom, in what had been the cellar of the old barn, was a gigantic swimming pool treated in still another architectural style—Byzantine?—with colored tiles and columns along the walls. When I saw it the water in the pool had turned

(349)

into a ghastly green slime, and the whole place, being unheated, was horribly cold and damp.

Amid all the gimcrack luxury those poor dead brothers, who had never learned, or did not dare, to have fun, lived much alone while they played out their financial chess games. M.J., a confirmed bachelor, did not even allow his younger brother to be married until he was old and sick. Standing by that vast basement pool, whence rose a foul stench, I contemplated the ruins of empire—as if I were a Gibbon at the Roman forum. The Van Sweringens had been mighty railroad kings in our business society and now their glory was gone; the flimsy monuments they had built were waiting for the wreckers. How quickly death had overtaken them; and also certain associates who planned to succeed them (before Young), such as the Cleveland financier Charles Bradley, and after him, Earl Baillie. The last, who was backed by the New York bankers against Young, had suddenly expired of a heart stroke in the stockholders' contest of 1938. A doom seemed to pursue all those who came to snatch the gold out of this bedeviled empire. As I left that miasma-ridden pool under the abandoned house of the Van Sweringens, I had the premonition that Young would never have much joy of his power, and not for long. Though he could be engaging in talk, I sensed an underlying sadness in the man. Tragedy had already marked him; his only daughter, whom he dearly loved, had recently perished in an airplane accident.

§ § §

The C & O board meeting, telescoped with directors' meetings of affiliated railways, was somewhat different in composition from those of other "blue chip" corporations. Among the Midwestern industrialists and railroad operating officers on the board, the presence of Young and his clan, including the lone wolf Cyrus K. Eaton, made for a difference in style. But still there were three New York bankers sitting in—for those people never really let go of anything if they can help it. One of them, a youngish vice-president of Guaranty Trust, hence wearing the "Morgan collar," was introduced to me, and he said briskly: "Well, Mr. Josephson, what are you doing in this galley? I thought you wrote for *The New Republic.*" He was James Nicely, a liberal, cultivated product of Harvard Law School who by chance had wound up in Wall Street instead of Washington. Young had made peace of a sort with the Morgan banks.

This directors' meeting was, in fact, like the Grand Council of the Venetian Republic at which doges speaking for rival interests came together. The ablest and most interesting person there was Cyrus Eaton, a man with a face suggestive of much finesse, like that of some cardinal of the Church in a Renaissance painting. After the collapse of his own holding companies in 1932, Eaton— though shown no mercy by the great New York banks—had worked his way back as an independent finance capitalist. I noticed that Young treated the older man with deference, for Eaton had given him strong support.

A horse of another color was a director named Erminger, a crusty, red-faced, white-haired lawyer from Chicago, who represented the Deering family holdings in C & O stock. Chairman Young had introduced me in a friendly way to the fifty or sixty persons connected with his various companies as a "distinguished guest" who was to write about the Alleghany System's story for *The Saturday Evening Post.* Young, himself an amateur writer and versifier, who often talked with wit and pungency of expression, remarked that he had looked me up and was pleasantly surprised to find that I had written "a whole series of well-regarded books," literary, historical, and political, even mentioning *The Robber Barons* as a realistic study in our financial history.

At this Mr. Erminger jumped up and sputtered something about their need to be careful of what they said "with a writer present." He insisted on knowing whether Mr. Young had arranged to see and approve of what I would write, in advance of publication.

Young answered crisply: "Mr. Josephson is going to write our story independently, without interference from anyone. I know he will be accurate." The testy Mr. Erminger subsided for a while.

After a discussion of financial and technical programs, Young and President Newton reported on the C & O's proposed advertising budget of $100,000 for time on the popular radio program: "Town Hall of the Air." There would be free debate among eminent speakers on all sorts of public issues.

The suspicious old Erminger rose again to protest at the idea of allowing "complete freedom" at such a radio forum. "Will people be permitted to attack the railroads, or advocate socialism, or the cause of the Soviets?" he asked scornfully. I found it hard to keep my face straight. Young and Newton tried to smooth things over; they even called on me, as a knowledgeable one, for comment. I held that at such forums the polite presentation of "two sides of a question tended to cancel out the arguments." An operating vice-president of the C & O, however, put in the assurance that "we will know beforehand what is going to be said." After the meeting Young apologized to me for the "old-fashioned director"; but I remarked that he was, at any rate, a man of candor and seemed to believe everything he said. (I had always suspected that extreme conservatives cared nothing for freedom of speech, but had never heard any of them say so.)

Young talked at length of large schemes for modernizing the C & O's passenger service, and taking the lead in winning back traffic for the railroads. (A while later he came out with his famous advertising slogan: "Even a pig can ride a train to the West Coast without changing at Chicago.") I thought that was all tosh for publicity, and that Young, as an accountant, knew well that his railroad's big profits lay in carrying coal, while it lost heavily on its very few passenger cars. There was something quite false in his pretended interest in updating service to human passengers, who were bound anyway to take to airlines, cars, and buses.

On returning from my journey I asked myself: Did the New Deal really work to reform the finance capitalists? (It is not easy to change an old and complicated economic system that has grown up like Topsy.) Despite the so-called "managerial revolution" Young had only contempt for the operating executives of his roads. "Their work is simple routine," he said. But on the other hand he argued that his job of financial house-cleaning was truly important. The old-line investment bankers charged far too much for the wholesale distribution of sound railroad bonds—they often took two or three millions for promoting an issue of mortgage bonds amounting to fifty or a hundred millions. The unduly high interest rates also added to the burden of debt.

"If you eliminate the gravy from financing you eliminate the Wall Street control," Young said. The introduction of competitive bidding definitely lowered costs and allowed independent financiers to operate as rivals of the old "monopolists." All that was useful, I could see, but it amounted only to a modest improvement. It opened the door to the "new money" crowd, including the R. R. Youngs, who were also finance capitalists seeking gain through the manipulation of railroad or industry capital.

The "crusade" for reform played a large part in the success of Young's raids on his adversaries. Shortly after buying into Alleghany, as I discovered, he had made a donation of $15,000 to Mr. Farley for the Democratic Party's chest. Roosevelt's lieutenants were ever on the lookout for friendly millionaires. But a few years later, in 1940, Young turned against Roosevelt and supported Wheeler's abortive campaign for the presidential nomination. In short, he had no real convictions about the New Deal: when its officials opposed some of his schemes, he found it "terribly bureaucratic." As far as I could tell he had no new light to shed on the economic problems of our society. When it suited his book he hounded the "damn bankers" of Wall Street, as he called them; or now he made peace and did business with them again.

I found it curious that Young, since 1928, had made his home in Newport, Rhode Island, where he eventually purchased a forty-room "cottage" on the cliff overlooking the harbor. On a weekend visit, I perceived that he and his wife had managed to push their way into that moribund society of rentiers by their conspicuous expenditures: $70,000 for one coming-out party for his daughter; and comparable sums for the entertainment of Young's most admired friends the Duke and Duchess of Windsor. Young attributed his own success to his superior brains; yet the company he surrounded himself with was dull and conformist. Actually, his life work was done while sitting on a terrace going over the balance sheets of railways with his pencil.

The honest thing would have been to dissolve the Alleghany

holding company; the government nowadays discouraged such corporate monstrosities. But, like the Van Sweringens, Young was bent on using its treasury for new acquisitions. Coal-carrying bored him, and for years he fought to gain control of the New York Central—another decrepit empire with frozen assets to be "liberated." He wanted the glamor of the old Vanderbilt line and its deluxe trains. I asked Young if the reports of his plans were true.

His voice rose to an angry shout at some implied criticism, and he gave me a tirade about what he proposed to do for the public, and how much the New York Central needed his improving hand. Then he calmed down, and we parted on friendly terms. In the conclusion of my articles I held that his claims to having achieved permanent financial reforms were dubious—though I credited him, and men like Cyrus Eaton, with having brought about certain improvements through the competitive bidding for bonds. Young wrote me indicating satisfaction with the fairness of my account.

In the end, with the help of the Murchison family of Texas, he succeeded in taking command of the New York Central. But only a year later, facing loss of control, and being weary, melancholy, and sick, Young took up his revolver again and this time shot and killed himself.

Chapter Seventeen

❧

The Writers and
the Popular Front

WHAT HAS ALWAYS SEEMED most amusing to me is the extraordinary variety of people I have met in my part-time capacity as a journalist writing about men of affairs. Thus on one day I would lunch with a fascist like Lawrence Dennis and patiently listen to him on the subject of religion, patriotism, and the frustrated middle classes; then in the evening I might dine with one of those generous and idealistic types of communist who expatiated for hours on end upon his idea of scientific socialism by which the world was surely and simply to be set aright. Or again, I might be consulting one of the New Deal officials on one day, and next day I would call on an officer of J. P. Morgan and Company to obtain a copy of their proposed reorganization plan for the Missouri–Pacific railroad.

It was then in the height of fashion for writers and intellectuals to participate in strikes of aggrieved workers, though not all were suited for such action. Everywhere labor was on the march and young writers were eager to go into the trenches with the embattled working class. In the winter of 1934 young Clifford Odets gave his attention to the taxi strike in New York, and not long afterward he wrote his powerful one-act play *Waiting for Lefty*. How rousing was the final curtain of that playlet, when news comes to the union men in their hall that Lefty will never come back, that he has been killed; the whole stage and the audience join in the cry: *"Strike, strike, strike!"* How much people romanticized the strike!

At length the class struggle invaded Grub Street itself. The Macaulay Company, the small publishing firm which several years earlier had issued my biography *Zola and His Time,* was suddenly in June 1934 struck by its editorial and clerical staff. The head of the concern, Lee Furman, was a kindly and likeable man; but two members of his editorial staff, Isidor Schneider and Susan Jenkins Brown, who were among the strikers, were good friends of mine and engaged my deeper loyalties. The trouble arose over a book-keeper who had been dismissed because of her union activities. Schneider and Mrs. Brown, assuming leadership in the strike, sent out urgent calls to writers to come to their aid. For several days the corner of Fourth Avenue and Twenty-first Street, adjoining the Macaulay Company offices, became the rendezvous of quite a group of notable men of letters serving as pickets. Among them were Dashiell Hammett, Edward Newhouse, Morley Callaghan, Tess Slessinger, Albert Halper, Michael Gold, Malcolm Cowley, and Kenneth Burke. I received a telephone call in the country asking me to join them, and I promised to do so the next day when I was to be in New York.

The next afternoon I hurried to the strike front. There I was furnished with a placard denouncing my former publishers for unfair labor practices, and thus equipped I marched up and down the sidewalk before their building in a line of novelists and literary critics. It was a sunlit day of late spring; and for us, who habitually worked alone, it was a joyful occasion to come together outdoors and give expression to our public spirit and our fellow feeling for the Macaulay clerks. The laughter, slogan-shouting, and singing made it one of the merriest literary parties I had ever attended. But I had only forty minutes to donate to the class struggle that day, since I had a prior appointment the same afternoon and had to catch a train home after that. I therefore surrendered my placard to a fellow agitator and hailed a taxi which took me uptown.

Three hours later, on boarding my train at Grand Central, what was my surprise to read on the front page of my afternoon news-paper (June 7, 1934) the story of that day's events:

AUTHORS ARRESTED AS STRIKE PICKETS

18 Loaded into Patrol Wagon after Demonstrating Before
Publishing House—Prisoners Sing in Cell

And the greatest surprise of all was to find my own name among those reported as arrested—though I was just then sitting in the train's club car enjoying a very bourgeois cocktail—and I laughed out loud. Someone had mistakenly handed in my name to the newspaper reporters as having been picked up with the others. Quite evidently it was expected that they would be apprehended and that I would be among the detained.

Only a minute or two after I had left, a police wagon had arrived in response to complaints of illegal picketing. The leaders of the strike had been warned, but they obviously did not mind how many literary pickets were arrested so long as they were well-known authors and would make good newspaper copy. My companions, however, were detained for only two hours in a precinct jail; a polite magistrate then released them with all charges dismissed. The bookish, peace-loving Kenneth Burke, finding himself incarcerated for the first and only time in his life, behaved as a Chevalier Bayard, *sans peur et sans reproche*. And Malcolm Cowley had kept all hands in good spirits with his singing of old chanteys such as "I'll go no more aroving"—an apt choice under the circumstances.

The tactic of linking the names of celebrities with strikes was characteristic of the 1930's and is, in fact, an ancient usage. Literary and intellectual volunteers entered into the economic struggles of the workers—once called by Engels their "school of war for the final battle"—with a fine amateur spirit. Their interest, however, proved transient. In later years repentant radicals, having turned informers, solemnly charged before the House Un-American Activities Committee that such affairs as the Macaulay Company strike were dark plots by communists exploiting well-known writers as stooges. We, nonetheless, found these actions entertaining, and we hoped we were being, in a small way, useful.

The little Macaulay strike of eleven office workers was of minor importance; but, perhaps owing to the good press it enjoyed, in hearings before the NRA Labor Board the strikers eventually won a favorable union settlement and were reinstated in their jobs. News of many such episodes had a cumulative effect on public opinion.

II.

To the latter-day simplifiers of our cultural history, those who have been writing so many laments for my liberal and radical generation, we were but political innocents allowing ourselves to be "tricked, betrayed, or manipulated." These judgments by the New Conservatives are distortions of the truth well calculated to support the posture of disillusionment, indifferentism, and reaction these younger critics assumed in the years following World War II.

I was in fairly close touch with many members of the intellectual generation that has been so much lamented, placed "on trial," and lapidated. It seems to me they were often sharply demarcated individuals in their opinions and were in no sense regimented; moreover their political action was only intermittent. During two or three years after the election of 1932 there were fewer common undertakings by the literary fellow travelers. For one thing, Roosevelt's great vigor in administering public relief and initiating government economic intervention served to reduce tension and remove the expectancy of social collapse.

Meanwhile the group of writers who had been associated in the campaign for Foster two years earlier had quite broken up. Several members of our group, including Sidney Hook, had severed relations with the communists and joined the faction supporting Leon Trotsky, recently exiled from Russia by Stalin. For the followers of Trotsky all that Soviet Russia did henceforth was to be rejected as evil. But to many of us, alarmed by the growing belligerency of the fascist bloc in Central Europe, the possibility of Russia's making common cause with the western democracies seemed greatly to be desired; the plan of forming a Popular Front with all liberal factions was germinating.

The men of the left in the thirties have too often been misrepresented as "idolizing" Stalin and all his works. In reality we knew little of him and, in the main, did not believe that he constituted a problem that was immediate to us in the United States. We saw him as the powerful committee chairman and boss of the Soviets. In a general way the Russian form of socialism or communism, as I wrote in 1935 to Kenneth Burke, seemed to me "a continuation of Western historical tendencies and cultural movement of the eighteenth century." We hoped that their society would evolve and that ours too would become both more humane and more scientific. Even our adherence to the Popular Front, though it seemed imperative to us, was not regarded as the be-all and end-all of everything. "We may work with the Marxist 'school,' and we must also look beyond it," I wrote at the time. "Our usefulness would reside always in our ability to look farther ahead. If ever it becomes dishonorable to doubt, to reflect for ourselves, or use disinterested judgment, then it will be too late for everything. . . ."

Writers of the thirties have also been accused of submitting to the demands of communist pundits that they follow the canons of "Marxist criticism" and produce a purely "proletarian literature." I find however no such unanimity in ideology among the fellow travelers; on the contrary, many passages in my correspondence suggest that most of us trusted in no such dogmas. In 1935 I was writing: "There has been so much idiotic confusion about 'Marxian literary criticism' that it is high time to clear the air. . . ." This whole debate, I remarked, was being conducted in the most "discouragingly low tone."

There was, to be sure, a Marxian orthodoxy propounded by the then literary editor of *The New Masses*, Granville Hicks, the former theological student who seemed to have found in communism the authority of a revealed religion; or, as he defined it: "a unified system capable of evaluating all literature past and present, proletarian and bourgeois, by a single standard." Literature must henceforth be cast in the mold of socialist realism; it must be the "weapon" of the proletariat and must work systematically to change the world. To be a good writer a man must first become a proper communist, he argued; the man who looked at life from the point of view of the exploiting class inevitably distorted life; only the partisan of the proletarians was capable of true and clarifying interpretations.

Like an implacable Robespierre judging his erring brother citizens in the name of the Goddess of Reason, Hicks operated a sort of ideological guillotine to sever the heads of unworthy authors. Among those condemned because, in his estimation, their writings "showed traces of bourgeois corruption," were André Malraux and John Dos Passos. James T. Farrell's novels and, still worse, Edward Dahlberg's *Bottom Dog*, that frightening document of the Inferno of our urban slums, were also severely censured because of their pessimistic view of the common people. In short Hicks, who was sometimes called the "literary terrorist of the left," was more intolerant of heresy than the most sectarian expounder of the Party line. He himself was forced to admit on one occasion that he tended, perhaps excessively, to "schematize things" and to "dogmatize" and "proscribe."

The English writer Charlotte Haldane, in analyzing the middle-class convert to communism in the thirties, defined the type as one who having suffered psychological strains in childhood and adolescence, "rejects the discipline in which he has been brought up . . . to seek another still more rigorous discipline." Such Granville Hicks seems to have been when he became a member of the Communist Party; such he was also when he bitterly abjured it five years later. In time his attitude hardened into hatred of his former friends—whom he nevertheless remembered as being "generous" and "idealistic"—and during the McCarthian terror he denounced them before the inquisitors of the United States Congress. For his new patriotic pieties obliged him to serve as an informer about the left groups he had been associated with. It is amusing to recall that this future recanter was the very one whose narrow interpretation of the Party line in literature most offended the young writers of the left.

After a while the editors of *The New Masses* invited the writers who had been murmuring against Hicks's pronunciamentos to contribute to a symposium on the question of Marxian criticism. Most of them responded by falling upon the new literary editor (in the issue of July 3, 1934) and belaboring him for his pretensions to a superior revolutionary virtue.

For my part I felt much distaste for the theorists of proletarian literature, such as Hicks, and said as much in an article in *The New Republic*, February 8, 1933, on the subject of Zola and his novels. Zola was of course the most famous example in recent times of the novelist with a social conscience, not only because of his descriptions of lower-class lives but because of his intervention in the Dreyfus Case.

Zola's career reflected the two distinct roles he filled: that of the devoted man of letters, and later that of the good citizen taking action in a social crisis. In the first phase, in writing his naturalistic *Tendenzromanen*, he observed men and things scrupulously, but seemed not to take sides. Accused of slandering the Parisian working class in *L'Assomoir*, he denied it; then, when he wrote *Germinal*, and was called a partisan of the socialist miners, he denied this too. In other words, he believed in holding by his concepts of rightness in art and his understanding of nature, without engaging in propaganda. But on the other hand, when his community was in danger, he might well leave his study, go out into the street and help put out the fire, or defend his city, or fight to save his people from disaster. Thus Zola came into the public forum with *J'Accuse!* It was my contention that a man might do well to keep his obligations to his art separate from his duties as citizen in his community, and try to perform both roles with honor.

Several years later, while the Battle of the Books went on among the writers of the left, I returned to the same theme in a preface written for a new edition of Zola's *Germinal* (1937). Here I argued that in his dramatic account of a strike of coal miners, Zola wrote nothing like what was later called "proletarian" or "revolutionary" fiction. Yet his novel induced in the reader the strongest feelings of compassion and involvement. I observed also that in his preparatory notes he reminds himself that the character representing management and capital, "while being the incarnation of money and money-getting must be that *without being a bad man.*" The result was one of the most effective of all social novels.

In reality Marx had never established any canons of "proletarian literature," and Lenin's favorite writer was the heretical Christian Tolstoy. Stalin threw out some vague ideas about the writer performing as an "engineer of human souls," but that is really the function of all who teach.

On this whole subject of revolutionary literature I find myself in accord with C. Day Lewis, who in his essay *A Hope for Poetry* declared his belief that a man's poetic function should not be dominated by explicit political doctrines, but rather that these should help form his character and "fix his humanity—with which his poetic creation would be permeated. . . . The man must pass the idea through the medium of his emotion before the poet can get to work on it."

Even Clifford Odets, who, as Harold Clurman has related, had overnight become the central figure of the left movement in the theater, came under the fire of *The New Masses*. Odets was trying to make the Revolution a joyful progress—and for this reason, apparently, was found wanting.

In April 1935, I wrote a letter to *The New Masses* protesting at the review of *Awake and Sing!* by their drama critic, Michael Blankfort:

> A young playwright, Clifford Odets, who merits all possible encouragement, produces a work of humor and satire which pictures the frustrations of a lower middle-class family; whereupon a left wing critic of the most dogmatic kind falls upon the playwright and reproaches him for his sense of humor, for his "wisecracking," for "allowing his flair for language and humor to run out of hand," etc. This critic certainly gave the impression that the proletarians might never laugh again, if he had *his* way; he simply ignores the fact that humor and irony may be the most powerful agents in forming public opinion; and that the revolutionary movement can scarcely have enough of such qualities. . . .

III.

We were now at the time of Mussolini's manifest preparations to invade Ethiopia. The threat of aggression by a rearmed Germany under Hitler was more appalling still. The campaign for a Popular Front against war and fascism offered a last great hope. All that they had learned of the four years' slaughter in World War I had turned young men coming out of college in America and England toward pacifism and, at the same time, toward making common cause with the left. From England and France many voices called us to join the crusade of the peaceful against fascism: Harold Laski's the socialist, as Strachey's, then the voice of communism. In France André Gide underwent a famous conversion; though a man of independent wealth and a lifelong Protestant, he now declared that not only capitalism but Christianity too had failed us. His new hope was placed in the "communism of love," love of his poor brothers in all lands. In this spirit in 1935 Gide made his first pilgrimage to Soviet Russia, of which he wrote in all enthusiasm in *Voyage à l'U.R.S.S.* (A year later his second visit would yield the sorely disillusioned *Retour de l'U.R.S.S.* yet the effect of Gide's conversion had been powerful for his intellectual public.)

In the autumn of 1934 a Congress of Soviet Writers was held in Moscow. It was attended by foreign delegations of mainly European writers of the left. This Congress was significant because its resolutions foreshadowed the turn of Soviet Russia toward the program of the Popular Front. In imitation of the left writers' conferences in Europe, the American communists sponsored a similar congress of American writers of various shades of liberal and antifascist opinion. The communists already had their affiliated John Reed Clubs of artists and writers with branches in the larger cities such as New York, Chicago, and San Francisco. These however became the social gathering places of mostly unemployed young men who neither wrote nor painted anything. There was some talent to be found in these clubs of often famished and angry youth: in Chicago the young Negro writer Richard Wright met with encouragement instead of scorn for his race, and so "found a home" for a while among the communists of the John Reed Club. In San Francisco the poet Kenneth Rexroth also figured as a leading spirit in his unit.

The elders of the Communist Party however, including Alex-

ander Trachtenberg, head of its International Press, now desired to
replace the John Reed Clubs with a broad-spectrum organization
welcoming liberals and fellow travelers who had won standing in the
literary profession. Hence the idea of convoking a congress of American writers in the spring of 1935, for which Granville Hicks wrote
the call. Many years later, Hicks contended that the whole operation was nothing but a Party front manipulated by Trachtenberg so
that it would be dominated by reliable fellow travelers, and that its
new liberalized line supporting the Popular Front was only "a
trick, a device for strengthening Soviet foreign policy." But to many
liberals the new line seemed entirely reasonable, as it offered hope
of arousing opinion in the western nations to the danger of war.

The purge of the John Reed Clubs was said to have been carried out in a high-handed way by Trachtenberg and the Communist
Party, who simply declared them abolished. A revolutionary of long
ago from czarist Russia, Trachtenberg seemed an amiable and cultivated sort of man who had long served as a faithful Party wheel-
horse. Swarthy, and wearing long mustachios which he stroked
thoughtfully, he looked somewhat like a stage caricature of a secret
agent from the Levant. He was in fact represented in that fashion in
some of the spine-chilling accounts of America's "Red decade" so
freely produced in the 1950's. To me Trachtenberg encircled by his
apostles had only the air of an anxious mother hen guiding her
chicks around.

On the evening before the Congress convened, Earl Browder,
secretary of the Party, gave a welcoming address at its open meeting
before a large public in Mecca Temple in New York. Conciliatory
in tone, Browder declared that he desired to fix no Party line in the
field of literature and art.

The call to the Congress of American Writers spoke of the
crumbling of the social order, and the danger to culture offered by
fascism. Well, it was true that in Europe books were being burned
and their authors thrown into prison. Many others, innocent of
wrongdoing—liberal or working-class leaders—were being arrested,
tortured, and even killed because of their political affiliations or
because of their race. Josephine Herbst, who had just got out of
Nazi Germany "by the skin of her teeth," made these episodes vivid

for us in her talk at the Congress. The attack upon civilization itself
had begun.

Writers (whatever their shortcomings) had been singled out for
special attention by the new barbarians as being a dangerous breed
because of their attachment to the values of humanistic civilization,
and because they were conveyors of such values. The writers felt
they should return the compliment by directing their attention to
the fascists.

What could a few writers do, what could a whole federation of
them do in the face of the dark forces marshaled against them?
They could do much, I told myself, as they had in the past: by determinedly speaking the truth, by the power of eloquence or irony.
They could spread ideas about. Zola had written in *J'Accuse!*:
"When truth has been long buried it accumulates an irresistible
force that must one day explode!"

The Popular Front called men of good will to take their stand.
As writers we could at any rate use words to awaken our people to
the peril around us and to petition our government. (Our statesmen
and academic authorities had said nothing as yet.) It is not surprising, therefore, that many non-communists willingly signed the call
to the American Writers' Congress.

I have read subsequently in books lamenting the grim thirties
that those of us who, though not communists, attended that Congress were given but a spurious sense of participation in the campaign against fascism by the conspirators of the Communist Party
who manipulated or tricked and betrayed us. My own eye-witness
impressions were quite the contrary. The Congress generated a
considerable enthusiasm, especially among youthful writers and
intellectuals just out of college who were finding jobs extremely rare
and already saw a new world war in their future. The older literary
men generally worked in isolation, as more than one remarked; in
this time of crisis they came out to meet the younger element
among their public, and this was mutually profitable. I greatly enjoyed talking with these eager young persons of twenty or so, some
of whom had hitchhiked from St. Louis, Missouri, or Madison,
Wisconsin, and were roughly dressed, hatless, and tieless. Their
tatters were not a bohemian affectation; they were honestly earned!

(365)

A goodly number of the John Reed Club boys, doctrinaires of proletarian culture, were on hand to call for a literature that would arouse the workers to action. Jack Conroy, a former steelworker and author of *The Disinherited,* a novel of the world of labor, girded against the "aesthetic" literature of recent years that men contrived for snobbish audiences. One young man urged that writers should turn out bulletins to be posted on the walls of union meeting places; another spoke for a group of poets who were inventing beautiful slogans for workers on strike, in the manner of the Russian poet Maiakovsky. These were often tremendously solemn young radicals; but on the other hand some of the more gifted ones, like Muriel Rukeyser, were evidently learning well the old secrets of their art and would cling to them.

Many of these young writers had a great will to identify themselves with the working class. Robert Cantwell was one who had captured the atmosphere of the factory truly; Edward Newhouse had gone to live in the "jungles" of the unemployed in order to speak for them in his novel. There was also much artless talk about eliminating the petty bourgeois in oneself and becoming class conscious and an integral part of the workers' movement. Malcolm Cowley, though he was one of the initiators of the American Writers' Congress, confessed that he was "not a proletarian writer" and doubted that he would ever become one. His whole family background and education had stamped him as petty bourgeois, but still he now desired to make common cause with the workers. (But Marx, Engels, and Lenin were also bourgeois, as I used to argue, and their grand object was to eliminate the proletarians!)

The closed sessions for writers at which papers were read and discussed from the floor were attended by about four hundred persons during two days. These often turned into high-spirited debates that got out of hand or, in unexpected ways, provoked laughter. A gathering of writers is quite likely to be the scene of conflict between highly charged egos.

Yet where is there the writer of mettle who is without an over-mastering ego-drive, who does not say, in effect, "The world can only be saved by reading *my* book!" Edward Dahlberg was such: the author of *Bottom Dog* stood before us ranting against the fascism and anti-Semitism of a T. S. Eliot. But then, amid general laughter, he suddenly turned his guns against the Marxist critics who had dared to write disparagingly of his own prose. Though his time for argument had elapsed, and many shouted for him to leave the platform, Dahlberg held forth in a voice of thunder; he was stronger for revolution than anyone else, but it was the Dahlberg Revolution he stood for, and he "talked Dahlberg" to us.

The non-Party characters accounted for at least a good half of the proceedings. Waldo Frank, an older writer than most of those present, spoke in his habitually Messianic vein in favor of "wholeness," of freedom for art, freedom from sexual repression, and freedom from money-seeking too! Meanwhile he rejected the idea of a proletarian literature as a schematization that would limit a writer's "revolutionary vision."

Dos Passos's paper contained a timely warning against the stultifying force of bureaucratic controls and committees directing writers' minds. "To fight oppression, to work for a sane society we do not have to abandon the state of freedom. . . . The dilemma that faces honest writers is how to combat the imperial and bureaucratic tendencies of the groups whose aims they accept, without giving aid or comfort to the enemy."

Dos Passos had originally formed friendly connections with the communists as a gesture of individual revolt, in the twenties, when they were few and had few friends. Now they were quite an army and thoroughly organized, and Dos Passos did not enjoy that. He was already en route from a position on the far left all the way to the far right. It is my recollection that he did not appear in person at the Congress but sent in his paper to be read.

My own paper was on the subject of "The Writer in the Soviet Union," based on impressions formed during my visit to Russia the year before. I described the advance of education in the formerly illiterate land and the ferment of activity it caused among journalists and writers. Perhaps (considering now how ephemeral their security proved to be) I spoke with excessive optimism of the superior economic status and prosperity of Soviet authors. However, I found the current literature of Russia, which consisted largely of journalism or topical novels, "not uniformly successful." Its weaknesses, I said, "were sometimes . . . only too apparent, and American writers who would create a revolutionary literature must study and avoid them. . . . To write under the influence of revolutionary necessities and hopes, to embrace the Marxist concept of society and its conflicts . . . ensures no one of excellence in this field."

§   §   §

Earlier in the proceedings there had been messages read by the chairman from exiled German authors, such as Bertolt Brecht and Heinrich Mann, and from the French writers Henri Barbusse, Romain Rolland, and Louis Aragon. The message from Aragon was especially moving to Malcolm Cowley and myself, who had been associated with him in the artistic revolutions of Dada and Surrealism. His paper in some measure traced our own intellectual pilgrimage from commitment in the wars of art to engagement in the social action of our time; or, "From Dada to Red Front," as Aragon defined it:

> I was a writer who boasted of having gone through the world war without having written a word about it. . . . My rebellion against the world around me found its outlet quite naturally in Dadaism. The quarrel in which I was joined . . . set the writer against the public.
>
> So it was that the Dadaists, my friends and I, with a few Americans too, Malcolm Cowley and Matthew Josephson, continued the tradition of Rimbaud, and that of Vigny, the poet of the Ivory Tower.

The time had come, however, when he had had enough of literary nihilism. Aragon had experienced an awakening of his social conscience, had said good-bye to his friends the Surrealists, and joined those who, in his conviction, were the continuators of the French Revolution.

To one of the younger members of the audience, Murray Kempton (who must have been a collegian then), the change of front of these literary men of the avant-garde appeared incredible. He remarked with an air of astonishment: "There was Matthew Josephson, the playboy of the revolution of the word in the twenties . . . previously identified with . . . *Secession, Transition* and

Dada. And there was Malcolm Cowley, who had been a friend of Dada in Paris." [1]

Certainly we had changed; history had changed us. Malcolm Cowley, for one, had thoroughly overhauled his ideas since the days of the American expatriates in Paris, to which he bade farewell in his recently published memoir, *Exile's Return*. Now he was saying to the earnest and hungry young men in that audience that the interior monologues of James Joyce and the chiseled verses of T. S. Eliot were *passé* in the 1930's. [2] The American scene before the Crash had been all sham and corruption. Cowley had tried to live within that social order, he said, but felt himself, like many other American writers, emotionally starved with every path to creativeness seemingly closed. In down-to-earth fashion he now talked of "What the Revolutionary Movement Can Do for a Writer." It could not offer an easy salvation or miracles, he warned. But the writers of the left would be faced with the challenge of new subject matter; they would surely gain in morale by abandoning the middle class that was fated to decline and associating themselves with the rising class. The workers and their friends would provide writers with increasingly responsive audiences. He then gave in illustration an account of the recent experience of Archibald MacLeish. Only two years before MacLeish had been appealing for leadership "to the Young Men of Wall Street" and lampooning the communists. But recently he had decided to hold a special performance of his new play, *Panic*, at an off-Broadway theater for the benefit of *The New Masses*.

I happened to have attended that performance, and I remember how after the final curtain the author came out and invited the audience to criticize his play. They responded with much warmth, mincing no words. The theme of the little drama was the market Crash of 1929; but it was written with the rhetorical excesses char-

[1] Murray Kempton: *Part of Our Time* (New York: Simon & Schuster; 1955), p. 121.

[2] It was true that Joyce and Eliot were then in some disfavor, though I suspected that they would continue to be read. But I remember entering strenuous objections, in conversations with Malcolm Cowley, to his statement in that paper that Wordsworth, Baudelaire, and Heine were good poets only so long as they were partisans of the revolutionary movements of their times (1789 and 1848) and went into decline after turning away from the revolutionaries.

acteristic of MacLeish and as drama was rather thin. Members of the audience offered intelligent comments on the defects of the work; some of them remarked that he had made a beginning in attempting a social play and exhorted the playwright to speak out more effectively for the common people. Apparently this confrontation greatly affected MacLeish, who ended up with tears in his eyes, thanking the public for their serious attention and their helpful criticisms. Thenceforth MacLeish was won over to the Popular Front.

In describing this episode, Cowley remarked: "This poet who had won the Pulitzer Prize had to turn to a revolutionary audience in order to get that sort of response, without which any writer feels that he is living in a vacuum and writing with invisible ink."

§   §   §

Controversy illustrating the differences between the orthodox communists and the independent intellectuals arose when Kenneth Burke read his paper on "Revolutionary Symbolism." Formerly an exponent of the "new criticism" of the twenties concerned with form and technique in literature, Burke of late years had plunged into long studies of metapsychology and semantics. He now offered new tools for the directors of social revolution.

All the world was symbol and myth, he held, which men used in living and working together. In periods of deep social crisis what actually happened was that people exchanged their allegiance to one set of symbols for another and more usable set. Today the capitalist slogans were losing their potency; but what of the symbol of "worker" to which the communists tried to attach men's loyalties? Did the majority of the people really prefer this symbol as applying to themselves? Or did they not rather dislike seeing themselves as only "human cogs" in a factory? Burke therefore proposed that in place of the terms "worker" or "proletarian," the word "people" be used instead. It spoke for a broader unity that would embrace the numerous petty bourgeois. If we hoped to accomplish more than to "convince the already convinced," then improvements in the current propagandistic vocabulary were in order.

The orthodox Marxists at the Congress promptly fell on Burke with great gusto. Mike Gold warned that Burke's proposals would turn their revolutionary movement into a petty bourgeois affair, adding that Burke had misconstrued the whole process of class struggle, as of class consciousness, and made of them mere myths to be juggled about or exchanged for other myths. Joseph Freeman, in more avuncular fashion, read Burke a lecture in which he argued that the use of the term "people" arose from the bourgeois revolutions of the eighteenth century, when the abolition of special political privileges was demanded. Marx's concept of the division of people into economic classes and of the predestined triumph of the workers was developed later, in the Communist Manifesto of 1848. Since then demagogues of the lowest type habitually addressed their appeals to the "people" against the "workers." Other speakers pointed out that the Nazi leaders always used the word "people" (*Volk*) in their propaganda.

Poor Burke was overborne by so much censure, but he held his ground, smiling, and allowed that he had expected there would be an unfavorable reaction. In truth he had worked better than he knew. The spokesmen for the Party line were the ones who were out of tune with the times. Two months after the American Writers' Congress was held, the Comintern in Moscow issued its formal resolution in favor of a "People's Front" in which the Communist Party would ally itself with the liberals and bourgeois of all lands. Thus the term "people," which Burke had proposed in place of "worker" as a superior instrument of exhortation, received official approval and was thereafter freely used by the very persons who in bureaucratic spirit had rebuked him for preferring it.

Chapter Eighteen

~

Art Under
the New Deal

ONE UNEXPECTED BLESSING of our De-
pression economy was the establishment in the summer of 1935 of
the federal government's several art projects as part of its expanded
relief program under the Works Progress Administration. Suddenly
there were excellent dramatic productions that could be seen for
fifty cents or less; one could also hear numerous concerts of a high
order that were generally free to the public. Besides this, WPA art
shows were presented in many cities, and modern mural paintings
were appearing on the walls of public buildings. Thousands upon
thousands of artists, writers, and performers, who for years had
been idle and hungry, were now cheerfully employed at such work.

It was something wholly new. America had lagged far behind
other nations such as France, Denmark, and Sweden in public support of the arts. Our people had been especially undereducated in
serious theater, music, and painting. Now, thanks to government
subsidies, the fine arts were brought into the lives of millions of
citizens. Masses of people encountered our native artists, musicians,
composers, and theater workers; and the artists met their public—
a very important confrontation and of immeasurable significance
for the advancement of cultural life in the United States. It turned
out that multitudes had been fairly starved for art and liked it
beyond a doubt. For several years the New Deal provided not only
bread but circuses. The thirties which some have misrepresented as

somber became an epoch of lively artistic ferment. A young generation of gifted painters was kept alive through employment by the WPA Federal Art Project, the very men who after World War II brought international fame to the "American School."

I have often wondered why this whole episode of the Federal Art Project under the WPA—one of the signal achievements of the Roosevelt era—has not been more fully recorded. About 80 per cent of the country's artists were then destitute, but they were enabled to survive and go on painting. Over a period of years some of them, as well as numbers of the WPA musicians and writers, told me stories of those strange days when their art was supported by the "world's greatest art patron," the federal government! I have tried to put down here what I could remember of their common experience.

§   §   §

In the first thrust of Federal Emergency Relief in 1933 the indomitable Harry Hopkins, in charge of the whole program, acted with characteristic speed to put four million people on the relief rolls by means of light projects for the Civil Work Administration. But Roosevelt was under pressure to reduce expenditures; after the heavy winter of 1934 he cut off the CWA's "made work" and directed Hopkins to carry on with the cheaper program of Federal Emergency Relief, which simply provided small doles for more people. Nevertheless Hopkins strongly favored work relief as helping to sustain the morale of the unemployed much better than the dole.

A confidential memorandum to Roosevelt from an experienced aide who toured the country in 1934 reported that the CWA alone had helped "avert one of the most serious crises in our history . . . a kind of revolution, or at least the threat of it." [1] When Roosevelt next won large appropriations from Congress in the spring of 1935 he came around to Hopkins's scheme for an ambitious work relief program. Hopkins was now allowed nearly $2 billion, and he quickly organized the WPA.

Three years earlier charity and state relief funds had been used

[1] Robert Sherwood: *Roosevelt and Hopkins* (New York: Harper; 1948), p. 35.

in New York to employ a few artists to decorate public buildings. In May 1933 George Biddle, a man of independent means who ranked as an accomplished professional artist, wrote a letter to the President—whom he had known long before at Groton School— pleading for work relief for his destitute fellow painters. Biddle proposed that an American mural painters' project be initiated under which qualified artists would be engaged to depict on the walls of federal buildings the "historic social revolution" of our time, much as the famous school of Mexican muralists had done under the leadership of Diego Rivera. But just then Rivera's frescoes in Rockefeller Center were the subject of a heated controversy between the buildings' owners—who had covered the pictures with a tarpaulin and begun suit against the artist for alleged violation of contract—and Rivera and his admirers. In reply the President wrote Biddle a rather cagey letter reflecting doubt about the expediency of having revolutionary images painted on our walls by Mr. Biddle's young artist friends.

Nevertheless Mrs. Eleanor Roosevelt and Harry Hopkins were extremely eager to have needy artists and musicians work at relief tasks for which they were suited. Hopkins was indignant at finding professional violinists employed to dig drainage ditches in parks. Through the CWA he temporarily hired about three thousand artists and musicians to do mural paintings or hold free concerts, and at the Treasury Department Edward Bruce, a corporation lawyer turned artist, was instrumental in having some small funds allotted to artists for the decoration of public buildings.

There was a drumfire of criticism directed by conservative members of Congress and by the newspapers at the New Deal's "boondoggling." That the government should provide artists and white-collar people with "useless" projects was stigmatized as both immoral and ruinous for our economy. Hopkins, a man of pungent speech, said in reply: "Hell, artists are people. They have to eat, don't they?" He also declared that the fact that many highly trained persons were losing their skills constituted a serious loss to society. Artists and musicians then suffered the highest ratio of unemployment.

The CWA, however, lasted but six months; the dismissed artists and sculptors, who had formed a union, paraded sadly about New York on several occasions with placards calling for relief.

My friends who worked under Hopkins at Washington all acquired a passionate loyalty to him. This native of Iowa, who had much experience in welfare work in New York, was a complete nonconformist in high office. He was convinced that an economic system that could engender such a great depression *must* support all who were made jobless against their will. Hopkins had a strong core of idealism in him, but he was also a driving administrator managing legions of officials in branches throughout the country almost without use of red tape. As head of the new WPA program, Hopkins was able to operate on a vastly expanded scale; he initiated as many as a quarter of a million light projects, ranging from local airports and stadiums to canning centers and needlecraft shops where people on relief could help sustain themselves. Beyond a doubt such spending spread buying power and, combined with the larger public construction at last under way, triggered economic recovery.

Meanwhile Hopkins had by no means forgotten his indigent artists and theater workers. Theaters, concert halls, and studios loomed large in the new program. Within a few months the WPA had more than 38,000 artists, writers, musicians, actors, dancers, and even circus performers working at programs specially designed for them. $46 million of the WPA's $2 billion were allotted to the creative and performing arts.

Hopkins had been searching for programs that would employ the largest possible number of idle hands. One of many proposals laid before him was a memorandum from the veteran playwright and producer Elmer Rice, who had much experience of repertory theaters. Rice advised the establishment of a chain of many community theaters and traveling companies. Hopkins kindled to the idea, and it became the pattern for other art projects organized around regional units in many cities. For the directing personnel Hopkins soon found able people: he himself chose Mrs. Hallie Flanagan (a fellow Iowan who had attended Grinnell College when he studied there) to head the Federal Theatre Project. Mrs. Flanagan had become known for her work at the Vassar College experimental theater. The veteran orchestra conductor Nikolai Sokoloff was chosen as director of the Music Project; Henry G. Alsberg, well-known newspaper correspondent and editor, who had close ties with people in the theatrical and literary world, headed the Writers' Project; and on the advice of Jacob Baker, Hopkins's administrative deputy, Holger Cahill was named director of the Art Project. Cahill, whom I had known since the early twenties when he was a student of art history, was then a curator of the Newark Museum; he had also been associated at times with the Museum of Modern Art in New York. He was an able writer on art and an expert in American folk art; at the same time he was the friend and sponsor of some of the best artists of the contemporary American school, and he proved a most fortunate choice for his office.

I I .

The Writers' Project under genial Henry Alsberg faced special problems: it was supposed to employ great numbers of writers certified for the relief rolls, but was not to compete with the literary business of private publishers. What was wanted was some enormous piece of research work, and Alsberg conceived the idea of compiling a sort of encyclopedia or continental Baedeker, to contain regional histories and guides to all parts of America as well as details of its folk history, its landmarks, and its monuments. This was a long-needed compendium such as other countries already possessed, but which no commercial publisher then could have afforded. Alsberg soon had an army of 1,400 writers and reporters working at Federal Writers' regional units in thirty states.

In the thirties American art and literature became more nationalistic than ever before, though this tendency was already marked in the twenties. Our art movements were distinguished by a passionate interest in all that was native to America. Not only writers but artists also, even when doing genre paintings in the style of social realism, studied our past, rediscovering not only our folklore but the early American crafts. In the field of music men on relief made important compilations of folk songs, Negro spirituals, and native jazz; several of the WPA's young composers were inspired, like Earl Robinson, to write popular airs in the manner of American folk music.

Alsberg explained to me later that it was foreseen that most of the writers on relief would be neither profound scholars nor creative artists. "It was not a question of the federal agencies' acting as patron for a few literary geniuses, but of their hiring crowds of writers of all kinds, even the mediocre, and using them for a large common task." At any rate, in Boston the regional Writers' Project had the services of the distinguished poet and novelist Conrad Aiken, then forty-six and recently a winner of the Pulitzer Prize for poetry; he was happy to avail himself of the WPA's $94 a month for contributions to its Massachusetts Guide. During that period Aiken turned in such excellent pieces of regional history as the story of Deerfield. The entries in the regional guides by men like Aiken, Vardis Fisher (of the Idaho Writers' Project), and many others were what made those volumes invaluable source works.

At the largest unit of the FWP employing 1,500 literary workers in New York, there was among the mass of workaday journalists a very decent quota of talented young people. My friend James McGraw, a newspaper reporter who served as regional director after 1936, remembers among those hired at various periods John Cheever, Richard Wright, Muriel Rukeyser, Tillie Lerner Olson, and Edward Dahlberg, as well as the young literary critics Harold Rosenberg and Alfred Kazin. At the Chicago center there were fledgling writers such as Nelson Algren. The New York FWP headquarters were located in a bleak loft building on West Forty-second Street. There the FWP writers were supposed to report every day, or at stated intervals, if not engaged in research outside. Alsberg arranged that qualified writers should be excused from regular attendance at headquarters and allowed to do their work at home. However, Colonel Brehon Somervell, Hopkins's deputy, insisted that writers working at home turn in some completed copy at regular intervals. Since Richard Wright was much troubled by such rules, McGraw arranged that he might "bring in any old thing" every fortnight, even if it was written long before. The WPA directors treated their often temperamental personnel with a good deal of tolerance; as a result Wright was encouraged to compose his early sketches of Negro life and his masterful autobiography of childhood and youth, *Black Boy*. By 1936 he was also launched on the writing of *Native Son*.

As a class, professional writers proved more resourceful than workers in the other arts in riding out the Depression by turning to journalism or teaching. The WPA's literary personnel were mostly young unknowns, yet a number of them were destined to win eminence; this was certainly furthered by their release from nagging anxiety and actual hunger during a year or two in which they could work out their first stories, poems, or novels. To have rescued a modicum of true literary talent, even at the cost of sustaining many incompetents, was an important net gain for the nation.

§   §   §

It was the Federal Theatre Project that made by far the strongest impact on the public mind. In the commercial theater of Broadway only by chance did one or two meritorious plays appear in a whole season. Little Theater groups were at work here and there, but they were in straits. Mrs. Flanagan had been a leader in the Little Theater movement of the twenties and the program of the Federal Theatre Project reflected her forward-looking spirit. Unemployed actors, directors, and playwrights of the avant-garde were brought into the Federal Theatre Project and gave it its strongly experimental character. The mood of the times favored social protest, but also artistic innovation.

For years it had been almost impossible to see Shakespeare. By the winter of 1936 we had not only Shakespeare but Christopher Marlowe and classical authors ranging from Euripides to Molière, as well as the modern masters Ibsen, Shaw, Synge, and Chekhov. Almost overnight a broad repertory of great drama was made available to us. There were also plays by contemporary Americans, such as Sinclair Lewis's *It Can't Happen Here*, an adaptation of his novel about native fascism, and John Howard Lawson's

Processional. The Federal Theatre in New York also produced, for the first time in this country, T. S. Eliot's superb verse drama *Murder in the Cathedral.* What was surprising was that such a difficult poetic tragedy as Eliot's played to full houses for twelve weeks in one of the largest theaters. Other literary productions, like Marlowe's *Dr. Faustus* and Voltaire's *Candide,* were sent on tour; and the total audiences mounted into the hundreds of thousands. Such success, even though ticket prices were low, revealed how greatly the commercial theater had underestimated the public's taste.

Mrs. Flanagan was able to engage directors of ability, including Elmer Rice, the regional director at New York; James Light, formerly of the Provincetown Playhouse; and Orson Welles, who soon became the boy wonder of the Federal Theatre. In her spirited memoir of the Federal Theatre venture, *Arena* (1940), Mrs. Flanagan has explained how she was obliged to spend most of her funds on salaries to workers—eventually over 12,000—leaving only 10 per cent of the budget for costumes and stage sets. Under the circumstances, the fact that the Federal Theatre usually attained excellent professional standards speaks well for the producers. Our community repertory theaters in many cities became powerful media for education and entertainment, as they were in other cultivated nations having subsidized theaters. They also served as popular gathering places where the emotional experiences of crowds of people, under the sway of players and dramatic authors, were focussed and shared.

Since the Federal Theatre people were looking for ways of employing actors in large numbers, they devised the novel entertainments known as the "living newspaper." These were skits or dramatic tableaux based on episodes of recent history or some burning issue of the time, such as the plight of America's farmers in *Triple-A Plowed Under,* or the housing problem pictured in *One Third of the Nation.* These productions, often in a satirical or burlesque style, used in part the device of the "camera's eye" that John Dos Passos had employed in his novels; vignettes of public personages figuring in the news of the day appeared as digressions in the text. They also borrowed some techniques from motion

(379)

picture documentaries and newsreels, the whole being worked out by teams of writers, actors, and scene designers.

The first "living newspaper" was produced early in 1936 in New York by Elmer Rice. Entitled *Ethiopia*, its theme was the recent invasion of that country by Mussolini's legions. Following months of preparation a huge company of Negroes and whites gave a dress rehearsal for newspaper reviewers and government officials. The WPA deputy administrator Jacob Baker had already given orders (under pressure of the State Department) that impersonations of foreign government leaders such as Mussolini and Haile Selassie be eliminated. After the rehearsal even citations from their public speeches were ordered stricken before the play could open. Rice thereupon resigned in protest, declaring in an interview that he had long fought censorship of the theater and would not accept it now at the hands of the government; *Ethiopia* died stillborn.

In this case problems of foreign diplomacy had arisen for the WPA; but in other cases all sorts of motives—religious, moral, or political—prompted the mayors of cities such as Boston and Chicago to have even plays by classical authors censored or suppressed. Harry Hopkins loved the theater and was no prude, but he was learning to play politics and gave his aides to understand that if they ran afoul of the authorities they could shift for themselves.

Managing a nationwide theater chain under a government bureaucracy became a pernickety affair for Mrs. Flanagan and her staff. More trouble arose later when the gifted young composer Marc Blitzstein completed *The Cradle Will Rock* for the New York Federal Theatre. Orson Welles and John Houseman, fired with enthusiasm for this authentic American *opéra bouffe*, arranged a notable production. In days when union labor was on the war path and sit-down strikes held the headlines, Blitzstein had composed a social satire which featured a "Mr. Mister," the sinister steel capitalist, along with angry workers and cops, a professional "moll" and other personages who were not quite respectable. It was my good fortune to attend the dress rehearsal, before an invited audience that gave the opera a magnificent reception. However, the high command of the WPA acted promptly to halt production. The next day, while many ticket buyers were being turned away, Orson Welles on the spur of the moment took the production to a private theater. There an improvised version was performed on a bare stage, with Blitzstein playing only the piano score and the actors—owing to trade union rules—speaking their parts from seats in the auditorium. The effect was such that commercial interests immediately underwrote Welles's impromptu version and he was enabled to launch his own theater.

A group of left-wing playwrights and directors who came over from the workers' theater movement of the early thirties, including Elia Kazan, Paul Peters, and Michael Gold, managed to function within the WPA while observing certain taboos. Mrs. Flanagan acted to discourage patent propaganda, but when Michael Gold built a play around John Brown she backed it, holding that such plays made propaganda for the traditional American form of democracy.

Conservative Congressmen of both parties, however, made the Federal Theatre the target of their most derisive speeches. That it was becoming a powerful agency of popular education was a fact not relished by some retrograde politicians representing poll-tax districts. In 1938 the Federal Theatre came under prolonged investigation by the newly established House Un-American Activities Committee under its first chairman, Martin Dies of Texas. "This Marlowe . . . is he a communist?" was one of the more memorable questions raised at a Dies Committee hearing.

Harry Hopkins, though often assailed in Congress, refused to give ground to the undereducated statesmen and newspaper publishers who regarded artists and even scientists on the WPA as inferior beings and demanded that they all be put to work with pick and shovel. "That is all they think about, money to repair the streets. . . . We are not backing down on any of these projects," Hopkins said. "I think these things are good in life. They are important. . . . The plain fact is we haven't done enough."

III.

Of the WPA's four art projects the section for plastic and graphic arts administered by Holger Cahill had perhaps a more lasting effect than the others; in itself it constituted a sort of cultural revolution. During the years when our museums and galleries were consecrated to the dead, Cahill had helped to interest the public in contemporary Americans such as Edward Hopper, Charles Sheeler, Stuart Davis, Ben Shahn, and Peter Blume. But under the WPA his problem involved more than aiding a few choice talents: he had to take over thousands of artists from the relief rolls. Ultimately 5,500 were employed.

There had been a few commissions awarded for murals; Cahill expanded these with a liberality that would have astonished Lorenzo de' Medici. By the end of 1936 approximately a thousand such wall paintings were completed or under way in schools, post offices, and other public buildings all over America. These frescoes or oil panels treated historical subjects or depicted our rural and industrial civilization. About six hundred art centers were also established where artists worked in diverse media, including industrial design. Qualified artists were permitted to work at their own studios, if they had them, and bring in completed pictures at stated intervals to receive $23.86 a week. Others taught classes, sometimes in remote rural regions where people had never before seen an original painting on canvas. The teaching of art at the high school age, often abandoned during the Depression, was strongly revived; the WPA teachers had sixty thousand pupils.

Cahill wrote at the time that he sought to create "not a school for a few solitary geniuses" in the interests of some wealthy patrons, "but a general movement to maintain art activities and . . . a great reservoir of art in many forms as a vital function of society." Many who later achieved fame had been obliged to work at other trades, when they could find work, to support their spare-time painting. "Under the WPA I could at last devote *all* my time to my art," was a common remark I heard. Out of such activity and ferment true artists and invaluable art works would emerge in the future.

With 80 per cent of professional artists in straits, the FAP was able to call on the services of men who had already attained high standing in their field. In New York these included Stuart Davis, Julian Levi, Raphael Soyer, Yasuo Kuniyoshi, Adolph Dehn, William Gropper, and Philip Evergood, as well as a crowd of young unknowns such as Jackson Pollock, Arshile Gorky, and Willem de Kooning. In Chicago Mitchell Siporin became the teacher of a notable group of easel and mural painters. In Boston the FAP turned up with such promising youngsters as Jack Levine, then just twenty-one. Exhibitions of artists on relief at federal art galleries in many cities attracted a surprisingly large public and won enthusiastic reviews in the press. Cahill also sent traveling exhibitions barnstorming in the hinterland of America; the response of the people to art shows in small towns in Tennessee, Oklahoma, or Utah revealed a veritable hunger for authentic works of art. The Federal Arts Project thus awakened a larger popular interest in the plastic arts, while stimulating work and study by persons with aptitudes hitherto undiscovered. Many of the WPA artists were able to sell their pictures, though at low values to be sure. Much bad art was produced too, but on the whole the project achieved what Cahill had hoped for: a reservoir of artistic production and an appreciative audience for a native American art movement.

§   §   §

Cahill's other interests, besides painters of the modern school, were antiquarian and archaeological and centered on American folk art. Inspired by John Cotton Dana in the early twenties he had long collected examples of Indian artifacts, Spanish Colonial religious objects, Shaker furniture, and "primitive" American paintings. As the Federal Art Project got under way, the artist Ruth Reeves came forward with a proposal that would permit the employment of hundreds of lesser artists and graphic artists: it was to set teams to work compiling an extensive pictorial and documentary record, drawn from all quarters of America, of examples of old American design and craftsmanship in textiles, furniture, ceramics, metal working, wood carving, glass, and costumery. The creations of earlier Americans of talent were to be rescued from oblivion. A group of scholars at the New York Public Library, including Mrs. Reeves, had already made a small beginning on such a compilation.

The FAP director took up this scheme with enthusiasm: at the different regional centers teams of searchers went forth to collect, classify, and record specimens of decorative art that belonged to an earlier tradition—old-time family portraits by naive journeymen, or "American baroque" paintings in taverns or hotels, figureheads of old ships, weather vanes, or ancient signs. Descriptions and measurements were taken down and more than eight thousand color or line drawings were made, as well as an equal number of photographs; these eventually composed the famous project later known as the "Index of American Design." Numerous separate portfolios in color drawn from this large collection were later published by commercial firms, so that fresh or virtually unknown aspects of America's arts were revealed. The huge program, which only the widespread personnel of the WPA could have carried out, thus yielded a large view of the whole country's artistic past and reminded men that, in contrast with the present landscape of "urban desolation," an everyday scene of good taste and fine craftsmanship had been known to earlier Americans.

Almost every day the newspapers, especially the Hearst press, published articles ridiculing the WPA's "Bohemian chiselers" who "defaced" our public buildings. When Arshile Gorky in 1938 completed a mural for the La Guardia Airport Terminal, not only the press but Mayor La Guardia too singled him out for abuse. As in other such cases, Cahill stoutly defended his artists and usually had the backing of Hopkins in matters of artistic freedom. In his later phase as an Abstract Expressionist, Gorky—especially after his suicide in 1948—became the hero of a widespread art cult so that his work, purchased so cheaply by the government, attained a fabulous value.

The mural painters, however, often felt they were running an obstacle race with censors political and moral. Philip Evergood, who for a while headed the American Artists' Union, was given an assignment to decorate a post office in a Georgia town with a mural on the theme of cotton. He journeyed about the region, studied the cotton pickers, and sent preliminary sketches and cartoons to

Washington for the approval of the authorities. He recollected for me: "I had the notion of placing a female figure in the foreground, with a suckling infant at her breast, to suggest the fertility that created the army of cotton pickers all about her. Before I had gone very far I had long-distance calls from Mr. Edward Bruce at the Treasury Department, ordering me to take out that half-nude female figure." But why? he asked. "The Southern people using that post office will be sure to think she is a *camp follower*—a loose woman pursuing the roving cotton pickers." Evergood protested but was warned that payments due him would be cut off. In place of the nursing mother he was ordered to put in "a bush, just an ornamental bush," though it destroyed the scheme of the composition. Broken-hearted he submitted, for he was then desperately in need of money.

IV.

Before the WPA came to their rescue a good many artists, especially in the great New York art center, were in a bitter mood and of a mind to make trouble. "During the depression we were the most forgotten of the Forgotten Men," Julian Levi, in later life a winner of many awards, said in recollection. To cite his case as one among many, he had known a brief season or two in which he, Stuart Davis, Adolph Dehn, Charles Sheeler, Niles Spencer, and a few other Americans regularly exhibited and occasionally sold pictures through New York galleries to a few patrons. When the market for contemporary Americans collapsed, Levi found himself on the beach at Cape Cod, where he had a studio. A little later he went on to New York, where the artists tried to help each other first by forming an Artists' Unemployed Council and then, in 1934, the left-oriented American Artists' Union.

Formerly they had been unpolitical; now they were ready to listen to those who spoke for communism. They had felt themselves alone and lost, as Levi recalled, but their small Artists' Union gave them hope. "We marched in the streets together—call it 'togetherness' if you will, but we enjoyed it," he said. Adolph Dehn, also a prize-winning painter, remembers that he felt ready to "join anything." The squat, beetle-browed Stuart Davis used to remind his union brothers in his rasping whisky baritone (as in a speech of 1936) that "it was only by going out in the streets and demanding support of the government as creative workers that they had obtained help." Artists were fed up with the sort of painting they had been turning out for the rich, whose patronage anyway had all but disappeared. (Davis, one of the most intelligent and gifted men of his day, made a great pretense of being gruff and tough in talk.)

The impact the WPA had on the everyday life of artists was described to me in jocular tone by my friend Henry Billings, who lived then in the old art colony of Woodstock, New York. By 1932 that village with its two hundred artists and art students seemed to have become completely moribund. Out of habit people stood before their easels painting pictures they knew no one would buy. Then came some federal relief in 1933.

Federal relief took effect, according to Billings, in three stages: "The first thing artists did when they began to earn $23.86 a week was to go and have their teeth repaired or get new dentures. Many had not seen a dentist since 1929. Second, several of them moved in and lived with that girl they had been going with all along. Finally, some of them got a divorce and married the girl."

The Depression years hardened the mood of the left group among the painters; such men as Hugo Gellert and Joe Jones, who depicted the class struggle in the communist press, called on their fellows to stop making pictures for the rich and paint political posters that would arouse the masses; or better still monumental wall paintings having the same militant purpose.

The inspiration for the movement toward a social art came not from Soviet Russia but from Mexico, where Diego Rivera, José Clemente Orozco, and David Siqueiros had brought about a great revival of mural painting. Toward 1926 Mexico's government, through its ministry of art and education, allotted four pesos a day to artists working on murals for public buildings. Rivera, who had formerly been a member of the School of Paris, returned from

France to work on frescoes depicting the history and legends of Mexico. Hundreds of European and American artists journeyed to Mexico in the late twenties to see the monumental frescoes of Rivera and Orozco, executed with an art all but lost since the days of the Renaissance in Europe.

The subsequent visit of Rivera to the United States, where he had been commissioned to do frescoes for buildings in several cities in 1931 to 1933, had mighty repercussions in our art world. Just before he began his decorations of the lobby of the RCA Building in New York he had journeyed to Soviet Russia, and in his volatile and mischievous way he became an impassioned partisan of communism (though not for long). The theme of the panels for the RCA Building, by agreement with the architects, was to be: "Man at the Crossroads Looking with Hope. . . ." But the crossroads for him now led away from the capitalist order. He was highly resolved, as he said, to make a series of frescoes that would be "useful to the working people of New York by showing them the true situation of society . . . hunger, oppression, war." But, according to the Rockefeller family's version of the affair, his preliminary sketches neither made his intentions clear nor revealed that he intended to include in his gallery of latter-day saints a portrait of Lenin!

The work in progress soon became the issue of a public quarrel between the artist and his patrons. Only a few American admirers of Rivera managed to see the incomplete panels; judging from photographs that remain they expressed, in his mannered style, his particular vision of our American machine age; certainly nothing equal to those frescoes had ever been attempted in this country. At first a tarpaulin was placed around these panels; then one morning in May 1933 the burly Mexican artist and several assistants were forcibly removed from the scaffold on which they were working by a team of Rockefeller Center agents. Outside on Fifth Avenue a little group of unemployed artists held a feeble demonstration in protest, but were soon routed by the police. Eminent artists and men of letters such as Boardman Robinson, Waldo Peirce, Van Wyck Brooks, H. L. Mencken, and Lewis Mumford voiced in letters to the newspapers their outrage at the suppression of the

(387)

frescoes. But several months later, in February 1934, wrecking crews came and reduced these wall paintings to rubble (for they could not be removed).

The horror felt by art lovers in New York and throughout the world at this act of vandalism was still recalled with much emotion three years later by several speakers at the first Artists' Congress held in New York in June 1936. One after another expressed the resolve to emulate Rivera as artist-hero "guiding the exploited masses"—his own estimate of his role at that time.

"For long centuries the artist had to fight his battles single-handed, depending entirely on his wits; society made of him a recluse, an exquisite, a Bohemian, a romantic fellow in velvet trousers, a clown and a bum." Thus spoke Henry Billings at the Artists' Congress. The artist at last recognized the need to join with his fellow craftsmen in working for a common goal, he went on; he must leave his "ivory" studio, and be done with art for art's sake.

§ § §

The social realists of the thirties in many ways derived from the "Ashcan School" of twenty years earlier and the work of John Sloan, George Bellows, and the early William James Glackens, who discovered the cruel landscape of America's cities. Others reflected the regionalism of Grant Wood. At all events many artists now went forth to paint America's "dark satanic mills," or her "factories in the fields." Among the more eminent beneficiaries of the WPA Art Project was Joe Jones, a former housepainter from St. Louis who depicted the plain people from the hills in his primitive style. Raphael Soyer portrayed the men and women of the slums with a serene sympathy rather than anger, and with a muted poetry of line and color. The young Jack Levine's crowded canvases of politicians on soapboxes, or of street scenes recalled the satirical spirit of Hogarth.

While the best of the WPA easel painters taken together gave an excellent performance, the "social" artists and the mural painters whose posterlike works were then so widely reproduced in left publications were generally sloppy and unimaginative. There was much talk of the need for art in the style of Goya and Daumier, but no American Daumiers turned up.

Only Siporin's murals seemed to approach the range of the Mexicans; and later Anton Refregier appeared with skillful frescoes, particularly his panels of California's history in the central post office of San Francisco. On the whole the revival of mural painting in America under government patronage was a partial failure; its practitioners, one of them remarked, "lacked the consistent revolutionary vision" of the great Mexicans.

Untypically, Stuart Davis would not leave off his neo-Cubist abstractions, inspired, as he claimed, by the rhythms of American jazz music. Afterward he said that he became so emotionally involved, so agonized by the Spanish Civil War, the sit-down strikes in America, and the Artists' Union demonstrations, that he spent several years without being able to paint. My neighbor Peter Blume was another who continued to move on his own course, working in a modified Surrealist manner which usually permitted no direct intrusion of the social question. But in the foreground of his grandiose canvas "The Eternal City" (1938) there is the hideous head of Mussolini as a jack-in-the-box, a jarring political statement coming, as Stendhal once said, "like a pistol shot in the middle of a concert."

Adolf Dehn remembered how the "social artists" used to appeal to the others to change their ways. "But I can't paint workers and machines," Dehn would protest, "I'm only happy when I do still lifes."

At the Artists' Congress of 1936 in New York, Orozco turned up among a foreign delegation. Though he was heart and soul for the popular revolution in Mexico, Orozco did not profess Marxism-in-art (as did Rivera in his fickle manner); the value of his own work was certainly not based on propaganda, but on the mastery of classical techniques. As Dehn once told me, Joe Jones and Hugo Gellert tried to draw Orozco into a discussion of what kind of art the workers preferred, and how artists might best appeal to them. On display were pictures of muscular and gloomy-looking machine laborers. What did the great Mexican think of them? And Orozco said smiling: "Perhaps the workers would like better something sweet—maybe a pin-up girl."

§   §   §

Roosevelt followed a wonderfully inconsistent course in the matter of federal relief expenditures. One year he would expand such outlays, but the next he might order sweeping reductions in the WPA budget.

The overwhelming election victory of 1936 had been attributed by the President's opponents, and a great part of the press, to Harry Hopkins's "buying of votes" among the unemployed. Certainly many of the light construction projects, even the location of federal theaters, were easily exploited as pork barrel affairs by "deserving" Democrats. Though Hopkins had vowed he would resign rather than lend himself to such partisan deals, he was evidently persuaded by Roosevelt to tolerate them; and in the end, went all out, as he said, for party politics. And so Hopkins, who figured so largely in the "spending and electing" process, came under the heaviest fire of the daily press and the news weeklies; ridicule of the "immoral" and "wasteful" art projects resounded through the country. It was not surprising, therefore, that follow-ing the good election tidings of November 1936, Hopkins got orders from the President to economize—orders which he always loyally carried out—and announced to his aides that he must drop 500,000 people from the WPA rolls.

The reliefers suffered above all from the sense of insecurity. For a season or two they might be happily occupied at useful or artistic labors; the next, seemingly without reason, they might be out on the street. Whenever large numbers were dropped, all the project workers walked out on strike—and what a paradox that these near-paupers, subsisting on the government's charity, should strike! Yet the Workers Alliance, principal union of the reliefers, insisted that strikes and "sit-ins," because of their nuisance value, were their only recourse. In New York and in other cities, writers, actors, stage hands, musicians, artists, and even artists' models on relief, carried out stormy demonstrations at regular intervals.

Alfred Kazin, who found employment at the FWP in New York just after graduation from college, has described such a scene in his reminiscences of the "Grim Thirties." Arriving at FWP headquarters one afternoon in 1937, he found all the personnel, a hundred or more in number, lying on the floor face down, as if they were devotees of Mahatma Gandhi.

Administrator Alsberg would come up from Washington to parley with the rebels sitting in at the New York center. His argument would run: "It doesn't make sense for you to stop working. This is not a commercial proposition—it's you who need the work." Nevertheless Alsberg was criticized by the press for "softness" in dealing with the WPA "ingrates." As he explained it to me afterward: "Of course I felt sorry for those people on the Writers' Project. They were told they would be doing useful work, and then were often dismissed without cause. The newspapers and the politicians mocked at them—and yet they had few chances of getting jobs outside. And so they felt frustrated: for they were living in an *unreal world*. It was to save their own self-respect that they joined the unions run by the communists."

In effect the federal government had socialized poverty in the work relief projects of the WPA. Roosevelt had remarked privately in 1933 that the United States would be forced to try some of the socialistic experiments known to Europe. In many respects our Federal Art Projects then surpassed in scale those of western Europe (though not in theaters and operas). But, on the other hand, there was little hope or glory offered the "socialized" relief workers in the arts. The artists on relief generally had no good prospects before them in the free-enterprise system outside the government which, in effect, treated them as "redundant." Meanwhile, the Government Art Projects became a confusion of ambitious schemes or programs that could be changed or dropped at any moment, because of political considerations. It is not surprising therefore that they hearkened to the spokesmen of communism and also of "Trotskyism," who were more radical still.

Regional director McGraw, at the New York FWP, remembered at least seven different unions among his 1,500 writers, the largest being the Workers Alliance (which had risen out of the

Unemployed Councils). Several smaller union locals were vociferous anticommunist "splinters" and had to be dealt with separately.[2] The communist locals were not only strongly organized among the WPA workers (who considered them the reliefers' best friends) but by the late thirties there were also labor spies and paid informers among them.

Harold Rosenberg, today the well-known critic and interpreter of modern art movements, then one of the employees of the PWA, once described for me the tangled web of political intrigue that was spun in those circles. It seems there was an old Communist Party hack named Banta on the FWP who claimed to have been a journalist in earlier days. He would formulate the Party line with authority, give orders to the communist contingent, collect dues from them. Generally he was well liked and trusted. One day, late in 1938, he was informed that he was to be "retired" from the rolls (the limit of employment being eighteen months), and his many co-workers, thereupon, arranged to give a party in his honor, each bringing his own beer with him. On this occasion they presented him with a book, W. Z. Foster's *Toward a Soviet America*. Banta, evidently touched by their kindness, asked the sixty or seventy persons present to write something appropriate in that book and sign it. Nearly everyone obliged, using phrases such as: "Yours for a Soviet America," or "Revolutionary greetings," or "Comradely Good Wishes."

Two or three weeks later all those autographs turned up in the hands of the House-Un-American Activities Committee under Martin Dies, who put the names of those WPA writers on the public record as communists, and called them to testify before his committee. The communists, however, had signed their real names and not their secret "Party names," and so there was no way of proving membership.

Later it was discovered by WPA officials that "Comrade" Banta had never been a reporter, as he claimed, but had once

[2] My only contact with the Writers' Project was in the form of a letter from an official at its Washington center inviting me to come and mediate the disputes between the communists and the Trotskyists—the invitation coming, by agreement, from both factions. I declined, because of pressure of my own work at the time, and was very glad I had done so.

worked for the Hearst organization as an industrial spy, and recently had been in the pay of the FBI.

Whenever WPA people were lopped off the budget, pink slips reached them by mail signifying their dismissal. In the late autumn of 1936 about 15 per cent of the personnel at the Federal Arts Project in New York were suddenly dropped from the rolls. (A historic canvas by Evergood, "The Pink Slip," commemorates such episodes.) This was the signal for all the artists to go out on strike, throwing their pickets around the FAP headquarters, an old loft building at East Thirty-ninth Street. At such times Administrator Cahill, a frail-looking man with kindly blue eyes, would come up from Washington to observe the scene of conflict. Out in the street, his friend and favorite drinking companion, Stuart Davis, stocky, black-haired, grim-mouthed, clad in a leather jacket, would march up and down at the head of the Artists' Union cohorts, who carried placards denouncing the government's action.

On this occasion, the afternoon of December 1, 1936, the FAP workers used tactics then coming into vogue at the great assembly-line factories of Ohio and Michigan. A body of more than two hundred men and women, painters, sculptors, etchers, draftsmen, and artists' models, arrived at the Thirty-ninth Street building, climbed up eight flights of stairs to the offices and studios of the FAP, and took possession. They ordered the clerical staff to stop work, cut off telephone lines, and held the regional director, Mrs. Audrey McMahon, as their virtual prisoner. Then the whole crowd sat down on the floor.

In such situations the WPA executives usually remained calm and waited the demonstrators out. But this time the building superintendent called the police, who arrived two hours later in a large body, with several police vans in readiness outside. Stuyvesant Van Veen, a member of the Artists' Union (but not on relief), who was equipped with a press card, accompanied the police detachment of seventy-four patrolmen and later described in detail the brawl that followed.

A police lieutenant began by ordering the strikers to leave the premises. Their leader, Paul Block, a solidly built sculptor, called on his people to hold their ground but to avoid violence. As the police started to move furniture and partitions out of the way, the strikers rose, moved toward the walls, locked hands, and formed a human chain all around the floor, with the police inside the circle. At a given signal the police, swinging their nightsticks charged the people lined up against the walls, then seized them, women as well as men, and dragged them off to the freight elevators, where they were carried down to the police vans outside. But this was not easily done. Some of the crowd seemed to go into a frenzy. Artists and sculptors exchanged hard blows with the police; the women kicked and bit them. One talented young woman artist, Ruth Gikow (later Mrs. Jack Levine), who was injured during the melee, said long afterward: "We were desperate; we were afraid we might be hurt or killed, but we were ready to go to any lengths, even to die in that fight." The brawling became fairly bloody: four policemen and thirteen artists, including three women, required hospital treatment. Philip Evergood had his nose broken by a policeman's billy. The newspapers the next morning reported: "219 ARTISTS AND MODELS ARRESTED IN WPA RIOT BATTLING POLICE."

Those were strange times when even artists, usually given to quarreling among themselves, gave battle to the police. Mayor La Guardia expressed concern because so much violence had erupted, and himself went to Washington in an effort to persuade WPA authorities to modify their orders. He had no success. A few months later another round of dismissals of WPA writers and artists was announced.

Chapter Nineteen

❧

The Labor
Movement Unbound

DURING SEVERAL YEARS after 1935—in
the period described as the Second New Deal—the revived labor
movement engaged our highest hopes. The American working class
seemed truly exalted. While some feared the rise of giant labor,
others believed its resistless advance might well bring about the
social revolution in our time.

Today America's labor organizations appear fat, contented, and
in some measure—like a good part of the body politic—corrupt
also; and it seems strange to recall how much enthusiasm was attached to the reborn unions of the 1930's. But our workers then
had suddenly to perform miracles in order to catch up with the
times. Except for a skilled minority in the AFL (some 10 per cent),
and employees in a favorable situation such as the railway industry,
they were unorganized, they had no job tenure, social security,
retirement pensions, or sickness benefits. In this field our social
laws lagged far behind those of western Europe.

Our intellectuals had long reasoned about the "lag" of our
working-class movement in terms of the historical pattern of
Europe. There laborers since 1848 had been building up their own
"ideological" parties in great strength. As our own industrial revolution had come later, so we hoped that our workers would eventually
follow a parallel course to that of their European brothers, combining economic power with political action.

At last, in November 1935, came the "breakaway" movement of an important group of AFL unions, led by John L. Lewis, of the United Mine Workers, Sidney Hillman, and others. Repudiating the AFL's craft union program, the dissidents formed the Committee for Industrial Organization, which was to unionize the semi-skilled mass production workers along the lines of "industrial," or plant-wide organizations. At the same time the CIO bloc—not yet in open schism with the AFL—helped create new political bodies in 1936 that would directly support the Roosevelt administration. Labor's Non-Partisan League acted on the national level to get union men (of both factions) to the polls; at the local level, such newly formed groups as the American Labor Party in New York State contributed mightily to the Democrats' landslide victory that year.

All through 1936 the industrial union "crusade" rolled on in high gear. Lewis and his organizers worked wonders in the heavy industries, such as steel, automobiles, and rubber, gathering in members by the hundred thousand. Hillman undertook the unionization of a million workers in the sprawling textile field. At this stage crowds of intellectuals came flocking to the banner of the CIO.

It was the golden day of the Popular Front and the "united front" in labor. In New York, rank-and-file organizers fought bloody battles with the city's racketeers and the AFL's "business unionists" to launch the CIO's National Maritime Union. An idealistic young intellectual of my acquaintance, Leo Huberman, who had been a progressive schoolteacher, became their educational director. Nowadays many collegians, active in the American Students' Union, used their summer vacations to organize white and Negro workers in the South for the CIO. There they lived dangerously and loved it.

In Washington too one could sense the impact of giant labor in the political field. A number of high-spirited New Deal officials had lately gone over to the CIO. One of these was Gardner Jackson, who after being purged from the AAA joined John L. Lewis as his press relations officer. Jackson, who had formerly hero-worshipped Henry Wallace, now talked of Lewis as if he were a demigod. (Later, this idol too would be lost to him.) Meanwhile Jackson brought in Lee Pressman, who had also been fired from the AAA; and that quick-witted young lawyer soon rose to be General Counsel of the CIO and Lewis's trusted adviser.

It was a revelation to see Lewis, in his fifties, formerly one of the AFL's stolid "labor bosses," now furiously engaged as a militant leader in organizing the unorganized. He not only called insurgents to his side, but also accepted communists. When he was warned against employing communists, he observed that "they worked well at their assignments"; he would not hold any inquisition into men's ultimate beliefs and was sure he was "man enough to take care of the communists," if need be.[1]

I met Lee Pressman while he was working under Lewis and asked him wonderingly: "How did that old 'leopard' Lewis happen to change his spots?"

Pressman shrugged his shoulders and replied: "What Lewis said to me was simply, 'It takes some men a long time to find their way.'" The young lawyer, whom Washington sometimes called "The Brain," was delighted to find himself at the very center of the militant union movement; and he was plainly captivated by Lewis's swashbuckling personality. He described him as not only a perfect showman, but also an opportunist, enormously ambitious, and with "a sure nose for power."

I was extremely eager to meet the great man in person, but did not have the opportunity until some years after the wars of 1936 and 1937. Though barrel-chested and burly, he had a certain animal magnetism, and could be all charm when he chose. In retrospective mood, he held me spellbound for two hours while he reviewed his record, speaking with uninhibited arrogance of the leading part he had played in American labor's heroic age. His talk was full of "I's." He exclaimed: "I made them put the 7(a) clause in the NRA" (though there were many other hands in that). He would say, with a short laugh: "True, I am not a modest man. People

[1] The day-to-day work of the union officer, handling wage negotiations, grievances, job-giving, can become wearing and dreary. The most energetic union officers I have known have been: (1) communists, who have their faith and count on compensation in the Heavenly Cities of the Future, and (2) racketeers who believe in gravy now, but like political bosses "take good care" of their followers.

shouldn't want leaders. But human nature is such that they tend to follow 'em."

Those who followed Lewis's career have generally agreed that his abiding sin was pride. In earlier days, in his imperious way, he had sometimes led his miners' union to heavy defeat. Later, in his disputes with President Roosevelt, in 1940, he lost out again. Through pride he broke with Hillman's pro-Roosevelt faction and saw himself replaced as chairman of the CIO by his own lieutenant Philip Murray. Since 1936 Roosevelt instinctively disliked and feared the headstrong Lewis, who seemed then a kind of demi-urge of the masses, and whose character Roosevelt sometimes likened to that of Huey Long. Lewis was capable of trying to browbeat the President of the United States himself. He made loud complaints because Roosevelt did not seek his counsel, though the Mine Workers had donated a huge sum to the Democratic Party fund. He was also furious because the President preferred, as his labor adviser, the soft-spoken, resourceful Hillman, and believed, as did many others, that Roosevelt used Hillman in order to "cut Lewis down to size." "Do you think I was not aware of *all that?*" he exclaimed in speaking with me of his relations with the President and Hillman.

In the great days of 1936, however, the CIO leaders and prima donnas all worked in harmony, so far as one could see; and Lewis's ego-drive was perfectly fused with the upsurge of labor. The new industrial unions were then heavily engaged in the history-making sit-down strikes.

§   §   §

There was much more to building a labor movement than calling men out on strike; there was a great deal of necessary spadework to be done, legal, legislative, and propagandistic. In those areas a key group of left intellectuals played a vital part—and among them were some communists and their sympathizers, who moved into the CIO as well as the old AFL unions.

Prior to the New Deal, we really had no written law governing labor relations. The vaguely conceived "magna carta for labor" of

1933 was annulled by the Supreme Court in May 1935. Immediately afterward Congress, with Roosevelt's support, passed the Wagner Labor Relations Act, which sought to restore labor's rights before the law. This bill also established a special federal agency, the National Labor Relations Board, empowered to supervise union elections, restrain "unfair labor practices," and even curb company unions. Our existing body of laws up to that time defended property rights primarily. The processes of judging anti-union discrimination, and supervising free union elections, were all to be charted; for the first time the "inherent rights of labor" were recognized and legally defined.

Large employers, being advised by their lawyers that the Wagner Act would be found unconstitutional, used the tactics of artful delay by filing an immense number of law suits or injunction proceedings during nearly two years (before the Supreme Court passed judgment on the Wagner Act). Corporate interests also made covert efforts, as often in the past, to "capture" the officials of the government commission that was to regulate their conduct. But in the late 1930's the three commissioners of the new Labor Board, the famous team of Smith, Madden, and Smith, showed themselves without fear in their judicial-administrative rulings; and if they showed favor it was toward the freely elected unions, which was the intent of the new law. Then it turned out that the NLRB's executive secretary was Nathan Witt, a zealous young lawyer who had lately resigned from the AAA's legal division. While the Board waited for the Supreme Court's decision, Witt and his associates busied themselves in compiling a huge dossier, based on investigations of thousands of cases of unfair labor practice and other violations of the Wagner Act. This material, in the form of a massive Brandeisian brief, was used with telling effect before the high court, which in April 1937 finally reversed its position and upheld the Wagner Act.

Another who made large contributions to the improved status of labor was my "Fabian" friend Heber Blankenhorn, who had seen service on the NRA's first Labor Board, and had been an adviser to Senator Wagner in the drafting of the new act. In 1935 "Blank" became the press officer of the NLRB, but actually carried out all sorts of roving assignments for the Board. A Midwesterner, Blankenhorn, at fifty, had had a varied experience as a newspaperman—he was for some years night city editor of *The New York Sun*—and as a correspondent for the labor press who was familiar with the British and European trade union movements. In this capacity he had served in World War I as a captain on General Pershing's staff in charge of psychological warfare, strewing millions of copies of Wilson's Fourteen Points by airplane behind the German lines. While in Army Intelligence, Blankenhorn had discovered that the only secret service activity the Army then operated depended on contacts with agencies of American industrial spies, such as Pinkerton's and Burns'. In 1919 he carried out a memorable work of labor research on the great steel strike of that year for the Interchurch World Council. Thereafter he was indefatigable in his studies of industrial espionage and strike-breaking agencies, to whom he attributed a great deal of American labor's former "backwardness."

During the spreading labor disorders of the time many good union men were being spied upon, blacklisted, beaten, arrested, or just shot. It was Blankenhorn who, together with Gardner Jackson, urged Senator La Follette to establish a Senate Civil Liberties Committee to investigate violations of free speech and interference with the rights of labor. (The La Follette Committee was set up by a resolution of Congress early in 1936.)

Blank, who seemed so mild and self-effacing, was possessed of a great passion for his chosen cause; but he was also tough-minded, and had the disposition of a strategist. Not only senators and congressmen, but eminent labor leaders such as Lewis and Walter Reuther, in later years, used him as a consultant. His interest lay, not in Marxist economic doctrine, but in the practical day-to-day struggle of organized labor. A famous drinking companion and storyteller, Blank drew together a whole circle of young enthusiasts at the NLRB. Among them were young writers such as Malcolm Ross and Robert Wohlforth, and here and there a fervent minister who had given up church service to preside at shop elections for the NLRB.

Meanwhile Blank (a small, gray-headed, quiet-spoken man with

silver-rimmed spectacles) was "loaned" by the NLRB to the La
Follette Committee, and began to investigate both the industrial
espionage agencies and their clients, such as General Motors.

§ § §

The first sit-down strikes of that era had been called by the rubber
workers at the Firestone plant in Akron, Ohio, in January 1936.
Despite gunfire and tear gas shells discharged at them by police
and guards, they stayed within the plants; their success led to the
organizing of eighty thousand rubber workers in a new CIO union.

A few months later, at Christmas 1936, the CIO's United Auto
Workers struck by "sitting in" at General Motors' Chevrolet
factories in Flint, Michigan. Court injunctions could not be enforced; and Governor Frank Murphy of Michigan delayed, as long
as possible, use of the National Guard.

President William S. Knudsen of General Motors (with whom
I talked of the affair in later years) said his greatest anxiety in those
days was for the safety of his beloved machinery. The silence of
his factories seemed catastrophic: "The greatest wrong labor has
done was to stop the machines," Knudsen declared at the time.

The drama of the sit-down strike in Michigan gripped the
entire country for weeks on end. The gargantuan firm of General
Motors had always hired labor on its own terms, as individuals.
Now the men in the plant said they were done with such feudal
rule, and demanded collective representation. The Democratic
Governor Murphy, elected recently with the help of labor, had
fifteen hundred state troops in readiness at Flint. However, he was
in constant communication by telephone with Roosevelt who
worked unremittingly to settle the affair in his own way.

The besieged strikers sent the Governor a message promising
that they would not damage the assembly-line machinery they had
taken under their charge, and concluding:

> Unarmed as we are . . . we have decided to stay in the plants. We
> have no illusions about the sacrifice which this decision will en-
> tail. . . . Many of us will be killed, and we take this means of making

it known to our wives, our children, to the people of Michigan and
the country that . . . you must be held responsible for our deaths.

Was there not a profound meaning in these unprecedented
actions, in the sit-down that suddenly imposed an unbearable strain
upon our political and legal institutions? The mass production
plants had long posed their social problems, turning the individual
laborer more completely than ever into a cog in the machine. The
CIO provided its answer: the one big union. Long ago Thorstein
Veblen had prophesied that the one big union would be the new
institution that would bring us to industrial democracy. At last
the toolless laborers of the belt-lines, with Promethean force, had
broken their chains; by their instinctive revolutionary act they
had created a social crisis demanding a new solution. The workers had
formerly been as helpless automatons serving the assembly-lines;
now, embittered by years of Depression, they fought for a new
kind of independence: the worker's proprietory "right to the job."
I wrote at the time:

> By the stay-in or sit-down action they (the workers) break old
> bonds, throw off the curse of landlessness and toollessness. The
> workers have not attacked property (like the old Luddites in Eng-
> land); they have sat down faithfully by the side of the machines
> which are life and death to them, and guarded them. In the absence
> of real social control . . . the workers have instituted a deliberate
> surveillance of the means of production, so that they may be directed
> more and more to creative social ends, rather than remain irrespon-
> sible and uncontrolled.

In Washington the real boss of General Motors, Alfred P.
Sloan, had been trying to bring pressure on the President and members of Congress to have the strikers expelled by armed force.
Most of the nation's press clamored for such action. Meanwhile
John L. Lewis also remonstrated with the President, calling on him
to help the workers against the "economic royalists." The President, very much in character, administered a rebuke to both Lewis
and Sloan.

In masterly fashion, Roosevelt acted to end the deadlock by
removing the whole dispute from Washington to Michigan. He

urged Governor Murphy to continue efforts to bring the two parties together, while avoiding bloodshed. Meanwhile Lewis was given the hint that he should go to Detroit and prepare to negotiate with the managers of GM. Roosevelt at his end of the telephone in Washington would deal with both sides at arm's length.

In a message to Knudsen, Roosevelt finally "insisted" that the corporation negotiate directly with the United Auto Workers and with Lewis as head of the CIO. The GM executives had hitherto flatly refused to do anything of the sort, maintaining that a company union had been "properly chosen" to represent their personnel. But faced with Roosevelt's virtual ultimatum they yielded and agreed to meet with Lewis and the Auto Workers' officers—which they had never done before.

Our friend Heber Blankenhorn, meanwhile, had not stood idly by. During the sit-down strike at Flint the La Follette Committee sent investigators to the scene. Blankenhorn and John Abt, the Committee's counsel, with the help of Robert Wohlforth, had already called up officers of the Pinkerton Detective Agency before the Committee in Washington, and laid bare their record of industrial espionage and strike-breaking. On January 22 and January 25, 1937, just as final negotiations between the two parties at Detroit were to begin, the La Follette Committee released stories to the newspapers describing how General Motors had spent $995,000 for strike-breakers and labor spies, and for the purchase of machine guns, ammunition, and tear gas shells. Basing his estimates on documents he had gathered, Blankenhorn charged that American industry spent $80 million a year to support about forty thousand labor spies. He reported that spies "shadowed" not only Walter Reuther of the UAW but also President Green of the AFL, and a professor of economics who advised him. Such stories, appearing just then on the front pages of newspapers throughout the country, strikingly affected public estimation of General Motors.

Roosevelt's next move, on February 5, 1937, was the announcement that he would recommend to Congress the immediate passage of a bill to reform, and, in truth, "pack" the membership of the Supreme Court. For nearly two years the High Court had delayed enforcement of the Wagner Act, which might have settled such disputes as that in the Chevrolet plant. If the President's bill went through, as seemed likely, then the Supreme Court would no longer serve as a bulwark of conservative jurisprudence.[2]

"Right there was the handwriting on the wall for GM," Blankenhorn said to me in reviewing these events. The corporation decided to surrender without delay, granting the conditions the UAW needed to complete their organizing drive. The union was inside the plants for good, and the way was open to unionizing the other motor companies. Three weeks later came news that the U. S. Steel Corporation had also reached full agreement with John L. Lewis and the CIO's Steel Workers' Organizing Committee. For half a century the gigantic mills founded by Andrew Carnegie had been America's strongest citadel of antiunionism.

I believed then (and do to this day) that labor was moving to right the balance of our society; and I hold that many intellectuals in the thirties made important contributions to this end. Later, during the dark ages of Senator Joseph McCarthy, the New Conservatives would charge that it was all a "plot" to "betray" our democratic society. In effect, these people actively schemed to raise the status of America's workers and farmers.

I talked with Lee Pressman in Washington after the sit-down strike at Flint. Pressman said in recapitulation: "The sit-down, the occupation of the factories, was clearly a 'revolutionary' step, and of course, unlawful. However, in 1937, it led to the greatest victories ever won by organized labor in America. Think of it, all that tremendous advance of unionism was therefore based on an *illegality*."

"Like the Boston Tea Party," I remarked.

---

[2] Roosevelt lost in the Senate on the issue of the court-packing bill; but won through forcing the retirement of certain Justices and bringing about a change of heart in the Court.

Chapter Twenty

~

Hemingway

Goes to Spain

DURING THE EARLY THIRTIES it was our own domestic convulsions, economic and political, that absorbed our attention almost exclusively. By 1936 however I was convinced that we Americans would somehow "muddle through," but thereafter my most anxious thoughts turned to the world abroad, toward Europe. There the mounting aggressions of Germany and Italy and the agonizing of Republican Spain in civil war gave the clearest warnings of world catastrophe.

In the summer of 1934 a letter had come from one of my friends in Madrid, actually an American citizen of Hispanic-American origin. It said: "I am writing you from a hiding place, as my home is being watched night and day. I am considered a 'dangerous foreigner' and they plan to expel me from Spain. The political situation is becoming cleared up to such an extent that government repression is inevitable, and I think we will have revolt soon."

What my friend predicted happened three months later: the far-right Catholic bloc led by Gil Robles at that period was awarded three ministries in the coalition cabinet of Premier Alejandro Lerroux—a concession the Republic had hitherto avoided, for Robles and his Falangist allies had vowed they would do away with parliamentary rule. Now Largo Caballero, leader of the Socialist Labor Federation (the UGT), called a general strike in Madrid. As the anarchist unions failed to join in the action, it developed no strength and its street demonstrations ended in confusion. Caballero and other socialist leaders were placed under arrest, as were the leaders of the Catalan rising in Barcelona. However in the province of Asturias on the northern coast a united front of socialists, anarchists, communists, and other left factions was formed; led by dynamite-slinging miners, the insurgents seized the industrial city of Oviedo and set up "revolutionary soviets" in the surrounding villages.

The Madrid government now called on General Francisco Franco, one of the heroes of the Moroccan War and commander of Spain's Foreign Legion, to quell the revolt in the north. This Franco accomplished in a fortnight of ferocious fighting, during which the Legionnaires and Moroccans gave little quarter to the Asturians. This operation, with its massacres of prisoners, gave a foretaste of what full-scale civil war in Spain would be like.

As many socialists and liberals were arrested, including even former Minister Azana, I felt great anxiety for my friends in Madrid until I learned that Rafael and Maria Teresa Alberti had managed to escape to Paris. In 1935 the couple turned up in New York in the course of a tour of lectures Rafael was to give in Latin America.

One would have thought their spirits would be thoroughly dampened by what had happened to them, but the irrepressible Albertis bubbled with hope and joy of life. It was as if they and their friends had lost a close game but counted on winning the next. Alberti, who exuded a romantic optimism, assured us that the present ministerial regime was only a caretaker government that would soon be swept aside. The last elections had not fairly represented the greater numerical strength of the left and anti-clerical parties. Alberti was certain that the two labor federations would soon reach agreement and, together with Azana's liberal group, win the next election. This was precisely what happened in less than a year. But that was what the implacable men of the right, the Spanish Church and the military crowd, would never bring themselves to accept.

We had been reading in the newspapers of the aggressions of

Italy and Japan in Africa and on the mainland of Asia; and many of us observed with growing dismay that these movements went unopposed by the western Allies. In March 1936 the reoccupation of the Rhineland by the German Army at Hitler's command provided a still greater shock. I remember saying at the time, what many clearly realized, that this was the last chance to halt the drift of Europe toward a new world war.

A few months later, on July 18, came news of the military rebellion in Spanish Morocco and fighting in the streets of Barcelona and Madrid between insurgent military detachments and mobs of citizen militia loyal to the Republic. The first reports showed that the insurrection of the generals had little popular support. To be sure, the rebels made good the landing of foreign mercenaries and Moors from Africa in the southwestern ports of Seville and Cadiz; but they met with strong resistance in all the populous centers, notably Madrid, Barcelona, Bilbao, and Malaga. Where sufficient arms were issued to the loyal citizens these prevailed, for the common people displayed a passionate devotion to the Republic. But within a fortnight Italian planes and German "volunteers" were reported to be aiding the rebels. Capronis bombed the loyalist-held cities, and soon twenty thousand Italian soldiers were sent to Spain by Mussolini.

Even from our side of the ocean we could distinguish clearly the design of the warmakers. They were beginning to overrun Europe. Victory for the fascists in Spain would mean the encirclement of democratic France and control of the Mediterranean. How could France and England fail to help the loyalists? And why did Russia wait?

I should never have believed that I would be so moved by any action taking place in a distant land, and it was surprising to see how many other Americans felt similar emotions. My fear was that Spain, as a vital part of European civilization with her enlightened traditions that had grown so strong since 1898, would be lost to us; the good books they were writing would be burned, the lights would go out. The cry of the rebel army was *"Viva la muerte!"* and of the Falangists: "Death to the Intelligence!"

We took some comfort from the fact that the French had

recently turned to a Popular Front ministry with Léon Blum as premier; they were half willing to help the Spanish Republicans but half fearful of being involved in a new continental war. In any case the British worked effectively to restrain the French from intervention. The policy of the Tories under Stanley Baldwin was that of elaborate compromise: they had voted formal disapproval through the League of Nations of Mussolini's attack on Ethiopia, but at the same time they continued to sell Italy petroleum for her ships and warplanes. In the United States public sentiment was strongly pacific and isolationist. In Russia André Gide, during his second visit in July 1936, appeared at a banquet and offered a toast to Republican Spain; but his hosts remained silent. Everyone waited on Stalin and Stalin bided his time. The British and French meanwhile worked up a sort of diplomatic effigy in the name of international order, the "nonintervention agreement," to which they hoped the fascist powers and the Soviets would conform, thus confining the war; and Russia, at first, accepted it. By September the modest professional army of Franco neared Madrid and was held up there.

I was in the country; two of my friends, Malcolm Cowley and Robert Cantwell, were visiting me and our talk was of Spain.

"This civil war is decisive not only for Europe but for the Americas," I said. "We can't afford to lose Spain. And why haven't the Russians come forward to help?"

Both men looked glum. Cantwell, then still an ardent fellow traveler, remarked: "We cannot endanger or perhaps sacrifice the security of 180 million Russians, the socialist fatherland, for the sake of a small country of 20 million like Spain."

"Danger—sacrifice—rubbish!" I exclaimed impatiently. "If things go on like this Russia and everything else will be sacrificed." In the United States the people on the left, liberal or communist, had not said a word or made a move. The communists operated like a cumbersome bureaucracy, I protested; their committees and the bureaucrats had not yet made up their minds, as in Russia, about what was to be done. "Well, I have made up my mind. I am thankful that I don't belong to anybody and don't have to wait six months or a year to have someone else, some higher-up or some committee, tell me what I ought to think."

I proposed that those of us who felt involved in the fate of Spain form some sort of ad hoc committee to arouse public opinion and arrange to help the loyalists with money and supplies. It seems that both Cowley and Cantwell were doubtful, at that stage of affairs, about such action. I wrote letters to various persons who might be of help, but my first efforts met with little response. There was a League against War and Fascism, supposedly sponsored by the communists but supported by many liberals; it too moved very slowly in dealing with the question of Spain.

In later years, during the repressive phase of the cold war in America, those who had supported the Spanish loyalists were denounced as "stooges" or servile followers of the Communist Party. My clear recollection is that my own concern for Spain preceded the line of the Party by several months.

The indifference of most Americans in those early months of the Spanish Civil War was disheartening. Not only were our people disposed to keep out of Europe's wars, but Congress the year before had passed the Neutrality Act inspired by the Nye Committee's exposures of the munitions industry. Although its restrictive provisions did not apply to civil wars the Roosevelt administration took steps to embargo arms shipment from the United States to *both sides* in Spain.

The university intellectuals in England, who widely propagated the Oxford oath, were more ardently pacifist than any others; but they were quick to change their ground. The newly formed Left Book Club, headed by Strachey, Laski, and Victor Gollancz, led the way to commitment on the side of the Spanish Republic. "Spain offered the twentieth century an 1848," wrote Stephen Spender; and W. H. Auden avowed, in a memorable poem: "*Yes, I am Spain.*" John Strachey asked what else there was to do with one's life if not "to take part in the struggle . . . for peace and a just society?" Young English intellectuals and former pacifists were among the first foreign friends of the Republic to drive ambulances for the loyalists.

By the autumn of 1936, while Madrid barely managed to defend itself with an army in overalls, the first antifascist volunteers began to arrive from all parts of Europe. As Auden wrote:

They clung like burrs to the long expresses that lurch
Through the unjust lands, through the night, through the Alpine tunnel;
They floated over the oceans;
They walked the passes; they came to present their lives.

The mobile army of Africa, driving up from the south, steadily outmaneuvered the crowds of socialist-communist youth and anarchist workers who fought now with utter recklessness or now turned into panic-ridden mobs. It was almost November; Franco's forces neared the gates of Madrid before we heard of Russian matériel arriving for the loyalists. This reflected a change of policy provoked by the arms and troops sent to Franco from Italy and Germany.

At last, on November 7, the first two battalions of the International Brigade with artillery and tanks came clanking into Madrid and abruptly halted the enemy army of 20,000 at the western edge of the capital.

Frustrated on the ground, Franco ordered an air bombardment of Madrid, mainly by German planes, as a first large-scale experiment in terror. Thousands died in the street; soon much of the city was in flames. Yet there was no rout. The inspiring voice of Dolores Ibarruri ("La Pasionaria") continued to resound over the front. The Republican radio sent forth appeals to all the world in expressions memorable for their eloquence: "Madrid is the frontier that separates liberty from slavery . . . love against hate, the fraternity of Christ against the tyranny of the Church. . . . This is Madrid. It is fighting for Spain, for humanity, for justice, and with its mantle of blood shelters all mankind!" Red Berlin had fallen; socialist Vienna too; but Madrid, surrounded on three sides, withstood its siege for years on end. Since its roads remained open on the eastward side to half of Spain the fortified city remained a deep salient in fascist-held territory, a great promontory of man's hope. The Madrilenos's cry: "*No Pasaran!*" echoed around the world, and all who felt morally engaged identified themselves with the

Spanish people's struggle. Madrid was the "miracle" from which all the antifascists drew courage.

The farce of nonintervention continued. A wavering border control in France allowed some arms to flow to the loyalists; munitions and planes also came by sea from Russia though subject to submarine attack. But at least four times the amount of supplies and personnel reached the rebels. For the barbarians in Germany and Italy who brewed world war, Spain served as testing ground. But for those who believed in the life of reason and the attainability of a humane social order, Spain also became the proving ground of their will to overcome the enemies of civilization. André Malraux flew in with fighter planes to reinforce the small loyalist air force; the Catholic Georges Bernanos and the communist Louis Aragon were among the first French writers who, from besieged Madrid, sent appeals to the world for aid.

In the United States earlier hesitancy about Spain's civil war began to give way to outright enthusiasm for the Republic among antifascists of every color. Early in 1937 an "underground railway" extending from California to the French-Spanish border was organized under Communist Party direction and eventually carried more than 2,800 American volunteers for the Abraham Lincoln Brigade. From 1937 on a number of Spanish aid committees with branches in many cities were actively raising funds for food and medical supplies for the loyalists. I supported or sponsored all such activities without hesitation. That war was an evil affair and civil war generally more cruel than other forms of warfare, I did not doubt. A good many of us felt reservations about official Soviet policy, for it was the time of the Moscow Trials of the "old Bolsheviks," and I wrote then of my own incredulity about the justice of those trials. Nevertheless Russian support of Republican Spain was vital; very little in the way of munitions came from other countries. If Stalin's conduct in Moscow was that of a ruthless dictator he was at least disposed to help the antifascist cause in Spain, whereas the behavior of such "democratic" statesmen as Baldwin and Hoare in England seemed hypocritical and noxious and no less ruthless than Stalin's. They were concerned with British capital investments in Spain and, in the hope of confining the war, persisted in wooing

Mussolini and Hitler. Above all the Tory leaders feared the victory of the left as the greater evil, and they suffered the open interventions of the fascists and Nazis (called "nonintervention") as the lesser evil. Our own State Department under Cordell Hull meanwhile pursued a policy of uncalculating neutrality, paralleling Britain's efforts to confine the war.

Alas, our choices in an actual crisis are seldom as clear or morally satisfying as we would wish them to be; neither are they often as ideologically consistent or as perfectly attuned to our finer sentiments as we might hope. Nevertheless, it was plain that we were witnessing the full-dress rehearsal of world war in the tragic Iberian Peninsula, and it was borne in upon us that if only the enemy could be defeated there the world would be spared far greater horrors. Otherwise, who could say that we Americans would not eventually be forced one day to take our part in the bigger show that was being prepared?

§ § §

We who believed in creating an international Popular Front of all the democratic nations, together with Soviet Russia, for our collective security, carried on a prolonged agitation for lifting the ill-conceived embargo on arms for Spain. On every side we met with vigorous opposition, especially from those who favored isolation. One of these was my old friend Charles Beard, who warned me that I was overzealous and that views such as mine, if widely accepted, would involve the United States in new foreign wars.

In World War I Beard had favored our intervention on the side of the western Allies, though he also engaged in a famous free speech fight at Columbia University. He had embraced, as he said, the Wilsonian hope for a League of Nations. "But I was wrong then," he went on, "and now I am weary of the national quarrels and the ancient hatreds of old Europe and believe we should keep out at all costs. How lucky that we have the broad oceans between us and the others and can easily defend ourselves. I say let us rather build a strong, democratic society in our island continent by intelligent planning." In short he was for a Little America and feared that Roosevelt might be tempted "to seek big adventures in foreign wars."

I argued simply that peace was "indivisible," that each aggression of the fascist powers that we tolerated emboldened them to raise their price; and so, in avoiding trouble now we would "pay more later." Beard and I agreed in "everything save opinions," as he remarked, yet respected each other's motives and remained good friends.

Roosevelt was said to have supported the specific embargo of arms for Spain because of the pressure of leading Catholics in the Democratic Party such as James A. Farley and Joseph P. Kennedy. It was well known that the President heartily detested Mussolini, Hitler, and company. At some time in 1937 I heard that Roosevelt, growing more concerned with the foreign crisis, invited Charles Beard to write a memorandum for him on what policy the United States should pursue. Beard of course produced a strongly argued tract for isolation. As was his habit, Roosevelt also called upon another adviser, the historian James T. Shotwell, known to hold views antithetical to Beard's. Shotwell urged full cooperation with the democratic powers in exerting pressure against the Axis. Roosevelt then dropped Beard's memorandum in the wastebasket and, in a speech given at Chicago in October 1937, made his bid for an internationalist policy of collective security in which he proposed that we "quarantine" the aggressor nations. If it was a trial balloon then the response of the home public seemed uncertain, while the British leaders were indifferent; and so the President turned to other issues.

Beard never forgave Roosevelt for that "quarantine" speech; he became so exercised about the danger of our being involved in a foreign war that, toward 1940, he associated himself with the America First Committee. On one occasion some of his friends learned that he was to speak at a meeting in Hartford in the company of leaders of the German-American Bund and other questionable characters, with the isolationist Senator Burton K. Wheeler presiding. At the last moment his friends persuaded Beard to cancel his speech. He was greatly troubled about this affair, saying to me: "I wanted to speak out for peace. But I found that the wrong kind of people were in that camp, while those I like all seem to be on the other side."

§ § §

In the winter of 1936, during a blizzard in the country, I came down with pneumonia and did not recover full strength until the early spring. Then with the return of cold weather in December I fell sick again with a respiratory illness that alarmed my doctor, who ordered me to go south before the snow began to fly. As soon as I could get up I set off by train for Key West, Florida, where friends of mine wintered, leaving my wife and children at Sherman. A plan I had entertained around that time to visit Spain was put aside.

Key West, a little city out in the sea at the end of the Florida Keys, had an unsubstantial look; it had not only suffered from hard times but had also been much battered by a hurricane and tidal waves the year before, so that the long railroad causeway leading to it had been destroyed and one spent the better part of a day reaching the place from Miami by buses and ferries. The bankrupt town, with its dilapidated buildings and pot-holed streets, had become the ward of the WPA. There were few tourists; most of the native population—Cubans, Negroes, and Florida "crackers"—worked for Harry Hopkins's organization to rehabilitate the old port that had been the repair of pirates, fishermen, and rumrunners. With its brilliant light, its subtropical shore and its many lagoons, Key West was a sort of poor man's Venice with no palaces and cathedrals but unpainted, tumble-down woodframe houses—well suited to rest and revive me.

For several years a little Bohemian society had been growing up here, as the place was unpretentious and cheap; Ernest Hemingway's residence in Key West in recent times contributed to this development. There were always two or three artists in town, as well as an author or two of detective stories or historical novels. Certain New Dealers, such as Hopkins, Tugwell, and Henderson, also liked to visit Key West from time to time. I was to stay at the cottage of Canby Chambers, a writer of popular fiction whom I had known since the twenties in Greenwich Village and Paris. Other winter residents were the aged writer Hutchins Hapgood and his wife. Hapgood had been a popular author (like his more famous brother Norman) back in the days of President McKinley and Richard Harding Davis, and he and his wife had been pillars of the Washington Square colony since 1908. Mary Heaton Vorse, the novelist and magazine writer, who had been reporting the labor uprisings in the Midwest, was also taking her winter vacation here. An old associate of the Wobblies of prewar days, she talked in a finishing-school voice as she described a gun battle between strikers and police at Youngstown, Ohio, which she had witnessed recently. To be sure she had tried to take cover, but a submachine gun bullet ricocheted and grazed her forehead, leaving a slight scar which she made light of.

For a vacation period I can think of no company more restful than a circle of good-humored, well-spoken Bohemians such as I had in Key West. After a week of sun and sea I felt so well that I decided to stay and work here. I rented a house, hired a cook, then, in a quite fervent telegram, sent for my wife, my children, my books, and my papers.

The man I had been visiting with, Canby Chambers, then a little under forty, had been a wheelchair case for seven years as a consequence of polio. He was a large, handsome man, with a big head, wide jaw, and powerful torso. Physically he reminded one of President Roosevelt—though it must be said there were great contrasts too. Unlike Roosevelt, who after paralysis drew on reserves of courage and energy, Canby had given up all mental activity, spending his days sitting up in his chair with a magnum (!) of gin by his side and sometimes a light novel or cards. Formerly he had been successful at light magazine fiction; but an inheritance gained at the time of his sickness permitted retirement to this immobilized life. He gave up writing because, as he confessed, he had no respect whatsoever for anything he had written.

Many persons came to visit and help him, for he was caressing with women, and his conversation was marked by a light raillery and risqué humor. He was also given to the black nights of an alcoholic that sometimes made his companions despair of him. For years

Ernest Hemingway used to come to take him fishing and swimming, and help drive away his glooms. (There are suggestions of the
liverish Canby sketched in Hemingway's often photographic prose.)

Just before I moved to my own quarters on the Key two miles out
of town, Canby Chambers and his wife gave a cocktail party for me
and invited Ernest Hemingway. Hemingway arrived looking much
heavier than I had expected and very healthy, for he had just returned to town after a long fishing trip off Cuba. With a breezy
Midwestern cordiality he bade me welcome to his domain of Key
West and the Caribbean Sea, adding that if the Chamberses didn't
feed me enough I was to "come and raid his icebox any time." We
had several mutual friends, especially Harold Loeb, whom he had
harshly satirized, and the poet of the racetracks Evan Shipman,
whom he loved, and we soon chattered away as if we had known
each other all our lives.

Almost the first thing he spoke of was the Spanish Civil War.
What did I think of it? What did others think? He exclaimed: "If
the fascists win in Spain it will mean a new world war for sure."

As we were talking in a corner of Chambers's living room,
Pauline Hemingway came over to join us. She looked somewhat
blank when she heard us talking of Spain. Hemingway changed the
subject.

He had been married then about ten years to his second wife,
former Pauline Pfeiffer of St. Louis, a rich girl who had been a
friend of his first wife. Pauline was small and fine-boned with black
hair and dark eyes, a vivacious woman rather than a pretty one.
One felt there were, or had been, strong bonds of affection between
them; she, at any rate, often used Ernest's turns of speech and
sometimes even the tone of characters in his books. She talked
Hemingway. He spoke of her sometimes with admiration, remarking to me on one occasion that she had really saved his life during
their African safari, a year or two earlier, by her quick application
of first aid and her nursing when he nearly died of dysentery.

After this first meeting I said to Chambers: "Considering that
Hemingway has had a sort of Lord Byron glory since his early years,
he is not a bad fellow at all." Others described him as the big
bumptious boy, but he could be very simple and friendly when he

chose to be. There was certainly nothing slow about him: his even brown eyes had a very keen look. He posed as undereducated or lowbrow, but I found on further acquaintance that he read widely in his own field and, despite his antiintellectual pose, was every inch a literary fellow with much natural equipment for his métier. While there were many glasses of liquor drained off in his stories and novels, Hemingway himself, I perceived, was no heavy drinker. He rose early and worked until one o'clock, when he stopped to eat and then for relaxation went sailing or fishing or for target practice down the shore.

To be sure he did a bit of blowing about his prowess as sportsman and told us his fish stories; there was certainly a full-grown ego in the man, and he sometimes sounded harshly competitive, as in speaking of his literary friends, often regarded as rivals. But we got on much better than I expected, for our interests were rather different and we were not competing. I did not by any means address him, as some others did, as "the world's great literary genius," and I sometimes expressed firm disagreement with his opinions, which often seemed to me prejudices. On the other hand, I felt and admitted to a strong admiration for the economy and the poetic and painterly qualities of his prose. In some of our good intimate talks he showed the humility about his own work that true artists generally retain.

During two months we met two or three times a week at the beach, at tennis, at occasional cocktail gatherings at his home or elsewhere, and regularly on Saturday nights at Sloppy Joe's café, where there was a native rhumba band and dancing. On Saturday nights Hemingway drank liberally, but he carried his liquor well enough in those days.

The Hemingways lived in one of the few substantial houses on the island, West Indian colonial in style with ironwork balconies and a tropical garden, all of it well restored by Pauline, who was its owner. They had also the big black fishing yacht *Pilar* that he said cost $60,000, which Pauline's uncle had presented to them. (Pauline's St. Louis family, I gathered, loomed large in beer-brewing and cosmetics too.) Some throat ailment made Hemingway avoid winters in Paris or New York in favor of a warm climate. Though he would have preferred to live in Havana, he found Key West a good compromise, because his two boys could receive American schooling there at its one good school, which was Catholic. "Papa" was Protestant-bred, but some years ago he had adopted the faith of his wife and attended Sunday services with his family.

A few days after I had first met him, on Christmas Eve, I stopped in at Sloppy Joe's for a drink while awaiting the evening bus from Miami on which my wife and children were just then arriving to join me. At the other end of the long bar Ernest was standing with a tall, handsome blonde. He waved in friendly greeting. I had seen that young woman at the beach, for she had the cabana next to mine and appeared there each day in the company of her mother and a younger brother. As they were leaving Ernest came and introduced her as Martha Gellhorn.

I told him that I was waiting for the bus to bring my wife and sons in time for dinner, and I must have looked cheerful as I said this.

Ernest said he too was going home soon to join his family for dinner. Then abruptly he asked me: "Do you love your wife?"

"I do," I replied.

He went behind the bar, selected a bottle of champagne from the shelves, and brought it to me saying: "Give it to her. For your reunion. It'll do you both good." I protested, but he insisted it was a Christmas gift, and he went off with his rolling boxer's gait.

II.

One of the subjects on which we did not agree was bullfighting, talk of which bored me. To the author of *Death in the Afternoon*, the matador, of course, embodied the Spanish tradition of physical courage and honor, and practiced the "cult of death," as Hemingway said, "with skill and grace."

In his marked taste for violent sports Hemingway reminded me of that earlier amateur boxer, big-game hunter, and man of letters, Theodore Roosevelt, who had been our "red-blooded" President when I was a small boy. Mussolini also propagated the cult of the "manly arts," such as sports and war, as part of the "new" fascist ideology. On the one hand Hemingway seemed to share some notions that made up the fascist mystique about violence and death, except that he was not a systematic thinker. On the other hand, he detested Mussolini because "that bastard" had banned the publication in Italy of his novel *A Farewell to Arms*, owing to its reflections on the Italian Army. When Italy invaded Ethiopia, Hemingway issued a strong public protest which was widely reported in the newspapers.

Meanwhile the leftward drift of opinion here was not without effect upon him. A number of his friends, including Dos Passos, who had stayed in Key West the previous winter, and Archibald MacLeish, participated in the politics of the left. Hemingway had little interest in politics, but like other successful authors, was sensitive to the movements of popular opinion in the era of the New Deal and was disposed not only to go along with them but to put himself at the head of them.

As for his attitude toward the common people and the poor workers, he contended that he knew them much better than did "those communist intellectuals in New York." He himself had worked as a dishwasher on a Great Lakes boat, and as a waiter when he was a high school student. Some of the friendships he found most comfortable were with such persons as Parker, the giant Negro bartender at Sloppy Joe's, the Key West "Conchs" who were former rumrunners, the genial, broad-beamed Sullivan, a machinist, and Sidney Franklin the Jewish bullfighter from Brooklyn.

The Marxist critics a while ago had slated him severely for his *The Green Hills of Africa*, a work steeped in "romantic pessimism." He, for his part, railed at the literary Marxists who just learned about the poor by reading some books, and cited to me the example of John Herrman, former newspaper reporter and author of a novel, whom he had known in Paris. The winter before, Herrman, with his wife, Josephine Herbst, had come to visit him and they had gone out fishing in the *Pilar*. All during the run Herrman sat there girding at Hemingway as a complacent bourgeois who went off on African safaris, or amused himself at depraved bullfights in Spain. Such talk made Hemingway almost speechless with rage. Then, as he related to me, he thought of an expedient: he went down into the cabin of the boat, fetched up a bottle of Old Methuselah, a twelve-year-old whisky he had acquired in Havana, and offered it to Herrman.

"There, you god-damn Bolshevik," he exclaimed, "drink some of that—it's Old Methuselah, and you can't find it in the United States." Herrman had a nose for liquor, took some good gulps, and agreed it was right good.

"Well, it's capitalist liquor, earned by a well-paid bourgeois writer—and you like it just the same. Go ahead, have some more, feel good, and the hell with your Revolution."

However, he was quick to show compassion—in fact, pain and suffering fascinated him. In September 1935, a hurricane struck southern Florida and drove a huge tidal wave over the neighboring Matecumbe Key, engulfing the government hospital for war veterans; two hundred of them were drowned. Learning of this the next morning Hemingway rushed to the scene in his boat, brought in emergency supplies, and helped volunteers gather in the bodies of the drowned men. Then he wrote a ten-page piece describing the disaster, full of anger at the failure of the authorities to protect a place where the crippled heroes of Belleau Wood and the Argonne had been put out of sight. On the impulse of the moment he sent the article, entitled "Who Murdered the Vets," to *The New Masses*, which published it in its issue of September 17, 1935.

He had already created the myth of the Lost Generation who, after the war, wandered disconsolately about Europe, drinking away their days in its pothouses, or giving themselves to sexual adventures that left them only more disenchanted, and believing in *nada* and "out of *nada, nada.*" But now we were in the thirties: the Great Depression was highly visible in wretched, hungry Key West, a "disaster area," and Hemingway was writing *To Have and To Have Not*, his only approach to the novel of social consciousness.

By the winter of 1937 he was putting the finishing touches on this novel. I was told that he had kept shifting and rearranging its episodes, yet remained despondent about the results.

One Sunday in January he came to my house, early in the morning, after attending six o'clock Mass. My wife and I were both

asleep, but our two boys, aged six and ten, were up and offered to
call me.

He said: "No, don't wake your father. We'll wait." And he sat
down on the floor of the living room and played quietly with the
two boys. He showed them a new stopwatch and other such objects
he had in his pocket, and told them stories that kept them laughing.
It was quite the way he performed with his own two small boys (by
Pauline), to whom he was greatly attached. After a while my wife
heard them and roused me.

He had brought with him the corrected manuscript of his new
novel and said he would like me to read it and give him my frank
opinion. It was fairly short; in two or three days I brought it back
with some notes I had jotted down for him.

The novel's central figure, Harry Morgan, a charter-boat sailor
of Key West, is represented as a helpless victim of the slump.
His adventures assume the quality of melodrama. In his dying words
are framed the realization that he had simply been caught in a huge
trap with multitudes of other unfortunates, that his desperate exertions were vain, and that "one man alone can't win." Such was the
rather *simpliste* message of this story of a romantic individual's
revolt against society.

Together with Morgan's story is interwoven a second plot concerning a frustrated, rather unprepossessing writer, Richard Gordon,
who had come to Florida to write of the rich "like a stranger spying
out the land." I found the two parts of the novel did not gibe, and
were even incongruous in tone. In fact I learned that Hemingway
had written the later episodes after a long interruption; the passages
about the rich folk at Palm Beach, and the society woman who
seduces Morgan, and those about the writer Gordon were not well
drawn and not credible as satire—in contrast with the colorful opening scenes of the wharfside workers and Cuban insurrectos done in
his best vein.

With some embarrassment I expressed my reservations about
the second half of the novel, but spoke with enthusiasm about the
opening scenes at Havana and the descriptions of sea journeys.
Hemingway received these observations with good grace, though
I sensed that he was unhappy about them. He made some self-

deprecating remark about the passages I had singled out for praise, to the effect that: "Sometimes, when the thing sounds really good, I feel as if somebody else must have written it."

"Your rich people," I went on to say, "seem less real than the others; it must be hard to know what the motives of rich people are." I said I had written of some who were long dead, but did not know this new breed at Nassau and Palm Beach. Then I made the error of mentioning that Scott Fitzgerald had written stories of the wealthy, as in *Rich Boy*, which reflected a fine understanding of the particular values they lived by.

Hemingway snorted in anger at the mention of Fitzgerald. They had been having some rows of late in correspondence. In the early days Fitzgerald had given generous help to the fledgling writer Hemingway. Now the positions were reversed: the highly successful Ernest pressed his advice upon the unhappy Fitzgerald, who was in deep trouble, and severely criticized his behavior. In the original version of Hemingway's story "The Snows of Kilimanjaro," Hemingway had made a wounding reference to "poor old Scott Fitzgerald and his romantic awe of 'the rich.'" Fitzgerald then had written asking Ernest not to use his name in future pieces of fiction, and the sentence was changed when reprinted in book form.

According to Hemingway, Fitzgerald had "run after rich people" all his life; he had tried to ape them, and then discovered they weren't as fine as he had believed. Scott had also done too much "money-writing" for *The Saturday Evening Post*, whereas Ernest wrote as he pleased. In *Tender Is the Night* Fitzgerald had written, in Hemingway's opinion, a bad autobiographical novel, in which he whined too much about the insanity of his wife, his own decline, and his generally unhappy lot. Even worse was his confession, published recently in *Esquire*, of his alcoholism and mental breakdown, the essay entitled *The Crack-Up*, which to Hemingway exposed a pitiable Fitzgerald without courage for life. (I thought *The Crack-Up* was literature anyway.) Ernest had his own moods of anxiety about his writing power, or his sexual potency, or, as I thought, simply about *not being twenty-five years old* any longer— yet he managed. Fitzgerald, Hemingway said, so charming on the surface, could be "the meanest drunk in the world." *Tender Is the*

Night also revealed, as Hemingway knew, Fitzgerald's own dilemma: his love for a psychotic woman, his wife, who was insanely jealous of his work, tried to ruin him, and took another man for her lover. Hemingway despised Fitzgerald for having accepted the role of cuckold.

On a later occasion we happened to touch again on the subject of the very rich, and also on the character of the woman in *To Have and To Have Not* who so brazenly seduced her employee, Harry Morgan, and I remarked that to me she seemed "unreal."

"Oh, hell,—*that* woman!" he blurted. "I tell you I knew her *very well*. We went fishing in her yacht off Bimini. Why, the bitch!—she gave me a dose of the syph—"

I began to commiserate with him, but he quickly waved aside my condolences, and expatiated on a curious theory he held of the possible creative value of venereal disease. "A man can't really be a good writer unless he has had syphilis," he asserted; just as one could not be a good soldier without having undergone the baptism of fire. I said that if this were true than I was "sunk," because I had never contracted v.d. and lived in the simple faith that one might enjoy women and sex without such contretemps. But he would listen to nothing I said. Was it that guilt and suffering loomed large in his intuitive ethical system? Or simply that when he tried to reason or generalize about things Hemingway "talked like a child"—as old Goethe had once said of Byron. (This point was originally made in a review of *The Green Hills of Africa* by C. P. Fadiman.)

Violence and pain and death were the major themes of his writing; he held also that to write of such things one must be schooled to face danger with sangfroid. In this quality he found many writers wanting—as for instance his friend Archibald MacLeish. The winter before he had taken MacLeish and Dos Passos on a trip to one of the tiny islands of the Bahamas chain. They had anchored the boat, walked into the jungle, and soon lost their way. MacLeish, according to Hemingway, became excited as they blundered about in the thickets of oleanders, crying out repeatedly: "My God—we're lost!" The near-sighted Dos Passos merely seemed distrait; and Hemingway, one supposes, was enjoying himself mali ciously. At length he climbed a tree and found the shortest route to the shore. "It was only a tiny island," he related, "and once at the shore we only had to circle it a little while to reach the boat. But, my God, how could Archie, though he had got the Pulitzer Prize for *The Conquistadores*, pretend to write with any understanding about men like Cortéz and his troops?"

I found this again one of Ernest's more absurd fulminations, and protested that neither MacLeish nor any other poet was required to kill a lot of Indians with his own hands in order to write of Cortéz. But Hemingway would not yield on this point.

Fame, and the whole Byronic legend that grew up about him, had its inconveniences. Young boys just out of prep school or college hitchhiked to Key West to call on Hemingway. One day I found a pallid young English lord, who waited for three days at Sloppy Joe's for a glimpse of the great man. There were also the idle rich and lady snobs who pursued him; he laughed about the glory of the "well-known Ernie Hemingstein," but really saw no harm in it.

The year before, the poet Wallace Stevens had turned up at Key West for his winter vacation, staying at the Casa Marina, the island's only luxury hotel. This subtle and rather précieux poet was, in private life, the corporation counsel and vice-president of an insurance company in Hartford, Connecticut, working soberly at his business in the daytime and writing poetry at night or on Sundays. It was Stevens's habit then to go off on winter vacations alone, frequently at Havana, and relax by sipping whisky for days on end—which was his condition at that time.

One morning he came over to Thompson's Dock, saw Ernest working over his boat, and mumbled something that sounded like: "You think you're Ernest Hemingway?" then challenged him to put up his hands. Stevens was of good height and had been an amateur boxer, but he was nearly sixty and very tight. Ernest, usually pugnacious, this time urged the older man to go away and sober up. But Stevens threw a punch at him; and there followed a bare-knuckled fight on the dock in which Stevens put up a good show of resistance, but was badly battered. The next day he left for Miami to have the cuts about his head dressed. I should never have believed that the shy and sedate Stevens would have acted as he did if several eyewitnesses had not told me of the affair, in which they testified that he alone was at fault. Under his mask of reserve, there must have been great emotional tensions building up periodically in Wallace Stevens, respectable lawyer and devoted paterfamilias.

III.

One night at the café Hemingway took me aside and began to talk to me earnestly about Spain, saying he had about made up his mind to go there. He had been negotiating with the North American Newspaper Syndicate (affiliated with *The New York Times*) to write special articles from the war front and, of course, from the Republican side.

"Have you any idea of what is going on? Do you really believe in the loyalists? Are they on the level?" Such were the questions he put, while his brown eyes bored into me. At the time there were many reports of atrocities committed by Republican mobs as well as by the fascists, also of alleged communist plots to seize power in the Republic. I replied that there was no question in my mind as to who had precipitated the Civil War: it was the generals, the fascists, and the ultraconservatives of the Church. The people had had their fill of dictatorship for long years prior to 1931; in the last elections under the Republic they had won a decisive victory over the right bloc, and it was just when they were to institute long-delayed agrarian reforms, by which land was to be distributed among poor peasants, that the generals and the Falangists rose in counterrevolution.

That winter of 1937 the loyalists had rallied strongly in the region of Madrid, despite the new and horrible experiments in terror-bombing of civilian populations. I held that given sufficient arms the more populous half of Spain, containing its big industrial cities, would in all likelihood prevail over the enemy. If Hemingway and others like him spoke in support of loyalist Spain, public opinion would be aroused, and the farce of nonintervention might be brought to an end. Hemingway indicated emphatic agreement.

(425)

"It's the prelude to world war," he said. But perhaps there was still time and ground for hope.

Pauline Hemingway came to join us during the latter part of our talk and said: "If Ernest goes to Spain it will not be to take one side or the other, the socialists' or the Catholics', but to show what war is. We are just antiwar, war of any kind. Maybe he can be of help in this way." Pauline was liberal by disposition but she was also a practicing Catholic; I had the feeling she had no enthusiasm for this adventure of Ernest's, and for this reason and others she felt rather blue. Hemingway had his own ideas, though he did not dispute with his wife.

It was by now visible to most of us in the Key West circle that the marriage of Ernest and Pauline had reached a delicate stage. She was trying to be patient and also fighting to hold him. But for Hemingway the journey to the Spanish war front would be a departure in more ways than one. He felt he must renew his powers as a writer and needed, as he put it, "to be where things are happening, for a man had to live his books." Spain was the central crisis of our time and would provide a big enough subject. He was now resolved to put himself at the front of the antifascist movement.

The possibility of renewal in a more personal or earthy sense also arose for him just then. Another woman, younger than his second wife, had come into the picture. Martha Gellhorn was then one of those novice writers for whom only the counsels of Ernest Hemingway would suffice. And so she had come to seek him out. After a while her mother and brother left and she stayed on. Hemingway frequently came to see her and read her early writings, which were not without promise; besides she was uncommonly pretty and dressed in winter resort clothes of Riviera chic.

My wife and I became acquainted with Miss Gellhorn and found she had more serious interests in life than most handsome young women. In 1930, after graduating from college, she had worked on the staff of *The New Republic* for several months as an editorial assistant. After that, she said, she had gone to France and there married a French intellectual, Robert de Jouvenel, of a noble family prominent in public life. For a while Martha was *la marquise*. Her husband wrote on political economy—he became quite well known later on—but they were poor and lived in the country near St. Tropez. Soon they were divorced and Martha was back in the United States (in 1934), working as a field investigator for federal relief. Her reports on reliefers and poor farmers all around the country earned her the commendation not only of Hopkins but of Mrs. Eleanor Roosevelt. Out of her notes on inspection tours she had contrived a first book of stories, *The Trouble I've Seen*, published in 1936 and well received by the press. A copy of this she presented to us. We found her charming—with a touch of the bluestocking—also capable and ambitious.

§ § §

A few days after our talk about Spain Hemingway invited my wife and me and a half dozen other winter residents to go sailing with him on his boat. On this trip Miss Gellhorn was not among the guests, but Pauline was with us. It was to be a farewell cruise as the *Pilar* was soon to be dry-docked, and Ernest was to leave for New York, en route to Madrid, two days later.

The day was dazzling out in the Gulf Stream; the blazing light and the deep greens and blues made that tropical sea one of the most beautiful regions on earth. On the little bridge deck above the cabin Ernest, clad in ragged shorts and torn cap, pointed the diesel-engined boat westward along the edge of the great deep between the Florida Keys and Cuba, where the game fish came up to feed at the reefs. We guests took turns at trolling a line from the fishing chairs in the stern; or sat about eating and drinking in a state of joyful stupefaction.

From his perch on the little bridge Ernest with binoculars watched out for signs of the beasts of the sea, sometimes shouting instructions to us. After a turn in the fishing chair—during which I managed, though almost exhausted by the struggle, to reel in a four-foot barracuda—I went up the gangway to talk with Ernest on the bridge. "Game fishing isn't the lazy life I thought it was," I panted. He grinned. "You had a real man-killer there."

He trolled the boat slowly and managed a rambling monologue above the diesel motors, interrupted from time to time by the excitement of fish striking our lines. Ernest knew this sea lane well, every mile of it, and loved his boat. I allowed that the *Pilar* and the Gulf of Mexico were well worth the expenditure of time and money required.

He said: "I've got this nice boat and the house in Key West— but they're both really Pauline's. I could stay on here forever, but it's a soft life. Nothing's really happening to me here and I've got to get out. . . . In Spain maybe it's the big parade starting again." His talk went on as a soliloquy, as if he were ruminating over his plans for the future: "The children are provided for. . . . If anything happens to me, Pauline has enough for the two boys; I've supported myself, at any rate, and taken care of my older son, John."

These half-confidences suggested that his approaching journey might be more than a temporary change of climate, such as he often indulged in. (I remembered on one or two occasions, when Ernest was absent, hearing Pauline say in a tone at once ironical and world weary: "I suppose Ernest is busy again helping Miss Gellhorn with her writing.") He himself spoke with evident awareness that his friendship for Miss Gellhorn had caused talk, for he remarked with a laugh: "Oh, I'm a fool with women—I always feel I have to marry 'em." He had left his first wife, Hadley, whom he said later he loved more than anyone else, because the other woman Pauline had been determined in her pursuit of him. Now there was the encounter with the tall, handsome Martha, and he was not yet clear what would come of it. (He was to marry her too several years later, and he would also divorce her in turn to marry again.)

I had the feeling that Hemingway was not by disposition a great womanizer. Certainly women, especially lion-hunting women, found him attractive and entertaining. At times he talked of womanflesh in an offhand, overtly masculine way, and in his prose he celebrated the physiology of love with an explicitness then almost novel. And yet those passages are not convincing; the favored women in his books are maternal, submissive, and sometimes almost blank. In reality Hemingway was no Don Juan, but a man ridden by the anxieties of the writer or artist, which periodically disturbed his sex life.

In his play *The Fifth Column*, set in Madrid under siege, the hero Philip Rawlings has as his mistress a tall blonde young American who has lately given up the comforts of St. Tropez in order to join him. Is she "only a very handsome commodity?" he asks himself in her absence; and he goes on debating with himself: "Granted she's lazy and spoiled and rather stupid and enormously on the make. Still she's very beautiful . . . charming and rather innocent—and quite brave." But Rawlings has other important commitments and cannot give himself unreservedly to her because: "We're in for fifty years of war, and I've signed up for the duration."

We held a farewell party for Ernest in the backroom at Joe's on the Saturday night before his departure. His Key West cronies were there, as were Pauline and Martha Gellhorn. The small band played its bravest rhumbas and the crowd kept dancing, except that Pauline was sad and Ernest was morose. He said his knee bothered him and suggested to me: "Why don't you dance with Martha?" As we danced and conversed in a confidential shout Miss Gellhorn confided that she too was leaving either by the bus that night or by airplane the next day.

The next morning—it was late February—several of us were playing tennis at the old Navy Yard when the Pan-American flying boat carrying Hemingway took off for Miami and New York. Miss Gellhorn had finally decided to make her departure by the same conveyance. From the edge of the dock we waved good-bye toward the cumbersome hydroplane that splashed furiously around the little harbor, then rose majestically in air.

I V .

By the time he arrived in Madrid a fortnight later Hemingway had gathered quite a train of helpmates. At New York he had agreed to be chairman of a committee furnishing hospital supplies and ambulance units for the loyalists, and by his own efforts he raised large funds for it. Stopping in Paris, he also arranged to write the script for a proposed film of Republican Spain at war; the cameraman was to be Joris Ivens, a young Dutchman. Originally John Dos Passos, who followed Hemingway to Spain a little later, was to have shared in the writing of the film script, but he soon changed his mind about that. In Paris too Hemingway had meetings with the Spanish underground. He also found our mutual friend Evan Shipman, whom he persuaded to drive groups of volunteers for the International Brigade across the border into Spain. Finally Martha Gellhorn also turned up in Paris around the same time, and though warned that Madrid was under heavy bombardment she went there and stayed a while as a correspondent for *Collier's Weekly*.

The case of Evan Shipman illustrates how enthusiasm for the Republican cause gripped many young Americans who formerly had shown no interest whatsoever in political questions. The skinny, long-legged Shipman, descendant on his mother's side of a distinguished American family (the Biddles) and son of the once popular playwright whose name he bore, had two ruling passions: these were horse racing and poetry, leaving aside wine and women—with whom he had poorer luck than with the horses. In his posthumous memoir *A Moveable Feast*, Hemingway testifies to Shipman's charm as a friend and drinking companion; he describes him as probably the only poet who did not seem to care whether his poems were printed or lost. (Evan used to mail them to his friends in lieu of letters, and they were often quite good.) So amiable and disarming was Evan about his little vices that when he lost at the races his friends really enjoyed pulling him out of scrapes; I would occasionally drive to fetch him from wherever he was stranded, and Hemingway more than once sent him the railroad fare to bring him to Key West. He looked somewhat motheaten at times because of his drinking habits, but even in worn clothes he had the casual elegance of an inveterate racetrack follower. It seemed incredible that Shipman could be driving a truck full of volunteers down from Perpignan and over the Pyrenees to Spain. Such activity was intermittently forbidden (whenever nonintervention was being observed), and by mischance Evan and his passengers were arrested by the French authorities and thrown into jail at Perpignan.

For several weeks, as he related afterward, he lived in a common prison cell with a band of ragged young men who had come from all parts of Europe—France, Germany, Yugoslavia—and were ready to lay down their lives in the war against the fascists. "I had known nothing about either communism or fascism," he said, "but those people really got through to me. I thought them the finest men I had ever met in all my life; they had the most magnificent spirit about what they were doing. Half of them died in action later. When we were all suddenly released from prison, as happened under the crazy French control, and allowed to go on our way, the customs guards just shutting their eyes, I decided on the impulse of the moment to join them." He was wounded in action, flown to France to recover, and early in 1938 returned to Spain where he served on the headquarters staff of the International Brigade under their political commissar André Marty.[1]

The spring of 1937 was a time of hope in Republican Spain: near Guadalajara an army of thirty thousand Italians had been routed just before Hemingway arrived. The antifascists had shown they could beat the enemy whenever they accumulated some armor and aircraft. Hemingway reported that the Republic could now be expected to win out "in a year."

Whatever he may have promised Pauline about staying neutral, he soon showed himself a convinced partisan of the loyalists. Like the hero of his novel *For Whom the Bell Tolls*, Hemingway found that the Civil War was "quite an education" for him. The communists in the loyalist army were harsh disciplinarians trying to make good soldiers out of the untrained militia; there was also a lot of "bureaucracy and inefficiency and party strife," he wrote. But still "you felt that you were taking part in a crusade. . . . You have to put many things in abeyance to win a war. If this war is lost all of those things are lost."

Everyone thought Hemingway behaved very well in Spain. He frequently toured the front lines during periods of action, writing excellent background sketches for the press. On one occasion, driving in a night time convoy, the truck ahead of him overturned; several soldiers were killed or wounded, and Hemingway jumped in to administer first aid while the other newspaper correspondents simply looked on in horror. In Madrid he chose as his living quar-

[1] It was Evan Shipman who told Hemingway about operations at the International Brigade's headquarters and described the character of the fanatical Marty, of whom a striking portrait is given in *For Whom the Bell Tolls*. Hemingway himself did not know Marty.

ters the Hotel Florida, though it was under direct bombardment
(or because of that fact). In his battered room he held open
house and shared scarce food packages and drink with all who
came, especially American combat soldiers. It was an arduous life;
visitors found him greatly changed, no longer the young writer who
lived only to cultivate his sacred ego, but a serious, compassionate
Hemingway. The Spanish Republicans idolized him.

Very different was the attitude of his friend Dos Passos. On an
earlier visit to Spain in 1931 he had judged "the Republic of Honest
Men," as he called it, too weak to deal with the realities of the social
revolution in progress. Now he found the same Republic, in time
of Civil War, imposing an iron discipline which he disliked. Political opposition, anarchist or Trotskyite, was sternly suppressed.
Fear of the "fifth column" (of which Franco openly boasted) was
everywhere. The rising communist faction seemed to be policing
people behind the lines, under the guidance of Russian agents. Dos
Passos, who had sometimes fancied himself a revolutionary, found
he did not like the real thing when he encountered it in Spain.

He had been turning against communism even before he came
to Spain. A year earlier, in January 1936, in response to a letter of
mine appealing for harmony among the people associated with the
Popular Front movement, he had written me that he was completely fed up with the "narrow sectarians" of the Communist
Party. He had taken his stand with them when they were small and
weak, but now they seemed to him to have grown arrogant and
bureaucratic.

Hemingway had made some rather acid comments to me about
Dos Passos having "a bleeding heart for the proletarians" but usually preferring to keep them at a distance. Dos Passos himself has
related that his real sympathies lay with the anarchists and the
P.O.U.M. faction just then being suppressed in Spain. Before leaving New York in March he consulted Carlo Tresca, romantic
leader of the Italian anarchists, and was warned that the small
Communist Party of Spain, thanks to the favor of the Russians,
was seizing control of the Republic and would "make a monkey"
out of Dos Passos if he did not go along with them.

During 1937 he wrote some travel sketches of Spain in wartime which were included with other essays published in book form in 1938 as *Journeys Between Wars*. In this first edition he did not reveal anything about the troubles he encountered in Spain (which his friends knew about). Perhaps, though privately disillusioned, he was still on the fence politically. Later, in 1952, he retouched those sketches and interlarded some bitter reflections on his own attitude of that time as "typical of the blundering of well-intentioned American liberals trying to make themselves useful."

In truth he had come to Spain as one already disenchanted. Then there was the unhappy affair of his friend José Robles, who used to teach Spanish in American colleges and had translated Dos Passos's novels: Robles was reported to have been imprisoned on charges of "treason." At Valencia, the loyalist capital, Dos Passos searched for Robles and asked for him persistently but was given no answer. Josephine Herbst, who was in Spain as a correspondent, happened to learn—through some official's confidence—that Robles had already been shot by the security police. She gave this still secret information to Hemingway, who sadly conveyed it to Dos Passos. Some of my loyalist friends told me afterward that they thought the execution of Robles was a mistake—the communist-dominated secret service was often trigger happy—and that Robles had probably been guilty only of some indiscretions.

Evan Shipman remembered meeting Dos Passos while on leave in Madrid and talking with him of the Robles case. Warning him that he was courting danger for himself, Evan told Dos he would do well to leave Spain. As Shipman related the incident to me: "Dos Passos seemed greatly shocked at what I had said. He went right out of that restaurant, took the first conveyance he could get, and went back to Paris." Dos Passos also had some differences with Hemingway about the script of the film *Spanish Earth*, and he judged later that Hemingway had come under the sway of the communists and swallowed their propaganda. But Hemingway thought only of "getting on with the war."

Dos Passos's change of heart was honest enough, but like that of George Orwell it derived from his concern for maintaining his and others' individual liberty even in wartime. The libertarian Orwell, also drawn to the anarchist and P.O.U.M. faction, joined

(433)

them in street fighting in Barcelona in May 1937 against government troops who eventually suppressed the dissidents. But Orwell admits apologetically, in *Homage to Catalonia*, that he actually "knew nothing about the internal politics of the Spanish."

The Spanish anarchists were charming fellows, sometimes showing a mad courage in battle, at others refusing to obey military orders. Amid the confusion of war they attempted to set up cooperative villages and shops. The P.O.U.M., a small heretical Marxist faction under Andrés Nin, also agitated for social revolution in wartime rather than later and was crushed at the order of the coalition government.

Dr. Juan Negrin, the moderate socialist who had succeeded Caballero as Premier, maintained a close working alliance with the Russians whether he liked it or not, because they supplied the bulk of military aid coming from outside. Negrin labored at the same time to create a moderate type of ministry that would dispel native radical or separatist dissension and gain the confidence of the British and French governments. The Cabinet was made up mainly of socialists but included two communists and some liberals. Stalin, after much vacillation, had come to favor such a moderate coalition on diplomatic grounds, for he and Litvinov still hoped to complete a defensive military alliance against Hitler with the French and British.

In strong contrast stood the repressive domestic policy of Stalin in Russia, then in the time of the great purges, during which not only his old Bolshevik opponents but also many Red Army officers were executed. The spirit of fanatical repression evidently carried over from the N.K.V.D. in Russia to the Soviet agents in Spain. Even so, the brilliant Negrin worked effectively to build up the Republic's native army until it needed only to overcome its shortage of munitions in order to defeat the fascists.

§ § §

Enthusiasm for loyalist Spain reached its crest in the years 1937 and 1938. The Second American Writers' Congress, convened at New York in June 1937, made its opening night a festival in honor of the defenders of the Republic. Hemingway, back from Spain, for the first time in his life gave a public address to an audience of 3,500 at Carnegie Hall. At the same time he presented the documentary film *Spanish Earth*, with its scenes of cities under siege and peasants raising crops at the edge of battlefields. In this film Hemingway's is the voice of the narrator, and he performed very simply and well.

By 1938 many Americans were busily engaged in raising funds amounting to several million dollars a year for shipments of medicines and food to Republican Spain; people who were predominantly liberal and charitable, including many Protestant ministers, then worked in close concert with those on the left. We heard much of young men going off by the "underground railway" to join the Abraham Lincoln Brigade (such foreign military service was forbidden American citizens). There would be a CIO organizer leaving his union local to fight the fascists in Spain; or a young schoolteacher in my neighborhood of Connecticut would quit his classroom to serve and die in Spain; or there were young men just out of college, like James Lardner, son of Ring Lardner, who joined the Lincoln Brigade and was killed in a night patrol.

John Maynard Keynes said then of the "intellectual communists under thirty-five" who made up most of the British volunteers in Spain that "they were the nearest thing we now have to the typical . . . English gentleman who went to the Crusades, made the Reformation, fought the Great Rebellion, and won us our civil and religious liberties." The same could surely be said of the Americans who served among the International Brigade volunteers.

By the late summer of 1938 a popular poll in America showed 44 per cent favoring repeal of the embargo on arms shipments; only 28 per cent were opposed, with the rest undecided. Even Senator Nye had come to realize that the embargo he had espoused worked to the advantage of the Franco movement, since it benefited from the uninterrupted flow of arms from Italy and Germany. In the autumn of that year the Spanish aid groups, with Mrs. Roosevelt at their head, made a determined lobbying effort to win key Congressmen for repeal of the embargo. I was in Washington and tried to help in this action, but it was too late.

It was generally anticipated that the dictator states, through their mounting aggressions, would at last force the western democracies and Soviet Russia to confront them with ultimatums of peace or war, and that the forthcoming showdown would bring some viable solution for Spain—if only the Republic could endure for another year or two.

Hitler's occupation of Austria in March 1938 was, however, swallowed without challenge. Despite the outcries of Winston Churchill in Parliament, Neville Chamberlain clung to the policy of conciliating Hitler and Mussolini under the formula of non-intervention.

After Austria, Hitler set up a cry for Germany's irredentist territories in Czechoslovakia and for the Polish Corridor. In July the Spanish Republican forces, after having been split by the rebels' drive to the east coast, rallied strongly and with a massive counter-movement drove Franco's armies back from the Ebro River. But in September Chamberlain and Daladier went to Munich to confer with Hitler on the "solution" of the Czechoslovak question. It seemed that the final confrontation had come. While the French Army mobilized at the Maginot Line, the most contradictory reports reached us, even one suggesting a possible mediation of the Spanish conflict. Then on September 22 came news of the pact of Munich and of the British and French surrender to Hitler's demands. Now we knew that the Spanish Republicans were doomed.

Chapter Twenty-one

❧

Going West: The Lost Ones of Hollywood

DURING THE WINTER that followed our stay in Key West I went south again, for I was still fighting my way back to full health. This time, accompanied by my wife and two boys, I journeyed in the family sedan as far as Tucson, Arizona, where we remained for three months. On our way out we skidded through snowstorms and returning crept through dust storms that were still blowing in 1938. Depression afflicted the country once more; the grimy mill towns of Virginia and Kentucky seemed stagnant, and one sensed a mood of disappointment in people we talked with along our route.

Depression again? But the New Deal had exerted itself to plan and spend for recovery. There had been a couple of years of the "Roosevelt prosperity cycle" up to the summer of 1937, during which the volume of business activity surpassed that of 1929; unemployment had declined noticeably. In self-confident mood President Roosevelt declared early in 1937 that the government's pump-priming had worked well, remarking: "We planned it that way." But the old-fashioned speculative boom that flared up soon ended in one of the sharpest slumps in our history. At the same time, unfortunately, the government reduced its spending for relief.

On my journey south I had stopped in Washington for a few days and found my New Deal acquaintances drawing long faces. Benjamin Cohen said—and his words seemed very perceptive then—

"The government really spent too little to ensure full recovery and then reduced its spending too soon." Now it would have to try the same restoratives used before. A congressional election loomed ahead and the New Deal was fully determined to woo the restive voters—with relief payments and public works if need be.

From the beginning of his second term the President had met with severe rebuffs at the hands of Congress, though he had been given an overwhelming popular mandate in the last election. His sudden decision in early 1937 to introduce a bill to change the composition of the Supreme Court had inspired fierce resistance in the Senate. Leading figures in his own Party joined with Republicans in attacking the bill because of the dubious grounds on which its proposed reforms were based: old age and the alleged inefficiency of the Court. Frankfurter, who had not been consulted, was deeply shocked at the terms of this bill. But Tommy Corcoran, who lobbied for its passage by the Senate, told me afterward that he had never seen the President so implacable in mood. The "nine old men," to his mind, barred his advance and simply had to be subdued. "Roosevelt was then at the very height of his power," Corcoran added. "He could not stop—he had to go on and on." In any case the bill was lost in the Senate. To be sure one of the conservative justices resigned, while two others shifted ground, and so Roosevelt at last was able to reverse the Court's five to four opposition. But the long-drawn-out struggle bred serious discord among the Democrats. Regional leaders within his own Party, such as Senator Wheeler, provided the strongest opposition the President had faced throughout his rule.

Roosevelt now determined to purge the Democratic Party of its anti-New Dealers in Congress. His loyal lieutenants, especially Harry Hopkins, went to work with great zeal to get out the vote for the pro-Roosevelt candidates—perhaps they used too much zeal.

I believed at the time that Roosevelt's attempted purge of his Party was one of the most courageous actions of his entire career. What he tried to do was to transform a highly professional bipartisan Party system, made up of office-seekers without an ideology, into an alignment of two "belief parties," the one progressive, the other conservative. For several years I had been engaged in writing a book entitled *The Politicos*, an analytical history of our century-old Party apparatus regarded as an institution. Governors, senators, and presidents came and went; but the Party organization lived on long after them. Our parties, except at intervals of crisis, embodied no consistent political ideas, but only the functioning of an army of opportunists in the local ward as on the national level. At long last Roosevelt was making a Promethean effort to change our professional Party institution from that of rival congeries of office-seekers into something resembling the European political system with clearly defined social goals and ideology.

The New Deal, for example, had made the old Democratic Party in part a movement of farmers and workers linked with the liberal middle class. It had introduced certain radical welfare measures. But these public enterprises had always to be presented, by various subterfuges or disguises, as being without long-range social purpose, in essence only temporary experiments or "yardsticks" used for an emergency period. The New Deal thus had the fatal flaw of always abjuring belief in any distinct body of social doctrines and of improvising curative measures without an over-all plan. In part this condition derived from the rigidity of the old Party bureaucracy, which permitted senior members of the majority Party to remain in standing committees of Congress where they opposed their own Party and its leader. In no other country was a political organization run in such a paradoxical manner. In trying to purge the Democratic Party of its conservative opposition, Roosevelt worked to clear the air and make way for open dialogue in our public life between liberal progressive and conservative classes.

The purge campaign enlisted my deepest sympathies. To my dismay however this salutary action was frustrated both by the great hue and cry against the "dictator" in the White House that was raised in the mainly anti-New Deal press and by the rebellious action of many local bosses. One of my good friends in Washington, Thomas G. Stokes, a columnist for the Scripps-Howard chain of newspapers, though himself a staunch ally of the New Deal, happened to come upon scandalous reports of WPA officials lining up relief roll voters in Kentucky. To his own regret, as Stokes related to me afterward, he felt obliged to publish these reports in syndi-

cated articles which produced a nationwide scandal and gave fuel
to the conservatives in the 1938 elections. Thus many fewer New
Deal adherents were elected than previously, while the President's
most powerful enemies within his Party—Tydings of Maryland and
George of Georgia—were easily reelected. The coalition of Southern Democrats and Republicans was more firmly cemented than
ever; and though he had a technical majority in Congress, Roosevelt faced complete stalemate after November 1938.

§   §   §

It was much earlier in that year, around January I believe, that I
had moved on from Washington, en route to Tucson. We drove all
day over the Appalachians, through the rural slums of eastern
Kentucky and Tennessee. Here were poor, tiny, unpainted villages
below the Cumberland ridges; clinging to the slopes were small
slattern tobacco farms with rickety cottages and tumble-down sheds.
Nowhere in the world did rural poverty appear more painful to the
sight than in our land of abundance.

Suddenly at dusk we came down over the hills into Norris to see
the TVA, and it was as if we had arrived in a new world, a new age
placed fifty years in the future. The towering Norris Dam loomed
before us as one of the most beautiful structures in the world, at
once light-giving and life-giving. Placed in this region of eroded soil,
it owned the largest source of cheap hydroelectric power and of
cheap agricultural chemicals as well, which it distributed to farmers
in seven states. This huge complex of dams, reservoirs, and generating and flood-control stations had been built up with great dispatch
during only a few years by thousands of workers who had formerly
been idle. The sight of this biggest of all engineering tasks gave, as
it seemed to me, a wonderful foretaste of what Americans could
achieve in the way of large public enterprises.

We stopped at the National Park Service hostel in Norris, the
model town that was built for the employees of the TVA. Walking
about the little planned community that gave on the broad lake
made out of the Tennessee River, coming on its flower gardens set
out among the shops and business buildings, we thought it the
prettiest town we had seen in all America. In my enthusiasm I ex-

claimed to my wife and sons: "Look, we have seen the future here! We in the United States could easily, if we wished, have *the most successful form of socialism in the world.*" The TVA, Senator Norris's dream of long ago, became for me the perfect symbol of New Deal accomplishment in its most constructive phase. Economic depression had come to afflict us again. Why then should we not launch fifty or a hundred such big regional development projects and make a thousand planned communities like Norris?

The restorative effect of the TVA upon its desolate environment was to be such that in later years one could no longer see such wretched and eroded farms as were there in 1937. Yet in the 1950's when there was talk of suppressing or even burning books, I heard that a high school text containing passages approving the work of the TVA was actually removed from the use of students in certain states, as if the whole subject were something shameful or wicked! It seemed then that what our benighted mentors desired was that our youth might grow up in ignorance of the great projects for human welfare their elders had undertaken in the generation before theirs.

II.

How spacious and also how incredibly arid was our great West, its lovely tumbled land so often scarred by ugly wounds left by mining and improvident agriculture. Where but in Texas could one ride under a low cloud of burning oil that extended, I would have said, for sixty miles out of Houston along the road to Austin? And in New Mexico a coal mine reared its dreary bunkers beside a beautiful old Pueblo raised by Indian architects.

That year the wide desert of the Rockies marched eastward until it reached the uplands of western Kansas. Dust storms darkened the sky; in the little square of Taos our car was stranded for three days while sand mounted to the level of its hub caps. We saw many families of "Okies" riding westward, out of the Dust Bowl, in jalopies or worn trucks loaded with all their poor household goods.

In Tucson where we stayed at the edge of town in a house that not long before had been the home of a rancher, surrounded by open cattle range, we found ourselves in an enclave of the proud Western middle class that would have none of the New Deal. Through the good offices of Mrs. Ada McCormick, sister of the painter Waldo Peirce, we met many residents of the town, university people, invalid pensioners, ranchers, and men of business. As the luncheon guest of a ranchowner with three thousand head of cattle I sat and listened as patiently, as blandly as possible while my host ranted against the Roosevelt administration—although the government, in effect, had "socialized" the price of beef steer so that his ranch prospered. The publisher of the Arizona *Daily Star*, also present, applauded his words. Yet even in Tucson there were dissenters, like the cultivated Irishman who had fled here from the civil strife in his country in 1917 only to encounter the naked violence of labor conflict in the copper mines of Arizona. Another happy chance encounter was with Christine Weston, an Englishwoman from India, then residing with her American husband in Arizona; Mrs. Weston had not yet begun to write her extraordinary novels about her native India, such as *Indigo*, but her intelligence and wit gave clear promise of such things. With a few such "eccentrics" we made up a little circle that stood against the Hate-Roosevelt element of that region—though we found we were not entirely alone.

We hired saddle horses occasionally and rode in that sun-drenched desert, desolate and astonishingly handsome—its colors the despair of painters. The cowboy who groomed our horses told me that he worked for the tourist trade in the winter months and for the WPA the rest of the year. A WPA for cowboys? "Yes, we love the WPA," he said. "I don't know what we would have done without it, with the cattle trade in decline."

How much the Western cowboy—once the very model of rugged individualism—had changed! He no longer pursued adventure or gold wherever he pleased, but counted on the helping hand of government.

§   §   §

While in Arizona that winter I corresponded with Professor Thurman Arnold of the Yale Law School, author of the recently published *Folklore of Capitalism*, that highly original and amusing commentary on our business society. With the weapons of wit and epigram Arnold in his short book demolished a great many myths about the "American way of life," to the delight of the New Dealers.

What was my surprise, one day in March, to receive a letter from Arnold posted from Washington under the severe letterhead of the Department of Justice. In the course of it he remarked that he had lately been appointed by the President as Assistant Attorney General in charge of the Anti-Trust Division. This seemed as paradoxical as Arnold's own writings, for he had previously treated trust prosecution as one of this country's most farcical myths. Americans, he wrote, had regarded the industrial trust as something that should be kept in bounds by the police yet also tolerated—"as if it were a necessary social evil" like prostitution. He had also jested at politicians such as Senator Borah, who had made a career of attacking monopolies. Now Arnold himself was engaged in battle with the trusts and, as he wrote me, expected to have a good deal of fun.

The Roosevelt administration in 1938 had not only turned to increased deficit spending, but also to criminal prosecution of trusts under the Sherman Act of 1890. Such a change of policy meant a complete reversal of the first New Deal program, which had freely encouraged combinations in industry. The change of view stemmed from Roosevelt's strong conviction that big business was "on strike" and merited chastisement. Some of his advisers, such as Leon Henderson, had pointed to the excessive rise in prices that had taken place in 1936 and 1937 and seemed to have contributed to the severity of the renewed deflation. A new theory also fascinated the government economists, that of "monopolistic competition" advanced by Professor Edward H. Chamberlain of Harvard. He maintained (putting it simply) that administered prices in industries controlled by cartels fostered rigidity and malfunctioning of the free enterprise system, tended to create underconsumption, and thus prolonged the downward business cycles. The solution for the

men who had earlier conceived the trust-favoring NRA law was
now to undertake a grand onslaught upon the same trusts.

Later that year, after returning to the East, I went to call on the
new Assistant Attorney General. He was a ruddy-complexioned,
breezy, broad-framed Westerner from the mountains of Wyoming
who spoke with a pleasant drawl but was given to forthright and
pungent language. Yet he was no provincial, for he had been educated at Princeton and at Harvard Law School and had served as an
officer of the AEF in France. The practice of law in Wyoming, his
election to the state legislature, and a brief term as mayor of
the frontier town of Laramie had all helped round him out as a
humorous philosopher. His former colleague at Yale Law School,
William O. Douglas, and his friend Robert Jackson had been instrumental in bringing him back to Washington, where earlier he
had helped the legal staff of the AAA.

Arnold received me very kindly and invited me to a staff luncheon with his assistants at the Justice Department. I had written a
good deal about the operations of the old-time monopolists but
had never really believed in pure and simple trust-busting. I expressed some curiosity about what Arnold and his young men hoped
to accomplish by returning to the old-fashioned procedures of
Theodore Roosevelt.

In less than a year, Arnold said, he had begun the vigorous prosecution of more trusts than we had ever heard about in four decades.
Formerly his Anti-Trust Division had been a do-nothing affair with
a tiny personnel of four or five; he engaged eventually some two
hundred lawyers and a strong research team. One of his young fer-
rets was Joseph Borkin, who tracked down the international cartels;
another was my old acquaintance Robert Wohlforth. Thus Arnold
literally made the fur fly as he fell upon corporate giants one after
another, among them Alcoa, General Electric, General Motors, and
the like. Nor did he spare certain labor unions in the building trades
that were indicted for alleged conspiracy and featherbedding.

In a suit against General Motors the government exposed practices that were shocking enough by any ethical standard. In a sort
of reign of terror they had forced their installment-plan subsidiary
upon thousands of car dealers, who were made to charge 24 per cent

for loans to their customers. But Arnold looked beyond such current evils to the prosecution of cartels based on the international control of patents, as in electronics and the glass and chemical industries, where the progress of technology was long retarded with intent. Everywhere he found dominant corporations stifling new energy in order to protect their obsolete capital, worn-out machinery, or out-moded products. By indicting them he hoped to liberate the competitive energies of modern men. "We are faced with the old problems," he said, "which confronted the world after the industrial revolution of the eighteenth century. Nevertheless the new energy is going to break through." The American people could take their choice: full government control of business or antitrust enforcement that would restore competitive enterprise. Arnold crusaded for pure competition.

I ventured to object that antitrust action had been tried in the past; Thurman Arnold himself had made mock of such prosecution as folk myth. But restoring competition would not solve the problem of idle machines and idle men. True, monopoly without responsibility—like absolute power—corrupted everything and needed policing. But I saw no objection to big units like Ford's that produced useful articles at low cost nor to government-owned monopolies like the TVA working in the interests of human welfare. I was for bringing monopolists and competitive interests alike into an over-all economic plan rather than returning to the anarchy of the market.

Arnold's contention was that our awkward attempts at economic planning in the early stages of the New Deal "had created only confusion and bitterness and the constant backing and filling that went on during those years." The business groups waged long contests in all the legislatures and courts, and the country was filled with the resentments aroused by "extreme theoretical positions in conflict." Antitrust enforcement, he argued, was the proper way to salutary economic results.

In pursuing this course moreover he had now the ardent support of the President; for two years he was the pride and joy of the Second New Deal. Roosevelt relished the fierce assaults of his Justice Department on certain big business adversaries. I heard that one of these, A. P. Giannini (a former Roosevelt supporter), suffering a long-drawn-out government suit against his chain banking monopoly in California, tried to win immunity by making large donations to the Democratic Party chest. The court suit thereafter experienced some delay but was resumed with great severity after the election. After war began in Europe, however, Roosevelt suddenly reversed his course, and the harrying of business conspirators came to a halt. Thurman Arnold and his staff for a while were left with almost nothing to do.

II.

From Tucson it was but a day's ride to southern California, and I was keen to visit Hollywood before returning home. Since the talking pictures had arrived in 1929 it had become—in its way, alas!—a center for many writers working on play scripts. The film companies had lately bought rights to two of my books, using only a few dramatic scenes but providing me with windfalls that helped us survive. Could it be true, as old Tolstoy had predicted on first seeing the flickering Edison pictures of 1904, that this was to be the literary medium of the future? I was also curious to learn if I could ever adjust myself to life in that reputedly weird community. Finally, there were several writers there I wanted to see, including Scott Fitzgerald, with whom I had had some correspondence in recent years. In 1934 he had sent me a copy of his last novel, *Tender Is the Night*, with a long inscription on its flyleaf declaring that: "Save for the swell organization of your '*Zola*' and your reproduction of it, this would never have reached the stalls. . . ." What he referred to was actually the appendix of my biography in which I translated Zola's detailed notes on the working plan of the Rougon-Macquart cycle of novels; this may have inspired Fitzgerald, after a prolonged period of inactivity, to complete his own novel.

At the time I felt certain reservations about *Tender Is the Night* and thought its picture of idle rich expatriates on the Riviera out of key with the arduous times we were living through. (Later, with added perspective and in the light of the author's early death, I revised my opinion and came to see the novel as a work of sheer tragedy.) Many commentators in the thirties tended to reproach Fitzgerald as having remained an incorrigible playboy of the jazz age and wanting in social conscience. Such criticisms, as well as poor sales, had evidently contributed to Fitzgerald's depression at the time. He had made a public confession of all that two years earlier in his *Crack-up at Forty*. I refused however to believe that the author of *The Great Gatsby*, probably the most delicately contrived satire in American literature, was all washed up. Moreover many finely poetic passages in his last book had led me to reread his earlier works, which I deeply enjoyed. I wrote him to that effect, remarking that even his youthful literary pastiche, *This Side of Paradise*, had assumed historical and nostalgic qualities. Fitzgerald however seemed vexed by any reference to that first novel, which he now scorned.

On arriving in Hollywood at the end of February I telephoned Fitzgerald, and at his friendly invitation I went out to the Paramount lot to lunch with him at the commissary. After all I had heard through mutual friends about his alcoholism I was surprised to find him as handsome as he was said to have been in youth. With his delicate and regular features, very fair complexion, and fine mouth—almost like a woman's—he was quite what we used to call a "pretty boy" though there was nothing effeminate about him. At forty-two he looked at first glance much younger, but there were lines of strain in his face and its skin seemed drawn tight.

One of my friends had described for me how Scott had become completely alcoholized at the time when his wife was under treatment in an asylum as a psychotic. Mornings he would tie a towel around his jaw to keep his teeth from chattering. He used to tell people that he had earned "a million dollars" by his writing, but that it was all gone and he was in debt "a hundred thousand." Besides he no longer seemed able to turn out the "money" stories he used to do in the old *Saturday Evening Post* formula. Yet I thought his memoir *Crack-up at Forty* a true piece of literature. The young French writers I knew began writing of their breakdowns at eighteen or twenty, like Flaubert in *Septembre*, and sometimes continued to turn the same subject into literature for the rest of their lives. Despair before life was an old literary stage property. Its usage did not signify that Scott was done for.

He was, to my astonishment, drinking water while I had beer. I was in high spirits at the time, footloose and fancy free, having sent off the corrected proofs of my last book. Scott's mood was serious, though he was also thoughtful of me and charming. He talked with fine competence of his work in films, of the technique of the novel, of various books he had read recently. Many then thought him a man of light mind, but I was surprised at the keenness of his reflections on the work of the writer and the discriminating expression he gave to his ideas. His was the conversation of a brilliant craftsman, and I wish I could recapture some of it, though its particular flavor is also to be found in many of his letters. I was enjoying him and was also much impressed because near our table sat world-famous directors and some nice-looking stars—though I did not know who they were as I seldom if ever saw their pictures.

Scott kindly devoted the afternoon to giving me an escorted tour of the movie lot, pointing out groups at work in studio sets, or watching films that were being cut—"the most important part of the job," he remarked. Indeed he seemed then full of enthusiasm for his métier, holding forth at great length and very informatively I thought on the "potential" of the film. Nevertheless he pointed out that the original script of the writer amounted in the end to only about "10 per cent" of the finished product. Starting out with the story, it was all subjected to the will of the director then altered further according to the preferences or whims of the stars and the limitations of stage architecture. Finally the business regime, with eyes only on the box office, moved in and brought about a reduction that left the story only a tenuous shadow of the original script. The writer was no longer alone, as he explained it, but had to work with a large team so that in the end he might scarcely recognize the thing he had started with. To me it all sounded disenchanting.

We stopped to watch Director Frank Borzage shooting a scene from Erich Remarque's *Three Comrades*, in whose script Fitzgerald had had a hand. Over and over again, in most wearying fashion, the players went through the same brief play of entrance and departure. Nor did they work over scenes in the sequence of a drama, but rather in an order set by some rule of efficiency. And yet for several years Scott had clung to his dream of being a big shot in Hollywood. I gathered somewhat later that after a while he had been given unpleasing assignments, and that these were sometimes rewritten by others. He had struggled with the special problems here, become frustrated, drunk too much, perpetrated ugly scenes that outraged the movie community, and then started all over again. His salary was minimal for one of his standing, and his tenure was uncertain.

I felt the undertone of gloom in him as he talked, and I tried to jolly him. But he would only give me his sad little smile then turn solemn again. Well, I thought to myself, he surely had his troubles to think about, especially his poor beloved Zelda. By chance I had once met her in New York a few years earlier when she had given an exhibition of her quite amateurish paintings at a small gallery; I saw them definitely as the products of a schizophrenic. She was taller than Scott, had enormous eyes, and was beautiful in a strange way, like no other woman I had ever seen. When I said a few words to her she seemed inarticulate. My impressions were probably colored by what my friends, who took me to the place, told me in advance about her having just been released from a mental institution—to which she soon returned.

Scott seemed rather reserved toward people whom we met on our tour of the studio sets. Everybody in Hollywood knew about his troubles, and the knowledge that they felt sorry for him or were tired of him did not make the confirmed alcoholic the happier. From what he said I judged that he kept a good deal to himself these days.

I remember that when I mentioned having seen Hemingway the year before he froze up. I made some little speech to him as I left, about my hope that he would be giving us some great new books, and he said briefly that he was working at something of his own. (The fragments of his unfinished novel *The Last Tycoon*, and his posthumous notes on it, date from this period.)

In the course of our talk I asked him if it were true that many Hollywood writers had gone left. He nodded, looking thoughtful, then ventured: "I have been reading Marx too—very impressive." But he added that he was also in regular communication with a Jesuit priest who acted as his spiritual director. Certainly Fitzgerald did not seem like a man with a taste for abstract systems of thought; I wondered what he found in Marx. In the years of Depression, fascism, Spain—to which so many of his contemporaries in their way tried to respond—he may have searched at times for guidance, for authority.

The next evening I looked up Nathanael West, whom I had encountered several years earlier at Robert Coates's in Connecticut. I had read aloud to friends passages from his *Miss Lonelyhearts*, that masterpiece of literary irony, in 1933. His vein was a devastating sort of black humor, and I could not imagine what a fellow of his kidney would be doing in Hollywood.

"Pep" West was a tall, dark-haired young man, a little over thirty then, with large sad eyes, a wide mouth, and a mirthless smile. He had lived in Paris for a year or so, then returned to work as a night clerk in a small hotel in New York (owned by his family) while he wrote *Miss Lonelyhearts*.

We walked up and down Wiltshire and Hollywood Boulevards most of the night, sometimes stopping at cafés for beer, while he delivered himself of a rambling monologue that was generally saturnine in tone, sometimes quietly comical by its underemphasis and self-disparagement, but seldom cheerful. He had a dim view of human nature; he expected everything would turn out badly for him and all others, and yet he kept laughing in his bitter way.

His experience here, he said, might serve as a model for that of most others. *Miss Lonelyhearts* had won him a little fame in literary circles; at length the film people showed an interest in it, and so West had come out to Hollywood in 1935. The results of that first project were nothing famous. West was above all the man who made mock of the fake sentimentality and standardized emotions by which Hollywood lived, and yet he stayed on. His brother-in-law, S. J. Perelman, who had established himself successfully as the writer of the four Marx Brothers' comedies, was of help to him.

"I'm turning into a competent writer of Grade C scripts," West went on, "for that is all they regularly assign me. I do dog stories.

And more dog stories. (He hunted and kept hounds.) The directors seldom read anything I do, but if their wives find I have put enough *schmaltz* into the thing, and cry over it, they buy. And so I earn enough to last a few weeks or months; after that I wait again."

He grew vehement: "But if you think I'm in the soup, look at that big man with the cauliflower ears at the other end of the bar." That battered-looking individual had been a hero of the prize ring, or of some sensational adventures that had made him nationally famous for a weekend; and so they had brought him out here to do the story of his life in film. But after that one chance he had sunk out of sight. It was a parable of West's own case—and of Scott Fitzgerald's, for that matter. This bit of California desert was filled with such derelicts, West asserted. They had nothing to live on and were unable to leave; they waited and continued to hope that "something might turn up." West however managed to survive, while working during less than a third of his time at Grade B or C scripts; and he was to complete two more novels, one of them *The Day of the Locusts*.

The next day S. J. Perelman, that sophisticated man of letters turned humorist, lectured me with surprising severity: "You already own that white house with green shutters in Connecticut that most film writers dream of escaping to. You should never think of coming to work here. . . ." I heeded him. The gifted Mr. Perelman, who had aspirations to write stage plays and stories in the Dadaist or free-association form, eventually extricated himself from the high-salaried madhouse of Hollywood (as he defined it) to live and work in Bucks County, Pennsylvania. Several years later when a Hollywood agent telephoned me at my home in Connecticut to offer me a "Grade A" contract with Metro-Goldwyn-Mayer I refused it, remembering Perelman's warnings (though my friends, but not my wife, thought I was mad to do so).

The star system in the film industry had made for an extremely high ceiling in salaries for players and directors; as a consequence the writers, though receiving only a fraction of what the performing artists received, became the best-rewarded literary group in the country. Most of them however, like West, were occupied for half the year or less with low-grade scripts that earned them $150 to

$300 a week. To many who had starved in New York's Grub Street while trying to publish fiction or write plays, this was reason enough to migrate to the film capital in California.

For all its palm trees, gardens, blue skies, pretty car-hop girls at gas stations, and oranges at ten cents a dozen, Hollywood was for most of these people a Heartbreak House. The writers in particular believed themselves the most insulted and injured of any group in their field. The crassest of businessmen had fastened themselves long ago upon this mass entertainment industry; they aimed to standardize its product for the lowest common denominator of the public taste, and to this end they censored and reduced the quality of all films. It was impossible even to put through a little plug for the New Deal, let alone propaganda for communism (as the witch-hunters in Congress later pretended was being done). Meanwhile quite a group of writers, some six hundred, had gathered here, among them able and high-minded young fellows such as those formerly associated with the little theater movement in New York. They had their visions of what great things could be done, as shown by the modern German and Russian films, to which the vulgar Hollywood operation for which they were hired stood in painful contrast. It was not surprising that many of these writers during the turbulent 1930's turned left.

In 1938 and again during a visit several years later I encountered a number of the leftists, such as John Howard Lawson and Lester Cole, who were then working zealously to build up the Screen Writers' Guild as a politically advanced union. It was to save them from remaining lackeys of the entertainment industry, they hoped. They also carried on an agitation for the various Popular Front or peace committees and for Spanish aid. In effect they worked out in the movie lots in the morning as "prostitutes" and in the evening as social idealists. Their movement, essentially one of moral revulsion rather than of economic necessity, eventually attracted many high-salaried liberals who were subject to guilt feelings or were agonized by Spain, fascism, anti-Semitism. They dreamed of changing and redeeming the art of the film some day. Joseph Freeman told me later that he was able to raise as much as $10,000 a night for Spanish aid at meetings in the homes of Hollywood personages.

The happiest man I met in Hollywood proved to be G., who was one of the poorest. After starving in New York while publishing some highly praised literary works, he had come with his wife and children to the film capital. There he got only a few commissions for low-grade scripts and was forced to live in a sort of middle-class slum of Los Angeles. But still it was a life spent out of doors; they took their meals in a garden under an orange tree and food was cheap. G. said his part-time work was degrading, but nights he went to the docks of San Pedro to give lectures on Marxism and labor unions to sailors and stevedores; and he spoke of the pleasure he found in such activities, for he had his faith. He was working for the future. The films of the Russian directors Eisenstein and Pudovkin gave him a great hope—perhaps a grand illusion—of what true works of art might yet be achieved under some form of socialism, even the authoritarian regime of the Soviets. Such ideas about enhanced freedom for the arts under dictatorships have, of course, been proved simplistic.

For my last evening of the week in Hollywood I had a dinner appointment with the playwright Sidney Howard and his wife, the former Polly Damrosch, whom I had known for some years.

Howard was a character in his own way. A native of San Francisco and a newspaper reporter in his youth, he had served as an ambulance driver in France in 1917 and afterward as a bomber pilot in the American Air Force. With the coming of peace he had joined the staff of *The New Republic* and specialized in writing on the labor movement. Later in the twenties he had turned to writing plays that reflected his considerable talent for social comedy, such as *The Late Christopher Bean* and *They Knew What They Wanted*, which enjoyed a huge box-office success. With the advent of the sound movies he had naturally come into demand in Hollywood, where he worked not only on original scripts but also as an expert "doctor" or adapter of plays by other hands. He told me that he made it a habit to come to Hollywood only for the winter months, working at his own terms and then returning to his home in the East to occupy himself with his stage plays. It was as if he held the company executives here *in terrorem*, I suggested. And he quipped: "Yes, I'm quite ruthless with them." For all his riches

Howard had remained something of a political radical, though unaffiliated. In 1932 he had even signed the manifesto of the fifty-three writers in favor of the presidential candidacy of W. Z. Foster. He had also been an active head of the Screen Writers' Guild, though of late he had grown weary of the quarrels of the right and left and tended to avoid them.

I told him of having seen Scott Fitzgerald, also that he was staying sober and that I hoped to see him again before leaving. Thereupon Howard and his wife decided to ask him to join us for dinner, and it seemed that Scott was very pleased to come. He and his friend Sheila Graham appeared promptly at the restaurant fixed upon, which was one of the favorite rendezvous of the film stars. The maitre d'hotel and waiters bowed so low as the long-legged Howard and his tall wife came in with me that their noses seemed to touch the red carpet. I supposed that Howard rated as a king in filmdom, and he looked it. Scott was with us for three or four hours, drinking only beer; he and Howard talked shop with an expertise that was impressive.

But we ranged over much other ground too. Both Howard and Polly were by nature very gracious. They were solicitous of Scott and infinitely tactful; in return the latter's fine smile came out more often. I remember that we laughed a great deal over each others' pleasantries. Miss Graham, a blond young Englishwoman, then Hollywood correspondent for the London *Times*, had been here only about a year and was rather shy and all but silent.

After Scott and his friend had left, Howard remarked: "Miss Graham seems very good for him—they say she's keeping him off the bottle." He thought Scott had looked for the moment much like his old self, before Zelda's breakdown, and we both felt much hope that he would find the road back. In truth, everything went badly for him during the year that followed.

I was never to see Fitzgerald or Howard again—nor Nathanael West. A little more than a year later, in the summer of 1939, Howard suffered a fatal accident at his farm in Stockbridge, Massachusetts, when a tractor he was trying to start with its hand crank crushed him against a wall. He was then but forty-seven, in the prime of life. Then in December 1940 I read the news of poor Scott

Fitzgerald's sudden death while undergoing surgery. And at almost the same time a press dispatch from Los Angeles reported that the thirty-four-year-old Nathanael West and his wife, whom he had but recently married (the former Eileen McKinney), had been killed in a road accident. Sidney Howard had shown quality as a playwright and was much loved; Scott Fitzgerald and Nathanael West possessed superb literary gifts. West's last book reached again the brilliant satirical powers of his first novel, and judging from the fragments of Scott's *The Last Tycoon* he was well on the way—despite lapses into alcoholism and illness—to completion of one of the richest and most mature of his novels. It seemed a veritable massacre of high literary talent.

Chapter Twenty-two

~~~

The Eve of

World War II

"WE LIVE BY the newspaper headlines from one day to another," Hamilton Basso wrote me in March 1938 from his village in the North Carolina mountains. "What next? What, now, do you think of the Situation?" This was written as Austria was suddenly occupied by Hitler's troops.

The Situation could be defined as a long series of crises played out on the installment plan, with the separate installments taking their titles from the capital cities in which their action was centered. Thus we had from 1936 on: Madrid, the Moscow Trials, Vienna, Munich, Prague, and finally Danzig. With the rearmament of Germany the balance of power in Europe, as fixed by the Treaty of Versailles, had been overthrown. Thereafter the triumphal progress of Hitler held us with a sort of horrible fascination.

For a long period we cherished the hope that the leading nations that were disposed to peace-keeping—and we tended to include Soviet Russia in that category—would be led eventually to combine and, with their superior wealth and population, face up to the Nazi-fascist bloc. But even before the Munich Conference in September 1938 our calculations about Russia's playing a decisive role in a future system of collective security had been thrown into confusion by the Moscow Trials that began in August 1936.

The regime of Stalin had a paradoxical character: on the one hand it pursued a conciliatory policy toward the capitalist democracies of the West, aiming at defensive military alliances and a popular front against fascism; meanwhile, on the domestic front, Stalin carried out the most ruthless repression of potential opponents or mere suspects.

Among the intelligentsia in New York debate now raged over the "show trials" in Moscow and their significance for those who had believed in the Soviet state as the model for the world movement toward socialism. The charges against Kamenev, Zinovieff, and company were that they had engaged in an actual conspiracy to overthrow the Soviet state directed from abroad by Trotsky. Was Trotsky a traitor to the state he had helped found? Or was his now the true voice of revolutionary socialism?

Malcolm Cowley, in an article in *The New Republic* disapproving of Stalin, held that Trotsky had probably been guilty of plotting against the head of the state. Sidney Hook wrote in reply: "Since when does it follow that because an individual desires to overthrow a government, he therefore is guilty of sabotage, arson, espionage, in the service of the enemy. On Mr. Cowley's view it would be justifiable for an American patriot to charge members of the Communist Party with all sorts of crimes, from arson to assassination, merely because they desire to overthrow the Government. This is precisely what Red-baiters do here, and what Hitler does in Germany." [1]

Soon afterward Sidney Hook, Dwight Macdonald, and several others organized a Trotsky Defense Committee, which set up a commission of inquiry to meet in Mexico City and question Trotsky in person; John Dewey presided. Trotsky was duly exonerated of the charges made against him in Moscow, and the persons participating in the trial were in turn fiercely assailed in the communist press in America as "enemies of the people."

I had been in Russia during an era of good feeling. A year later, after the assassination of Kirov, the atmosphere had completely changed. It became more difficult to approach people; they showed evident fear when one broached political questions, for they lived again in terror of the secret police. So Edmund Wilson reported in

[1] *The New Republic*, letter of June 7, 1937.

articles written during a journey of five months in the USSR, re-published in book form as *Travels in Two Democracies* (1936). Still he found ground for hope in the impressive social improvements introduced by Bolshevism.

In his book Wilson—like many others—made allowances for the shortcomings of the Russians, holding that it was "foolish to make an issue of the bad aspects of the Soviet dictatorship." We Americans with our excellent democratic institutions still seemed unable, as of 1935, to feed and clothe all our people adequately; Americans were therefore in no position to reproach the Russians until they could show the way to a socialistic society free from the defects of the Soviet bureaucracy. Thus Wilson, describing the United States of the Depression Era in half of his book and devoting the rest to his Russian tour, still defined *both* countries as democracies, different though they were: ours was a political democracy, though far from a just society, theirs a society seeking economic justice but wanting in freedom.

Wilson had come late to the study of the Marxist dialectic. The way to understanding the historic forces that made for the evolution of human society toward scientific socialism, he then believed, was through mastering the science of history as taught by Marx and adapted later by Lenin. I remember visiting him in the summer of 1934 at Cape Cod and being invited by him to read proofs of *The New Republic* articles that later appeared in his book *To the Finland Station*. This work was then quite a mixed bag of essays on such people as Michelet, the romantic historian of the French Revolution, and Anatole France, and it also contained a series of excellent biographical studies of Marx, Engels, and Lenin. The book then (as in its revised form) reflected Wilson's scholarly and critical spirit, but it also revealed wide gaps in his knowledge of the literature of the social sciences and economics. What seems most interesting here is that the various revisions of *To the Finland Station,* made during the seven years that he was engaged with it, closely paralleled the changing views of many American intellectual fellow travelers during that whole period.

After about two years' work on his book Wilson interrupted it and went to visit Russia, where he bravely applied himself to the study of the language. At that time he seemed convinced that Marx's materialist philosophy made it possible to predict the course of history and, in some measure, even control it. Lenin was certainly an example of one who, inspired with the certainties he received from Marx, mastered practice as well as theory and finally, in 1917, rode in the famous sealed train through the German lines to his rendezvous with world history at the Finland Station of St. Petersburg.

Wilson's sojourn in Russia created some doubts in his mind about the Soviets; the Moscow Trials later strengthened these doubts. Meanwhile his work on *To the Finland Station*, which was to have been a firm exposition of the science of history, suffered extended delays as well as changes of attitude; it was not published until 1940, seven years after he had begun writing it. By then its concluding sections were written in full contradiction of his earlier views: after having begun as a believer in Marxism he came out several years later as an anti-Marxist. Already in articles written in 1937 he declared himself fed up with the "grim" Russian form of socialism. As he came to the end of his book *To the Finland Station*, Wilson himself denied its main thesis that a predictable science of history existed, and he dismissed the whole Marxist dialectic as so much "myth" and a "hocus pocus of German mysticism."

Thus a minority of the political avant-garde of the thirties, typified by Wilson, Dos Passos, and Hook, ceased to be fellow travelers and broke away from the Popular Front movement (though the great majority held to that line throughout the years of the Spanish Civil War). Some of these disillusioned radicals carried on angry polemics in which they waged a sort of literary class war against those with whom they had formerly been so closely allied. Generally they echoed the arguments of Leon Trotsky to the effect that the revolutionary state in Russia had reached the phase of Thermidor, like the French Republic in 1794, and degenerated into a servile bureaucracy ruled by the new Bonaparte, Stalin. It became fashionable to hold that the Soviet regime had not only abandoned its earlier social ideals, but had betrayed the German working class and the Spanish Republic alike. Indeed James Burnham, in his pamphlet *The People's Front: a New Betrayal* (1937), held that Stalin had not only compromised the whole revolutionary movement by his external policy of collaborating with the bourgeoisie abroad, but that Soviet Russia itself had been converted by him into a society ruled by an elite of privileged officials. Thus to his mind the whole system could be equated perfectly with that of National Socialism under Hitler. Burnham, in his later phase of disillusionment with Marxism, went so far that even Trotsky, his former master, denounced him as a "witch doctor" forever concocting different theoretical broths, each stronger than the last. (By 1947 Burnham's shift to the extremism of the right would lead him to theoretics about starting an unprovoked nuclear war against the communist nations.)

Those who experienced disappointment in the camp of the left found at different stages different reasons for quitting it. Some even objected to the success the American Communist Party had enjoyed in recent years, during which their small membership increased from about twelve thousand in 1932 to four times that number, while they also received support from hundreds of thousands of non-Party members in their "front" organizations.

In those days Earl Browder proclaimed communism as "twentieth-century Americanism" and Jefferson and Lincoln were installed as patron saints in the Communist Party calendar. The Party had turned into a moderate and respectable movement for socialism at some future date, much postponed, while at the same time it gained prestige in leading the fight for Republican Spain.

The very success of the Party in its democratic and unitary phase was enough to disconcert men like Dos Passos and Edmund Wilson. It was as an expression of their own prickly nonconformity, of their individual revolt, that they had originally joined with the people of the left. But now that the communists were a flourishing organization, Wilson remarked in the scolding tone he sometimes used:

> There was a time when literary Communists were few and when they were the spokesmen for a very important point of view which had hardly got into the liberal weeklies, let alone the old family monthlies. . . . But today, when half the world has turned leftist,

the Communist point of view is no longer a rarity, and we have a right to call its exponents to account.[2]

With the passage of time Dos Passos's attitude froze into hatred of everything connected with communism. In later years, reviewing his commitments of 1932 in favor of the Communist Party's presidential ticket, he declared that it had been "a mere protest vote" and also an act of folly. In the topical novel entitled *The Story of a Young Man* (1939), in which he gave vent to his own disappointment in his former associates, he argued that the three years' struggle in Spain against the fascists was in vain. Indeed Dos Passos went on in later writing to subject the Roosevelt administration itself to his sweeping condemnation; in his political novel *District of Columbia* (1956) he satirized certain fictive characters resembling the leading figures of the New Deal as carpetbaggers seeking only power and plunder. Whereas he had formerly, in his trilogy *U. S. A.*, written a prose edged with anger at the capitalist class and at the hamfisted police and government authorities protecting its property interests, in his later phase he represents the men of business as "parfit gentil knights." Finally the police themselves are transformed, in the novels of Dos Passos's later years, from gargantuan brutes into scholars and gentlemen. Thus when a group of communist-led workers form a picket line at the fence of the White House, the Washington police address them with the greatest consideration: "Not on this side of the street, please. . . . Please! You may march on the opposite side of the avenue." And the police behave with such courtesy as they guide the pickets across Pennsylvania Avenue that they seem almost to pick up their hats for them!

A spate of books devoted to reappraisal of the Russian experiment appeared in the autumn of 1937; they were preponderantly works of special pleading pro and con, mostly con. I chose to read mainly those that "said their worst" for the Soviets, as if to correct my own judgment; and wrote my commentary in an article at the time. The books in question bore such titles as *The End of Socialism*, by Max Eastman; *Russia Twenty Years After*, by Victor Serge;

[2] *The New Republic* (January 20, 1937).

Retouches à mon retour de l'URSS, by André Gide; and *Assignment to Utopia,* by Eugene Lyons. Among these generally well-informed observers—save for Serge, who was an old opponent of the ruling power—were persons who had come to Russia from the outside infatuated with their preconceived idea of her society. Gide had undergone a religious conversion in one season and lost his faith in the next. Eastman went to Russia to see "the future Socialist society," and Lyons claimed he went "in search of Utopia . . . the land of our dreams." It was like the era of the French Revolution at the end of the eighteenth century, when intellectuals looking on from outside, such as Coleridge and Burke in England and Jefferson in America, debated their hopes or fears for the new order with passion or in terms of their own emotional engagements; almost none spoke with objectivity. I wrote of the October Revolution twenty years after: "Today Soviet Russia still offers a picture of violent contrasts; a society in the throes of 'becoming,' whose realities exceed the frames set by optimists and skeptics alike. Enormous social gains are achieved; and there are also retreats and compromises; exploitation by capitalists is eliminated; but the termites of bureaucracy invade the state and breed new evils. There is order and peace among a federation of seventy different races; there is incessant preparation for war. There is the promise of liberty in the new constitution, and there is terror, a fearful armed vigilance, invoked against enemies within." [3]

As the First French Republic after its heroic years had become consolidated into the Directory and the Consulate, so the Russian Republic had in some measure degenerated during its second decade into a socialist dictatorship that was less than ideal. Far from turning "bourgeois," however, Stalin had pressed on with the Five-Year Industrial Plans and the collectivization of the farms.

[3] Matthew Josephson: "Russia and Some Utopians," *The New Republic* (December 1, 1937). In diary notes of November 3, 1937, I wrote under the head of *The Russian Enigma,* referring to the Moscow Trials: "I find (according to my knowledge of their past) much atavism, callousness, ineptitude. The face of the Party Machine and the Boss is implacable. . . ." One often heard then expressions of admiration for Stalin's cleverness and resolution, but very seldom a word of sympathy or liking for him. Isaac Deutscher's biography is probably the most balanced estimate of Stalin's tenacious strength and paranoid personality, written long before Khrushchev's revelations about him at the sessions of the Twentieth Soviet Congress in 1956.

But had not the German sociologist Max Weber, who was the opponent of Marxism, long ago warned that the workers under socialism might have *"everything to lose but their chains"*? In his fear of coming invasions, perhaps on two vast fronts, Stalin conducted a crisis regime. Meanwhile he cried for more factories, more food production, and more arms. The form of discipline was pitiless, but then Stalin knew that there had long been many Oblomovs in that country—I refer to Goncharov's classical novel whose hero, for days on end, is unable to make up his mind to get up out of bed and take some action. How stupidly naive to go to Russia with the illusion that one would find a utopia there! Marx, and Lenin after him, had warned that the working-class society they envisaged for the future would be in no sense utopian.

11.

In those days people prepared themselves for the end of the world every three or six months. The terror-bombing of populous cities such as Madrid and Barcelona with high explosives, and the destruction of whole towns such as Guernica, then constituted the highest point of military barbarism modern man had known.

The western Allies were war weary in advance, and Hitler brazened his way from one diplomatic victory to another, loudly warning everyone of what his "ten thousand airplanes" would do to London and Paris. The ruling statesmen in London and Paris, abandoning the hollow formulas of the League of Nations, employed themselves with ingenious schemes for satisfying the land hunger of the "have-not" powers at someone else's cost. Our own American ambassadors in Europe, Joseph P. Kennedy at London, William C. Bullitt at Paris, and William Phillips at Rome, then strongly approved of the Anglo-French policy of trying to pacify Nazi Germany and Italy. "I can't for the life of me understand why anybody would want to go to war to save the Czechs," Ambassador Kennedy said at the time. The indiscreet Mr. Kennedy assured Prime Minister Chamberlain that the American people would do nothing to help the Allies if they went to war with Germany over the Czechs.[4]

I wrote in my journal on October 8, 1938:

> The last week of September, especially the 28th, saw the Czechoslovak crisis at its worst. Tension grew unbearable. I believed that war, however, would be [temporarily] avoided by the Western Powers. At the eleventh hour the heads of the British and French Governments, assuming the pose of men who had "saved" the world's peace, were able to persuade their public and even the Czechs to accept the Nazis' demands. Jules Sauerwein ("Pertinax") of *Paris-Soir*, wrote bluntly that "the prospect of fighting a war in which Germany would be overcome with Soviet Russia's help was not relished."

We imagined that the future war would assume the form of terror-bombing advocated by the Italian air strategist General Douhet. In anticipation I wrote in my journal on the same date: "The island of Minorca in the Balearics, still held by the Loyalists, has defended itself successfully against all attempts at invasion by sea or air during two years. It is honeycombed with caves dating from the Stone Age and thus offers natural bombproof shelters. My best advice now is for us to become Cave Dwellers."

A few weeks after the crisis over Munich had passed one of my Wall Street friends, an émigré from Germany, drove up to my house in the country with a visiting German industrialist just arrived from Berlin. The man was a huge, beetle-browed fellow looking like a caricature of a Prussian, and he was actually engaged, as he told me, in armament manufacture for the *Reichswehr*. Because he was one of the leading metallurgical technicians he had been allowed to travel abroad to buy rare metal. He himself was secretly anti-Nazi; he was also a man of literary taste, and searched through my house for recent books by banned German authors which he was eager to read during his journey abroad.

"*Hitler has peace for sale*," was the explanation he gave us. No one in Europe and almost none in Germany really wanted war. Hitler would continue his threats until the last provisions of the

[4] Richard J. Whelan: *The Founding Father; Joseph P. Kennedy* (New York: New American Library; 1964), p. 237.

Versailles Treaty that had dismembered Germany were undone, and there would be peace—at his price.

I refused to believe the visitor from Germany and argued that Hitler would invade Russia at a suitable time, as he had long promised to do. I was told that an accord with the Soviets would probably be brought about through similar threats. The same thought occurred to others at the time, including editors of *The New Republic* who pointed out that though Russia had offered to support France—if war came over Czechoslovakia and France honored her military pact with the Czechs—Russia was now left isolated by the accord at Munich. Stalin might have no other recourse but to seek an accommodation with Hitler.[5]

Meanwhile the *cordon sanitaire*, made up of military pacts between the French and the East European nations encircling Germany, was broken. There had been not merely appeasement of the aggressor, but surrender without a real *quid pro quo*. The general war from which the pacific nations shrank had merely been postponed. President Roosevelt, who voiced approval of the settlement at Munich, was saying privately that there would probably be war in Europe in a year or two. Many predicted that if general war came the United States would be in it later. In Europe the Nazis renewed the "war of nerves," now aimed at Poland.

III.

Was fascism the wave of the future, as Colonel Charles A. Lindbergh and his wife assured us nowadays? Should we simply wait for the Nazis to come and bomb our cities and burn our books? In November 1938, after the assassination of a minor German official in Paris by a young Jewish refugee, the Nazi mobs carried out a pogrom against the Jews in Germany ("the Night of Broken Glass"), smashing their shops, burning their synagogues, arresting and beating them. It was not an inviting prospect the Nazis offered even to Aryans. Yet in New York the German-American Bund filled Madison Square Garden with

[5] *The New Republic* (October 5, 1938).

twenty-two thousand people at a meeting of pro-fascist groups early in 1939. There were even a few instances around that time in which local anti-Semites assaulted Jews in the New York subways and in Boston and in Philadelphia.

Some of my friends assumed an attitude of deep pessimism about the chances of the democracies ever resisting fascism effectively. Several of these who had journeyed to Europe in 1938 returned full of forebodings about the coming defeat of France and England. They found the French along the Riviera cynical and defeatist. (To be sure, they might have gained a different impression at the Place de la République on the east side of Paris.)

Apprehensive though I was, I did not share my friends' pessimism but felt the need to overhaul our old stock of ideas about fascism. In the official Marxist view it was the last desperate resort of capitalist nations in their decline; to forestall drastic social reforms they turned to wars of conquest for foreign colonies or neighboring territories. However, the procedures of our modern fascists now looked less simple than they had seemed. The National Socialists under Hitler had in fact grown rich and confident with success. In the face of the timid policies of their opponents, the Chamberlains, Halifaxes, and Hoares, the Nazis looked even stronger than they were as they went about smashing up the Anglo-French balance of power in Europe. At home they had gathered in the middle classes and the unemployed proletarians as well as the men of capital; it was done partly by terror, but also by propaganda (even a lying propaganda) appealing to national prejudice and passion and by their eyefilling circuses. They operated with great energy and very planfully, using a variety of economic stratagems including autarchy and rigorous state controls by which they pretended to save their country from socialism or communism, but they actually instituted a hybrid state capitalism with management generally left to the capitalists under Nazi surveillance. Such was the famous fascist synthesis which recreated the nation in arms and worked above all to socialize warmaking. Thus Italy was able to wage small-scale foreign wars while Germany could expand public construction, housing, and arms industries and generate full employment.

These opportunists and Machiavellians drew their ideas from ancient and modern sources: from Sparta and the Roman Empire, from the Prussia of Frederick II, and from Bismarck, who propagated racism and the *Kulturkampf*. Indeed Curzio Malaparte, a disciple of Mussolini, held that the mass organization of the Fascisti was originally an imitation of Lenin's monolithic party. But whereas the Marxists believed in the science of history and espoused mass education and social improvement, the fascists' interest in education seemed directed mainly to improving the technology of war. The fascists and Nazis were antihistorical; Lewis Mumford held that they derived their hatred of humanitarian ideas and their admiration for the "irrational" from Oswald Spengler, author of *The Decline of the West*. Like Vilfredo Pareto, they rejected history and saw in it only eternal recurrence and the "circulation of elites."

In the end the fascists and Nazis, with their mixed programs and promises, their big lies, and their methods of spreading terror, had managed to draw powerful support from the channeled emotional drives of the mass-man. This meant that the citizens in the more or less civilized nations would not long be left to live in peace.

My rather summary reflections on the march of fascism and the hard choices it presented to us came up in the course of conversations with friends, especially in an extended correspondence with Hamilton Basso. He used to inveigh against me—though always in friendly terms—for clinging to eighteenth-century ideas of progress. But my notion of progress, I always insisted, was based on the long historical view of *homo faber*, on belief in man's courage and will to liberate himself in the face of a hostile nature or evil circumstances. My special hero of the eighteenth-century Enlightenment was the positivistic *philosophe* Condorcet, who wrote his essay "The Ten Tablets of the Laws of Human Progress" while he himself lay in hiding from the terror in Paris; waiting to be arrested and sent to the guillotine, he continued to believe in the social good the French Revolution wrought.

It was my assumption at the time that the logic of events would ultimately bring together the large nations such as England, France, Russia, China, and perhaps even the United States in a concerted defense against the Axis Powers and that their combined weight of population and resources would finally prevail. To Basso such anticipations based on the rational action of men seemed false and misleading, and he wrote me with some heat: "The trouble with you is that you believe in reason, in economic determinism, in the quantitative strength of the Western nations; whereas Hitler and Mussolini are 'irrational' and so are able to defy your laws of economics. . . . They summon up mysterious new forces, psychological and emotional, which confound reason. If you wish they use *magic.* . . ."

A good many of my friends were drawing long faces; they attributed to the enemy the powers of the Devil. Basso went on: "What I feel, after Munich, when the great tides of history are in flow, is the rank uselessness of all these elaborate 'systems'—as demonstrated by experience. Talk to me of 'systems' of fascism and communism, and all I see is rivers of blood. I see a way of life based on one thing I truly hate, and that is hate itself."

Basso opposed the agitation being carried on in the press by persons like Dorothy Thompson and Lewis Mumford, who wished to prepare public opinion for our future intervention against the fascist powers. They would lead us, he held, only to a new massacre of the innocents, "the slaughter of millions upon millions." He was against those who prated of principles; the barbarians too claimed their own principles. He had none, except his Christian spirit of compassion, and preferred to go back to "cultivating his own garden" and resign himself to whatever was in store for us.

Gloom lay thick among us after Munich; quite a number of persons spoke as if they believed the tides if history were running against us and no useful purpose would be served in undertaking any public action. In an article written in memory of the downfall of the Spanish Republic in March 1939 I took issue with those who had fallen prey to the prevailing mood of pessimism and dared to find hope in the very tragedy of Spain.

Some wonder even if the Fascists do not possess some unknown magic or wizardry which helps them to victory both in the economic and military fields, and makes resistance vain. Others have begun to entertain doubts about the rule of reason itself, and about the humanistic doctrine underlying democratic and socialist societies.

The answer to the argument of "magic" is simple. Even I might be able to overthrow the Spanish Republic, if I had not only the help of Spain's owning class and military organization, but also that of Italy and Germany, together with indirect assistance from the British and French as well. To me the magic and wonder of it all is to be seen in the three-years' resistance of the Spanish people, without trained armies and with insufficient arms and food. It is a miracle to me that the common people and their leaders delayed seriously the "time-table" the Fascist powers had undoubtedly set for [the conquest of] Europe. So a century ago the plain people of Spain repeatedly disturbed the plans of another imperial invader, Napoleon I, while at the other end of Europe Russia waited to complete the overthrow of the French Caesar.

. . . Dictators usually follow a historical pattern of action essential to their business. A deep inward necessity drives them to speed things up and overextend themselves—as may have been done in the Spanish adventure. The invasion and partition of Czechoslovakia may seem like a clever coup. But then it may well mark the point at which fascist aggression begins to provoke worldwide, concerted opposition, and prepares its own ruin.

The fascists might be antihistorical and bent on destroying the monuments and literature of the past, but I would not throw away my history books.

We must cling to our common sense, to our human sense of proportion; in spite of provocations. We must not become . . . infected, debauched by our contemporaries of Central Europe. . . .

Every so often the fight against the barbarians and the witch burners and bookburners must be fought all over again. What liberties, what human rights were ever won without being fought for?

In the Spanish Civil War—to say nothing of the volunteers who bore arms and died for the Republic—it was notable that "behind the lines" American intellectuals and writers volunteered their services with an energy and devotion rarely shown before in a similar "idealistic" cause. The defeat has been hard. But if one may take some comfort from this misfortune, it is that the partisans of the Spanish Republic performed near miracles in arousing public opinion in our own country, usually so indifferent to events abroad.

Instead of turning from this experience with a sense of defeat, I hope that the friends of democracy who fought together . . . will keep always with them an awareness of the potential strength they showed when unified in defense of a great cause. All this generosity, this spontaneity, is not only something to remember, but something to hold—for equivalent needs or emergencies, should they arise.

IV.

During the late thirties crowds of German-speaking refugees arrived in this country for asylum; the spring of 1939 saw a new flood of émigrés reaching New York, and now they were Spanish. Two of my friends of several years ago in Madrid, Emilio Delgado and Jose Lopez Carmona, had walked over the border into France in the final mass exodus of 400,000 loyalists, then sailed to America. They looked hungry and thin, so we took them to Connecticut, and filled them with good food for days on end. Our Spanish friends, in most cases, were not permitted to remain long in the United States, and soon moved on to Mexico and other Latin American countries.

After the Spaniards had gone, Louis Aragon with his wife Elsa Triolet arrived from France at the end of April. Their visa had been held up for a while; whereupon Archie MacLeish, Malcolm Cowley and I and many other admirers of Aragon sent urgent appeals to Washington by telegraph, so that they were permitted entry at the order of Undersecretary of State Sumner Welles.

Aragon, at forty-two, with his black hair graying, looked handsomer than ever and seemed at the height of his powers. In his restless way he spread himself in a multitude of activities, writing articles and editing the large communist daily *L'Humanité* while working at a series of novels and other books—several of which were published here in translation.

Part of his business in this country was to attend a presidential press conference at the White House, which he reported to Paris by cable. Another reason for Aragon's journey was his scheduled

(470)

appearance as a speaker at the Third Congress of American Writers, whose opening session on June 2, 1939, was a public meeting at Carnegie Hall attended by 3,500. That gathering became the occasion of elegies and impassioned demonstrations in honor of the two republics that had just fallen to the fascists: Czechoslovakia and Spain. Earl Browder, for the American Communist Party, opened the proceedings; President Edouard Benès appeared as the principal speaker and was followed by Spain's ambassador to the United States Fernando de Los Rios, and by Thomas Mann, who after long hesitation now aligned himself with the Popular Front.

Benès's talk had an undertone of bitterness and grief; he ventured the prediction that the sacrifice of his country would not spare the western Allies the pains of a war with the Central Powers. Aragon spoke for collective security of all the democratic states against the aggressor nations. Though this meeting was obviously managed by the communists, it was significant that among the guests of honor on the platform there were not only numerous liberals such as Heywood Broun, but also one Republican City Councillor of New York and a prominent Catholic intellectual.

Although Aragon put on a brave face in public, I found in private talk that he had the darkest forebodings about the immediate future for France and for himself. As a reserve officer he had been called to the Army during the mobilization of last September. He told me that he feared he would be called again at the end of the summer, this time for "the real thing."

He and his wife visited us for a week in the country, and as we discussed the dismal prospects before us—and especially for him—he spoke with calmness and sang-froid. "We will just not think about it any more," he said. The springtime in our American countryside seemed more beautiful than anything he had imagined, and for the present he was going to enjoy it to the full.

In his happier moods none could be more vivacious, more entertaining than our old companion of the 1920's in Montparnasse. Aragon's gaiety in those June days (when everyone sensed war approaching) was infectious. Even his way of writing while on his travels kept us amused. He was then carrying on with a prodi-

giously long novel, *Les Voyageurs de l'impériale* (later translated by
my wife and published in this country in 1941 as *The Century
Was Young*); and he seemed to write at any odd hours of the
night or early morning. He would come down for breakfast in the
highest spirits and recite for us in all detail whole chapters of the
novel which he had composed in his head, for his memory was
prodigious.

We held a garden party for the Aragons, and our friends of the
neighborhood all came. Among them were Charles and Mary
Beard, and our talk soon became a raging debate over the continuing crisis in Europe. Aragon urged upon Beard, of all people,
the necessity to arouse Americans from their dreams of isolation.
If only our full weight could be brought to bear on the side of
France and England we might yet be spared a new general war.

"Uncle Charlie," then in his middle sixties and looking like a
staunch old Roman, was at fighting pitch; he always enjoyed a
little opposition. The United States, he argued, had generously
helped the Allies in the last war but had been overruled when it
came to making the peace settlement—which was perfectly designed by our Allies to breed new wars such as now impended.
Why should America intervene again? England and France were
the most "ruthless" of imperialist powers—here he cited for Aragon
the terms of Lenin—recalling how they still exploited hundreds of
millions of coolie laborers in their Asian and African colonies. And
who could regard such nations as defenders of democracy in the
light of their "nonintervention agreement" on Spain and their
betrayal of Czechoslovakia? "We in America," Beard wound up,
"still don't seem to know how to manage our own business and
deal with our problem of ten million unemployed. And yet we are
in a position to do great things for our own society. We must stay
here and tend to our own affairs!"

Beard made it an oration: his blue eyes flashed, his sharp voice
rang strong; after the delivery of one of his heaviest broadsides he
bounced off. Aragon shook his head, saying: "What a droll type!
I am sorry he feels the way he does."

Aragon went on long walks in our neighborhood and he swam
every day in our big brook. Then he would sit with us in the little

garden on the knoll behind our house overlooking the valley. He
thought that we lived an ideal existence in the peace of rural
Connecticut, being able to do our work among the flowers and
trees and with our growing children near us. "This must be one of
the few happy places left in the world," he said. "Indeed, I believe
these are probably the last happy days of my life. I feel I don't
want to leave ever."

In early June, nevertheless, he returned to France and two
months later was called up to serve in a tank division near the
Belgian border. For a long time we heard no more from him.
"I will not grieve for Louis," I said to my wife. "Whatever may
come, he will face it with courage. I pity much more those who are
ruled by fear."

§   §   §

Ruth McKenney had come into our lives in the autumn of 1936
when she and her fabled sister Eileen made their home in the
neighboring village of New Milford. Ruth was a buxom young
woman, then twenty-five, of Scotch-Irish type, with a snub nose, a
mass of curly auburn hair, and blue eyes full of mirth, while her
smile was rather composed and bland. Wherever Ruth was there
was laughter. Her conversation given in her pleasant Midwestern
drawl was exactly in the tone of those sketches of her girlhood in
Ohio and of her farcical adventures in Greenwich Village that were
then appearing week by week in *The New Yorker* and, when published in book form as *My Sister Eileen*, won for her an enormous
popular success. Compared with other humorous or satirical writers
among her contemporaries, such as Nathanael West and Dawn
Powell, Ruth McKenney's stories were in kindly vein; and she herself had great warmth and generosity of spirit. Her humor refreshed and heartened us during the several years that our
friendship lasted—until it was abruptly severed under circumstances
beyond our control, determined by the strange times we lived in.

Even before the Great Crash, Ruth McKenney had learned to
laugh at hard times. Her mother having died when she was young,
she and her sister had been raised in Ohio by a severe stepmother
and an aunt in a middle-class poverty made painful by its efforts at

concealment. The comic spirit of her stories derived from her keen perception of the contrast between the pretensions of the middle-class poor and the hard realities of their life.

A child of the Depression years, she came naturally to the politics of the left. During the labor conflicts of 1935 and 1936 she happened to cover the first sit-down strikes in the Akron rubber factories as a reporter for the New York *Post,* and did so with a cool competence that won her citations. Her strongest friendships then were with the left-wing people of the CIO.

Ruth was often accompanied by her younger sister Eileen, a pretty and slender brunette, toward whom Ruth habitually assumed a protective air. In her fiction she represented Eileen as a light-headed little siren to whom all men, including Ruth's admirers, were fatally drawn. Eileen became, in the play and the motion picture about her, a national legend; yet in real life she was rather average, while her elder sister actually possessed more charm and interest.

In the late summer of 1937 Ruth came to visit us with a new friend, Richard Bransten, then one of the editors of *The New Masses.* He was a native of San Francisco, of a family well known in trade, and a graduate of Harvard. From what Ruth told us, he had taken up communism in rebellion against his moneyed family. Bransten had a nervous manner, but seemed very intelligent and high-willed. His first marriage to a California heiress had ended in divorce; his second, to Ruth McKenney, which took place only a fortnight after they met, proved more enduring. Ruth loved her husband and the married state, but nothing came easily to Richard Bransten.

By that time I felt strong differences between myself and the orthodox sort of communist, though I continued to see some of them because of my interest in maintaining the Popular Front, and because I thought some of them were fine, courageous human beings who had "got religion." Now Richard was nothing if not pious; he devoted all his time and much of his money to *The New Masses* and to a left publishing enterprise, the Modern Age Press. Meanwhile Ruth, thanks to the success of *My Sister Eileen,* also helped the cause. Richard became a big wheel in the Party, and both he and Ruth regularly gave their evenings to "Party work," to organizing the unorganized, or helping the Negroes. But Richard followed the Stalin line so strictly—he fairly lived and breathed communist politics—that I, as a habitual infidel, found it uncomfortable to discuss political matters with him and, as a rule, tried (not always with success) to avoid argument. Ruth, in the meantime, had become utterly, immitigably "serious," as she termed it. Instead of continuing with her humorous sketches, which showed such a fine sense of social comedy, she tended to accept her husband's censure of such work as "middlebrow" or vulgar, and dropped it entirely to write of the labor movement, as in her next book *Industrial Valley* (1938). In her arch manner, really *faux naif,* she would prattle on about her attempts to master the "dialectic," or of her "serious revolutionary duties"; so that I found her both odd and diverting, an Epworth Leaguer in communist guise.

The flavor of the left's breathless social life in the late thirties in New York is caught in a few of the letters she addressed to us in the country. Now she tells of a "modern music night," arranged for one of the Popular Front groups, with Virgil Thomson, Marc Blitzstein, and Harold Rome playing their own musical compositions. "Everybody worth his salt in radical literary, musical and bookish circles was present, including CIO organizers and playwright Clifford Odets. Two lovely Group Theatre actresses were reported to have been squeezed to death on the stairways. . . . As for the music . . . my taste is not to be trusted." In another it is a publishers' tea she describes, in honor of John Dos Passos, whose novel *Adventures of a Young Man* had just appeared. As it is considered an attack on Republican Spain, the literary people on the left, including Ruth McKenney, stay at the far end of the room "looking daggers" at the new anticommunists, Dos Passos and James T. Farrell, whom they regard as "traitors." Dissensions among the literary fraternity seemed to be growing ever stronger in that eve of war period.

V.

For four years past the Communist Party in America had pursued a policy of collaboration with socialists, liberals, and church organizations in order to make common cause against fascism and war. Whereas formerly their critics had assailed the communists for aping the Russians and not "talking American," of late the party's guiding genius Earl Browder had thoroughly Americanized himself, while some of his literary disciples published books with titles such as *I Like America* and *The Great Tradition*, in which Jefferson, Emerson, Thoreau, and Whitman were reinterpreted as the true precursors of latter-day Marxism. Indeed communism greatly resembled the quite legal and gradual movement of our socialist grandfathers; and its ideological compromises, its *embourgeoisement*, made it the subject of much derisive comment.

Undoubtedly a large public now supported the Communist Party and its front organizations; to this body should be added several important unions in the CIO and some large locals in the AFL also. The communists in 1939 were probably at the apogee of their influence as a minority movement that could now hardly be called radical.

A good many forward-looking young men just out of college chose to make their careers in the left wing of the labor movement, which was now able to confer some patronage in the way of jobs and funds for organizing campaigns—a very important factor. As one of these young men recalled to me in later years: "We were organizing Negro and white tobacco workers in the backward South under communist leaders, but we were building real industrial unions for those workers, who had been in a desperate plight; we knew nothing about Soviet Russia or its ideological doctrines."

The shifts in policy in far off Moscow nevertheless had unpredictable and unfortunate effects on the communist-influenced unions and front organizations. We had rumors of a possible turnabout in Stalin's foreign policy after the Munich Pact and again later, in March 1939, after the occupation of all Czechoslovakia by Hitler's troops when Stalin was quoted as having said that "Russia was not just going to pull other people's chestnuts out of the fire."

A British-French mission was then in Moscow, discussing the terms for a possible military treaty with Russia. But Mr. Chamberlain's diplomats were wary while the Russians were suspicious and resentful, having seen themselves excluded at Munich and Hitler given a free hand to move against them in the East.

At Martha's Vineyard, which I visited early in August 1939, Roger Baldwin, then director of the American Civil Liberties Union, and his wife gave shelter at their estate to two German refugees who had formerly been communists active in underground resistance against Hitler. They seemed disillusioned and without hope, and one suggested that Stalin was "going to make some deal with Hitler." I said this was impossible, and Roger Baldwin agreed with me that the Soviet communists and the Nazis could not lie down together.

A few days after that conversation a circular reached me at Martha's Vineyard containing an "Open Letter to Supporters of Peace and Democracy"; it called for a friendlier understanding and cooperation with Russia, while repudiating assertions that the USSR and the fascist states were "identical" and to be condemned alike as "totalitarian." There had lately been much propaganda in the press and much talk in Congress against Russia and communism; but the signers of the open letter held that it might be useful to keep Russia as a friend and ally of the democracies and a "bulwark against war and the persecution of minorities." Among the signers, four hundred in number, were many liberal journalists such as Vincent Sheean and Max Lerner, as well as writers like Ernest Hemingway, Clifford Odets, and William Carlos Williams. I signed this Open Letter and Roger Baldwin also signed it. It was dated August 10, 1939, and appeared as a newspaper advertisement on August 19—only a few days before the whole picture was suddenly and completely changed.

On August 23, 1939, came the stunning news of the German-Russian pact of nonaggression and trade. The Hitlerian uproar against Poland was then at its height; under the circumstances the new pact made war a certainty and moved its opening date forward. The Ribbentrop-Molotov agreement gave Nazi Germany a free hand against Poland.

(477)

The western Allies themselves had allowed Hitler a free hand in Czechoslovakia only the year before, trusting that the German armies might afterward become engaged upon the wide spaces of eastern Europe in an exhausting conflict with Russia. Now Stalin had turned the tables on the clumsy Machiavellis of London and Paris. At the last hour they, England and France, had given firm commitments to aid Poland and thus obliged themselves to declare war on Germany—though Poland was beyond help. We now perceive, a generation later, that the immense stupidity of *all* the Great Powers played a large role in precipitating World War II: the western Allies did not make their stand against Germany until it was too late; Hitler followed his intuitions and went on to finish off a weak Poland; Stalin, who had observed how faithless Hitler had been in agreements with England and France, signed a pact of friendship with him in order to win time and space for Russia, though it helped little in the end.

America in September 1939 was frozen in the position of neutrality. Those Americans who were associated with the antifascist movement were as dumfounded as anyone else both at the reversal of the Nazis, sworn to wage holy war against Bolshevism, and at the about-face of Stalin, who was pledged to fight for "the liberation of mankind from fascist barbarism" as recently as *Pravda's* issue of August 14, 1939. Rumors of a possible German-Russian rapprochement had been denounced as "vicious slanders" in the New York *Daily Worker*. But two days after the pact was reported Comrade Earl Browder, recovering from his own initial bewilderment, defined it as "a master stroke for peace" intended to balk some new "Munich treachery" on the part of the British. The war now under way was a mere conflict of imperialists, he held. In *The New Masses* Richard Rovere wrote an emphatic apologia for Stalin's new policy in an article entitled "What Every Appeaser Should Know"; in it he argued that Russia had perpetrated "no betrayal" of anyone and had merely continued its previously declared program of "maintaining peace and trade with *all countries*." [6]

[6] Richard Rovere: "What Every Appeaser Should Know," *The New Masses* (September 5, 1939). The young Mr. Rovere would soon execute a rapid turnaround to assume the posture of an anti-Stalinist.

Most of the liberals who had formerly championed Soviet Russia in the press joined in a stampede to reverse themselves. Vincent Sheean now declared that the Soviet dictator was only another Bonaparte who enslaved his people and helped unleash war in Europe. The veteran Moscow correspondent for *The Nation*, Louis Fischer, and Max Lerner, associate editor of the same journal, also said their good-byes to Russia. Lerner considered himself a close student of Marx but had long been a critic of the official communist line. Now he observed that "the Nazi-Soviet Pact, combined with the intellectual antics of the Communist Party that accompanied it, and the war itself had inevitably plunged radicals of every kind into a state of disenchantment and despair."

Most of the Communist Party's intellectuals who had not yet left the Party in 1937 during the Moscow Trials now hastened to resign. One was Joseph Freeman, who found the new line indefensible. Granville Hicks, literary editor of *The New Masses*, also resigned, as he wrote in a public letter, because membership in the party could no longer serve the ends of a democratic front—though he "did not condemn the pact itself." At the same time Hicks wrote me as to one who, like himself, was not in sympathy with the Communist Party's new policy, sending me a mimeographed bulletin in which he outlined plans for the organization of an Independent Left.[7]

James Wechsler, who had been a leader of the American Students' Union and taken a prominent part in the Depression period "revolt on the campus," in later years recalled the bombshell effect of the German-Soviet pact:

> For a brief period following the Nazi-Soviet alliance there was an attempt to create some American replica of the "New Beginnings"

[7] By 1953 Granville Hicks had moved on to a higher stage of his "apostasy," so that he felt compelled in all conscience to appear as a cooperative witness before the House UnAmerican Activities Committee and denounce his associates on the Harvard and Smith College faculties as former members of an alleged communist cell. Hicks himself relates that he "put the finger" on at least eight university teachers, who were thereupon subpoenaed by the congressional witch-hunters. Part of Hicks's testimony, by his own admission, was false and misleading, for he relates: "And I know of one innocent person . . . who was hurt by me and might have been badly hurt." This case involved a young instructor, with a family to support, who was put to great trouble and expense to save himself from professional ruin. Granville Hicks: *Where We Came Out* (New York: Viking Press; 1954), pp. 137, 138, 139.

group [in England]. Among the participants in the informal sessions that initiated—and terminated—this move were Max Lerner, Granville Hicks, Matthew Josephson, I. F. Stone, Malcolm Cowley, Leo Huberman, and I. Quite a few others dropped in. . . . There seemed to be general agreement that the time had come for reconstruction of the American left. . . . But there was a good deal of ambiguity and disagreement about what was to be done next.[8]

During that gloomy autumn of 1939 about a dozen of us gathered on Sunday evenings at the home of Max Lerner, that ambitious, articulate, and congenial young professor and editor who often acted as a catalyst. There was continued discussion, without agreement, about drafting a new program and establishing a clear position on the crisis. Robert Lynd, who joined us, urged that we must now make a great effort to "think things through." Hicks wanted a new periodical with thousands of readers and lecture forums. I was for running a sort of Jacobin Club that would attempt to clarify and guide public opinion. As I wrote to Lynd at the time, it seemed to me we did not need a new political organization that would be another splinter party.

> The Comrades have been magnificent organizers. Being either destitute WPA clients, or wealthy, they have had leisure to work long hours. Only the Tammany Hall people have been more disciplined in the dreary day-to-day canvassing that makes up our politics.
>
> The trouble with us whom you kindly call "intelligent folk" is that we would give a weekend, then go back to breadwinning or paying off bills.
>
> Recognizing our predicament . . . I therefore urged . . . keeping a record of honest talk by people with some information, and passing this around. In other words leaving ideas out like milk bottles so that they can be "stolen," that is, used for others' nourishment.

The left had split; but I hoped that the Popular Front might somehow, someday be reunited. Now Lerner, Hicks, and others wanted to develop a specifically anticommunist or anti-Soviet movement. These persons already began to see Russia as "total evil"—the phrase is Mrs. Diana Trilling's. I could not find the Rus-

[8] James Wechsler: *The Age of Suspicion* (New York: Random House; 1953), p. 153.

sians more immoral politically than the Anglo-French bloc the year before at Munich.

I remember saying: "The Soviets have made a power play for their own good reasons. Stalin thinks of Russia's interests, not of you and me—he never asked *me* whether I would like this. I will have no part of any such pact with the Nazis; I was antifascist yesterday and I am holding the same ground today. Power politics brings together queer bedfellows, but history is moving very fast now. This marriage of convenience between the Comintern and the Anti-Commintern may fall apart one day. Perhaps the Russians may come back to *us*, and we may find them useful again."

Max Lerner considered my views with only a passing interest, then resumed his denunciations of the "unspeakable" Stalin. For him the future would be anticommunist, and it would be a fairly prosperous future. But then Max Lerner was an amiable liberal who never pretended that he was out to sacrifice himself for the human race.

It was difficult to judge the moves of the great card players of history when one could not see the cards they held, or thought they held. Besides, the interval during which the western Allies remained passive behind the Maginot Line added to our confusion. Stalin's prompt signing of a nonaggression pact with Japan did not bespeak trust in the future intentions of Hitler; nor was the Russian aggression in Finland committed with the thought of making things easier for the Germans.

At *The New Republic* there was also high argument over what was to be done now. Malcolm Cowley felt as disconcerted as anyone else. On November 2, 1939, he wrote inviting me to a dinner gathering at which a group of writers were to discuss the great shift in Russian policy and the war. Our exchange of ideas, it was hoped, would lead to articles that might help clear the air. Malcolm desired among other things that we reconsider Marxism and communism, which "in spite of its opposition to religion had itself become a religion, with a pope, a priesthood, a standard of ethics, and a heaven placed in the future." I came and, after our discussion, wrote a memorandum on the German-Russian pact which together with other statements of opinion was incorporated in a *New Re-*

public leader on the altered world situation. That, however, was for me an unsatisfactory composite; I find my own statement reflected more of the mental stress we felt as we stared at the world catastrophe so long dreaded and which we had hoped to avert.

In my memorandum of autumn 1939 I said:

We must struggle to collect our thoughts. . . . At all events the European democracies have not capitulated as at Munich last year, but have taken up arms "to save the world from lawless aggression." So far so good. But Soviet Russia which yesterday worked to the same end has turned to . . . alliance with Nazi Germany. Hitler has joined hands with the Bolshevists!

In the real world of power politics the choices are not always of the most desirable kind. Moreover, Lenin urged that the Soviet Communists must be ready to conclude alliances and compromises with their opponents, or retreat, if need be, in order to advance again. Other admirable political leaders, including Lincoln, made compromise bargains . . . then returned to pursue ultimate objectives.

But whatever the ground for Stalin's strategic retreat, whatever advantage or delay it may gain, means nothing to us who work for a democratic reconstruction of our own country and for the preservation of peace abroad. We must not abandon our own convictions. We have no business to follow Stalin, or the Communists who cleave to him. Their recent maneuvers serve to alienate liberal and progressive men everywhere, and make it impossible for them to march with us toward common goals.

Two years ago, I wrote of the Soviet Communists that they were our "awkward allies." Their direction would sometimes approach ours, or now diverge. Well, Stalin and Soviet Communism have left us. We have parted company, perhaps for the time being, perhaps for good.

We must continue to hold our ground as anti-Fascists, come what may. We must also prepare to play a constructive part in the peace that must follow the war.

I am for carrying on with the Popular Front at home, and feel that factional quarrels among liberals, radicals and Marxians of various kinds would serve no useful purpose.

We must keep America an outpost of sanity.

(482)

We may well feel despondent and ask ourselves if it is true, as Spengler held, that men are but "beasts of prey." Is the future, then, all to the barbarians? But if that were true, where would the war-lovers and pirates of bygone ages have found loot, or food and drink? Most human beings were rational and constructive creatures. There was always *homo faber*—but for whom there would be nothing to plunder or destroy.

At heart I was for American intervention on the side of the western Allies, for war against the Nazis. But there were other and very estimable people already agitating for military assistance to the Allies—through the Committee to Defend America by Aiding the Allies, whose chairman was William Allen White. Its sponsors included Henry L. Stimson, Felix Frankfurter, Dorothy Thompson, Lewis Mumford, and Archibald MacLeish. But I could not bring myself to speak for our actual entrance into war, as I wrote Max Lerner. The force of events would determine that question sooner or later. Lerner wrote me in the summer of 1940: "Do you remember an essay of Randolph Bourne in which he advised people not to resist war, but not to help it in any way? I presume that's how you feel."

§   §   §

The German-Russian pact and the onset of war produced upheavals in private life as well as in our political relations. Friendships were broken; people quarreled with each other and resigned from various front committees or left organizations. Van Wyck Brooks, for example, quietly withdrew from the League of American Writers; I did likewise. The Popular Front was falling apart.

Ruth McKenney, who had settled with her husband in Westport, Connecticut, wrote us a doleful account of the ordeal that all loyal followers of the Communist Party line then underwent. Richard, she reported, felt as though "he bore the whole brunt of the crisis"; night after night he went forth to speak at meetings of "honestly bewildered people" about his faith in the Soviet Union and in the Communist Party as the true medium of the socialist movement. Their friend Earl Browder meanwhile was sentenced to prison for having traveled abroad on a false passport. Ruth wondered how much longer she and Richard would be allowed their freedom.

Several months had passed since the signing of the pact when they drove to our house for dinner. Though our relations had been entirely cordial and Richard was grateful for some kindness I had shown him, he and I were soon engaged in a dispute that raged for hours. I said that while I could understand Stalin's "appeasement" of Germany on military grounds, I could not condone a political party in America that professed democratic principles and ideals of social justice yet held itself bound to the changing policies of Russia's Foreign Office.

"Stalin never considered how people like me would feel about his pact," I went on. "I cannot just stop feeling myself an antifascist on being given such orders. If you fellows are wrong I must say so. I will not allow any party or committee of bureaucrats to do my thinking for me."

Richard retorted with much heat that by questioning the intelligence and integrity of the Soviet Union and the communists in this country I was being inconsiderate and even insulting to him. He then became greatly agitated (as I continued to differ with him) and rose from the dining table, exclaiming with tears in his eyes: "The Soviet Union and the Communist Party are to me the last best hope in the world. If I should ever lose my faith, the only thing that has sustained me for many years, I would feel myself utterly lost and life not worth living!"

It was like a quarrel over religion. There was partial truth in Malcolm Cowley's idea that communism had become a kind of religion. But in the case of the somewhat neurotic Bransten its secular fraternity provided him with group therapy as well. His words about the danger for him of loss of faith proved fatally correct. In later years when he became an apostate he was indeed an unhappy and lonely soul. As they left that night Ruth showed great mental distress over our dispute, which I had tried to keep impersonal; she at any rate was deeply attached to us, especially to my wife, and now foresaw the rupture of our friendship.

VI.

The German offensive in western Europe began in Holland and Belgium in the second week of May 1940 and soon swept into northern France with a force and speed beyond anything men had imagined. During the climactic week of the Battle of France I was so shaken by these events overseas that I was utterly unable to work at my book *The President Makers*. By a coincidence the book's last chapters were devoted to the period of the Wilson administration when America turned from its task of domestic reform to enter the war raging then too in Europe. It was such a reversal of our policy that I foresaw would recur under Franklin Roosevelt; of course many persons had the expectation that history would soon repeat itself.

The President Makers: 1896–1919, the third in a series of studies in recent American history that began with *The Robber Barons* and *The Politicos*, attempted an analysis of the reform era of Theodore Roosevelt and Woodrow Wilson. Our statesmen of those days were concerned with political improvements primarily, rather than with such measures of social reform and economic relief as were undertaken during the New Deal; they wanted to curb the machine in politics and the trusts in industry. The march of reform, national and local, during the 1900's had been inspired by the very excesses of the Robber Barons and politicos during the preceding generation. Meanwhile the general war in Europe in 1914 halted the reformatory movement in the United States, its advance in any case having slowed down as if approaching natural limits. In his campaign for reelection President Wilson had pledged that he would not send Americans to fight in a foreign war; Franklin Roosevelt also promised as much in 1940 while campaigning for reelection for a third term.

For about twenty years before 1914 American statesmen and military strategists had come to regard the Atlantic Ocean as *Mare Nostrum* and tended to accept the ideas of our Admiral Edward T. Mahan concerning the vital importance of sea power or control of the main sea lanes of the world. England's hegemony during three centuries, of course, furnished the inspiration for Mahan's doctrine.

With some surprise I discovered that the typical progressives and reformers of the Roosevelt-Wilson era—so humane in all other respects—were with few exceptions great warlovers and ardent imperialists. They desired that the United States "as a great people should play a great part in the world" and enter into the competitions of the Great Powers for colonies and new markets. Theodore Roosevelt urged that fighting for one's country was a nobler thing and more "red-blooded" than merely filling one's pocketbook. The ideology of American imperialism, model 1898, was fostered not only by the "yellow press" but by intellectuals of the upper crust like Roosevelt, Lodge, and Beveridge. For them the "manifest destiny" of America was to be a key nation in the so-called "Atlantic System," in alliance with England and France, who as our nearest neighbors on our common ocean had a longtime interest in maintaining friendship with us. The others, the "continental powers" Germany and Russia, were to be prevented from gaining dominance over the Atlantic.

In 1905 during the international crisis over Morocco, which carried the threat of war between France and Germany, Henry Adams wrote to one of Theodore Roosevelt's intimates that "we must support France against Germany and fortify an Atlantic System . . . for if Germany breaks down England or France, she becomes the center of a military world, and we are lost." Adams echoed Mahan's seapower doctrine which guided America's statesmen in two world wars. Now it seemed likely that the second Roosevelt would tend to follow similar concepts of America's military interests.

Theodore Roosevelt's steel "battle wagons" were no longer the queens of battle, for by 1939 air power had diminished the size of the oceans. Earlier Franklin Roosevelt had begun expanding our Navy; after the summer of 1939 he pressed for revision of our neutrality laws restricting arms shipments and seriously warned the country of the danger of air invasion. As in 1917 material interests, nationalist sentiment, and fear of future military enemies worked to bring America into alignment with England; more or less consciously Roosevelt would try to shore up the old balance of power formerly maintained by the British Empire, to whom we had been in effect junior partner.

The President Makers was a historical parable for our times; it did not propose, it sought only to expose. It carried however the warning that when the impetus of reform movements dies down "there is always a war," and the wrong people take charge of our wars. C. Vann Woodward (then a graduate student in American history), on reading an advance copy of the book, wrote me: "The reviewers will probably call you a fifth-columnist appeaser." In truth the press either ignored or attacked the book, though it held much appeal for the younger generation of historians and was reprinted in 1964.

§   §   §

In the latter part of June 1940 I was back in Washington again, trying to gather some idea of the government's direction by looking up old acquaintances among the New Dealers. A kind of panic seemed to possess almost everyone I saw, for as I arrived the news came that France under Marshal Pétain had signed an armistice with Hitler.

On that day, June 22, I happened to see Benjamin V. Cohen, who was acting as a White House assistant to President Roosevelt. "What is going to become of France?" he asked me in a tone of despair. I said I was resigned to seeing her occupied and enslaved for a long while, or until the Nazis were persuaded to leave.

"But where is the French Navy?—What are they going to do with the French Navy?" Mr. Cohen exclaimed. Usually a poised man, he was frightfully agitated, and while I sat with him he kept telephoning to various federal departments to ask officials there the same question. His anxiety reflected the terrible fears preying on the President's mind. Roosevelt evidently reasoned that the German and French fleets combined might well overcome the Royal Navy, and then America's Atlantic coast would be left naked. Mr. Churchill and the Royal Navy, however, soon tried to settle the question by proceeding to attack and sink as many vessels of the French fleet as could be found. Later that summer, after the Luft-

waffe had suffered inacceptable losses in the air battles over London
and had been forced to terminate its attacks, people in Washington
recovered their spirits.

After the autumn of 1939, when the Neutrality Act was revised,
a boom in the export of airplanes and armor for the Allies began; it
continued at a rising tempo when Roosevelt, in the summer of
1940—while France fell to the Germans—obtained from Congress
appropriations of $2 billion for "50,000 airplanes" and other arms
with which to safeguard America.

§   §   §

For long weeks in 1940 we lived under the pall of burning cities in
Europe; in imagination we shared the agony of masses of civilians
in flight down the roads of France, bombed or gunned down as they
went. Every few days refugees arrived here whom we knew or met
through friends—instead of being Jews, Germans, or Spaniards they
were now French or old American residents of France—and their
tales of horror or of eleventh-hour escapes added to the mood of
panic. Many of us saw that America would not long remain shel-
tered from the widening circle of catastrophe.

The mass of refugees was handled of course by the organized
charity bureaus such as the Red Cross and the Friends' Service. In
individual cases of French families known to us we tried to help
with household supplies or spare blankets, as they came out almost
empty-handed. Our neighbors Alexander and Louisa Calder, old
residents of Paris, were especially generous in giving shelter and
help to many artists arriving from France.

It was at the house of the Calders that I met the American
architect Paul Nelson, who with his French wife had fled from his
home in France to England a few steps ahead of the German tanks.
In his state of excitement Nelson spoke as if the Germans used the
Devil's own magic in air and land warfare. He quoted the poet
Paul Éluard as having written recently (though evidently as hyper-
bole) that the French soldiers were momentarily dazzled, while
engaged in battle, when the Germans dropped parachutists into
their lines who were "disguised as naked women." Nelson went on
to say darkly: "England will fall in two weeks; three weeks later
Hitler will attack the United States."

I felt and expressed my exasperation at such fantasies of gloom and doom and argued that there were many logistical difficulties preventing the transport of the German military machine to England, let alone this country. In the event of war with Germany I foresaw that the United States would bring to bear its "overwhelming and pitiless industrial power"—to which Ludendorff had attributed Germany's defeat in 1918.

Lewis Mumford, visiting us at the time, also seemed beside himself with anger at those who wanted to bide their time and opposed our entering the war against Germany and Japan. He spoke as if we in America were already in deadly danger and yet were behaving like "cowards and degenerates." Lewis indeed was capable of a splendid power of moral indignation, which he now manifested in various articles and polemical books devoted to the war crisis, such as *Men Must Act* (1939) and *Faith for the Living* (1940). In the latter work he advocated that we begin at once to refortify our nation and pursue a program by which our people would become hardened for the rigors of war; we were to return to the land, eat simple food, give up artificial luxuries, and even have our women avoid the use of rouge or lipstick (!)

Archibald MacLeish, then librarian of Congress, also engaged in heated argument against those whom he called "the Irresponsibles." They were the intellectuals and literary men of the left who still spoke for keeping the peace and who were joined by a strange conglomeration of allies: the communists, the isolationist *Chicago Tribune*, the America First Committee, the followers of Father Coughlan, and the fascists of Gerald K. Smith. Somewhat in the style of the author of *J'Accuse!* MacLeish made sweeping charges that "the generation to which I belong" had "corrupted" our youth and undermined our courage by teaching mistrust of ideas like patriotism and abhorrence of war. MacLeish warned us that "only liberty for which men are willing to fight . . . can survive."

Edmund Wilson, commenting on MacLeish's invocations to the martial spirit, said: "In his career he has struck a greater variety of attitudes, and been led to repudiate them faster than any other writer of our time."

In discussions with Mumford, I pointed out that we Americans were faced with the paradoxical situation of needing to arm ourselves to give battle to the fascists without becoming like fascists ourselves. I found it natural and human that Mumford, MacLeish, and others should be aroused against the Nazis; but I refused to believe that Americans were too craven to take action if need be.

Mumford became wrought up over my attitude of restraint and my determination neither to resist nor help the movement toward war. I myself was disqualified from military service through impaired hearing, and I refused to take the position of urging other and younger persons to go to war in my place. (My eldest son in 1943 would leave college at eighteen to volunteer for the Air Force; and I recall in sorrow that Lewis's charming son Geddes was fated to die in combat in Italy.)

I found myself writing letters to Lewis and not mailing them:

> I hope you will bear with me, for I esteem you above ninety-nine out of a hundred of my contemporaries. But I feel that you have taken the spirit and method of the enemy. This does not surprise or shock me, because with all who go to war the principle is the same. I am no pacifist. However I do believe there are possibilities of *democratic* mobilization against external danger, which you have unfortunately passed over (in *Faith for Living*) and which would help our people make a far stronger fight when the time comes. One of my friends, Robert Lynd, is working on just such a plan and has outlined a program. . . .

The New Deal was being abandoned, I went on, though until this war material business turned up we had ten million unemployed and wages were still low. Little had yet been done about "rebuilding America," a task that I knew meant much to Lewis in particular. Now we were about to turn away from our social program at home and risk everything under the arbitrament of war. I continued: "A war boom begins now! I have seen the crude faces of the dollar-a-year men in Washington again. The U. S. A. has the potential of the most gigantic military power the world has ever known. Hitler knows nothing of Detroit or Pittsburgh—you will see what they can do. But the war will be run by the wrong people. We may become a terrible military state. . . ."

Archibald MacLeish wanted the poets to begin writing war songs. I was reminded of what Goethe had said in 1813 when he was asked to write a national anthem: "Let Koerner do it." Goethe went on calmly with his wonted labors literary and scientific. But who remembers Koerner now?

§ § §

With the opposite faction, the newly converted pacifists, I had my troubles also. Many months had gone by and we had seen nothing more of the lovable Ruth McKenney or of her husband Richard. At last my wife wrote Ruth asking for news of them and in April 1941 received a long and melancholy letter. These were trying times for communists, and Ruth and her husband were busy working for the American Peace Mobilization. Ruth still loved us both beyond any other friends, she declared; and often she felt the impulse to get into her car and drive to our house but she "dared not" because her husband forbade such a visit. "Something lies between our husbands," she remarked. (The great autocrat of Moscow had come between us.) For her part, differences over political issues should mean nothing between true friends. But the times had made her husband very unforgiving. "Ah, it is a terrible thing to lose friends," she ended.

Within less than sixty days after that letter from Ruth McKenney signalizing the rupture of our friendship, the German armies, on June 22, 1941, attacked Russia's borders without warning. The world war now entered an entirely new phase; the whole picture changed, and the necessity for men like Bransten to sunder friendships along Party lines was ended.

There was to be a sequel to the chapter of our politically troubled relations with Ruth and Richard. Ruth was naturally formed to be a humorous writer, but her life was not cast along pleasant lines. Her sister Eileen, early in 1940, had met the young novelist Nathanael West in California; they had married and about six months later died together in an automobile crash, leaving an infant son (by Eileen's earlier marriage) who was adopted by Ruth and Richard. Several years passed; the Branstens worked in Hollywood while being active also in the high councils of the Communist Party. For the duration of the war the Soviet Russians were our "noble allies" and the American communists, who now showed intense loyalty in war service, were no less. Indeed the policies of the Communist Party in America had turned so much to collaboration with our government that at the end of the war Earl Browder was ousted as Secretary at the order of the Comintern, and the line became "hard" again. I read in the newspapers at the same time that Richard and Ruth had come under the censure of the Party on the somewhat different grounds of "left-wing deviation" and demands for the "petty bourgeois rights of free criticism."

At last I heard again from Richard, after four years of silence. In July 1945 came a letter from him of "profound apology for an inexcusable action on my part, in which Ruth participated unwillingly, and with regret." He now made confession that in the matter of my criticism of the communists' policy of 1939 to 1941 I had been right, and he had been "wrong, stupid, and self-righteous." Only after some time had passed did he come to realize, to his keen disappointment, that the denial of freedom of thought and criticism within his Party had permitted its leadership to follow a mistaken course (under Browder). Richard expressed himself as still dissatisfied with the new policies and said he felt the urgent need to consult me on this and other questions, but he realized that he had given me cause for resentment and that it might be hard to restore the relations of friendship he had so thoughtlessly disturbed.

I replied perhaps with more politeness than enthusiasm. His apologies had cost him much to write and had been volunteered in manly fashion; I thanked him and said I hoped we might meet soon and discuss everything freely, but I arranged no definite appointment.

The next year Richard and Ruth were expelled from the Party after another controversy reported in the newspapers, and with their two children the couple took passage for Europe. It seemed to me that Richard evinced fear both of meeting his former comrades and facing what he gloomily predicted would be a "coming fascist revolution" in the United States. Thereafter they lived abroad for many years. In 1955 Richard Bransten, in early middle age and while ill, took his own life.

Chapter Twenty-three

⌒

Our Arsenal
of Democracy

DURING AN INTERVAL of eighteen months after the fall of France the nation was no longer at peace and yet was not at war. It was an anxious and restless time. I had spent the past five years writing two books on America's political ideas and institutions; this period of seclusion at my country home was interrupted only by two winter journeys to the South when I was ill. Now as I came again to the last page of a new book in the spring of 1940, the world outside seemed all agog; I felt extremely eager to stir about and, if possible, place myself near the center of things.

As before I thought I would try to recuperate from the fatigue of long books by turning to journalism. The assignments that were offered me proved absorbing enough: I was to go to Washington again and write profiles of certain national figures for *The New Yorker,* one of which turned into an extended report on the emergency defense organization Roosevelt was setting up. After that there would be more of the same work for *The Saturday Evening Post* (which became a strong supporter of the wartime administration). My magazine writing kept me in Washington during the eve of war and much of the time of active war. Thus I was in the mainstream again—I could have said the "main maelstrom"—and could observe the swift transformation of our peacetime economy, the little world of the New Deal, into that of war production and armament boom.

Only the year before Congress, having turned anti-New Deal since the last elections, had fallen to haggling with the President over petty expenditures of a few millions, such as that for the Federal Theatre Project, which it eliminated. But now, with the danger of war looming ahead, Republicans and Democrats joined in voting funds for the fifty thousand airplanes and ten thousand tanks Roosevelt called for in his May 16 speech before Congress. Where they had formerly debated in terms of millions for relief or reform they now readily poured out billions for military defense.

In America war had come to be regarded not as a romantic adventure, or as an art, but as a business. Our military forces usually counted on winning not by Napoleonic stratagems but by an overwhelming weight of numbers, armor, and firepower.

The nation needed to be put on a war footing and to build or convert hurriedly many plants for the output of arms and airplanes. How should this program be managed and, at the same time, coordinated with the normal economic life of a country which was still at peace? To deal with the changed facts of life Roosevelt's answer in May 1940, as often before, was to appoint a wholly new federal agency to act under his authority, called the National Defense Advisory Commission. Its personnel at first glance resembled in composition that of earlier Rooseveltian agencies. Here again was the economist Leon Henderson working as a full-fledged member of the Commission on price stabilization programs; by his side was Sidney Hillman as adviser on labor relations in defense factories; there was also a member acting as representative of consumers' interests, another concerned with farm products and food, and a well-known railroad executive to deal with transport plans. But the overshadowing personage in the group—whom I was to write about—was definitely William S. Knudsen, former president of General Motors, who was in charge of production planning. The new Secretaries of War and Navy, Stimson and Knox, ex-officio members of the NDAC, were certainly not of the reformist stripe. There would be some debate within the Commission over maintaining New Deal policies, but the conservative element, supported by the quartermaster generals and admirals, would easily outweigh the others. The NDAC looked like one more pyramid of power in the Washington scene, but it soon towered over most of the other power structures.

During the summer, while London was being bombed, Washington fairly boiled with excitement. I haunted the headquarters of the NDAC in the new marble palace of the Federal Reserve Board on Constitution Avenue and saw with my own eyes how the power elite was changed. As in 1917 and again in 1933, under the Blue Eagle, a horde of dollar-a-year men converged on the capital to serve as deputies or assistants to the Defense Commissioners. The regular New Dealers, often seedy-looking professors or lawyers in baggy trousers, were quite outnumbered by the dollar-a-year men who stemmed from Wall Street, Chicago, or Detroit, and were usually spruce chaps in $200 suits. They came ostensibly to donate their services for the emergency as civilian patriots, but it was evident that they meant to keep a sharp eye out for their private business interests as well, since huge government contracts worth billions of dollars were being handed out day by day.

The New Deal had boasted a few "captive millionaires" like Henry Morgenthau, Jr., or Harold Ickes, who seemed in contrast with the newcomers to have been philanthropic, if sometimes eccentric gentlemen. The new breed were real operators, long accustomed to wielding power in big business affairs. Corporation lawyers like the aged Henry L. Stimson, Secretary of War, Robert L. Patterson, his Undersecretary, and Robert A. Lovett, Assistant Secretary for Air and former partner in Harriman Brothers, were all worth the high price they commanded in Wall Street. The same could be said for the shrewd investment banker James V. Forrestal, Undersecretary of the Navy.

When I talked with Patterson and Lovett, who had both seen service in the last war, I soon perceived they were no clods; they meant business. Lovett, an airman of World War I, told me that the United States must quickly win control of the skies and hold it after the war. It seemed incredible in view of the Germans' great power. "Why?" I asked him. "*I want the air!*" Lovett growled.

The others who made up the new power elite were also highly aggressive types; they moved in from General Motors, General

Electric, U. S. Steel, Standard Oil, Wright Aeronautical, or United Aircraft; in short, from the fifty giant corporations that controlled a third of America's industrial wealth. With them came some of the heirs of the old Morgan, Rockefeller, and Harriman dynasties whom Roosevelt used to stigmatize as economic royalists. One of these was Edward L. Stettinius; another was young Nelson Rockefeller.

"After all," remarked one of the dollar-a-year men, "if you want quantities of powder and shell casings you can't go to some New Deal professor to get them."

I called on one who formerly typified the "New Deal professor," Leon Henderson. In his years of service under Roosevelt he had shown himself supple enough to keep his footing but had also grown stout and ruddy. Up to recently he had been carrying on a searching inquiry into the affairs of the industrial monopolists for the TNEC. Now he found himself working hand in glove with the same monopolistic gentlemen. How did he like them? At first he felt quite uneasy among his new associates, he confessed; but as he was a confident and bouncy sort he soon managed to adapt himself very well.

One of the most curious side effects, a seeming paradox deriving from the operations of the Roosevelt welfare state in the thirties, had been its tendency to align a group of intellectuals vested with important bureaucratic power against the formidable private business blocs they were authorized to regulate and sometimes even to police. Thus you had "Tommie" Corcoran fighting for the SEC against the whole New York Stock Exchange; or another young government lawyer, David E. Lilienthal, defending the great TVA project against the private electric utility associations led by Wendell Wilkie the "Morgan man." The New Deal's lawyers and social workers were comparatively ill paid and hard pressed; the private business blocs deployed against them whole batteries of expensive corporation lawyers and lobbyists who fairly dripped money and had the support of most of the press and of conservative members of Congress. "Honest Harold" Ickes was perpetually worried lest some of the New Deal personnel go whoring after the rich corporations. Here and there an official would resign from the government service and take employment counselling the very private interests he had formerly regulated.

What was remarkable was that there was so little actual graft or overt bribe-taking under the New Deal; it was as nothing compared with the Grant administration after the Civil War, or the recent Teapot Dome affair under Harding.

The corporations' lobbyists sometimes directed their fire upon one obstreperous official—as in the case of my friend Jerome Frank in AAA—and tried to drive him from his office. It is interesting to note that the $200,000-a-year man Wendell Wilkie believed that the only reason why an able administrative man worked at low pay for the government was for the purpose of "building himself up for a private job later on at a better salary." Therefore he hinted (in an article published in *Fortune* in 1935) that a good way to influence such persons would be to let them understand that their resistance to agreement with private business views might impair their future chances for lucrative jobs outside the government service. In his candid *Journals* of that period, David Lilienthal recalls that the methods of temptation and threat were used alternately against him by the adversary.[1]

The paradox of government regulation in our divided economic society was reflected in the way in which the group of nonprofit-seeking bureaucrats, or "managers," of the New Deal found themselves ranged against the mass of private business interests, who could offer boundless material rewards to those who would join their camp. In his *Journals* Lilienthal gives frank expression to his self-satisfaction at having helped defeat the "power trust" after long years of court litigation; and he shows all the joy of finding himself a "big shot," a successful bureaucrat who has fought hard for the public welfare (though at low wages). Meanwhile the TVA chairman also confesses that, after having served in public office for more than ten years, he would dearly love to acquire some of the private power, the cash, even the fleshpots that the men of the

[1] *The Journals of David Lilienthal; I; The TVA Years* (New York: Harper; 1964), p. 712 (Appendix).

banks and the private utilities seem to enjoy. The time would come when Lilienthal too would leave the public service and try his skill at money getting.

During the national defense interlude and the war that followed—when deals for munitions contracts were being negotiated on a vast scale—Roosevelt's lawyers and professors kept their hands clean. However, *they also kept their professional shingles in full view* right on their desks, as if to say: "Today we are the counsellors of the state negotiating with you who represent private capital. But tomorrow will be another day, when we may go into business on our own." One after another the New Deal "commissars" would resign and enter private practice to serve as counsellors, or even lobbyists, for the same corporate interests they had formerly judged and regulated. The ex-New Dealers' intimate knowledge of the political machinery made them all the more valuable to their new employers. Thus men like Richberg, Corcoran, and Lilienthal, after having been honest public servants, wound up as millionaires in private life. The reconciliation came about during the interlude of national defense preparation when the New Deal officials sat down in friendly spirit at the same council table with the executives of the billionaire corporations and members of the old family dynasties, the Rockefellers and Harrimans, and worked with them in the common cause of winning the war.

The presence of a multitude of men in military uniform gave the effect of the players having made a quick change of costume. We had not seen much of the military brass in Washington these twenty years. Now a good many "desk soldiers" engaged in administrative service hurried in and out of the NDAC headquarters carrying brief cases with papers or forms in duplicate (sixteen copies). These colonels and captains, some of them veterans of the last war, jolly outdoor types with youthful faces, could scarcely conceal their pleasure at the new turn of events. After having been "starved" and "neglected"—as General Patton had remarked to me in 1934—they found that their country had need of them again. There would be unlimited Treasury funds, and swift promotion in rank; a first consignment of 1,200,000 draftees had just gone to the cantonments.

The pace of arms production, after a slow start, advanced little by little. But the boom in peacetime industries developed much faster. For the first time since 1929 motor manufacturers were running at full capacity, producing four million cars a year; and other consumer goods were being manufactured in large volume. Our moribund capitalist economy was awakened: employment rose to the full—a result which the New Deal, in years of peace, had struggled vainly to achieve. The painful thought was borne in upon me that we had not known how to reach full production and employment *without war*. It stayed with me like a shadow all through that cheerful boom.

§ § §

Given jobs or good business prospects—"guns *and* butter"—people seemed happier now. Most remarkable was the change of popular sentiment toward the question of our becoming involved in war. Only a year or two earlier most Americans were indifferent to the quarrels of the Europeans and the Asiatics. Roosevelt himself showed a marked detachment during the Spanish Civil War and behaved with restraint toward Japan, though she constantly extended her offensive in China. Moreover the strength of the America First movement made the President circumspect. During his third-term campaign in 1940, when he was provoked by his opponent Wendell Willkie to speak out on the possibility of our future intervention in the war, he was clearly disingenuous in promising that our soldiers would not again be sent abroad to fight in a foreign war. Yet even before the November election he had already approved in private the plans for the Lend-Lease agreement with Britain by which destroyers were to be exchanged for military bases. At this stage of affairs, however, Roosevelt showed little intention of going further than helping the British to defend themselves. It was quite in his character when in a dangerous situation to await developments and improvise measures accordingly.

I have often wondered who and what gives the decisive direction to our lumbering ship of state in a period of foreign crisis. In World War I we already leaned toward the Atlantic System: our great banks financed the Allies' war loans and their heavy purchases created an armament boom in America. Knowingly or not we had invested in victory for the Allies. But at the outset of World War II we were without similar commitments and had even enacted neutrality legislation to avoid involvement.

Moreover a feeling of pessimism about the prospects of our West European friends prevailed among some of the career officials of the State Department and was reflected in the views of certain influential ambassadors, such as Joseph P. Kennedy and William Phillips, that the Nazi-fascists would win out. They urged that we and everybody else should make the best terms we could with them. Some of our leading corporations maintained friendly and profitable trade relations with Germany. On a trip in 1938 to inspect G. M.'s Opel plant in Germany, William S. Knudsen himself had evinced enthusiasm over the achievements of the Hitler regime in bringing about an economic "miracle." Knudsen also had been a favored guest at Hermann Goering's country estate, and he pronounced the number two Nazi "very nice." His views were given as those of a production man, and he avoided airing opinions on Germany's politics. A while later however, in April 1940 when Knudsen's homeland, Denmark, was invaded, his feelings toward Germany underwent a violent change.

The average American gave little thought to troubles abroad. My village storekeeper in Connecticut, for example, showed an intelligent interest in local and national affairs; but he would always add: "I really know nothing about foreign politics." My other rural neighbors also had "no opinion" in such matters. There were however many business groups that were deeply engaged in foreign commerce and kept themselves closely informed about our foreign policy. Early in the war I happened to interview some executives of Pan-American Airways about their transport contracts with the Army Air Force. One day, after having talked with Pan-American's president Juan T. Trippe and two vice-presidents of his company, I set off for Washington by night train in order to see certain State Department officials the next morning. What was my surprise at finding the two Pan-American executives I had met the evening before camped in the vestibule of the State Department; they had preceded me in their airplane. It seemed that they practically lived there. Moreover they cheerfully introduced me to two other gentlemen waiting in the corridor who turned out to be Standard Oil Company vice-presidents. They too practically slept at the State Department.

The division chief I had come to see turned out to have been at some earlier period a roving representative of one of our international oil companies. He had been "loaned" to the State Department for war service, but in a year or two he expected to return to some oil company or some other international concern at higher pay. In fact the career men of diplomacy and the agents of oil, shipping, or airline corporations often seemed like interchangeable parts. Unlike my village storekeeper, those firms knew and cared a great deal about our foreign policy. They intended to go on trading everywhere no matter what happened, but they wanted to be informed about whether the Nazis would be allowed to preempt the commerce of South America or whether our Navy and Air Force would take preliminary measures to defend that region, as they did in secret from 1940 on.

Yet it was not fear of the loss of trade with Argentina and Brazil that caused opinion makers like Henry L. Stimson, Dorothy Thompson, or William Allen White to cry out for aid for England or even for intervention on her side. Nor did such concerns affect some of our leading writers such as Robert Sherwood and Walter Millis—both authors of antiwar books—who now joined the Committee to Defend Democracy by Aiding the Allies. The thought that free Americans in the future might not "own their own souls," Robert Sherwood wrote, made them fearful. They and others felt fear that America would be "beleaguered"; or, as President Roosevelt phrased it, we would become "a democratic island in a totalitarian sea."

Like Churchill, Roosevelt was intensely conscious of the strategic importance of sea power. The Axis formed by Japan with Germany and Italy in the late summer of 1940, and the advance of Japan to Indochina and the regions of oil and food, increasingly troubled Roosevelt and his advisers. The new air arm was a mighty instrument; but for England and America war would still be a maritime operation, with ships carrying the bulk of armor and personnel. As Churchill pointed out in his private correspondence with Roosevelt prior to the Lend-Lease agreement, it was the two great navies alone that could keep the democracies of England and the United States afloat. Foreseeing that this global war must end some day with a new settlement of the world balance of power Roosevelt and his advisers intended that the United States, in one way or another, should play a decisive part in that settlement.

§ § §

There was a mass of paper work to be done at the NDAC, embracing all sorts of plans and surveys of manpower, materials, and production schedules. Soon a white-collar army of 1,100 was mustered to handle it. But no one on the Commission seemed to have any real authority in his department and there was not even a chairman, as was Baruch on the 1918 War Industries Board. On first coming to Washington Knudsen had asked Roosevelt: "Who is to be the boss?" "I am," Roosevelt answered urbanely. Apparently he had no wish to install a "czar" over the arms industries but intended to keep control in his own hands with the Commissioners acting as his deputies.

During the first summer the press gave cheerful reports month by month of the gradually increasing output of airplanes, tanks, ships, and ammunition and of the conversion of factories to war production. But in the autumn of 1940, when I looked into these reports, I found they were only estimates and quite fuzzy at that. We were turning out scarcely 600 warplanes, though the target was 3,000 a month. Relatively few factories were being converted to arms manufacture, though some new airframe plants were going up. After all the President had pledged that there would be no profiteering and no new millionaires as a result of the arms business. Capital was being timid.

It was imperative that I see and talk with "Big Bill" Knudsen, and I was curious to meet him for a number of reasons. Though he was a former Liberty Leaguer of the General Motors–DuPont clan he had willingly joined the administration during the defense emergency. In fact his presence marked the Roosevelt administration's sharp turn to alliance with big business. As the old assembly-line king of Detroit he also embodied American managerial skill; he had turned out millions of Fords and as many Chevrolets. It was my guess that with men like Knudsen speeding things up we would soon be turning out armor in quantities that would stun the world.

I found it difficult however to arrange an appointment with the production boss, and for several days I was put off with statements that he was infernally busy. The trouble was that only some New Dealers had vouched for me, and it appeared that Knudsen and his aides were on distant terms with men such as they. At length I thought of an expedient: telephoning my old friend "Sell 'Em Ben" Smith, the Wall Street operator, I asked him to help me. He obliged by calling Secretary of Commerce Jesse Jones, and Jones promptly arranged my appointment with his good friend Knudsen for the next morning.

Though his reputation was that of a hard-boiled production man, Knudsen turned out to be a kindly looking, pink-complexioned giant of sixty with barrel chest, huge hands, and charming old-fashioned Danish manners. He talked of his work in the language of a plain mechanic, though showing himself well informed and not without imagination. As he related, he "was very moved" when Mr. Roosevelt called him, who had come here from Denmark forty years earlier as an immigant laborer, to "the biggest production job in the world."

The floor of his office was covered with blueprints of airplanes and tanks, and his desk was laden with contracts which he was supposed to review and either approve or object to—but he explained that he was only a "consultant" here, allowed to act only with the President's support.

The real planning and designing of armor, the real decisions, were all being made by the top Army and Navy procurement officers and by the Joint Army-Navy Munitions Board. It was their personnel who did business with ordnance experts and manufacturers. Although Knudsen could explain to me freely how many parts there were in a military tank and how it might be made on assembly lines, he could not order any; he could not even buy a shovel for the Army or Navy.

Knudsen was then much photographed and interviewed in the press as he toured the country inspecting war plants. But it struck me that he was actually little more than a figurehead who was being used by Roosevelt to cheer up the public and the business world. What Roosevelt had really counted on was that Big Bill Knudsen would be able to go out and persuade his old friends, the Detroit manufacturers, to convert their plants quickly into factories for war matériel while cutting down on pleasure cars. This the automobile magnates flatly refused to do so long as we were still at peace. They were in a boom and were earning profits of 20 per cent (after taxes), whereas the government arms contracts were then limiting profits to 8 per cent or less. The motorcar people also contended that it would be more expeditious to build new plants than to convert old ones for specialized arms output. But they were not building many new factories, and the obstreperous Mr. Ford even rejected large British and American orders for airplane engines. Roosevelt's attempt to use Knudsen's influence failed. After all, Knudsen had only been a "straw boss," never one of the real bosses.

The industrialists however made an interesting counter proposal: as the expanded or renovated plants might bring them losses after the war emergency had passed, let the government allow rapid depreciation charges amortizing the cost of such defense plants—at the high rate of 20 per cent a year against taxes. Eager to push on with rearmament, Roosevelt soon yielded and asked Congress to provide such tax rebates as incentive for undertaking military contracts. The Excess Profits Tax Rapid Amortization Bill was accordingly passed in October 1940, permitting defense contractors to obtain modern plants for about half their cost or less with the government paying for the rest. On the day that bill was passed manufacturers from all around the country fell over themselves to sign contracts for war matériel that had long been pending; Knudsen's division, which had been a quiet place in the first few months, did a land-office business, clearing about $4 billion of defense business in a single day. Capital, after having conducted a kind of strike, henceforth gave full cooperation to the defense program and was well paid for it.

§   §   §

It was actually the military brass, a bevy of generals and admirals, who specified and awarded the contracts to shipbuilders and munitions manufacturers with whom they had done business in the past. Of the first $10 billion in orders for arms about 75 per cent went to the fifty largest corporations. The military bureaucrats held fast to any added authority that came into their hands. In 1940 they assumed immense economic powers and took in the industrial giants who were entering the arms business as their working partners. Here were laid the foundations for that "military-industrial complex" of whose all-pervasive power Dwight Eisenhower himself, in his farewell message as President twenty years later, would warn the country.

Early in the war I ran into a whole informal and cosy club of generals, war contractors, and lobbyists that used to meet for cocktails and to talk shop at Bernard Baruch's suite in the Carlton Hotel at the end of the business day in Washington. They seemed like excellent fellows, some of them former corporation presidents in uniform. But in range of ideas and understanding of human and political relationships they seemed to me far beneath the former leaders of the New Deal.

Roosevelt was strongly minded to maintain good labor standards in defense plants doing business with the government, for he remembered the many strikes of the last war. Hence the appointment of Hillman as a defense commissioner ranking with Knudsen. Yet no definite labor policy was established. The military leaders in some cases expressed feelings of outrage because civilian workers demanded union wages and hours while soldiers, in the event of war, were expected to fight and die for a mere pittance. The Army and Navy freely awarded contracts to large employers such as Bethlehem Steel and Ford who persisted in maintaining nonunion shops. Though Hillman patiently raised objections to the labor provisions of such contracts, he was repeatedly overruled, since the military held that speed of delivery was paramount. The unionists grew restive; John L. Lewis, protesting loudly that the defense emergency was being used to undermine labor's hard-won rights, called strikes in the vital coalfields and forced sharp increases in wages. At length, at Hillman's urging, the President intervened in the case of an important order for $67 million of Army trucks, originally given to Ford, which he caused to be shifted to the unionized shops of Chrysler.

The loss of so much business, in addition to the denial of Ford's final appeal to the Supreme Court against National Labor Board rulings, led Henry Ford at last to change his ground and seek peace both with the Roosevelt administration and the CIO. For long years his tough private army led by Harry Bennett had banned all union agents from his plants and refused to permit free elections of union representatives. The report of Ford's surrender set off a whole day of fiesta in the Detroit region, during which 140,000 Ford workers walked out in a demonstration of union strength. To everyone's amazement Harry Bennett announced to the United Auto Workers' representative: "We're going to sign the best damn contract with any union around," and they did. The "Little Steel" companies also fell to the union men early in 1941. Thus it turned out that the war behind the front was to be fought under trade union standards—the brothers and fathers of the men in uniform working with great elan to raise output per man.

§   §   §

Scarcities of vital raw materials such as aluminum, rubber, and even steel created bottlenecks at an early stage of the expanded arms program. Roosevelt had started stockpiling in 1939 and had been assured by leading industrialists that supplies would be ample. Yet now they were short.

How could we help the British defend London and also build an air force of our own if we had not enough aluminum? At Knudsen's office I could find out little about why there were such shortages, and I determined to approach other sources of information. It occurred to me to go and see Assistant Attorney General Arnold, who had been actively prosecuting the industrial monopolies a year earlier. I heard that antitrust action had lately been much reduced, but that my friends in the Department of Justice would know a good deal about such things as rubber and aluminum.

Thurman Arnold smilingly assured me that the Anti-Trust Division had discovered for itself a new usefulness and was helping in its own way to speed up arms production. He attributed our worst scarcities entirely to the restrictive operations of the trusts and was hot on their trail. The Aluminum Corporation of America, for example, the single firm controlling all patents in its industry, had long restricted plant capacity for producing aluminum ingots, and other light metals such as magnesium. We would now need two years to expand our metallurgical mills. Similar restrictions in the output of synthetic rubber were traced to international cartel agreements between Germany's I. G. Farben Company, Standard Oil of New Jersey, and DuPont. The same condition held for much electronic equipment and for optical glass, produced only under limits imposed by the Zeiss Company of Germany. When Leon Henderson heard of these still existing cartel agreements he exclaimed: "The Nazis have already invaded America!" As a consequence Arnold and his aides directed their efforts against American members of the world cartels in order to break their patent contracts, "liberate" their industries, and introduce fresh competition among them. The government's suits to be sure might have met with long delays in the courts. Roosevelt, however, managed to reach a working agreement with ALCOA permitting several competitors to begin aluminum production under their patents. At the same time, it was reported that court suits against ALCOA, DuPont and others were to be suspended.

I was discussing the news of this abrupt change of front at the NDAC with Leon Henderson—an old adversary of the trusts—when he remarked: "That is very welcome news, at present." The government, he pointed out, could not keep ALCOA tied up in costly law suits and at the same time demand that they invest millions in added plants.

A few days later I saw Arnold again. He said that he had just returned from a conference with the President on pending trust prosecutions. The big cases, he confirmed, were now to be suspended, and he seemed a little cast down.

"How gloriously inconsistent is our President," I remarked. "One season he orders the prosecution of the trusts and the next he grants them immunity."

"That inconsistency," Arnold observed in his sententious way, "is part of Roosevelt's political genius." And reverting to a countryman's term, he added: "Roosevelt knows very well how to drive a two-horse team, now giving rein to the near-horse and now to the off-horse."

§ § §

The monstrous defense program that got under way with all the fine administrative confusion often characteristic of Rooseveltian projects shook itself down as it went along, and soon made astonishing progress. Knudsen (after Pearl Harbor) was displaced by other able citizens such as Donald Nelson of Sears, Roebuck and Charles E. Wilson of General Electric. A managerial consultant from Chicago came in and set up a viable organization chart for the defense production center, which helped. At the War Department an acquaintance of mine, Professor Stacy May, acted as chief of a new statistical bureau that measured the "input" and "output" of the entire national economy. Our planning work constantly improved; the War and Navy Departments were converted into huge business establishments run by executive types like Forrestal and Patterson, who with the help of the military chieftains fearlessly dispensed most of the $60 to $80 billion appropriated annually during the war's active phase. After all, the nation could boast of ample managerial talent and this had all been brought into play. The wartime expansion far exceeded the wildest estimates ever made of our industrial potential. Everything assumed astronomical proportions. Yet planning, rationing, and priorities, together with monetary controls, worked admirably to contain the tremendous inflationary forces that were being generated.

The arms economy inevitably strengthened monopoly in industry. The oligarchs of business moved into the centers of power

(508)

in close association with the military specialists. There was some show of distributing and subcontracting some of the arms manufacturing to small business units here and there, but in the main the Army and Navy brass displayed a marked preference for the large corporations commanding the big battalions of employees that had produced munitions and ships en masse in earlier wars. Some of their executives were brought into the War and Navy Departments and given uniforms and high ranks. After the war many of the professional generals and admirals reversed the process and transferred to executive posts with the corporations that had been their chief suppliers.

The splendid profit picture on the home front was not created out of graft or swindling—there was only a modicum of that—but through legally arranged bargains by the business element for the commodities they delivered. An advantage of a few cents a pound in copper or sulphur meant tens of millions gained; the subsidizing of war-essential plants was also a great boon to private industry. Despite Roosevelt's admonitions many contractors emerged as new millionaires.

During the war the capitalist class saw a great light. Whereas formerly its conservative leaders had clung to their old economic pieties about the virtues of public thrift, they now saw that the government's colossal borrowing and spending did not cause the heavens to fall. Capital had long feared a powerful political government; yet America's industries now had in the federal government the biggest customer they had ever dreamed of, and they found themselves prospering. Taxes were extremely high to be sure, but many corporate executives discovered the joys of the unlimited expense account. At all events our experience of wartime money and debt management, involving hundreds of billions of dollars, would make it impossible to pretend that we "could not afford" to plan for full employment. For American capital the ever-expanding economy had arrived.

In the thirties we had had no economic planning worth the name. But during the forties we had our Five Year Plan for recovery—through war. I had become thoroughly accustomed, indeed happily reconciled, to the little world of the New Dealers with their grand designs and huddle-muddle methods of achieving them; I longed that it might continue. We were legislating for the welfare state; some even hoped that we would achieve a degree of social justice equalling socialism, though it was forbidden to call it by that name. Many of the New Dealers were men of education and humane sentiments—pejoratively called "intellectuals"—who brought fresh imagination to the task of peaceful revolution and gave a brilliant style to the political era that was ending in war.

Yet as the thirties came to an end it was noticeable that the forward movement of the reformers was losing momentum; the leaders themselves appeared fatigued. And at such times, alas, as I wrote early in 1940 concerning the Wilsonian era, "there was always a war to turn to." [2]

Americans had been so deeply absorbed in their domestic problems that for many years most of them gave no thought to the deepening international crisis outside our borders. That the "have-not" nation states, Italy, Germany and Japan, were arming themselves for wars of aggression and were determined to destroy the old balance of power seemed at first of little import to Americans. Perhaps it was only a passing phase of atavism, with posturing military dictators threatening war for "territory and slaves" in order to wring concessions from the empires of England and France? It seemed unthinkable that men of Neanderthal minds would be allowed to lead their people again to the mass slaughter of 1914–18.

Some of us, to be sure, had taken up the cry for defensive action against the fascists in 1936, during the Spanish Civil War when such a course might have been pursued with far greater advantage. But only in 1940 had our government shown awareness that the aggressions of the dictator states posed an eventual threat to our own security. Our intervention in the world-wide contest, through being tardy, would demand all the greater expenditure of America's blood and treasure.

[2] Matthew Josephson: *The President Makers* (New York: Harcourt, Brace; 1940), Introduction, p. iv.

II.

For more than a year before December 7, 1941, the country continued in that state of semi-warfare later defined as "cold war." After the Germans invaded Russia at the beginning of the summer Americans breathed more easily, feeling that England was saved. Thereafter we shipped arms not only to England but also to Soviet Russia. Yet how stupid to believe that we could employ our resources to help one party to the conflict without becoming engaged sooner or later in hostilities with the other.

I remember, however, my feeling of sudden panic one night in mid-October when, dining with two friends in New York, I heard from one of them the rumor that we would be "at war with Japan almost any day." The man who said this was young Stewart Alsop, whose older brother Joseph had recently given up his work as a newspaper correspondent at Washington, volunteered for Naval Intelligence, and gone to China. For us "the war will start in the Pacific," Joseph Alsop said in a private communication to his family. My two young dinner companions were themselves making ready to volunteer for service, for it was enervating to sit and wait in an office for the war to reach out to them. Alsop's friend made some jest about the time having come for him to "take leave of his pretty wife and his bourgeois apartment" and go to the Air Force.

Now that we were far advanced in military preparations, in the autumn of 1941, the attitude of our government toward Japan had hardened. Embargoes on war materials had recently been imposed. When the Japanese aircraft carriers suddenly swooped down upon Pearl Harbor, the attack so disastrous for our fleet was something less than a surprise and ended an interval of tormenting uncertainty.

Modern military techniques, exemplified by the Germans and Japanese, counted heavily on the surprise attack and on speed of movement—not the forte of a democratic nation. We had been preparing ourselves yet seemed as unready as in our other wars. I had no fear, however, that the United States, with her matchless industrial and technological resources, would not prevail in mechanized warfare.

(511)

The expectation of a successful outcome, nevertheless, was not comforting in itself. Once again we and the other pretendedly civilized nations had failed in the test; the history of man's aggression was repeating itself in an orgy of destruction and genocide expanded in scale by modern machines. Sapient man could still be the most fantastically predatory of all the mammals.

As the war's fury mounted and its unheard-of magnitude imposed itself, while Americans died on the sea, on the shore, and in the skies, the mood of our people changed. The very air of the time seemed regressive. My constant fear was that power was going into the wrong hands, into the hands of the military, who were specialists in violence and policing and might wholly convert our people to their ends. I thought of the postwar future with apprehension—despite the talk of new parliaments of nations and world law—and saw it eventually assuming in this country the character of a Restoration Period which would revert to conservative doctrines.

In the interval of preparedness in 1940, while Soviet Russia was still apparently the ally of Nazi Germany, we actually had a foretaste of McCarthyism in the investigations by the House Un-American Activities Committee under Representative Martin Dies of suspected radicals and communists. (I published at the time a polemical piece in which I tried to heap ridicule upon Mr. Dies and his principal assistant.[3]) We were to wait only three or four years after the war's end to witness a renewal of such public inquisitions in more malignant form.

World War II was a repetition of World War I with a difference. What was different was the immense scale of the military operations and their destructiveness. This war's fabulous wastage, the huge numbers engaged in working and fighting, seemed to cause everything about us to expand. As before, war brought progress in technological invention—in means for making things swiftly and for destroying them instantaneously. And we "managed" our debt, our inflated money, and our rationed goods. Few

[3] Matthew Josephson and Russell T. Maloney: "The Way of a Sinner," *The New Yorker* (November 22, 1944). A profile of J. B. Matthews (Research Director of the Dies Committee).

could deny that wartime planning made for the health of the state.

In the winter of 1944 I attended a press conference given by President Roosevelt at the White House. It was but a few months before the landing in France; he had just returned from the fatiguing meetings at Teheran and looked utterly spent and sick, with yellow-green complexion as if jaundiced. I had never seen him from close up and now found myself standing in the crowd only a few feet from the man whom I believed even then to be dying, though he managed to survive for another year. Despite his condition, seeing him made quite an impact: he had a large and handsome head and also gave the impression of a man of large stature and special capabilities. This smiling man had carried on with the impossible task of being President of the United States in one of its most turbulent eras and had borne inhuman burdens. When he chanced to look at me for an instant, a stranger in the crowd of familiar journalists, his gaze seemed direct and friendly. The others present however told me afterward that he seemed more reserved than usual, almost enigmatic in response to questions put to him. But there was so much he could not tell us about what was going on, and about the preparations that were being made for the end of the war, least of all the unmentionable nuclear experiments. For not even Roosevelt could possibly read the future. Who could have foreseen that, in the course of that conflict, four of the Great Powers would utterly collapse and the United States would assume her new role as military superstate and arbiter of the world's destiny? One expected that the changes in America's status and power relations, though unpredictable, would be on the scale of the great war going on and that with its end we would cross over a sort of Great Divide in time. In the turmoil of the war days, I often thought of the popular movements and countermarches that had so engrossed our minds in the decade of the thirties, and they already assumed for me an air of remoteness, with something of the charm of the long ago. I feared that men would no longer remember well what had really happened; and so, during the time of war, I determined to preserve and set down, while they were still freshly remembered, my impressions of the way we were then, which formed the basis of these recollections.

Index

Index

Index

A NOTE about
the AUTHOR

MATTHEW JOSEPHSON was born in Brooklyn, New York, in 1899, and educated at Columbia University in New York City. In the 1920's he traveled to Europe and during two different periods of that decade was a member of the expatriate society there. He described that era in his recent memoir *Life Among the Surrealists*. His other books include *The Robber Barons*, a scathing indictment of the arrogant "captains of industry" of the late 1800's. He is also the author of several volumes of biography, including *Zola and His Time, Jean-Jacques Rousseau, Victor Hugo, Stendhal: or the Pursuit of Happiness*, and *Edison: A Biography* (which was awarded the Francis Parkman Prize in 1960); two works on politics, *The President Makers* and *The Politicos*; and five other books.

A NOTE on
the TYPE

The text of this book is set in Electra, a typeface designed by W(illiam) A(ddison) Dwiggins for the Mergenthaler Linotype Company and first made available in 1935. Electra cannot be classified as either "modern" or "old style." It is not based on any historical model, and hence does not echo any particular period or style of type design. It avoids the extreme contrast between "thick" and "thin" elements that marks most modern faces, and is without eccentricities which catch the eye and interfere with reading. In general, Electra is a simple, readable typeface which attempts to give a feeling of fluidity, power, and speed.

W. A. Dwiggins (1880–1956) was born in Martinsville, Ohio, and studied art in Chicago. In 1904 he moved to Hingham, Massachusetts, where he built a solid reputation as a designer of advertisements and as a calligrapher. He began an association with the Mergenthaler Linotype Company in 1929, and over the next twenty-seven years designed a number of book types, of which Metro, Electra, and Caledonia have been used very widely.

The book was composed, printed, and bound by American Book-Stratford Press, Inc., New York, N.Y. Typography and binding design by Kenneth Miyamoto.